AN INTRODUCTION TO

DATA ANALYSIS

Sara Miller McCune founded SAGE Publishing in 1965 to support the dissemination of usable knowledge and educate a global community. SAGE publishes more than 1000 journals and over 800 new books each year, spanning a wide range of subject areas. Our growing selection of library products includes archives, data, case studies and video. SAGE remains majority owned by our founder and after her lifetime will become owned by a charitable trust that secures the company's continued independence.

Los Angeles | London | New Delhi | Singapore | Washington DC | Melbourne

AN INTRODUCTION TO DATA ANALYSIS

QUANTITATIVE, QUALITATIVE AND MIXED METHODS

TIFFANY BERGIN

Los Angeles | London | New Delhi
Singapore | Washington DC | Melbourne

Los Angeles | London | New Delhi
Singapore | Washington DC | Melbourne

SAGE Publications Ltd
1 Oliver's Yard
55 City Road
London EC1Y 1SP

SAGE Publications Inc.
2455 Teller Road
Thousand Oaks, California 91320

SAGE Publications India Pvt Ltd
B 1/I 1 Mohan Cooperative Industrial Area
Mathura Road
New Delhi 110 044

SAGE Publications Asia-Pacific Pte Ltd
3 Church Street
#10-04 Samsung Hub
Singapore 049483

Editor: Jai Seaman
Editorial assistant: Shelley de Jong
Production editor: Ian Antcliff
Copyeditor: Richard Leigh
Proofreader: Thea Watson
Indexer: Martin Hargreaves
Marketing manager: Susheel Gokarakonda
Cover design: Lisa Harper-Wells
Typeset by: C&M Digitals (P) Ltd, Chennai, India
Printed and bound in Great Britain by Ashford
Colour Press Ltd

First published 2018

Library of Congress Control Number: 2018938086

British Library Cataloguing in Publication data

A catalogue record for this book is available from the British Library

ISBN 978-1-4462-9514-4
ISBN 978-1-4462-9515-1 (pbk)

Contents

List of Tables

List of Figures

Preface

The ability to analyse raw data is an increasingly important skill in numerous fields, including psychology, business, politics, media studies, international relations, criminology, sociology, medicine, and environmental studies. This book offers an interdisciplinary introduction to the fundamentals of data analysis and uses real-world case studies to illustrate both quantitative and qualitative data analysis techniques. Examples are drawn from a wide range of different social science fields. Hands-on exercises are also included, as the best way to learn how to analyse data is *by actually analysing data*.

The book is designed to be used as a comprehensive but digestible course textbook for undergraduate or graduate students with little previous exposure to data analysis methods. However, it could also be used as a self-teaching guide, since opportunities for self-assessment are included in each chapter. Its aims are to help you gain proficiency in data analysis and also encourage you to develop the critical thinking skills necessary to assess data analyses presented in academic journals and the popular media.

To that end, although the book focuses on data, some guidance is also provided on data *organization* and *presentation*. Technological developments mean that data is ubiquitous in modern life. Although exciting, the scale of the data now available to researchers presents emergent challenges. In particular, sorting through available or newly collected data, identifying which data will be analysed, and then organizing data into an analysable format are all paramount tasks. Similarly, the increasing emphasis on data-driven improvement in both the private and public sectors offers new opportunities for data analysts, but also requires such analysts to develop further skills. Specifically, the ability to clearly *communicate* the findings of data has become ever more fundamental. Up-and-coming data analysts today must consider how to accurately convey the findings, implications, and limitations of data to diverse audiences who may not be familiar with analytical techniques. Effective communication is essential for data to have a meaningful and lasting impact on the world.

Although quantitative data often seems to garner greater media attention, both quantitative and qualitative data analysis techniques are indispensable for understanding individuals and societies. (Quantitative data is numeric or focuses on numbers, while qualitative data does not focus on numbers but instead considers texts, images, or other sources.) Qualitative data analysis can uncover nuances and complexities that could not be ascertained through quantitative techniques alone; similarly, quantitative data analysis can detect patterns and relationships undetected in qualitative work. Although data analysts typically specialize in just one of these approaches, a working knowledge of both is required to fully engage with current developments in one's discipline. This book therefore explores quantitative approaches, qualitative approaches, and mixed-methods approaches (or approaches that draw upon both quantitative and qualitative methods). The theoretical background driving each of these approaches is discussed, and practical guidance is offered on when and how to implement these approaches. Finally, the limitations of quantitative, qualitative, and mixed-methods approaches are also each explored, since overconfidence in one's findings is a particularly alluring and dangerous temptation for many data analysts.

Any book of this kind must make a trade-off between breadth and depth. When dealing with a topic as expansive as data analysis, the implications of this trade-off are acute. For the textbook to remain manageable (and affordable!) for students, not all relevant material could be included. To decide which material to focus on, quantitative and qualitative breadth was privileged, with priority given to providing students with in-depth experience of actually *doing* data analysis. After reading this textbook, students should be able to interpret and critically evaluate the data analysis they encounter in everyday life, whether that be in the media, politicians' speeches, or the arguments of their lecturers. Students should also be able to embark on their own data analysis projects, using the basic and intermediate techniques for which detailed practical instruction is provided in the text. Students can then build on the knowledge acquired in this introduction for more advanced exploration of these and other techniques – a task facilitated by the suggestions for further reading given at the end of each chapter. A key tenet of this book is that data analysis involves a particular way of thinking, a rigorous, reflective, and methodological attitude to beliefs and questions about the world. Thus, although every specific data analysis technique cannot be covered in detail in this book, developing this attitude and way of thinking will equip students to more effectively explore additional data analysis methods on their own or in a more advanced course.

Data, in some form, is essential to all academic disciplines; acquiring data analysis skills has become an increasingly important component of university courses in a range of subjects. Since data analysis methods are often cross-disciplinary, this textbook is not aimed at a single discipline or subject-matter area. Indeed, advances in data analysis that are made in one discipline are often usefully applied to research in another discipline. The cross-disciplinary perspective of this book honours this intellectual cooperation and complements the recent rise of cross-disciplinarity in universities. In keeping with this approach, examples and case studies discussed in this text are taken from a diverse range of fields, particularly in the social sciences, and were chosen to interest a broad, general audience. Finally, it is important to note that, although the fundamentals of data analysis are not discipline-specific, each discipline does maintain unique conventions and customs – particularly regarding the selection of analytic techniques and the reporting of findings – which cannot always be discussed in detail in this book. Readers are therefore advised to seek out further information from colleagues in their discipline.

Although examples of data illiteracy on the part of politicians or media commentators abound, many more examples can be found of individuals using data in interesting, ethical ways to illuminate important phenomena – and even change the world. From the nineteenth-century efforts of Adolphe Quetelet (discussed in Chapter 1) to the insights (and risks) that 'big data' presents today, the potential of data to fuel human knowledge remains vast. Yet the usefulness of data depends on our ability to effectively *analyse* it. By learning the data analysis skills described in this book, you can begin to harness the power of data yourself.

How To Benefit From This Book

Through examples and hands-on exercises, this book offers an overview of key issues and techniques in data analysis. Data analysis is such a massive topic that we won't be able to explore all potentially relevant issues in detail. However, we will cover the most important issues you may come across in your research. Suggestions for further reading to increase your knowledge of particular topics will also be presented throughout the text. Here is a roadmap of the specific themes we will address in each of the book's chapters:

Chapters 1 and 2 introduce the general process of data analysis, illustrating why such analysis is now a critical skill across multiple disciplines and industries. These chapters aim to teach you the skills you need to *think* like a data analyst. Through real-world examples we will explore key concepts related to the analysis of both quantitative and qualitative data.

Chapter 3 focuses on finding, collecting, and organizing data. Guidance will be provided both for students interested in collecting their own data and for students who want to analyse data that has been collected by others. The importance of upholding ethical principles – and specific advice about how to uphold such principles – will also be discussed.

Chapters 4 and 5 investigate the analysis of quantitative data. We will examine concepts and procedures that apply to a wide variety of different quantitative techniques. We will then explore three different types of quantitative procedures in detail: correlations, *t*-tests, and chi-square tests.

Chapters 6 and 7 focus on qualitative data. We will explore the analysis of different types of qualitative data, such as interview transcripts and ethnographic field notes. The process of coding will then be probed in depth, with advice about when to implement different types of coding procedures.

Chapter 8 focuses on mixed-methods research, and how quantitative and qualitative approaches can be effectively synthesized. Rationales for using mixed methods are identified, and interesting real-world examples of mixed-methods research are discussed in depth.

Chapter 9 explores how to most effectively communicate your data analysis findings to other academics, the public, and even policy-makers. In particular, we will consider the growing field of data visualization and strategies for presenting your findings through bar charts, pie charts, network maps, and other visual means.

Chapter 10, the concluding chapter of the book, discusses key principles for becoming a data analyst. It also describes emerging trends in data analysis and highlights some potential directions for future development in this field.

At the very end of the book you'll find a glossary. The glossary defines key terms related to data analysis. Therefore, if you come across a term that you're not familiar with as you read the book, feel free to skip ahead to the glossary and search for a definition.

Additionally, each chapter includes both a preview of its content (presented at the beginning) and a summary of its key points (presented at the end). The end of each chapter also features a list of suggestions for further reading which provides a jumping-off point for learning more about themes or methods discussed in that chapter. A list of discussion questions is also provided; the goal of these questions is to get you thinking about the material covered in each chapter. It's worth contemplating these questions to make sure you get the most out of this book.

Finally, throughout each chapter, you'll sometimes notice the following prompts: 'Stop and think' and 'Let's try this!'. The 'Stop and think' prompt invites you to reflect on a particular theme or issue in more depth. The 'Let's try this!' prompt encourages you to try out some of the data analysis techniques described in the chapter. Since data analysis is best learned by *doing* rather than just *reading*, I'd strongly recommend taking advantage of these opportunities. Good luck!

Acknowledgements

I am deeply grateful to Jai Seaman, Alysha Owen, and the entire team at SAGE for their perceptive feedback and encouragement. I would also like to thank the anonymous reviewers for their helpful suggestions to improve the manuscript.

My thanks also go out to the many students and colleagues I encountered at the University of Cambridge and Kent State University who asked interesting questions about data analysis and prompted me to think more deeply about research methods. Good data analysis, after all, always begins with good research questions!

Of course, any errors are the responsibility of the author. Any opinions expressed in this book are those of the author and do not necessarily represent the views of any organizations with which she is – or has been – affiliated.

About the Author

Tiffany Bergin is Senior Research Analyst at the New York City Criminal Justice Agency. Previously she was Assistant Professor in the Department of Sociology at Kent State University and Sutasoma Trust Research Fellow and Director of Studies in Politics, Psychology, and Sociology at Lucy Cavendish College, University of Cambridge. She is the author of *The Evidence Enigma* (Ashgate, 2013) and *Regulating Alcohol around the World: Policy Cocktails* (Ashgate, 2013). With Emanuela Orlando, she is the editor of *Forging a Socio-Legal Approach to Environmental Harms: Global Perspectives* (Routledge, 2017). She received her PhD and MPhil in Criminology from the University of Cambridge, and her AB *summa cum laude* from the Woodrow Wilson School of Public and International Affairs at Princeton University.

Introducing Data

contents

Chapter Overview

By the end of this chapter, you will be able to:

- Describe the impact and lingering influence of data through historical examples
- Gain a first-hand perspective on what data analysis involves by making your own predictions and comparing these predictions with real-life data
- Define the term 'data'
- Describe the 'big data' phenomenon and its potential advantages and risks.

Data Surrounds Us

Data surrounds us. From stock prices on the morning news to records of calories burned on fitness machines, we all encounter colossal amounts of data – quantitative or qualitative information about ourselves, society, or the universe – every day. Analysing all of this data would be impossible; analysing *some* of it, however, can tell us a great deal about ourselves, our society, and the world we live in.

Data allows us to make discoveries that intuition or common sense cannot uncover. Data drives policy changes by governments. Data shapes the behaviour of companies and organizations. Data even changes the way people think. Given the power of data, the ability to analyse data is a special skill that is increasingly valued in society. However, because this skill is so potent, it can – like any type of power – be used for good or evil. While many data analysts strive to do good by accurately and clearly presenting their findings, others deliberately misrepresent data for selfish purposes. The goal of this book is to develop your data analysis skills to help you do good things in the world, and recognize when other data analysts are deliberately misrepresenting their findings.

The Power of Data: Fog, Pollution, and Catastrophe in London

Not yet convinced of the power of data? Let's look at one example of how data, painstakingly collected and clearly presented to the public, saved countless lives and permanently altered life in one of the world's great cities.

Imagine you are living in London in December 1952. Pollution emitted by the city's smokestacks and coal-burning fireplaces mixes with the winter fog, resulting in a thick, choking, and nearly immobilizing smog (MacNee & Donaldson, 2008, p. 121). The smog lasts for five days. Visibility becomes so poor that buses stop running and, even indoors, many theatrical events are cancelled because audiences cannot see the stage (BBC News, 2008; Wallace & Hobbs, 2006, p. 179). Even scarier is the fog's impact on human health. Between 5 December and 9 December 1952, overall hospital admissions increase by half, with many of these admissions due to respiratory conditions (MacNee & Donaldson, 2008, p. 121).

Although the December 1952 fog was particularly severe, similar air pollution events were alarmingly common in nineteenth- and early twentieth-century London. Several past smog incidents had killed hundreds of people in the late 1800s (Brimblecombe, 1987, p. 124). Yet these past tragedies did not prompt policy changes. Although some observers expressed concern about potential health consequences – in the late nineteenth century, for example, one meteorologist argued that elevated levels of bronchitis in London were partly due to smoky fogs (MacNee & Donaldson, 2008, p. 121; Russell, 1889) – data was not yet generally available to analyse this issue. However, by 1952, this had changed. The ability to accurately collect, analyse, and communicate findings from data about the fog's consequences changed everything.

For the 1952 fog, the first set of influential data was released by the health minister several weeks after the tragedy, revealing that 2800 extra deaths occurred in London during the fog as compared with the same week in 1951 (Thorsheim, 2006, p. 165).[1] This dramatic statistic received significant media attention, both in Britain and around the world ('Week of London fog...', 1952). It encouraged people to view the 1952 fog as a *preventable* tragedy that could be stopped through policy action on pollution (Thorsheim, 2004, p. 166). Public concern about the 1952 fog paved the way for adoption of the Clean Air Act of 1956 which regulated industrial emissions and mandated that most homes and businesses stop using coal fires – a massive societal change that did not occur in response to previous fogs (Thorsheim, 2006, pp. 173–174).

This example illustrates the power of data to sharply alter people's perceptions – and even to change policy. Such policy change only occurred after the public was given clear proof of the number of people who had been killed in the fog. In other words, accurately collected and clearly presented *data* was necessary to prompt this transformation.

The Lingering Influence of Data: The Work of Alexis de Tocqueville

The data that helped prompt action on air pollution was **quantitative data** – meaning that it consisted of *numbers* (in this case, a single alarming statistic about the number of people who had died). When we hear the word 'data', we often think about statistics like these. But data does not have to consist of numbers; it can, instead, consist of words, actions, behaviours, images, objects, and numerous other features of individual or social life. Data that is not numeric is known as **qualitative data** and, as with quantitative data, the analysis of qualitative data has similarly shaped policy and society in innumerable ways. Such influence can in fact resonate centuries into the future.

Let's look at one such example of the lingering influence of data: the landmark qualitative research of Alexis de Tocqueville. In 1831, de Tocqueville and his colleague Gustave Beaumont undertook a thorough nine-month journey throughout the Eastern, Midwest, and Southern

[1]Other reports have suggested that some 4000 people died due to fog-related respiratory difficulties (Wallace & Hobbs, 2006, p. 179), while a more comprehensive recent analysis found that as many as 12,000 additional deaths between December 1952 and February 1953 were related to the fog (Bell & Davis, 2001).

regions of the United States. Although tasked by the French government with studying the US prison system, de Tocqueville expanded the scope of his analysis to include all elements of social and political life in the young country. The lengthy, groundbreaking work that de Tocqueville produced, *Democracy in America* (1835), offers a multilayered analysis of democracy (and the appalling contradiction of slavery within a democracy), class, gender, cultural attitudes, and political values (Kurweil, 1999).

Although de Tocqueville's work is often considered a work of political philosophy, it's actually an 'example of productive qualitative inquiry', since, to produce the volume, de Tocqueville meticulously collected and analysed qualitative data about the attitudes of American citizens and the workings of their democratic government (Lingenfelter, 2016, Chapter 5). Specifically, de Tocqueville's work is an early example of 'participant observation' (Whitley, 2008, p. 98; see also Handler, 2005, p. 22; Kurweil, 1999, p. 153), a qualitative research method in which a researcher conducts extensive research in the field, and participates in activities or daily life routines within a particular area, organization, society, or group of interest. Participant observation allows a researcher to obtain first-hand insight into what it feels like to be a member of a specific group and engage in particular activities. De Tocqueville achieved such insight by travelling throughout the country's regions, conversing with numerous Americans, and participating broadly in community life. As an 'outsider', de Tocqueville was able to bring a uniquely observant perspective to the society he studied, and he is now recognized by some contemporary scholars as 'the first modern social scientist' (Kurweil, 1999, p. 153).

Perhaps the clearest illustration of the value of de Tocqueville's work is its lingering influence today. *Democracy in America* is still regularly referenced by cultural commentators and is widely assigned to social science students in US universities. A 2015 article in the *Washington Post*, for example, described de Tocqueville's work as '[t]he book every new American citizen – and every old one, too – should read' (Lozada, 2015); and a 2017 *BBC News* article entitled 'Can democracy survive Facebook?' referenced de Tocqueville's work (Rajan, 2017). The fact that de Tocqueville's findings are still considered relevant to a twenty-first-century discussion about social media and democracy illustrates that well-executed qualitative research – like quantitative research – can exert a long-lasting impact. If you're interested in learning more about participant observation and other forms of qualitative research, you can look forward to Chapter 6, where we'll discuss qualitative data analysis in detail.

1.5 The Questions that Drive Data Analysis: The Work of Adolphe Quetelet

Data analysis is driven by questions. Learning to ask interesting and thoughtful questions is the first step in conducting interesting and thoughtful social research. One of this book's goals is to inspire you to ask such questions about the world, and in each chapter we'll explore real-life examples of the kinds of fascinating questions data analysts have asked. In fact, let's start with one example now: the work of Lambert Adolphe Jacques (or simply Adolphe) Quetelet (1796–1874). Quetelet's pioneering *quantitative* research illustrates how well-thought-out questions can prompt innovative data analysis, and lead to surprising and fundamental insights about the social world. Quetelet, a brilliant early data analyst from Belgium, produced groundbreaking findings in a wide range of disciplines, including medicine and criminology. We'll focus on Quetelet's work in two controversial areas: human height and weight, and weather and crime.

1.5.1 Height and weight

How do height and weight change over the course of individuals' lives? Do gender, class, and geographic region affect such changes? These questions, which reverberate in today's discussions about rising obesity levels, also fascinated Quetelet in the 1840s. Yet in contrast to more speculative commentators, Quetelet analysed quantitative data to answer these questions rigorously. Quetelet's (1842) data was derived from a broad range of sources – including government registers in Belgium, measurements taken from infants at the Foundling Hospital in Brussels, measurements taken from children working in factories in Manchester and Stockport (in England), and measurements taken from undergraduates at the University of Cambridge.

Quetelet (1842) noted that wealthier individuals tended to be taller than average, and that the growth of poorer individuals was often stunted by poverty and deprivation.[2] He also observed that, for the average person, body weight measured in kilograms tended to be proportional to the square of their height measured in meters – an observation that remains deeply influential (Eknoyan, 2008, p. 48) as it helped form the basis of the Body Mass Index (BMI; Keys, Karvonen, Kimura, & Taylor, 1972). Today, the BMI is one of the most widely used measures for assessing whether an individual is underweight, at a healthy weight, overweight, or obese, and since obesity is now a significant global health concern, the BMI currently receives substantial attention from health professionals and the popular media. For example, the US Centers for Disease Control and Prevention (CDC, 2012) note that: 'For adults, overweight and obesity ranges are determined by using weight and height to calculate a number called the "body mass index"'. The BMI is also used to trace global trends in obesity, revealing that, from 1980 to 2013, the percentage of men around the world who were obese rose from 19% to 37%, while the percentage of women rose from 30% to 38% (Ng et al., 2014).

The BMI has many limitations. Since it does not distinguish between fat and muscle, it may not be helpful for all individuals (such as athletes with substantial muscle mass), but it can be useful at the population level, as the example of global obesity trends illustrates (see the discussion in Stephenson, 2013). Although more sophisticated methods for measuring obesity now exist, the simplicity and ease with which the BMI can be calculated likely reinforce its appeal. Additionally, as Wells (2014) has described, it is not clear whether some alternative measurements, such as waist size, are actually better indicators of the risk of developing chronic diseases than the BMI.

[2]Although Quetelet's (1842) overall work was based on the range of data sources already described, he used a more limited dataset to derive these specific findings. This dataset only included data from Brussels and the Belgian province of Brabant; therefore, Quetelet cautioned that his findings were only applicable to these areas, and were not guaranteed to hold true in other regions. Such explicit acknowledgement of the limitations of one's findings is essential for any data analyst.

The BMI's persistence and continuing value illustrate the potential impact of thoughtful and considered data analysis. Quetelet's observation about human height and weight that inspired the BMI was not based on speculation or intuition; as we have seen, Quetelet's (1842) observation was based on his considered analysis of data of the heights and weights of many different individuals. A more speculative observation would likely not have been as accurate or achieved the precision necessary to survive into the twenty-first century, as the BMI has done. Additionally, the BMI's persistence also highlights the importance of data presentation. Quetelet's (1842) original observation is just a simple formula, accessible to anyone, and this simplicity has likely helped the BMI to persist despite the availability of more sophisticated techniques for measuring obesity today.

1.5.2 Crime and weather

In addition to height and weight, Quetelet explored the contentious question of whether the weather can affect crime rates. This question has continued to interest scholars, and Quetelet's data-driven observations have proved influential in this area as well (see, for example, Rotton & Frey, 1985; Yan, 2004).

To consider this question, Quetelet (1842) examined data from France in the 1820s, determining that the *colder* months of the year typically witnessed more *property* crimes, while the *warmer* months of the year witnessed more *violent* crimes (see also Bray, 1994, p. 68). Quetelet explained this pattern by arguing that excessive heat fostered aggressive behaviour by individuals, which encouraged more violent crime; meanwhile, a dearth of food and other necessities for daily life in winter led to more property crime (Hipp, Bauer, Curran, & Bollen, 2004).

Although weather's influence on crime has not been examined as thoroughly as socio-economic or demographic factors, many researchers have expressed interest in this topic (Cohn, 1990). Like Quetelet, some scholars have theorized about a linkage between hot weather and aggression or hostility (see the discussion in Anderson, 2001). Additionally, warmer weather also means that individuals spend more time outdoors and come into contact with more people, perhaps raising the risk of violence and crime (Moser, 2012).

stop and think

Do you think weather affects crime rates? If so, do you agree with Quetelet's idea that violent crimes are more common in warmer periods and property crimes are more common in colder periods? Why or why not? If you wanted to conduct a data analysis to answer these questions, what data would you collect?

Quetelet's idea that violent crime is more common in warmer weather is supported by more recent data analysis. Butke and Sheridan (2010), for example, examined police records for 1999–2004 from the US city of Cleveland, focusing on the following crimes: domestic violence assault, non-aggravated assault, aggravated assault, robbery, rape, and homicide. Their data analysis revealed that these crimes tended to peak in the summer months and plummet in the winter months; similarly, these crimes also increased in tandem with rising temperatures.

McDowall, Loftin, and Pate (2012) explored similar questions using a broader geographical range and time series. Specifically, they examined monthly data for 1977–2000 for all US cities that had a population of at least 200,000 in 2000. They used the FBI's Uniform Crime Reports data – which registers crimes reported to law enforcement – to obtain information about homicide, rape, robbery, aggravated assault, burglary, larceny, and motor vehicle theft rates. They discovered that the rate for all of the crimes except robbery was highest in July or August and lowest in February. Although this finding partially matches Quetelet's hypothesis, burglary and larceny are traditionally considered property crimes and, in contrast to what Quetelet (1842) would suggest, these crimes also tended to be higher in warmer months.

Another valuable data analysis of the relationship between crime and weather was undertaken by Cohn and Rotton (2000), who analysed two years' worth of police crime data from the US city of Minneapolis. They also found that, in contrast to what Quetelet suggested, more property crimes were reported to police during warm periods than cold periods. They explained this finding by suggesting that, in warmer weather, more opportunities exist to commit certain property crimes, since potential victims are more likely to leave windows open or leave goods outside.

What are the implications of these findings for Quetelet's argument? Well, it seems his assertions about violent crime have received some support in more recent data analyses, although the link between heat and aggression – which Quetelet (1842) focused on – may not be the sole explanation. Quetelet's statements about property crime did not receive support in the more recent studies reviewed here. This divergence illustrates how social phenomena can change over time, and updated analyses are needed to assess new data. When the findings of an updated data analysis diverge from the findings of a previous analysis, it is important to step back and consider *why* this might be the case. Has the phenomenon of interest (i.e., in this example, the relationship between weather and crime) actually changed, or have different data analysis methods produced a new understanding of the phenomenon (which has not itself changed)?

Although Quetelet focused on temperature, other weather features might also affect crime rates. Before moving on, it is interesting to consider one of these features: rain. Although less explored than temperature, an analysis by the *New York Times* examined rainfall data and homicide data for New York City in 2003–2008 (Lehren & Hauser, 2009). The analysis found that *fewer* homicides occurred during *rainier* summers. Potential explanations for this finding include temperature (since rainy days tend to be cooler, one would expect to see fewer violent crimes, in keeping with the findings of the studies discussed above); or that rainy days offer fewer potential opportunities for stranger homicide, since potential victims are more likely to remain inside and less likely to meet people they don't know. (The authors note, however, that one limitation of the latter explanation is that most homicides are ***not*** stranger homicides (Lehren & Hauser, 2009).)

Interestingly, some evidence from other cities has detected a similar pattern. For example, data from Glasgow, Scotland, revealed that violent crimes were nearly 45% lower on rainy days, with overall reported crimes 25% lower ('Rainy days help…', 2011). However, the same pattern was not seen for rape ('Rainy days help...', 2011). In Los Angeles, during an unusually rainy week in 2005, violent crime was found to be 23% lower and property crime 25% lower than the equivalent week the previous year; however, child abuse and domestic violence were 25% higher compared to the same week the previous year (Winton & Lee, 2005). (This finding makes sense when one considers that these crimes are more likely to take place at home, and rain might make people less likely to spend time outside the home.) Ultimately, research has revealed that in pleasant weather, crime typically increases, while in inclement weather or excessively high or low temperatures, crime seems to fall (Winton & Lee, 2005).

stop and think

Now that you've explored data analysts' various findings about the relationship between weather and crime, do these findings support – or contradict – the suggestions you made in response to the previous 'Stop and think'? In other words, do these findings match your predictions? What remaining questions need to be answered in future research?

Believe it or not, by following this simple 'Stop and think' exercise, you have already taken the first step toward understanding one of the most fundamental processes in research: *hypothesis testing*. A hypothesis is a formal statement or argument that identifies a relationship or explains a phenomenon in the real world. As we will see throughout this book, researchers can test the veracity of a particular hypothesis by collecting and analysing data. Hypothesis testing is so fundamental in research that we will revisit it in more detail in Chapter 2.

1.6 Defining 'Data'

We have been discussing *data* in detail for a while now, but it's time to step back and think about this concept more formally. What is data? At the beginning of this chapter, we defined data as 'quantitative or qualitative information about ourselves, society, or the universe'. This is the definition that I'll employ throughout this book, as it highlights the diversity and wide-ranging nature of data. However, my definition is not the only definition of data that scholars have advanced. Van Beveren (2002, p. 19), for example, has asserted that data are 'raw facts'. For Meaden and Chi (1996, p. 12), data are 'purposeful observations which have been recorded and stored'. Polit and Hungler (1999, p. 267), on the other hand, argue that the term 'data' can be applied to all information found during the research or inquiry process. Scholars even diverge in their opinions about whether the word 'data' should be treated as a singular or plural noun; technically speaking, the word is plural (meaning that one should write 'The data are...'), but the word is also commonly expressed as a singular noun ('The data is...'). Indeed, the singular form is frequently used in this book. This grammatical disagreement underscores a much larger philosophical point: data is a heterogeneous concept, and no one single definition appeals to all data analysts (for more information about the numerous different approaches scholars have taken to define the term 'data', see the discussion in Fox, Levitin, & Redman, 1994, pp. 11–12).

Regardless of which specific definition of data you prefer, it's important to note that data typically needs to be managed or organized in some way to offer knowledge value to users (Hoffer, Prescott, & McFadden, 2002; Van Beveren, 2002, p. 19). Once data has been arranged into a useful form, it can be analysed to provide information (Meaden & Chi, 1996, p. 12). We will explore the question of how to most effectively organize data in preparation for analysis in detail in later chapters of this book.

1.6.1 Thinking creatively about data

Earlier in this chapter we investigated several examples of researchers thinking creatively about data. From de Tocqueville's thoughtful, qualitative observations of societal dynamics to Quetelet's innovative, quantitative examinations of weather's effects, it's clear that data can be analysed in a wide variety of diverse and original ways. As you embark upon your journey into data analysis, keep this point in mind: there is no single 'right' way to analyse data. Yes, there are best practices and ethical guidelines that all responsible data analysts must follow (which we'll discuss in Chapter 3), but, beyond these precepts, data analysts have significant freedom to choose different analytical approaches. To become a 'good' data analyst you must learn to use this freedom wisely, and to think creatively about how best to answer your research questions. Sometimes thinking creatively about data means *combining* different analytical techniques; for example, instead of relying solely on quantitative or qualitative methods alone, one might choose to combine their respective advantages.

A landmark real-world example of such a creative approach can be seen in the 'Middletown' studies, launched by the sociologists Robert S. Lynd and Helen Merrell Lynd in the 1920s. The Lynds wanted to understand how the economic growth and industrialization of the late nineteenth and early twentieth centuries impacted life in an 'average' mid-size American city. To answer these research questions, they conducted fieldwork over a three-year period in Muncie, Indiana – a city they referred to by the pseudonym 'Middletown' in their published findings (Geelhoed, 2000; Emmel, 2013). Lynd and Lynd (1929) used both quantitative and qualitative data to explore their research questions; specifically, they conducted interviews, analysed relevant documents such as local newspapers, and compiled key statistics. Their use of multiple types of data was an inspired strategy that allowed them to create a vivid portrait of this community. Although still novel in the Lynds' time, the use of both quantitative and qualitative methods in the same study is more popular today. This approach is known as *mixed methods*, and we will explore it in detail in Chapter 8.

The Lynds also brought a creative perspective to their work by trying to explore Muncie as 'outsiders' – in other words, they investigated industry, community, class, religion, and family life in Middletown as if they belonged to a foreign culture (Peters & Simonson, 2004, p. 58). (This kind of approach, if you recall, was also helpful for de Tocqueville.) The Lynds' goal was to use their single, in-depth case study of Middletown to formulate broader conclusions about how industrialization impacted people's lives – not just in Muncie, Indiana, but all over 'middle America' (Schreier, 2018). The book reporting their findings, *Middletown: A Study in Modern American Culture* (Lynd & Lynd, 1929), was extremely popular with the public, and was even 'displayed in bookstore windows alongside the leading novels of the time' (Horowitz, 2004, Chapter 32) – a testament to the ingenuity and magnitude of their work.

The book inspired numerous follow-up works, beginning with the Lynds' own effort in the 1930s to assess how the Great Depression and the subsequent increase in unemployment affected societal and family life in Middletown (Lynd & Lynd, 1937). In the 1970s a new generation of sociologists returned to Middletown and employed many of the same research methods that the Lynds had originally used, to assess how the town had changed in the 50 years since the Lynds' original work (Center for Middletown Studies, 2018). As part of this updated research, Caplow, Bahr, Chadwick, Hill, and Williamson (1982) administered surveys in the late 1970s to compile extensive quantitative data about myriad details of social life, such as the number of hours per week that mothers and fathers spent with their children (disaggregated by social class), and adults' self-reported frequency of church attendance. In the 1990s and 2000s, researchers also addressed the original study's failure to fully account for Middletown's diversity, and gave greater attention to the city's African-American and Jewish communities (Emmel, 2013; see also Lassiter, Goodall, Campbell, & Johnson, 2004; Rottenberg, 1997). Researchers have continued to study Middletown, and a Center for Middletown Studies (2018) is active at Ball State University in Muncie, Indiana (i.e., in the actual Middletown). As recently as 2015, a major new study was published exploring the books and other reading materials that were popular in Middletown, to better understand the community's values and culture (Felsenstein & Connolly, 2015).

This enduring interest in research about Middletown illustrates the tremendous and continual power of data to yield new and exciting insights about the world. By bringing fresh perspectives, asking creative research questions, and employing rigorous research methods, multiple generations of social scientists have been able to uncover fascinating insights about one 'ordinary' place. In other words, data analysis can help us see the 'ordinary' in new and exciting ways.

1.7 From 'Data' to 'Big Data'

In addition to the word 'data', you may also have encountered the phrase **big data**. This phrase has been used with increasing frequency in recent years, and refers to the broader range and larger scale of data that is now available due to technological advances. The internet, digital archives, smartphones, and social networking are just a few of the technological changes that have contributed to the enhanced availability of data. Big data is not just affecting a few limited industries; it has already started to impact a wide variety of sectors (see, for example, the discussion in Liebowitz, 2013). Even seemingly traditional areas of the economy such as agriculture have been impacted, with farmers using big data to help them make more efficient use of their land (Doering, 2014). Such transformations mean that right now is a fascinating time to explore data analysis, and that the opportunities and needs for competence in this area will continue to grow (Mayer-Schönberger & Cukier, 2013).

Despite the substantial promise of big data, some scholars have advocated caution, and warned of the need to better recognize its limitations. For example, Taleb (2013) has warned that big data has simply created an ever larger 'haystack' that needs to be searched to find the needle of important information. Building on this idea, one could argue that big data has in fact made the data analysis process *more* intricate and gruelling, and not more streamlined. In addition, although big data can detect associations or patterns that cannot be found in smaller datasets, it cannot identify which of these associations and patterns are actually valid and meaningful (Marcus & Davis, 2014). Finally, by allowing a researcher to identify more possible associations, larger datasets increase the potential for identifying false associations – or patterns that are the result of chance rather than real characteristics of the dataset.

Alongside these concerns about the impact of big data on data analysis, the growth of big data has also prompted widespread privacy fears about how companies and governments collect, store, and use personal data. Such concerns about privacy and technology are not new; in the 1960s similar fears were expressed when the US federal government began to use large mainframe computers to handle certain data related to tax returns (Lohr, 2013). Nevertheless, today the use of social networking, smartphones, GPS technology, and other big data-related developments have all multiplied the amount of personal data that we willingly or unwillingly share with technology providers and other entities. These developments have prompted discussions and policy recommendations about data privacy.

For example, in the USA, former President Barack Obama launched a review of big data and privacy issues in January 2014; members of the review panel included the Secretary of Commerce, Secretary of Energy, and the President's Science Advisor (Podesta, 2014). The panel's recommendations included the idea that individuals 'deserve clear, understandable, reasonable standards for how their personal information is used in the big data era' and the argument that 'a single national data breach standard' should be adopted to govern large-scale breaches of personal data (Podesta, 2014).

stop and think

Had you heard the phrase 'big data' before reading this book? Do you think the growth of big data is exciting, scary, or neither? In addition to the concerns just described, are there any other potential problems related to big data that you foresee?

1.8 Concluding Thoughts

Although the title of this chapter is 'Introducing Data', data really needs no introduction. Every day, as we go about our lives, we're surrounded by data; we are also regular creators of data as we surf the internet and click on links. In fact, in our technologically equipped world, it's almost impossible to avoid any interactions with data.

Given the ubiquity of data, the ability to make sense of it and therefore understand what the data actually means are essential skills. The goal of this textbook is to help you develop those skills. In the upcoming chapters we'll explore many different kinds of data – from numbers and statistics to words and human interactions – and examine the techniques you can employ to analyse these various data forms. We'll explore both the promise of data analysis and its drawbacks and limitations. As we just saw in our discussion of the 'big data' phenomenon, data analysis can pose significant ethical challenges, which any burgeoning data analyst must confront.

Summary

- Data surrounds us, and allows us to make discoveries that intuition or common sense alone could not uncover. The goal of this book is to develop your data analysis skills to help you harness data's power.
- The power of data can be seen in the policy impact of the data collected about London's December 1952 air pollution event, the long-term popularity of Alexis de Tocqueville's qualitative observations about the USA, and the continuing contemporary interest in the Body Mass Index (BMI), a statistic that emerged out of the work of the nineteenth-century data analyst Adolphe Quetelet.
- Different scholars have promoted a variety of definitions for the term 'data'.
- One of the most exciting recent developments in data analysis has been the emergence of 'big data'. Yet this phenomenon has also raised concerns, both for its potential impact on data analysis and for its potential impact on privacy.

Further Reading

Want to learn more about the London fog and the role of data in tackling air pollution? Take a look at the following compelling account:

Thorsheim, P. (2006). *Inventing pollution: Coal, smoke, and culture in Britain since 1800.* Athens, OH: Ohio University Press.

Seasonal patterns in crime rates are fascinating, and reveal the power of data analysis to illustrate large-scale relationships. For an interesting and sophisticated example of such analysis, see:

McDowall, D., Loftin, C., & Pate, M. (2012). Seasonal cycles in crime, and their variability. *Journal of Quantitative Criminology*, 28, 389–410.

In this chapter we explored why Adolphe Quetelet is considered to be one of the most innovative early thinkers in the field of data analysis. Why not investigate his work for yourself? Although some of his ideas are outdated, it is still interesting to follow the work of a data analyst grappling with social phenomena that had never been rigorously studied before. To find the original English translation of Quetelet's landmark work on height and weight, look for:

Quetelet, L. A. J. (1842). *A treatise on man and the development of his faculties*. Edinburgh: William and Robert Chambers. (Reprinted in: Hawkins, F. B. (1973). *Comparative statistics in the 19th century*. Farnborough: Gregg International Publishers.)

The exciting example of the 'Middletown' studies shows the power of data analysis to help us see the 'ordinary' world in new and exciting ways. If you're interested in finding out more about the history of Middletown research, as well as more recent scholarly efforts, take a look at the following website:

Center for Middletown Studies (2018). About the Center. Muncie, IN: Ball State University. Retrieved from http://cms.bsu.edu/academics/centersandinstitutes/middletown/about

The 'big data' phenomenon has reinvigorated interest in quantitative data analysis. Want to learn more about how big data might impact society in the coming years? For a fascinating but easy-to-read overview, see:

Mayer-Schönberger, V., & Cukier, K. (2013). *Big data: A revolution that will transform how we live, work, and think*. Boston: Houghton Mifflin Harcourt.

Discussion Questions

1. In thinking about the relationship between weather and crime in this chapter, one factor we failed to consider was the effect of different climates. The majority of studies we discussed were conducted in just one country: the United States. Do you think the same patterns described in this chapter would apply to different regions of the world, which experience very diverse weather patterns and climate conditions? Why or why not? (This question of whether findings are *generalizable* to other contexts and conditions is a fundamental theme in data analysis, and one we will return to in the next chapter.)
2. Does your answer to Question 1 change after learning that Yan (2004) examined data about theft and burglary in Hong Kong, a city with a subtropical climate, and found *no* seasonal patterns in rates of overall theft or burglary? Explain the reason(s) for your answer.
3. How do you define the term 'data'? Does your definition differ from the definitions presented in this chapter?
4. What explains the persistent popularity of the Body Mass Index (BMI) measure? Why do you think this nineteenth-century measure is still in use today?

Thinking like a Data Analyst

contents

Chapter Overview

By the end of this chapter, you will know how to:

- Cultivate the 'rigorous attitude' necessary for becoming a data analyst
- Explain what *positivist* and *interpretivist* frameworks are, and how they can each shape the data analysis process
- Discuss what *quantitative* and *qualitative* data analysis approaches are
- Define the term *hypothesis*, and articulate the differences between null and alternative hypotheses
- Identify alternative approaches to data analysis such as *grounded theory* research, *action research*, and *critical research*
- Discuss the different types of validity that are important in research, including *internal validity*, *construct validity*, *external validity*, and *descriptive validity*
- Define the term *triangulation* and explain its crucial role in data analysis.

Introduction: Developing a Rigorous, Reflective Attitude

Data analysis requires you to adopt a rigorous, reflective attitude and a rational and methodological approach to research questions about the world. This attitude will allow you to recognize both the strengths and weaknesses of your own data analysis methods, as well as the data analysis methods of other scholars. In order to cultivate a rigorous, reflective attitude, you must first select an appropriate theoretical framework (or combination of theoretical frameworks) to guide your data analysis. This framework will help you develop interesting research questions, design an effective research study, advance a methodological approach to analyse your data, assess your findings, and identify the limitations of your work. At each stage in the research process, your rigorous, methodological approach to data analysis will allow you to interrogate your assumptions about data, and identify intriguing findings or relationships that exist in the social world.

This chapter will help you cultivate a rigorous attitude by introducing different theoretical frameworks to guide your analysis. We will then begin to explore the two main types of data, *quantitative* and *qualitative*, and investigate different analytical techniques that can be used to analyse these data types. Next we will move into the process of *hypothesis testing* – the formal process of questioning and testing assumptions about data – that is an essential component of many but not all data analyses. The knowledge presented in this chapter will serve as a springboard for the later chapters, in which we will explore specific quantitative and qualitative data analysis procedures in detail.

Above all else, developing a rigorous, reflective attitude requires you to *think for yourself*. A good data analyst is always asking questions, both about the data she has collected and about the phenomena she is studying. A good data analyst does not rely on superstition, habit, or even 'common sense' to answer such questions. Instead, a good data analyst focuses only on *data* that has been scrupulously collected and analysed before drawing conclusions. Even then, a good data analyst takes time to thoroughly consider her findings' limitations, and acknowledge these limitations when presenting her results.

As you read this chapter, ask questions. Question your data. Question this book. Question your lecturer. Respond to the questions and exercises contained in this text. Think about where you stand on the data analysis debates discussed in this chapter. By doing each of these things you will develop a rigorous attitude about the world around you. And although data analysis is often conceptualized solely as a list of statistical procedures or coding techniques that must be learned, an essential first step in any data analysis is the development of this rigorous attitude.

2.3 Positivist and Interpretivist Frameworks

In order to cultivate a rigorous attitude, you must first select an appropriate theoretical framework (or combination of theoretical frameworks) to guide your data analysis. This framework will help you progress through each stage of the data analysis process, from beginning your study and developing your research questions, to presenting your results once the study is complete.

Previous data analysts have drawn upon many different theoretical frameworks to guide their work. You should take time before beginning any data analysis to consider which theoretical framework (or frameworks) is most appropriate for your study. Choosing a suitable framework is essential, as this decision will influence your overall approach and data analysis methods.

Although we won't be able to discuss all the potential frameworks you could choose, we will now review two general frameworks that have shaped many previous data analyses. One (or both) of these frameworks might appeal to you and help shape the perspective you bring to your data. However, even if none of the ideas discussed in the following paragraphs appeal to you, do not worry. Many additional theoretical frameworks exist; you will encounter some of these frameworks as you read more widely in your discipline, and as you investigate previous studies that have examined the topic you are interested in (or related topics). If you still have trouble selecting a framework even after reading more widely, consult the suggestions for further reading given at the end of this chapter. Several of the books on that list describe additional frameworks that may be relevant to you.

In this chapter, however, we will focus on two general frameworks that have substantially influenced much data analysis in the social sciences. These two frameworks are the **positivist tradition** and the **interpretivist tradition**. The *positivist* tradition posits that an objective reality exists which researchers can study through direct, rigorous observation. Ideally, for positivist researchers, such observation should include experiments or other tightly controlled analyses in which a researcher can isolate cause-and-effect relationships. (For more information about how to define the positivist tradition, see: Merriman, 2009, p. 8; Newman & Benz, 1998, p. 4; Wimmer & Dominick, 2014, p. 118.)

For example, suppose you are interested in exploring the question of whether a new drug treatment programme is more effective than the programme a treatment centre currently uses. To examine this issue from a positivist perspective, you might conduct an experiment in which you *randomly* assign individuals to the new drug treatment programme or to the current programme. Random assignment minimizes the possibility that any differences you observe are due to factors other than the type of treatment programme. If you did not randomly assign individuals to treatment programmes, some other factor – such as a difference in gender or average age of the groups – might actually be responsible for the different results you observe for the groups. The goal of positivist research is to limit and control such alternative possibilities, to increase confidence that your findings represent reality, and that you are actually studying the relationship or process that you intend to study.

Standing in sharp contrast to the positivist tradition is the *interpretivist* tradition. The interpretivist tradition (which is also known as the *constructivist* perspective) asserts that there is no singular, objective reality, as every individual interprets the world in his or her own way. According to the interpretivist perspective, our interpretations of the world are shaped by our experiences, and by the societies in which we live. The goal of interpretivist research, therefore, is to uncover research participants' different perspectives (Gratton & Jones, 2010, p. 28). As a result, much interpretivist research is actually fieldwork, undertaken 'in natural surroundings' so that a researcher can 'capture the normal flow of events' without worrying about creating a rigorously-controlled experimental setting (Wimmer & Dominick, 2014, p. 118). For example, let's imagine you were still interested in the question posed above – namely, whether a new drug treatment programme is more effective than the programme a treatment centre currently uses. To examine this question from an interpretivist perspective, you might be most interested in understanding the experiences of the individuals who participate in the two different programmes. Therefore you might conduct interviews with those individuals to uncover their opinions about the programmes, to assess whether, and in what ways, the programmes have impacted their lives.

Table 2.1 The positivist and interpretivist frameworks

Framework	Assumptions	Example
Positivist Tradition	An objective reality exists which researchers can uncover. By establishing rigorously controlled conditions, a researcher can isolate the effects of a particular variable or set of variables. Common techniques for increasing the rigour of research include randomly assigning research participants to different conditions, or considering alternative explanations during the analysis process.	A researcher wants to assess the effects of an online tutoring programme on undergraduates' performance in a research methods class. The undergraduates enrolled in a research methods class are randomly assigned to either receive online tutoring or not receive online tutoring. After 4 weeks, all the students are given an exam to test their research methods knowledge. The performance of the students who received the tutoring is compared to the performance of the students who did not receive the tutoring.
Interpretivist Tradition	No single objective reality exists. Researchers should instead focus on uncovering different individuals' interpretations of reality. Rather than trying to isolate the effects of particular variables, research should illuminate the nuances of individuals' perspectives.	A researcher wants to understand the experiences of newly qualified teachers. The researcher conducts in-depth interviews with 15 newly qualified teachers and asks them about their stress levels and attitudes towards their profession.

Table 2.1 summarizes the key components of the positivist and interpretivist perspectives, and offers an example of a research project for each tradition.

stop and think

In one or two sentences, explain what the positivist tradition is. Then explain what the interpretivist tradition is. What are the key differences between the positivist and interpretivist frameworks? If you have trouble identifying either perspective, take a look back at Table 2.1 before moving on to the next section.

Although *in theory* the divide between positivist and interpretivist traditions is vast, *in practice* the distinction between these two traditions is not always clear-cut. For example, many positivist researchers accept the interpretivist idea that a researcher's own beliefs and perspective can shape his approach to data analysis, although positivists may not describe these effects in as much detail as interpretivists (Weber, 2004, p. vi). Some researchers draw upon elements of both traditions when designing their data analysis projects. For example, a researcher might conduct an evaluation of a job training programme to determine its effectiveness; the same researcher might also conduct interviews with programme participants to understand their perspectives on the programme. The researcher might bring a positivist perspective to the first part of this study (the evaluation) and an interpretivist perspective to the second part of this study (the interviews).

Further complicating the distinction between the positivist and interpretivist traditions is that different researchers advance diverse interpretations of the two perspectives' principles. Even the term 'interpretivist' has been defined differently by researchers (Schwandt, 2006, p. 40). Despite this diversity of understandings, it is important to consider the distinctions between the positivist and interpretivist traditions, as these are among the most prominent theoretical perspectives in social science research.

Contrasting Quantitative and Qualitative Approaches

Traditionally, these two theoretical traditions – positivist and interpretivist – have been associated with different data analysis methods. While positivist approaches have been linked with the analysis of *quantitative* data, interpretivist approaches have been conventionally associated with *qualitative* data. However, these linkages are no longer fixed and some qualitative research has been expressly conducted in the positivist tradition (see the examples cited in Myers, 1997), and some quantitative research has been conducted in the interpretivist tradition (see the discussion in Westerman, 2006).

Quantitative research is research that focuses on numbers and the quantification of concepts or relationships between concepts. Statistical methods are typically used to determine the likelihood that an observed relationship between variables is not due to chance. Often the goal of quantitative research is to uncover findings that can be generalizable beyond a single case or context. As we will see in the next chapter, quantitative research can include experiments, evaluations, secondary data analysis (or analysis of data collected by other researchers), surveys, and a variety of other more specific research methods.

stop and think

Can you think of an example of quantitative research? What makes your example *quantitative*?

Qualitative research, in contrast, typically focuses on text or image-based sources rather than numbers and aims to achieve a deep and specific analysis of a particular process or setting, rather than more generalizable findings (Maxwell, 2013, p. viii). As we will see in Chapter 6, qualitative research can include interviews, ethnographies, content analysis, and a variety of other more specific research methods.

stop and think

Can you think of an example of qualitative research? What makes your example *qualitative*?

Quantitative and qualitative methods both have limitations, and have been subjected to specific critiques. Quantitative studies can be limited by the need to reduce complex phenomena or social structures to a selection of representative variables that do not offer a true 'feel' for the nuances and complexities of these structures (Bryman, 1989, p. 115). On the other hand, Mays and Pope (1995, p. 109) have described how traditional critiques levelled at qualitative research include the accusation that it is vulnerable 'to researcher bias' and difficult to replicate as 'the research is so personal to the researcher', and different researchers might interpret the same data differently. An interpretivist perspective might lead you to argue that this limitation is an inherent feature of research and therefore unproblematic; however, those interpretivist researchers who *do* consider this limitation to be problematic have devised several strategies for overcoming it, which we will explore in Chapter 6.

The prominence of quantitative and qualitative methods in social science research has varied over time. In the immediate post-World War II period, quantitative methods prevailed in social science, but by the 1960s, new perspectives emphasizing power dynamics and the complex 'value-laden nature of human social interactions' came to the forefront and cast doubt on whether quantitative techniques adapted from the natural or physical sciences were appropriate for studying the intricacies of individual lives and societal phenomena (Newman & Benz, 1998, p. 5). This theoretical shift brought increasing prominence to qualitative methods, although some scholars questioned whether qualitative research was given as much attention or esteem as quantitative methods (Dey, 1993, p. 4) – criticisms that still reverberate today.

The distinction between quantitative and qualitative methods is a central feature of many data analysis courses and textbooks (including this one!), but it's important to remember that the methods share many important similarities. Both types focus on rigorous analysis and are driven by a similar desire to understand the social world. Quantitative and qualitative methods are also increasingly being used together as part of the same research project. This type of research, known as *mixed-methods research*, allows a researcher to benefit from the advantages that both quantitative and qualitative methods offer. Conducting mixed-methods research also poses additional challenges though, and these challenges are discussed in detail in Chapter 8.

2.4.1 Case study: Using quantitative and qualitative methods to study policy-making

In my own work I have found that employing both quantitative and qualitative methods can reveal findings that would not have been discovered through the use of just one method on its own. For example, in my book *The Evidence Enigma* I explored why a particular criminal justice policy spread widely throughout the United States in the 1990s (Bergin, 2013). I used quantitative methods to probe whether US state governments' decisions to adopt this policy were related to economic and political conditions, crime rates, and other societal circumstances. In my quantitative data analysis, I represented each of these concepts through numerical values. For example, one way that I represented economic conditions was to include a measure of the unemployment rate in each state. In addition to quantitative methods, I also employed qualitative methods to explore the same research questions. Specifically, I used qualitative data when examining two case studies of the discourse surrounding states' decisions to adopt this policy. My sources for qualitative data included legislative transcripts, news reports, and policy-making documents.

By combining quantitative and qualitative methods I was able to produce findings that were both broad in scope (as all 50 states could be included in the quantitative analysis) and deep in scope (as the two case studies could be explored in great depth in the qualitative analysis). Additionally, several findings emerged in the quantitative analysis that could not have been uncovered through qualitative analysis alone, and several findings emerged in the qualitative analysis that could not have been uncovered through quantitative analysis alone. Such discoveries highlight the value of each of these methods, as well as the potential utility of employing both methods together. These issues will be covered in greater depth in Chapter 8.

2.5 Hypotheses and How to Test Them

In Chapter 1, you considered the question of whether the weather affects crime rates. Your initial answer to this question – either that 'the weather affects crime rates' or that 'the weather does not affect crime rates' – was a **hypothesis**. A hypothesis is a belief or argument about the social world based on experience, intuition, or the findings of previous research. In Chapter 1 you then engaged in an informal version of **hypothesis testing**, or examining whether your hypothesis actually matched data collected in the real world. Based on these findings, you then accepted, rejected, or revised your original hypothesis. This process is a central component of data analysis.

For research to be considered valid and objective, hypothesis testing must adhere to a formal, rule-based process to ensure that any researcher examining this particular dataset would achieve an identical result (Smith, Gratz, & Bousquet, 2009, p. 163). Hypothesis testing actually requires a researcher to formulate *two* hypotheses: an **alternative hypothesis** and a **null hypothesis**. These two hypotheses are opposites of each other (see Table 2.2). The alternative hypothesis posits that there *is* a relationship or a difference that the researcher is interested in, while the null hypothesis posits that there is *no* relationship or difference of interest. The null hypothesis always perfectly complements the alternative hypothesis. In research studies, the null hypothesis is denoted H_0 and the alternative hypothesis is denoted H_1. It is imperative to identify one's hypotheses *prior to* beginning the analysis process; hypotheses should not be edited or flipped around once your results are ready. Such practices can lead to erroneous or misleading results in some statistical tests.

Table 2.2 Null and alternative hypotheses

Type of hypothesis	Notation	Content	Example
Null hypothesis	H_0	There is *no* relationship or difference	Junior employees assigned a mentor are not more enthusiastic about their jobs than junior employees not assigned a mentor
Alternative hypothesis	H_1	There *is* a relationship or a difference	Junior employees assigned a mentor are more enthusiastic about their jobs than junior employees not assigned a mentor

Although a researcher is usually interested in the alternative hypothesis, technically she will test the null hypothesis. After analysing her data, she will report whether she has *rejected* the null hypothesis, or *failed to reject* the null hypothesis. If a researcher fails to reject the null hypothesis, she cannot say that she has 'proved' the null hypothesis, as collecting more data might result in a rejection (Howell, 2007, pp. 91–92). In this light, it is helpful to remember Smith, Gratz, and Bousquet's (2009, p. 163) advice that failing to reject the null should not be viewed as a disappointment, but as a first step towards 'more refined research'. It can prompt a researcher to look at her data more closely to consider whether more nuanced results are present for different groups in the dataset (for example, for men and for women). Trying to understand *why* the null hypothesis could not be rejected can be a very interesting and important question as well.

One prominent school of thought, most closely associated with the work of the twentieth-century philosopher Karl Popper (2002), sees hypothesis testing as a process of *falsification*. Popper posited that scientific hypotheses must be *falsifiable* or testable; this means that a hypothesis should be articulated in such a way that a scientific study could determine if the hypothesis was *untrue*. Although Popper's framework has been criticized (for a discussion of key criticisms, see Yazici, Lesaffre, & Yazici, 2014, p. 255), the framework does highlight a significant principle in data analysis. Specifically, Popper's work shows the importance of ensuring that your own hypotheses are falsifiable before embarking on a research project.

In addition to falsifiability, what are the other characteristics of a 'good' hypothesis? A good hypothesis must also be *logical*; it needs to make sense. A good hypothesis should also be *succinct*, or expressed as simply as possible (Balnaves & Caputi, 2001, p. 45). Check that your own hypothesis makes logical sense and is not too complex before proceeding too far with your research. Finally, a good hypothesis should be *specific*; hypotheses that are too general or vague can confuse readers and make it difficult to determine whether a research project has actually tested the hypothesis.

Hypotheses that do not make logical sense need to be reformulated; hypotheses that are too complex can sometimes be broken down into multiple good hypotheses and may form the basis for several research projects.

Although, in the social sciences, hypothesis testing is most associated with quantitative research, many qualitative researchers also engage in hypothesis testing. Indeed, there have been calls for this process of 'scientific inference' to be adopted more widely in qualitative research (King, Keohane, & Verba, 1994, p. ix). Not all qualitative research follows the process of hypothesis testing described in this section, however. Sometimes qualitative researchers construct their own theories and ideas from the data they have collected in the field, rather than formulate a hypothesis and then test it (Merriman, 2009, p. 14). In other words, researchers use data to *build* theories or hypotheses, rather than use data to *test* theories or hypotheses. This form of theory generation is known as ***grounded theory*** (Glaser & Strauss, 1967) and we will explore it in more detail in the next section of this chapter.

Finally, it is important to recognize that the process of hypothesis testing does not end once a single test (or single data analysis or research project) has been completed. Social science can instead be viewed as a continual process of testing hypotheses, developing results, and generating new hypotheses – thereby beginning the process all over again. Although this constant testing and hypothesis generating might seem tiring, it makes research exciting, and offers numerous opportunities for researchers to contribute new findings to their respective fields.

let's try this!

Think about an area of research that most interests you. What unanswered questions remain in that area of research? Perhaps uncertainty remains about whether a particular social intervention has positive effects, or whether a relationship exists between two different variables. Write down at least three questions and, if possible, share them with a classmate or friend also taking your course. Now think about how you might turn those questions into hypotheses and actually explore these questions through data. Keep in mind the criteria specified above and make sure your hypothesis is:

Falsifiable or testable

Logical

Succinct, or expressed as simply as possible

Specific.

Talk to your classmate or friend about your hypotheses and ask them for feedback. Do they agree that your hypotheses meet the criteria specified above? Do they have suggestions about how the hypotheses can be improved? By completing this process, you've achieved the first stage of research and data analysis – and maybe even generated some hypotheses to explore in a future research project or thesis!

2.6 Other Theoretical Approaches

2.6.1 Grounded theory

In contrast to the traditional process of hypothesis testing described in the previous section, some research employs a **grounded theory** approach which emphasizes formulating theories out of data, rather than relying on data to test hypotheses. Pioneered by Barney Glaser and Anselm Strauss (1965, 1967), the grounded theory approach stresses 'the constant comparative method' when analysing data, so that 'concepts or categories emerging from one stage of the data analysis are compared with concepts emerging from the next', and the connections between these concepts are then used to formulate a theoretical understanding of the phenomena or subjects of interest (Lacey & Luff, 2007, p. 10).

To engage in a true grounded theory approach, a researcher therefore must be careful not to be influenced by prior knowledge or fixed ideas before entering the field, but instead should be focused on 'grounding theory in data' (Noaks & Wincup, 2004, pp. 122–123). The grounded theory approach is more common in qualitative research than in quantitative research and stands in stark contrast to the traditional process of scientific inference as described by Popper in which 'theory precedes experiment' (Manzi, 2012, pp. 17–18). Of course, it is difficult for an analysis to be thoroughly grounded in the data, as every researcher, despite how hard they might try, will bring some ideas and preconceptions to the research process. The inevitable presence of such biases must, of course, be recognized by the researcher. (Indeed, as described at the beginning of this chapter, the *interpretivist* perspective directly acknowledges the importance of a researcher's own perspective in the research process. For example, if a researcher who is studying the news media is a former journalist, this past experience should be acknowledged. The researcher should consider how such experience might affect his or her analysis of current journalists' perspectives.) Additionally, even if themes appear spontaneously in a grounded theory analysis, the researcher is still the authority who must *identify* and *describe* those themes, illustrating the necessity of always acknowledging the researcher's influence over the analysis process. However, grounded theory is still very much 'a scientific method', since, like other data analysis approaches, it also emphasizes 'precision, rigor, and verification' throughout the research process (Strauss & Corbin, 1990, p. 27).

If you decide to adopt a grounded theory approach rather than a hypothesis-testing approach, you will need to adjust the procedures you employ to analyse your data. The chapters on qualitative data analysis techniques later in this book offer guidance about how a grounded theory approach specifically affects the coding and analysis processes.

stop and think

How does the *grounded theory* approach to data analysis differ from the *hypothesis-testing* approach?

2.6.2 Action research

Another very different theoretical approach you could choose to adopt in your research is the **action research** approach. As its name suggests, action research uses research to generate action – or, more specifically, to generate forward-thinking 'social change' (Greenwood & Levin, 2007, p. 5). The presence of this specific, practice-focused goal distinguishes action research from the *positivist, interpretivist,* and *grounded theory* approaches already presented. Indeed, action research emphasizes the production of applied, real-world findings that are 'useful to people in the everyday conduct of their lives' (Reason & Bradbury, 2006, p. 2). Any kind of research (including both quantitative and qualitative studies) can be conducted from an action research perspective, and interviews, statistical analyses, participant observation studies, and many other forms of research have all been undertaken within this paradigm. For example, an international development researcher might use interviews and participant observation with local community members to improve the design and implementation of development initiatives. (For an example of a development-oriented action research project, see Bacon, Mendez, & Brown, 2005. To see further examples of action research that illustrate the diversity of subjects and methods used in this approach, see the different chapters of Klein, 2012.)

2.6.3 Critical research

Sometimes qualitative researchers adopt a *critical* approach to their research topic. A critical approach identifies and critiques power imbalances throughout society, and seeks to understand how those power imbalances were created, and how such inequalities have been maintained. In other words, **critical research** questions current social structures. Given its focus on inequality, some – but by no means all – critical researchers utilize Marxist ideas questioning capitalism and the power dynamics present in market economies (Stahl, 2008, p. 10). Like action researchers, critical researchers may explore the causes of societal inequalities; however, critical researchers do not adopt the same action-based orientation that action researchers employ. A compelling real-world example of critical research is Xiao, Paterson, Henderson, and Kelton's (2008) study of how to train nursing students to treat elderly patients. In this qualitative study, Xiao et al. adopted a critical perspective to better ascertain the obstacles to establishing such training in this area, and design strategies to overcome those obstacles. The goal of Xiao et al.'s study, therefore, was not merely to research current practices but to actively *improve* those practices.

The alternative theoretical approaches discussed in this section – *grounded theory, action research,* and *critical research* – do not represent the full range of approaches available to data analysts. Nevertheless, their diversity illustrates that no single approach is appropriate for all researchers or research projects. Some data analysis projects require a more positivist approach, while others might be more suited to a critical approach. Certain researchers may find that one of these approaches is apposite in most of their work, while other researchers may feel more comfortable applying varying approaches in different projects. Sometimes a combination of approaches might be useful in a particular study. For example, a researcher may wish to bring a grounded theory perspective to a set of data, but then, based on the results of that analysis, engage in action research to improve current practices.

2.7 Different Types of Validity

Testing a hypothesis produces results. But how *valid* are these results? How do you know if you can trust the findings of a data analysis? As we saw at the beginning of this chapter, becoming a data analyst requires you to adopt a rigorous attitude. You must approach the findings of any data analysis – including your own – with a critical eye. We have all seen or heard news reports about 'scientific' studies whose conclusions seem strange or exaggerated. So how do we know if we can trust the findings of these studies? In this textbook, you will learn a variety of specific methods for assessing the rigour and 'trustworthiness' of data analysis findings. However, one general consideration is whether the study's findings are *valid*, a determination that can only be made by exploring the following four types of validity: *internal validity*, *construct validity*, *external validity*, and *descriptive validity*. In this section we will explore each of these types of validity in turn.

2.7.1 Internal validity

The first type of validity is **internal validity**, which considers whether your data analysis actually reflects the relationship or effect you are interested in. A study with high internal validity will allow you to conclude that an effect is actually due to a particular cause, and not due to alternative confounding explanations (Gonzalez, Yu, & Volling, 2012, p. 251). Rigorously conducted experiments feature a high level of internal validity, since these designs minimize the impact of confounding alternative causes for the phenomenon you are interested in (Walker, 2005, p. 574). Internal validity is an essential component in assessing the overall rigour of many studies, as studies that do not minimize or control for confounding explanations cannot make trustworthy conclusions about the causes of particular phenomena or the directions of relationships between different variables.

2.7.2 Construct validity

The second type of validity is **construct validity**, which considers whether the variables or measures you have included in your study accurately reflect the constructs or concepts they are intended to represent (Ary, Jacobs, Sorensen, & Walker, 2014). For instance, in the example from my own research on the spread of a criminal justice policy that I discussed in the case study in Section 2.4, I mentioned that I used the unemployment rate to partly represent economic conditions in US states (Bergin, 2013). Is the unemployment rate an accurate reflection of the construct 'economic conditions'? I think it is, but perhaps you disagree. (You don't have to agree with me just because I am the author of your book!) If the unemployment rate does not accurately reflect or capture 'economic conditions', then we must question the construct validity of this study. Ultimately, construct validity is essential because, as Dooley (2001, p. 270) has observed, even if a study features 'high internal and external validity, the findings say nothing about the constructs of interest' if construct validity is not present.

let's try this!

Think about a construct from your area of study. The construct should be a broad concept relevant to your field, such as 'poverty' or 'self-esteem' or 'violent crime'. Have you been assigned any readings for other classes that have addressed this construct? If so, revisit those readings. If not, take a brief moment to search for your construct in a scholarly database. In the documents you find, look carefully at how the authors *specifically* measure the construct. For example, perhaps poverty in a particular country is measured as the percentage of households with an annual income below a certain monetary level. Assess the construct validity of each of these specific measures. Do you think the measures adequately capture the construct they are intended to capture? Can you think of any ways to improve the construct validity of these measures?

The questions you just answered in the exercise above are particularly important in the social sciences. As Cartwright and Runhardt (2014, p. 284) have discussed, 'social science measures are often value-laden' because they focus on important issues – such as poverty or violent crime – that are connected to social values. Therefore, our decisions about how to represent constructs often intersect not only with practical research concerns but also with deeper questions of societal values.

2.7.3 External validity (or reliability)

The third type of validity, **external validity**, focuses on whether the findings of a single study can be *generalized* to additional settings, historical periods, groups, or societies. This is the exact issue that you considered in the previous chapter, when you explored whether findings from data analyses about the relationship between weather and crime also held true in different contexts (namely, in other regions of the world with diverse weather patterns and climates).

Even studies with high levels of internal validity and construct validity may exhibit low levels of external validity if their findings are not applicable in other settings. (For an interesting discussion of barriers and challenges related to external validity, see Wagner, 2003, pp. 64–66.) Indeed, rigorously conducted laboratory experiments with high internal validity may be particularly susceptible to external validity problems since 'laboratory settings are not, by definition, natural settings' (Balnaves & Caputi, 2001, p. 95).

How can we foster external validity in our own data analysis work? Utilizing larger and more diverse samples and replicating a study in different cultural contexts are two key methods for increasing external validity. For projects that involve an element of researcher judgement, such as qualitative analyses of textual data, you can increase external validity by asking other scholars to conduct their own analysis of your data to check whether their judgements match your own, thus promoting a type of external validity called *inter-rater* or *inter-coder reliability* (Armstrong, Gosling, Weinman, & Marteau, 1997; Lombard, Snyder-Duch, & Bracken, 2002). Other forms of research may require specific strategies to ensure external validity. For example, in historical research, an important component of external validity is the accuracy of information presented in historical documents; a responsible historical researcher should always investigate whether the information contained in one historical document is supported by evidence from other sources.

External validity, in slightly different forms, is an important consideration in many projects. However, not all projects endeavour to achieve high external validity. A researcher who examines a few particular cases in depth may have no intention of producing findings that also apply to other cases or time periods. Such researchers must be scrupulous, however, in acknowledging this lack of generalizability when they present their findings – a practice that reflects the next type of validity, *descriptive validity*, which we will examine below.

2.7.4 Descriptive validity

Although not traditionally emphasized in introductory textbooks, **descriptive validity** is gaining increasing attention among data analysts and is viewed by some researchers as one of the most important determinants of a study's rigour and quality (Farrington, 2003, p. 61). Descriptive validity involves accurately and comprehensively describing a study's data collection and analysis procedures (Perry, 2010). Accurate and detailed descriptions can help readers of the study determine whether the other types of validity were threatened during the study (Gill, 2011, p. 203), and can also help future researchers replicate a study's methods and findings. When writing up the findings of any data analysis, a researcher should be careful to describe his methods in detail so that readers can accurately assess whether the other types of validity have been achieved.

stop and think

Why is *descriptive validity* so important in social science research? What problems can arise when a study exhibits low descriptive validity?

The four types of validity discussed in this section – internal, construct, external, and descriptive – are not the only types of validity that scholars have identified, although their centrality in many data analysis procedures merits their inclusion here. (For more information on the additional types of validity that previous researchers have identified – including *theoretical validity* and *interpretive validity* – see Thomas, 2006). Ultimately, even the most assiduous researchers cannot always perfectly achieve (or even want to achieve) all types of validity in their research projects. Nevertheless, when designing your own data analysis or critiquing another researcher's work, it is important to keep these concepts in mind as they may help frame your assessment of a study's rigour.

2.8 Triangulation

How can we ensure that our data analysis contains all four types of validity? As we saw in the previous section, a range of tactics exist for probing the different types of validity. One general method that can be used to increase several types of validity and augment the overall 'trustworthiness' of data analysis findings is **triangulation**. Triangulation is the application of different data analysis methods, different datasets, or different researchers' perspectives to examine the same research question or theme. A researcher can compare the findings obtained from these different methods or data sources to help confirm or complicate his results.

The mixed-methods approach described in Section 2.4 in which both quantitative and qualitative methods are used to study the same topic or phenomenon, is one potential way of achieving triangulation. Mixed methodologists hope that the disadvantages of both quantitative and qualitative methods will be minimized (or compensated for) by employing both methods together, although, as Jick (1979, p. 604) has observed, this does not always happen in reality. Achieving similar results from both a quantitative and qualitative data analysis can help reinforce those findings; yet using both quantitative and qualitative methods can still be helpful even if the findings of the quantitative and qualitative components diverge (Jick, 1979, p. 608). Uncovering divergent findings offers a researcher a richer and more complicated portrait of the phenomenon of interest, helping to illuminate further complexities.

Triangulation is not a unitary concept. As we've discussed, it can include the use of multiple data collection methods, multiple data *analysis* methods, multiple datasets, or an additional researcher to independently investigate your data. All of these forms of triangulation are important, although some are more prominent in particular types of either quantitative or qualitative research. Each of these forms of triangulation will be revisited throughout this book as we discuss specific data analysis methods in detail.

stop and think

Why might it be helpful to ask another researcher to independently analyse your data? Why might it be helpful to use two different methods to analyse the same set of data?

2.9 Recognizing Our Limitations

The most important lesson to learn from this chapter is that, to become an effective data analyst, you must first develop a rigorous attitude. You should view all data analyses – including your own – with a critical eye, scrutinizing whether their theoretical approaches are appropriate, and whether they have achieved all four types of validity. As you proceed through this book and learn more about the specific procedures necessary for conducting rigorous quantitative and qualitative data analyses, you may find yourself surprised to encounter so many studies in the popular press – and even some academic journals – that do not undertake these procedures, or fail to meet the criteria we discuss. This unfortunate reality only underscores the need to view research from a critical standpoint.

However, one must temper this critical perspective with the recognition that social scientists study human beings and societies, both of which are complex and often unpredictable. In certain cases, it may not be possible or ethical to conduct research that perfectly achieves all four types of validity. As a data analyst, none of us can ever be an entirely neutral and objective observer of the world or of other human beings. Our personalities, previous experiences, cultural backgrounds, and numerous other considerations shape our perspectives and interactions. Therefore, even as researchers, any insights or understandings we develop about an issue will be personal to us, and affected by our own perspectives (Al-Najjar & Kans, 2006, p. 620). Thus it is essential to take time to consistently reflect on your work as you engage in data analysis, ensuring that you are aware of how your own perspective might affect your approach, even if it is impossible to ever fully eliminate such influences from our analysis. This point is one we will revisit in later chapters of this textbook.

Researchers are often drawn to particular fields of study because of their own personal experiences. For example, an excellent teacher might inspire someone to become an educational researcher; a family member's experiences with medical treatment might inspire someone else to become a public health researcher. Although such personal motivations are perfectly normal, it is essential to recognize how these and other personal factors might impact one's approach to research.

stop and think

Take a moment now and consider what motivated you to study your specific field of interest. How might those motivations affect your approach to research?

2.10 Concluding Thoughts

We've covered a lot of information in this chapter, so don't worry if you're feeling a bit overwhelmed. The goal of this chapter is *not* to force you to memorize the names of the different types of validity; instead, the goal is to encourage you to begin thinking like a data analyst. To think like a data analyst, you need to cultivate a rigorous attitude – and this is the most important lesson from Chapter 2. Ask questions and take time to reflect on your methodological choices. Take time also to think carefully about the methodological choices of others, as you read academic studies from your field. In upcoming chapters we'll revisit many of the themes we covered here, so feel free to return to Chapter 2 at any time to refresh your memory about hypothesis testing, validity, grounded theory, and the other concepts we've just explored.

2.11 Summary

- Becoming an effective data analyst requires you to develop a rigorous, reflective attitude, so that you view all data analyses – including your own – with a critical eye.
- Two general frameworks that have substantially influenced much data analysis in the social sciences are the *positivist* tradition (which promotes rigorously controlled studies to discover objective truth) and the *interpretivist* tradition (which probes the various realities that are true for different individuals).
- *Hypothesis testing* is an essential element of many quantitative and qualitative research studies. Good hypotheses should be falsifiable, logical, succinct, and specific.
- The formal process of hypothesis testing requires a researcher to formulate *two* hypotheses: the *alternative hypothesis* and the *null hypothesis*. While the alternative hypothesis states that there *is* a relationship or a difference that the researcher is interested in, the null hypothesis states that there is *no* relationship or difference.
- Many additional theoretical approaches also exist that can guide researchers, including *grounded theory* approaches, *action research* approaches, and *critical* approaches. Each of these approaches has its unique strengths and limitations.
- The *grounded theory* approach developed by Glaser and Strauss (1965, 1967) uses data to develop theories rather than to test hypotheses.
- Researchers must consider at least four different types of validity in any data analysis: *internal validity*, *construct validity*, *external validity*, and *descriptive validity*. Each form of validity is important for ensuring the 'trustworthiness' of one's research results.

2.12 Further Reading

For more information about the history of, and relationship between, quantitative and qualitative methods, see:

Newman, I., & Benz, C. R. (1998). *Qualitative-quantitative research methodology: Exploring the interactive continuum*. Carbondale, IL: Southern Illinois University Press.

Contemporary researchers are greatly indebted to the twentieth-century philosopher Karl Popper, who clarified many key issues regarding scientific inference. Why not take a look at his landmark work for yourself?

Popper, K. (2002). *The logic of scientific discovery*. London: Routledge. Originally published 1959.

Scholars have long debated the respective merits of positivist and interpretivist approaches to research. For one scholar's interesting take on the value of each of these traditions, see:

Weber, R. (2004). Editor's comments: The rhetoric of positivism versus interpretivism: A personal view. *MIS Quarterly*, *28*(1), iii–xii.

For an interesting perspective on interpretivist approaches to social research, see:

Schwandt, T. A. (2006). Constructivist, interpretivist approaches to human inquiry. In J. O'Brien (Ed.), *The production of reality: Essays and readings on social interaction* (4th ed., pp. 40–43). Thousand Oaks, CA: Pine Forge Press.

For a more detailed perspective on the grounded theory approach, take a look at the two original works in which Barney Glaser and Anselm Strauss pioneered this concept:

Glaser, B., & Strauss, A. (1965). *Awareness of dying*. Chicago: Aldine.

Glaser, B., & Strauss, A. (1967). *The discovery of grounded theory*. Chicago: Aldine.

Are you interested in further exploring issues of validity? If so, investigate Gill's (2011, p. 203) *descriptive validity matrix*, which provides a framework for assessing the descriptive validity of randomized controlled trials in criminology. Do you agree with Gill that such a matrix could help policy-makers determine the rigour of evidence in support of policy options? Do you think similar efforts could also be useful in other social science fields, in addition to criminology? Finally, consider that descriptive validity has typically received less attention from researchers than internal, external, or construct validity. Why do you think that is?

Gill, C. E. (2011). Missing links: How descriptive validity impacts the policy relevance of randomized controlled trials in criminology. *Journal of Experimental Criminology, 7,* 201–224.

Discussion Questions

1. Describe three key differences between the *positivist* and *interpretivist* theoretical orientations.
2. What is *falsification*? How is *falsification* related to the process of *hypothesis testing*?
3. What do you think are the most important *strengths* or *advantages* of the *grounded theory* approach? What are the most important *weaknesses* or *limitations* of the *grounded theory* approach?
4. In one or two sentences, define the *action research* approach. In one or two sentences, define the *critical research* approach and explain how it differs from the *action research* approach.
5. As Gonzalez et al. (2012, p. 251) have pointed out, some researchers perceive *internal validity* and *external validity* to be part of a 'zero-sum game' in which 'you can have one only at the expense of the other'. Do you agree with this view? Is it possible to maximize both internal and external validity in the same study? What about *construct validity* and *descriptive validity*?

3 Finding, Collecting, and Organizing Data

contents

Chapter Overview

In Chapter 3, we'll explore how to collect and organize the data that you want to analyse. By the end of this chapter, you will know how to:

- Develop research questions and appropriate hypotheses that you can explore through data analysis
- Design a practical research plan to guide a data analysis project
- Recognize the benefits of a *pilot study*
- Explain the differences among different methods for finding a *sample* of data
- Deal with, and minimize, issues such as *sampling error, non-response*, and *missing data*
- Recognize the importance of ethics in research design, and understand what *informed consent* means.

Data Sources: An Introduction

To analyse data, we first need to obtain data. It's an obvious point, but the question of *how* to obtain data does not have an obvious answer. Many different methods exist for obtaining data, but each of these methods has its own advantages and limitations. To see these complexities, we'll start by considering a few scenarios that are representative of situations researchers often encounter.

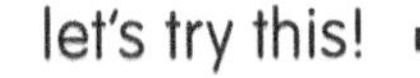

Take a moment to read the two scenarios and then answer the questions described below.

> Scenario A: A researcher is interested in the question of why some young adults don't vote in elections. To obtain data, the researcher plans to interview two dozen individuals between the ages of 18 and 24. He will recruit these individuals from student political organizations at local universities.
>
> Scenario B: A researcher is interested in the question of whether rates of binge drinking among adolescents have changed over time. Due to time and funding constraints, the researcher cannot collect her own data. However, she has found survey data online that the public is allowed to use. This survey was administered to a random sample of 1000 adolescents in 2005 and to a different random sample of 1500 adolescents in 2010. The survey includes the question: 'Approximately how many alcoholic drinks have you consumed in the past seven days?'

For both scenario A and scenario B, consider the following three questions:

1. What is one advantage of the data source the researcher has selected?
2. What is one disadvantage of the data source the researcher has selected?
3. Do you think the data source will allow the researcher to fully answer his/her research question? Why or why not?

The goal of this exercise is to get you thinking about the complexities of selecting a data source. Therefore, before continuing, make sure you've thought about the questions with respect to both scenarios A and B. Like the researcher in scenario A, you may prefer to collect your own data. If so, you'll need to think carefully about *how* you will recruit an appropriate sample. One potential limitation of the researcher's approach in scenario A – and perhaps this is a limitation you identified – is the choice to recruit interviewees from student political organizations. Such students are by definition politically engaged, and therefore probably *do* vote in elections. Would a sample consisting solely of such individuals be able to fully answer the researcher's question? This limitation illustrates a broader point: if you choose to collect data yourself, you need to think carefully about the sample you will recruit.

Alternatively, like the researcher in scenario B, you may choose to rely on *secondary data*, or data that you have not collected yourself. (In Chapters 4 and 6 we will explore some of the many sources that exist for obtaining secondary quantitative and qualitative data.) Perhaps, due to time or resource restrictions, you may not be able to collect data yourself and therefore have no choice *but* to use secondary data. When using secondary data, you need to select a data source that will allow you to adequately explore your research questions. You are obviously limited by the decisions of the researchers who originally collected the data. If they chose *not* to examine a particular issue or collect data on a specific question you are interested in, then you're out of luck and need to either select a different secondary dataset or modify your research questions so that they *are* answerable with the dataset you have selected. Think back to your analysis of question 3 for scenario B. Do you think the dataset will allow the researcher to answer her research question? Why or why not?

Ultimately, all three of the questions presented above about the strengths and limitations of data sources are worth considering before every data collection effort that you undertake. All datasets – whether collected by you or by others – have advantages and disadvantages, which should be considered carefully before, during, and after the data collection and analyses processes. Don't be surprised if no single, *perfect* dataset currently exists – or can be collected – to answer your research questions. However, some datasets will be more appropriate than others, and it is your task to discover which original or secondary dataset is best for your project. (In Section 3.11, we'll explore some special considerations you'll need to keep in mind if you're considering using secondary data.)

Unexpected Data Sources: A Long-Term Perspective on Crime

Sometimes extraordinary datasets can be found in unexpected places. One such dataset, analysed by John Laub and Robert Sampson (1993), offers insight into one of the most fundamental questions in criminology: Why do some people *stop* committing crimes?

In a basement at Harvard University's Law School, Laub found an extraordinary dataset that dated back to the 1930s ('John Laub and Robert Sampson...', 2011). Originally compiled by Sheldon and Eleanor Glueck, the dataset focused on a sample of 500 boys from Massachusetts with a history of delinquent behaviour (Shoemaker, 2010, p. 39). The Gluecks had collected data on the sample at three points in time: at age 14, age 25, and age 32

('John Laub and Robert Sampson...' 2011). After Laub found the dataset in 1986, Laub and Sampson (2003, p. 5) analysed the data, and added new data by following up with individuals from the original sample (who had now reached middle age).

By tracing the lives of individuals over such a long time span, Laub and Sampson were able to uncover not only why some of the individuals began committing crimes, but also why some of those who started committing crimes eventually stopped. Specifically, Laub and Sampson discovered that individuals often stopped committing crimes after they reached key 'turning points' in life, such as getting married or serving in the armed forces (Sampson & Laub, 1993). This finding, a landmark discovery in criminology, was only possible thanks to the unique dataset they had found and expanded ('John Laub and Robert Sampson...', 2011).

Although most data analysts are not fortunate enough to find a valuable and underappreciated dataset like the Gluecks' work, the example of Sampson and Laub highlights the importance of bringing a *proactive* and *resourceful* mindset to research. Being observant and cultivating contacts both within and outside your field can yield unexpected dividends. Even when a good data analyst is not 'working', he is still on the lookout for new potential data sources, collaborators, or insights from other fields that might be relevant for his own work. Great data sometimes emerges from unexpected places.

3.4 Developing Research Questions and Hypotheses

In Chapter 2 we saw that a central element of many data analyses is the process of hypothesis testing, in which a researcher formulates a *hypothesis*, which we defined as 'a belief or argument about the social world based on experience, intuition, or the findings of previous research'. A researcher then tests the hypothesis by exploring whether data collected in the real world matches or contradicts the hypothesis. One question that may have occurred to you during that discussion is how a researcher develops a hypothesis in the first place.

Rather than trying to develop a hypothesis immediately, it is often easier to start by identifying the key research questions you want to answer or explore in your project. Before you even begin to collect data, it is essential to have specific research questions in mind, as such questions can help narrow your focus and decide what kinds of research methods and data to focus on; as the project develops, you can refine your research questions to make them more specific (Flick, 2007b, p. 22). Don't be afraid to let your own personal experiences and interests influence the research questions you select. As Maxwell (2013, p. 24) has argued, choosing research questions that are meaningful to you can increase your willingness to finish the research project, a particularly important concern when trying to finish a dissertation or thesis on a tight deadline!

Formulating research questions often involves building on previous research. But how can you contribute something new to a field or topic that has already been studied by other scholars? Although this task might seem overwhelming at first – especially if you have only recently begun studying the topic that interests you – you *can* make a unique contribution to your field of interest. The social world is so complex that unanswered questions remain in almost every field. If you're having trouble generating a specific hypothesis, consider the following questions:

- Have past scholars neglected any particular aspects of the phenomenon you're interested in?
- Are there any potential causes of the phenomenon/relationship you're interested in that other scholars have overlooked?
- Has previous research hinted at a surprising relationship between variables that merits further analysis?
- Have previous studies on this topic been limited in some way that you can overcome in your own study?
- Have previous studies neglected a particular geographical region or cultural context that you have access to?

These are just a few examples of the specific questions you can ask yourself to help generate a hypothesis. As you can see from these questions, many possible avenues exist for you to make your own unique contribution to your area of interest.

Once you have settled on research questions, you can turn those questions into hypotheses, keeping in mind our discussion in Chapter 2 that good hypotheses should be falsifiable or testable, logical, succinct or expressed as simply as possible, and specific. Even if you are planning to conduct *grounded theory*-based research (and therefore do not intend to test hypotheses), it can still be a good idea to devise specific research question(s) to shape your data collection plans.

Since your own research will build upon the work of previous scholars, it is essential to investigate the findings of past research on your topic of interest. Before collecting data, researchers typically perform a thorough **literature review** to determine relevant findings or theories from past research. Compiling a literature review involves a thorough search of relevant research databases and library catalogues. The types of sources researchers look for include books, academic articles, government reports, and reports by non-profit or research organizations. For guidance about how to compile a literature review, visit your university or town library and speak to a librarian. Many university libraries employ librarians who are subject-matter experts and can help you access relevant databases and library catalogues to find previous relevant research on your topic.

let's try this!

What research databases or other resources does your university or local library offer which might be useful for your project? Take a moment to explore the website of your university library, or of a public library in your community. Are there databases or archives listed on the library's website that sound like they might be helpful? Are there any contact details listed for librarians or research specialists who might be able to help you? If not, are there other libraries nearby that look more useful? Are there any special procedures you will need to follow to gain access to the library?

Designing a Research Plan

Once you've developed your research questions and hypotheses, it is useful to step back and develop a plan for how you will collect your data and carry out your overall research project. Writing out each stage of this plan can be useful, particularly if you are coordinating a team of multiple researchers. Additionally, a written research proposal explaining the stages of the project can be an important component of applications to secure research funding from your university or external agencies. A written proposal might also be necessary to secure formal ethical approval for your data collection efforts through your university's research ethics committee or other research advisory body. (We will explore the issue of ethical approval in greater detail later in this chapter.) Ultimately, writing out a formal plan can help you think through each stage of your project beforehand, allowing you to better anticipate problems and prevent delays in your progress. As you formulate your research plan, spend a moment considering how you will analyse your data, and what formatting requirements such analysis requires. Although appropriately formatting and organizing data might seem like simple activities, they can eat up significant time and energy. By thinking carefully about these issues early on, and formatting your data appropriately as you collect it (or as soon as you obtain it from another source, if it is secondary data), you can save yourself much aggravation later.

3.6 Pilot Studies

Many larger-scale research projects begin with a **pilot study**. A pilot study is a preliminary, smaller-scale study that allows a researcher to test and refine research methodologies before conducting the actual, larger study (see Leon, Davis, & Kraemer, 2011, for an overview of the advantages of pilot studies). For example, if you're interested in survey research, you could conduct a pilot study first by testing your questionnaire with a small sample of participants. This pilot study would allow you to receive feedback from the participants about the question wording and general content of the survey, so that you could make appropriate revisions before conducting the full-scale study. Pilot studies can also be useful for other research designs, in addition to surveys. For example, a pilot study of interview-based research could give a researcher the opportunity to refine his interviewing technique. A pilot study of quantitative research could allow a researcher to try out an innovative statistical method before employing it in a much larger dataset.

An additional appealing characteristic of pilot studies is that, although their goal is to prepare and refine methods for a larger study, they can still yield interesting results that merit publication and spur more comprehensive research (e.g., Goodman, Meltzer, & Bailey, 1998; Basch, Hillyer, Basch, & Neugut, 2012). Even though you may not have the time or resources to conduct a full pilot study, it may still be worthwhile to pilot elements of your data collection process. For example, you could seek informal feedback from fellow students or professors about the interview questions you plan to ask.

stop and think

What is one potential benefit of conducting a pilot study?

Finding a Sample

Although many researchers are interested in an entire **population** (e.g., all university undergraduates in England and Wales), it is often impractical – or even impossible – to obtain data about a whole population. Instead, they can often only obtain data about a **sample** (or a selection of observations or cases from the population) and must use this sample to make inferences about the characteristics of the population. But how do researchers obtain samples? How can they be sure that their samples could be used to make inferences about the population? What if a researcher is not interested in an entire population, but in uncovering more detailed findings about a few special cases? What sampling strategy should be employed in that instance? We will now take a closer look at all of these questions, and the advantages and disadvantages of various approaches to quantitative sampling. Even if you plan on using secondary data, it is necessary to become familiar with different sampling approaches, so you can assess the sampling approach used in the secondary dataset you select. Is that sampling approach adequate? Will the sample allow you to answer your research questions? As we shall see, not all sampling approaches are appropriate for all research questions; therefore, before settling on a particular secondary dataset, you should think carefully about the strengths and limitations of its sampling strategy.

Popular sampling approaches include: *random* sampling; *stratified* sampling; *systematic* sampling; *cluster* sampling; *deliberate* (or *purposive*) sampling; *snowball* sampling; and *convenience* sampling. As we explore each of these methods below, think about what the **sampling frame** for each method might be. A *sampling frame* is the source from which you draw your sample. It might include voter rolls, or lists of all students attending a school, or the census data for an entire country. In order to actually locate your sample, you must first clearly identify the sampling frame.

3.7.1 Simple random sampling

One of the best-known sampling strategies is **simple random sampling**. As the name suggests, in a random sample, every unit (i.e., each individual or organization or other entity you are interested in) has an exactly equal probability of being selected for the sample. The sample is truly selected at random from the population. Figure 3.1, by Dan Kernler, offers a helpful visual representation of the simple random sampling process. On the left-hand side of the figure is the population we are interested in, and the arrows indicate how units from that population are selected for our sample (shown on the right-hand side of the figure).

Most statistical techniques presume that data is drawn from simple random samples, so simple random sampling is an important concept in quantitative data analysis. (In fact, we'll revisit

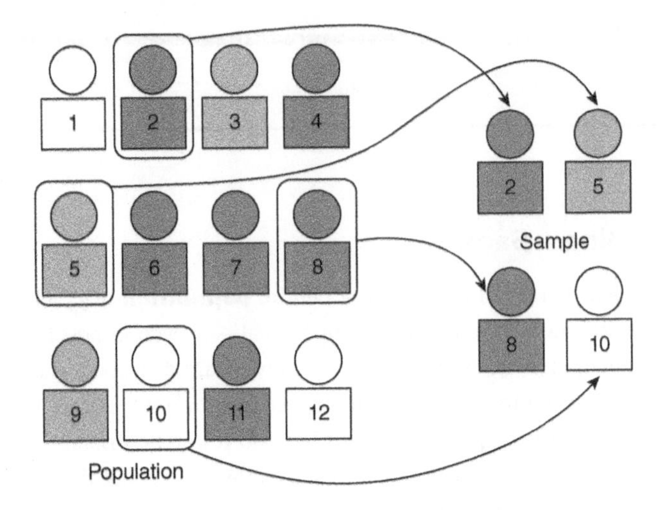

Figure 3.1 Simple random sampling. Image credit: Dan Kernler (2014). A visual representation of selecting a simple random sample. Licensed under CC BY-SA 4.0 https://creativecommons.org/licenses/by-sa/4.0/. Retrieved from https://commons.wikimedia.org/w/index.php?curid=36506020

this concept in the next chapter.) However, despite this emphasis on simple random sampling, the technique is not often employed in social science research, since sampling frames are often large and complex, and a simple random sample may not actually yield the type of sample a researcher is most interested in (Babbie, 2011, p. 228). The latter point will become clearer if we compare simple random sampling with a related alternative: *stratified random sampling*.

3.7.2 Stratified random sampling

Unlike simple random sampling, **stratified random sampling** begins by splitting a population into different categories (such as males and females, or different age brackets) and then choosing units at random from those different categories. Stratified sampling is useful when you want, for example, to achieve 'an equal representation of males and females in your sample', or if you want to ensure that certain age or other demographic groups are represented in your sample (Fink, 2009, p. 53). One strength of stratified random sampling is that it allows a researcher to easily compare and contrast different strata within the population, such as differences between men and women, for a particular variable (Rao, 2000, p. 83). To visualize how stratified random sampling might work in practice, take a look at Figure 3.2.

stop and think

Why would a researcher prefer to use *simple random sampling* instead of *stratified sampling*? Why might a researcher prefer to use stratified sampling instead of simple random sampling?

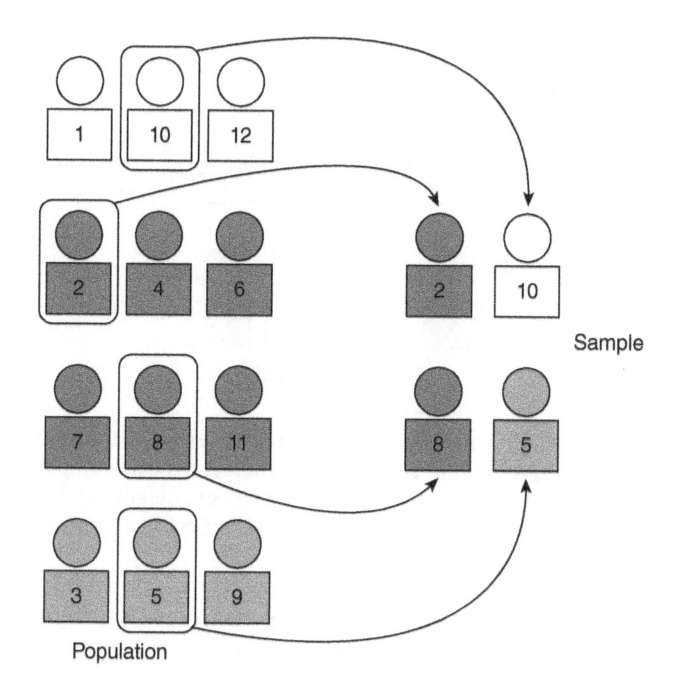

Figure 3.2 Stratified random sampling. Image credit: Dan Kernler (2014). A visual representation of selecting a random sample using the stratified sampling technique. Licensed under CC BY-SA 4.0 https://creativecommons.org/licenses/by-sa/4.0/. Retrieved from https://commons.wikimedia.org/wiki/File:Stratified_sampling.PNG

3.7.3 Systematic sampling

Despite their many advantages, both simple random sampling and stratified random sampling can be complex to execute in practice, as a researcher needs to have knowledge of the entire population and a foolproof mechanism (such as a random number generator) that will randomly select cases from the population or from strata within that population. Sometimes these circumstances are impossible (or too expensive) to obtain. A technique that may be easier to execute in practice is **systematic sampling**. Systematic sampling involves using sources such as phone number directories, lists of registered voters, or even just individuals randomly spotted in a given area, and choosing cases at regular intervals from these sources, such as 'every tenth person passing a certain location' (Rao, 2000, p. 49). Therefore this technique does not require you to have knowledge of the entire population, nor does it require you to have a robust mechanism for ensuring complete randomization, such as a random number generator. To see how this process might work in practice, take a look at Figure 3.3.

Although systematic sampling may sound more practicable than other sampling techniques, keep in mind that it won't necessarily generate a random sample from the population you are interested in. For example, if your population of interest includes all of the people in a given area, selecting every tenth individual listed in the local telephone directory won't give you a truly random sample as not all individuals may be listed in the phone book, and those

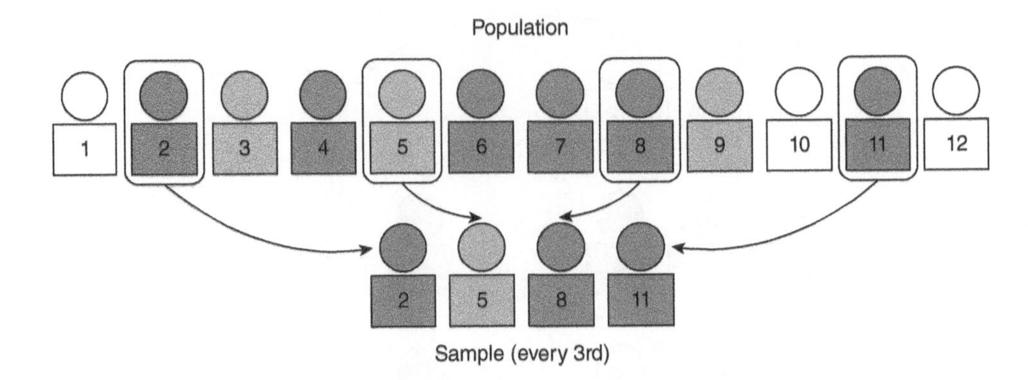

Figure 3.3 Systematic sampling. Image credit: Dan Kernler (2014). A visual representation of selecting a random sample using the systematic sampling technique. Licensed under CC BY-SA 4.0 https://creativecommons.org/licenses/by-sa/4.0/. Retrieved from https://commons.wikimedia.org/wiki/File:Systematic_sampling.PNG

individuals who are listed may be systematically different in some way from those individuals who are not (for instance, they may be less concerned about privacy).

3.7.4 Cluster sampling

Another sampling approach that can be easier to execute than the fully randomized processes described above is **cluster sampling**. Instead of sampling randomly from an entire population, the population is first divided into clusters such as schools, neighbourhoods, or counties, and clusters are randomly selected for inclusion in the sample. Like systematic sampling, cluster sampling also has the advantages of practicality and lower cost. It's usually easier and cheaper to focus on a few clusters than to find a random sample in an entire population. However, additional care must be taken when making estimates based upon clusters of different sizes (Lee & Forthofer, 2006, p. 6).

For a straightforward overview of what cluster sampling looks like, take a look at Figure 3.4.

3.7.5 Deliberate sampling

Sometimes researchers do not want a sample selected at random, but instead want a sample that exhibits particular characteristics. For example, perhaps a researcher is interested in comparing the views of current vegetarians and former vegetarians who now eat meat; such a specialized sample might be difficult to draw randomly from a population and may instead need to be deliberately sought out by the researcher. This sampling strategy is known as **deliberate sampling** or sometimes as *purposive sampling* (Boulmetis & Dutwin, 2005, p. 146). Although deliberate samples are, by definition, not generalizable, they allow a researcher to guarantee that individuals included in the sample exhibit particular characteristics, perhaps because

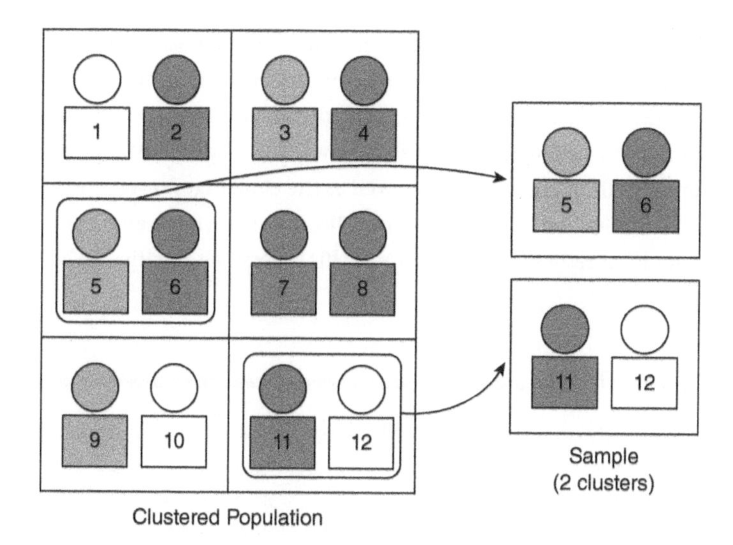

Figure 3.4 Cluster sampling. Image credit: Dan Kernler (2014). A visual representation of selecting a random sample using the cluster sampling technique. Licensed under CC BY-SA 4.0 https://creativecommons.org/licenses/by-sa/4.0/. Retrieved from https://en.wikipedia.org/wiki/Sampling_(statistics)#/media/File:Cluster_sampling.PNG

theoretical works or previous pilot research have highlighted the importance of including such individuals in the study (Berg, 1995, p. 179).

3.7.6 Snowball sampling

Another non-random sampling technique that researchers sometimes employ when studying individuals or other units that cannot be easily located is **snowball sampling**. Snowball sampling involves recruiting at least one individual, and then asking that individual for the names of other individuals who might also be appropriate to include in the sample; each of those individuals, if they agree to take part in the study, is then asked for the names of more individuals, and the sample grows like a rolling snowball (Blankenship, 2010, p. 88). For social scientists interested in highly specialized samples – such as surrogate mothers, or agricultural workers in a particular area – snowball sampling can be useful. Additionally, snowball sampling can be helpful for researchers studying social interactions, since this sampling strategy can illuminate how individuals are connected to each other within a larger social network, and how such individuals influence and interact with others (Monge & Contractor, 1988, p. 125).

One recent piece of research that fruitfully employed snowball sampling was Rajacich, Kane, Williston, and Cameron's (2013) study of men in the nursing profession in Canada. The study explored job satisfaction and work–life balance among the men, and offered suggestions for improving the inclusion of males in this profession. Since men constituted a minority of nurses in the area in which the study was conducted, snowball sampling was essential for locating enough eligible participants. Another recent study that used this sampling technique was Konstantopoulos et al.'s (2013) exploration of anti-trafficking service providers in eight different cities around the world (Los Angeles, Rio de Janeiro, New York City, Kolkata, Manila, London, Salvador, and Mumbai). The researchers wanted to gain insight into the needs and hardships of human trafficking survivors, as well as the challenges service providers face when providing care to this vulnerable population. Through snowball sampling, the researchers were able to locate local research participants in this diverse set of cities.

let's try this!

Before moving on, take a moment to review the six different sampling strategies already discussed: *simple random sampling*; *stratified random sampling*; *systematic sampling*; *cluster sampling*; *deliberate sampling*; and *snowball sampling*. After you've done a quick review, consider which sampling strategy would be most appropriate for answering each of the research questions listed below. Make sure you can defend your answer. For some of the research questions, more than one sampling strategy might be appropriate.

> Research Question 1. Are individuals aged 20–29 more likely to support the legalization of marijuana/cannabis than individuals aged 50–59?
>
> Research Question 2. What motivates hackers and other cyber criminals to commit their offences? Are they driven by the desire for money, or other factors?
>
> Research Question 3. Which of the following current issues are 16-year-olds in your city/town most concerned about: climate change, crime, education, poverty, terrorism, or something else?
>
> Research Question 4. What are the most important concerns of new mothers who have just given birth to premature babies?

Have you selected at least one sampling strategy for each of the research questions? Great! If possible, share your answers with a friend or classmate. Are their answers similar to yours? If your answers differ, discuss these differences.

If you're struggling to decide on a strategy for one or more of the questions, don't worry. Your struggle might just be a reflection of the inherent difficulties of translating research questions into actual research projects, with methods that a researcher can easily execute. As we will see in Chapter 4 (Section 4.6), this process of translation is known as *operationalizing* your research question.

Ultimately, there's no answer key for this thought exercise because there's no one correct answer. Instead, consider whether your answers make sense and are well supported. If you were interested in the research questions outlined above, which sampling strategies would you use?

3.7.7 Convenience sampling

All of the sampling strategies described thus far require planning and effort on the part of the researcher. However, researchers sometimes face significant time or resource constraints; it isn't always possible to undertake one of the six strategies discussed above. In such cases, the only sampling strategy available to a researcher may be **convenience sampling**, in which a researcher simply includes in the sample those units that are the most 'convenient' or easy to access, although the results from such a sample are not generalizable (Ary et al., 2014, p. 169). Convenience samples are typically only employed when it is not possible to engage in a more rigorous alternative; for example, a convenience sample might be used for a pilot study whose results are not intended to be generalizable, and to which only scant resources have been allocated (Davis & Cosenza, 1988, p. 231).

Confused about the different sampling strategies we've discussed in this section? We've discussed a wide range of choices, and it can be difficult to remember the differences among them. Let's quickly refresh our memory about the strategies we've discussed so far before

Table 3.1 Sampling strategies

Sampling strategy	Quick description
Simple random sampling	Units are chosen at random from the population of interest Every unit has a precisely equal chance of being selected for the sample *Advantage*: Many statistical techniques described later in this textbook assume the researcher is using a random sample *Disadvantage*: Requires access to the entire population, and can be expensive and time-consuming to execute
Stratified random sampling	A population is split into different categories (such as different age brackets) and units are selected at random from those different categories *Useful for*: Researchers who want to ensure that certain age or other demographic groups are represented in the sample
Systematic sampling	A researcher uses sources such as phone number directories or lists of registered voters and chooses cases at regular intervals from these sources (e.g., every 5th name) *Advantage*: A researcher does not need to have knowledge of the entire population to employ this technique *Disadvantage*: Technique does not necessarily generate a random sample
Cluster sampling	A researcher divides a population into clusters such as schools, neighbourhoods, or counties, and clusters are randomly selected for inclusion in the sample. *Advantage*: Easier and often cheaper than simple random sampling *Disadvantage*: Need to account for clustering when analysing your data
Deliberate sampling	A researcher *deliberately* selects a sample that exhibits particular characteristics (e.g., people who commute to work by bicycle) *Useful for*: Researchers who don't want a sample selected at random, but instead want a sample that exhibits certain characteristics
Snowball sampling	Each individual who agrees to participate in the study is asked for the names of more individuals who might be appropriate, causing the sample to grow like a rolling snowball *Useful for*: Researchers who are interested in highly specialized samples (e.g., surrogate mothers, or ex-gang members) that are impossible to randomly recruit *Useful for*: Researchers who want to map how individuals are connected to each other in a larger social network
Convenience sampling	Researcher samples those units that are the most 'convenient' or easy to access Typically only employed when resource constraints preclude a researcher from using an alternative sampling method, as results will not be generalizable

moving on to the next section. (The next section addresses strategies for finding a sample that differ substantially from the strategies we've discussed already, so it's a good place to stop!) Table 3.1 presents the names and quick descriptions of the sampling strategies. How many do you remember?

3.7.8 Most- or least-similar cases

One particular form of qualitative research, **case-study research**, explores a few specific cases in detail rather than one large sample. Each case is carefully selected and examined in comprehensive detail (Boeije, 2010, p. 36). Although the process of selecting cases can share similarities with the different sampling strategies described above, an important difference is that the researcher is typically only interested in understanding the selected cases rather than generalizing to any population (Ragin, 1987, p. 49). So a researcher typically does not use the 'sample' of cases to infer broader findings about the population.

Several different methods exist for selecting cases. One popular method is the *most-similar cases* approach, which, as the name implies, specifies that researchers should pick cases that are similar to each other but vary in one important respect – usually just a single independent or dependent variable that the researcher is interested in (Hirschl, 2006, p. 48). The presence of these similarities ensures that a researcher will not be distracted by confounding explanations, and can focus solely on the variable of interest. A second popular case-selection method is the *least-similar cases* approach, in which a data analyst chooses cases that differ from each other in many respects but exhibit a similar value for the dependent variable of interest, thereby allowing the analyst to understand the forces that produced that outcome under different circumstances (George & Bennett, 2004, p. 50). The least-similar cases approach helps a researcher understand the diversity of independent variables that are all associated with the same dependent variable or outcome. As the two examples above illustrate, choosing an appropriate case selection method in qualitative research can be as complex as selecting a suitable sampling strategy in quantitative research.

3.8 Minimizing Sampling Error

Whether your goal is to compute the mean and standard deviation of a single sample, or to use sample data to make inferences about a population, or compare differences between two samples, or achieve most other quantitative data analysis goals, you will want your conclusions to be as accurate as possible. In other words, you will want to minimize **sampling error**, or the variation we tend to see in different samples drawn from the same population, even if those samples are drawn randomly and no mistakes or biases impact the sampling process. Realistically, one wouldn't expect every sample drawn from a population to have the same exact mean; we'd expect to see some variation in the different samples' means. This variation is the sampling error. Therefore, although the term 'error' implies this variation is wrong or a mistake, keep in mind that the presence of some sampling error is often inevitable.

Sampling error can be reduced by obtaining *larger* samples from the population you're interested in. However, practical constraints – such as limited time or money – often limit the size of the samples social scientists are able to draw, meaning that a certain amount of sampling error exists in many data analyses.

3.9 Non-response

Although it may not be possible to completely reduce sampling error, researchers should endeavour to minimize other threats to validity, such as *non-response*, during the data collection process. Many popular data collection methods require some type of 'response' from individuals in the sample. For example, survey research requires individuals to answer questions and submit their completed surveys; interview research requires individuals to respond to questions asked by an interviewer. However, some respondents may fail to complete their surveys, and some interviewees may decline to answer certain questions. What should a data analyst do when individuals *fail* to respond? How should non-response be handled? The answers to these questions depend in part on the *type* of non-response encountered by the researcher. Non-response may be *complete* – meaning that some potential research participants did not answer *any* of the questions – which can indicate a failure to recruit appropriate participants or design an understandable survey instrument, or non-response may only be *partial*, indicating that only particular questions were avoided, perhaps because they were difficult to understand or involved sensitive topics (Hussmanns, Mehran, & Verma, 1990, p. 317). Complete non-response is particularly important to diagnose early in the research process, as it can indicate larger problems related to the adequacy of one's data collection efforts. If you are using secondary data that was originally collected through a survey, take a close look at the survey's response rate and any information about how the original researchers handled non-response.

A large body of research has investigated methods for improving response rates in surveys (for a comprehensive overview, see National Research Council, 2013). When considering survey response (or non-response) rates, it is useful to distinguish between different types of non-response, including *non-contact* (not being able to locate a particular respondent), *refusal* (an unwillingness by a respondent to participate in the survey or answer certain questions), and *inability* (or being unable to participate due to language barriers, medical issues, or other concerns) (Bethlehem, Cobben, & Schouten, 2011, p. 6). Logically a researcher should employ a different approach, depending upon which of these explanations is the reason for the non-response. For example, for individuals unable to participate due to language barriers, the use of 'proxy respondents' who can speak for those individuals might be an effective remedy (Biemer & Lyberg, 2003, p. 92). Such a remedy would not be appropriate, however, for non-response due to non-contact or refusal.

In addition to these strategies that are aimed at reducing non-response during the data *collection* process, other strategies to address non-response can also be employed during the data *analysis* process. Specifically, a researcher can attempt to account for non-response after a survey has been conducted through different data analysis strategies such as 'case weighting' (Groves & Couper, 1998, Section 1.2.5). Although the specifics of such procedures are beyond the scope of this introductory textbook, using weighting adjustments in data analysis to account for non-response has received significant attention in survey research (Kreuter et al., 2010). Readers interested in learning more about this technique can consider the sources discussed in the 'Further Reading' section at the end of this chapter. In the case of secondary data in which the original researchers did not effectively deal with issues of non-response bias, addressing such bias during the data analysis process may be the only recourse available.

Ultimately, despite a researcher's best efforts, most surveys will feature some level of non-response, which a researcher must consider when deciding what sample size to aim for. In particular, if a researcher is hoping to make comparisons among individuals with specific characteristics (e.g., between men over the age of 45, men under the age of 45, women over the age of 45, and women under the age of 45) then he must be particularly sensitive to non-response issues and the larger challenge of recruiting a large enough sample that retains enough individuals in each of these categories even after non-response (Bryman & Cramer, 1994, p. 104).

3.10 Missing Data

The issue of non-response in surveys is linked to a larger concern affecting all forms of research, including research with secondary data: how to handle missing data. In survey research, missing data can result from non-response, but missing data due to other causes can affect all types of quantitative research. Whether you are collecting your own data or examining secondary data, it is important not to use blanks or zeros to designate missing data, as this can cause confusion (Newton & Rudestam, 2013, p. 30). (Confusion could result, for example, if real zeros – representing a complete lack of the quantity of interest – are also present in your dataset, or if a software package fails to properly recognize the blanks you have used.) Instead, choose one of the widely accepted coding conventions for missing data, such as a value of '–99' (or another value that cannot possibly appear for real in the dataset).

In addition to correctly coding the missing data, it is imperative to determine *why* the missing data is missing. If the missing data is associated with some unmeasured variable – for example, data on younger people seems more likely to be missing, meaning that missingness may be associated with age – then we need to carefully examine the data for any evidence of 'selection bias' (Chan & McGarey, 2012, p. 375). In such scenarios you must first investigate these larger methodological concerns – such as bias – before worrying about how to code the missing data.

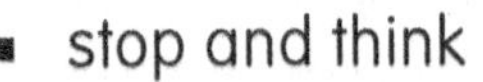

Why is it important to consider whether there is missing data in your dataset?

There are three main types of missing data, which are now conventionally known as: *data missing completely at random*; *data missing at random*; and *data not missing at random* (Little &

Rubin, 1987). Unfortunately these names can be easily confused, but the definitions of each of these data types are distinctive. The first type, data missing completely at random (sometimes abbreviated as MCAR), is data that is truly randomly missing, following no particular pattern (McKnight, McKnight, Sidani, & Figueredo, 2007, p. 53). The second type, data missing at random (MAR), is when missingness is associated with another variable that is available and can be added to the model (Graham, Cumsille, & Elek-Fisk, 2003, p. 89). For example, an MAR scenario could be present if some data on income is missing in your dataset, but you have data on education and education is correlated strongly with income (McKnight et al., 2007, p. 53). The third type of missing data is data not missing at random (MNAR), which is when data is more likely to be missing for units which exhibit certain characteristics (Newton & Rudestam, 2013, p. 191). In other words, missingness is clearly not distributed randomly. An example would be a dataset in which data on younger people seems more likely to be missing.

If this is the first time you're learning about missing data, don't worry if you're feeling a bit confused about the differences among these three types of missing data. Even seasoned researchers sometimes have difficulty remembering which type of missing data is which – a problem only exacerbated by the three types' similar-sounding names. Table 3.2 offers a quick definition of each type, to help you start to learn the differences. Don't be afraid to return to Table 3.2 in future if you find yourself confused. (In fact, I may need to return to Table 3.2 myself the next time I encounter missing data in one of my own projects!)

Table 3.2 Types of missing data, following Little and Rubin's (1987) typology

Name	Description
Missing completely at random (MCAR)	Data that is truly randomly missing, so there is no pattern to the missingness Data is not more likely to be missing for cases that exhibit particular characteristics, and missingness is not associated with any variables
Missing at random (MAR)	Missingness is associated with another variable This variable can be added to, and accounted for, in the model
Not missing at random (MNAR)	Data is not randomly missing, and missingness is not associated with another variable that can be easily added to the model Instead, data is more likely to be missing for cases that exhibit particular characteristics (e.g., data on younger people is more likely to be missing)

To clarify the differences among the three types of missing data, let's envision a hypothetical example of how the three types of missing data might emerge during a research project. Imagine that a researcher wants to conduct a survey of adolescents' attitudes towards social media. The researcher administers survey questionnaires to all 17-year-olds in a large school. However, pages from a few of the completed questionnaires were randomly dropped on the floor (and subsequently thrown away by the cleaning crew) before they were delivered to the researcher. This missing data is data missing completely at random (MCAR), since pages were dropped at random, and there is no pattern to the missingness.

Now let's suppose that many (but not all) of the students failed to fill in a question on the back of the survey. This question asked about the number of hours they spent studying per week. However, the researcher realizes that the number of hours spent studying is strongly associated with a student's grade point average (GPA), and the researcher *does* have data on GPA. This missing data, therefore, is data missing at random since the 'hours spent on homework/studying' variable can be accounted for by including GPA in the model instead.

Finally, a number of students were absent from school on the day the survey was administered. These absences had no clear pattern, as some students were ill, while others simply skipped school. Since this missing data is not random and does not seem to be associated with any other variable, it is data not missing at random.

Now that we've (hopefully!) clarified the differences among the three types of missing data, let's turn our attention to the most salient question: what should we *do* if we encounter missing data in our research? Not surprisingly, the most appropriate response for dealing with missing data depends on what type of missing-data problem you encounter. For data that are MCAR, one method for handling missingness – indeed, the standard method in most statistical software packages – is to use *case deletion* or *listwise deletion* procedures (Newton & Rudestam, 2013, p. 193). These methods involve simply deleting all cases that have missing data, from some or all analyses. These methods therefore have the advantage of being straightforward and easy to execute; however, since these methods reduce the number of cases available in the dataset, they can also reduce power and increase standard error in one's results – significant disadvantages (Newton & Rudestam, 2013, p. 193). If the missing data are MAR or MNAR, engaging in case deletion is often *inappropriate* and 'can bias estimates of treatment effects', since cases exhibiting particular characteristics might be more likely to be missing (Mark & Henry, 2006, p. 334).

An alternative strategy to deal with missing data is to use imputation, which is when a researcher develops estimates for the values that are missing, and then includes these estimates in calculations in place of the missing data (Newton & Rudestam, 2013, p. 194). The most straightforward form of imputation is called 'mean substitution' and consists of replacing the missing data points with the mean value for the data points that are not missing (Vogt, 2005, p. 150). More advanced imputation techniques, such as multiple imputation, have received increasing attention from methodologists in recent years (Rubin, 1987). In multiple imputation, a researcher uses data obtained from all the variables in the dataset to try to *impute* (or predict) the likely values of missing datapoints. (Although a full discussion of these more complex approaches is beyond the purview of this introductory textbook, readers interested in these techniques can consult the sources described in the 'Further Reading' section at the end of this chapter.) Despite this increased interest, however, imputation remains the subject of debate among some researchers, and disagreement persists about the appropriate circumstances in which to apply this method (Vogt, 2005, p. 150). Indeed, some researchers feel an instinctive reluctance to impute data, as it may feel like they are 'creating' data. In reality, the issue is more nuanced, as the imputed data is based on the collected data, and the decision *not* to impute data can also introduce serious biases. If you're intrigued by these issues, do take a look at the suggested further readings.

Ultimately, regardless of which approach you select to handle your missing data – whether you select casewise deletion, mean substitution, multiple imputation, or a different technique – it is essential to clearly explain which approach you employed, and why you selected this approach (Higgins & Green, 2011, Section 16.1.2). Additionally, it can be helpful to also perform 'sensitivity analyses', which allow you to determine how much small changes in your assumptions impact your results – a particularly important concern if you are assuming particular values for missing data (Higgins & Green, 2011, Section 16.1.2). Sensitivity analyses could be helpful, for example, if you have decided to impute data; such analyses could reveal how sensitive your results are to different imputation strategies.

Thinking about Secondary Data

All of the issues that we've discussed in this chapter – including sampling error, non-response, and missing data – are relevant whether you're analysing data you've collected yourself (known as **primary data**), or whether you're analysing data collected by other researchers (known as **secondary data**). Analysing secondary data has become increasingly popular in the social sciences in recent years, so it's highly likely that you'll use secondary data at some point – whether for a class activity, a paper, a project of your own, a thesis, or even a dissertation. It's therefore essential to familiarize yourself with the unique opportunities and challenges posed by secondary data.

Perhaps the greatest advantage of secondary data, and a key reason for its growing popularity, is its *convenience*. Many researchers – and many student researchers in particular – lack the time, institutional capacity, or resources necessary for collecting the primary data they need to answer their research questions. For example, you may find that it's simply not possible to recruit enough people to answer your survey, or to collect data over a long enough time period. Previous researchers, however, may have had more resources, time, or institutional capacity – and if they explored similar research questions, they may have collected exactly the kind of dataset you need! Even if the previous researchers did not examine *exactly* the same research questions, it's possible that they still collected potentially relevant data. In many large-scale, long-term studies, researchers collect data on a wide variety of variables, but don't end up including all of these variables in their analysis. Exploring such previously overlooked variables can be a promising opportunity to make an original contribution from secondary data.

Although not all researchers allow their datasets to be used for secondary analysis, an increasing number do. In Chapter 4 we'll identify places where you can obtain potentially relevant secondary *quantitative* datasets; in Chapter 6 we'll do the same for *qualitative* datasets. But before we explore *how* to obtain secondary data, we must first consider some precautions to keep in mind if you want to use secondary data in your own work.

The first precaution is to make sure you still take the time to become fully versed in the data collection procedures. In order to use secondary data accurately in your own work, you need to understand exactly how each variable was measured, how the sample was obtained, during what time period the data was collected, and all those other nuances of the data collection process. When you collect data yourself, you naturally wade into these details; however, when working with a secondary dataset, you may need to push yourself to get into these 'weeds'.

Secondary datasets are typically accompanied by some kind of documentation that describes the data collection process and defines key terms or variables in the dataset. Read through this documentation carefully. Unfortunately, there may not be enough documentation about particular issues – such as whether the data exhibits the different types of validity, which we discussed in Chapter 2 (Beer & Faulkner, 2014, p. 194) – and, in such cases, you'll need to proceed with caution (Hair, Celsi, Money, Samouel, & Page, 2011, p. 119). Even when extensive documentation is provided, simply reading this documentation is not enough. You also need to look carefully at the dataset itself. Before you jump into your specific analysis, make sure to allocate enough time to first become familiar with the dataset as a whole. Every dataset has idiosyncrasies – perhaps a variable is defined in a strange or non-standard way, or the dataset has a surprisingly large amount of missing data – which you must discern.

The second precaution is to not assume that secondary data obtained from a reputable source somehow represents the 'truth'. When obtained from a reputable source, such as a government agency or university, secondary data can acquire a sheen of 'officialness'. However, beneath this official gloss, secondary datasets – like all datasets – are influenced by researchers' 'subjective judgements' about which variables to include, how those variables should be measured, what criteria should be established for recruiting a sample, and so forth, and even datasets collected by prestigious government bodies, like national censuses, often 'reflect organizational priorities' as they were collected for a particular purpose (Hoggart, Lees, & Davies, 2014, p. 76). When you collect data yourself, you know that your own goals and perspective shaped the data collection process, since *you* decided which questions to ask, or which themes to focus on. When you analyse data collected by others, don't forget that some other researcher (or team of researchers) had to make these same decisions. Therefore, you need to consider how those original researchers' goals and perspectives shaped their data collection process as well.

As you reflect on the original researchers' goals, you may find that those goals differ from your own. Many analysts of secondary datasets focus on new research questions that don't match the research questions of the original researchers. There is nothing wrong with this practice; in fact, it's a great way to make a unique contribution from 'reused' data. However, you need to think about how this practice might shape or limit your analysis. If the original researchers focused on different research questions, did they still collect all the variables you need?

Another, related precaution when using secondary data is to think carefully about the original researchers' *sample*. Large-scale secondary datasets, such as data from the Office for National Statistics in the UK or the US Census Bureau, are often based on nationally representative data. If you want to explore nationwide trends, such a sample is ideal, but if you're interested in one local area or one very specific segment of society (e.g., university-educated parents who speak at least two languages), you may need a very different and more focused sample (Begun & Gregoire, 2014). Conversely, other datasets might have been collected in just one area, which may not be appropriate if you *do* want to generalize your findings to a broader population. Similarly, if you want to make conclusions about *current* conditions in society, you need to think carefully about the *age* of your dataset. By definition, secondary data was collected in the past; but there is an important difference between data collected one year ago and data collected 20 years ago. (Although even data collected one year ago may still be out of date if massive social or political changes have occurred in the meantime.) Make sure you know *when* a secondary dataset was collected, and think about how this timing – and the political, social, economic, and other conditions in place at that moment – may have affected the data.

Finally, consider carefully the issue of *access*. Although an increasing number of researchers allow their datasets to be used for secondary analysis, the practicalities of actually *obtaining* the dataset may not always be straightforward. Some secondary datasets are freely available to the public and can be easily downloaded online. Other secondary datasets require that researchers first submit a proposal or complete an application before access is granted. (For some secondary datasets, if an application fails to meet particular criteria, such as protecting research participants' privacy, access to the data may be denied.) An example of a well-known dataset that can only be accessed after a rigorous application review process is the Framingham Heart Study. The Framingham Heart Study (2018) is a landmark health study that was launched in Framingham, Massachusetts, in 1948 and has included almost 15,000 research participants from multiple generations. The study's large sample size and long-term duration mean that it is a rich source of potential health-related findings; indeed, a large number of important insights have emerged from both primary and secondary analysis of the study's data. However, due to the sensitive nature of health information, the Framingham Heart Study (2018) maintains a rigorous review process for secondary researchers who wish to use study data.

If you're thinking about using a particular secondary dataset, before you get too far into your research process, check what the access procedures/requirements are for that dataset. Is it freely downloadable, or do you need to submit some kind of proposal or application? If the latter, do you meet the application requirements? You don't want to spend months planning your dissertation around one secondary dataset only to find out that you won't be allowed access to that dataset.

3.12 Ethics and Research Design

Ethics should be central to all forms of data analysis – whether quantitative or qualitative, or based on primary or secondary data. Ethics can be defined as the 'principles of conduct that govern an individual or a group', and the 'moral duty and obligations' we must follow (Kromrey, 1993, p. 24). As a researcher, you have ethical responsibilities to your research participants, and to the research community at large. Good research practice requires a researcher to think through all potential risks and ethical concerns *before* embarking on any data collection or analysis. Since research is a *cumulative* activity – meaning that all researchers build upon the work of previous scholars – unethical research practices can have serious cascading consequences for entire social science disciplines (Israel & Hay, 2006, p. 5).

The issue of research ethics, which was initially prompted by concerns about the morality of medical research on human beings, has gained increasing prominence across numerous fields since the 1960s (Aguinis & Henle, 2002). Certain activities, such as fabricating data, plagiarizing the work of other researchers, and taking credit for other researchers' work, are clearly unethical. (For an expanded discussion of issues related to proper credit and control of research, see Cryer, 2006, p. 88.) However, research ethics also includes the responsibility to fully consider the harms and risks that a research project poses to research participants and other community members. Such harms must be minimized, and ethical researchers must carefully evaluate both the harms a project might produce, as well as the harms to society that might result if the research is *not* undertaken (Aguinis & Henle, 2002). In addition to protecting research participants from harm, ethical researchers must also be careful not to breach participants' privacy, or prevent participants from gaining access to the knowledge or other gains produced by the project (House, 1993; see also Shaw, 2003, pp. 14–15). This respectful approach to the individuals who take part in one's research is reflected in the term *research participants* – which we have used, and will continue to use, throughout this book – as it recognizes the active participation of individuals, as compared to the more passive term *research subjects*.

3.12.1 Confidentiality and reflexivity

Protecting the privacy of research participants is a particularly important – but sometimes complex – concern for researchers. Although the terms **confidentiality** and **anonymity** are often used interchangeably in discussions about privacy, these two concepts are actually very different (King & Horrocks, 2010, p. 117). In the formal context of research methods, *confidentiality* is the idea that certain information 'will remain private and not be repeated' at all, while *anonymity* involves 'concealing the identity of the participants in all documents resulting from the research' (King & Horrocks, 2010, p. 117). Since confidentiality conflicts with most researchers' desires to publicize and disseminate their findings, anonymity is a more prominent concept in social science research. However, anonymity can still be challenging to achieve in studies with small samples or in studies that focus on research participants' detailed personal stories or potentially identifiable information (Webster, Lewis, & Brown, 2014, p. 85). Researchers are typically expected to be upfront and forthright with research participants about the amount of confidentiality and anonymity the participants will be granted.

The issue of research participants' privacy can be even thornier in studies that address sensitive issues, such as research participants' involvement in antisocial activities. As Howard S. Becker observed, when conducting research on some social science topics, researchers will likely encounter attitudes or behaviours they 'may personally disapprove of'; such researchers must therefore adopt a 'deliberately tolerant attitude' to understand the perspectives of their research participants (Becker, 1970, p. 47). However, when research participants address behaviours that are not only repugnant but are also against the law, extra concerns arise for researchers. A researcher must recognize that, typically, her data does not enjoy 'the same privileged status as communications between doctor and patients or solicitors [lawyers] and clients', even if she has promised anonymity to the participants (Davies, 1999, p. 52); therefore, as Davies (1999, p. 52) has recommended, research participants 'should be warned against self-incrimination' if there is any potential that this might occur. If there is a risk that research participants may report illegal activities in your study, before collecting data, you should seek greater clarity on your specific legal and ethical responsibilities and consult with ethics committees/panels in your discipline. Later in this chapter we will discuss the specific activities and characteristics of such ethics committees/panels that promote ethical research practices at universities and other institutions.

Illegal activities are not the only subjects that can present ethical challenges to researchers. The exploration of other emotional or sensitive topics can also test researchers' 'professional boundaries', as researchers gain the trust of research participants and feel pressured to act in the professionally incompatible role of 'quasi-counsellor' (Webster et al., 2014, p. 84). In such situations, as well as other scenarios that challenge a researcher's objectivity, it is important for a researcher to retain a 'reflexive' perspective and consider how his own 'identity' has influenced the data collection and analysis processes (Banks, 2014, p. 296). Engaging in reflexivity – a practice that will be emphasized several times in this textbook – is not only a useful research technique, but also often an important component of ethical practice. Indeed, Pink (2007, p. 49) has argued that, when conducting certain types of qualitative research, researchers should adopt 'a reflexive approach to their own ethical beliefs' and recognize that different contexts exhibit a diversity of ethical codes. Although you may not agree with Pink's specific argument, it underscores the larger point about the centrality of reflexivity in the research process.

3.12.2 Informed consent

In addition to privacy and reflexivity, a third theme that is also essential in research ethics is **informed consent**, or the principle that research participants should be allowed to make an educated individual decision about whether they want to take part in a study. This principle of informed consent first emerged in medicine but is now widely recognized as central to social science research as well (Nathan, 2000, p. 71). Informed consent is typically recorded using a formal document that outlines the research project and is signed and dated by the research participant (Mayo Clinic, n.d.). Informed consent should always be continuous; a research participant should be allowed to revoke their consent and end their participation in a research project at any point, without experiencing any negative consequences (Smith, Todd, & Waldman, 2009, p. 90). The need to obtain informed consent is now a widely accepted principle in the social sciences; however, more complex questions remain about *how* to obtain informed consent in the most ethical and effective manner. For example, the question of how to ethically obtain informed consent from children is important, as the informed consent of 'parents, teachers or carers' might also be needed (Smith, Todd, & Waldman, 2009, p. 90).

One type of research in which researchers are not able to gain the informed consent of participants prior to the study is **covert research**, in which research participants are not informed that they are participating in a research project (Spicker, 2011). In covert research, researchers disguise their true intentions, and may mislead research participants in order to obtain data

(Davies, 1999, p. 53). The key advantage of covert research is that it can minimize 'observation effects', or the tendency of individuals to alter their behaviour when they are aware they are being observed (Mouton & Marais, 1996, p. 94). Since, in covert research, research participants do not know they are being observed, they will be more likely to exhibit their 'natural' behaviour. However, covert research can raise substantial ethical concerns, since it does not, by definition, allow researchers to obtain informed consent, and it may even intrude on research participants' privacy. If you are contemplating covert research, you *must* think carefully about these ethical issues and take steps to minimize their impact. One such step that covert researchers have adopted in the past 'involves asking the permission of the subject to use the information gathered immediately upon completion of the study' and 'ensuring the anonymity of the subject' in all published results (Mouton & Marais, 1996, p. 94). If you are contemplating covert research, you must first familiarize yourself with its unique ethical risks – as well as with the wider debate among researchers about whether such research should be conducted at all. To gain such knowledge, take a look at the 'Further Reading' section at the end of this chapter, which describes several good sources for obtaining more information about the controversies and ethical issues surrounding covert research.

3.12.3 Case study: The nocebo effect

Let's take a look at a real-life research phenomenon, the **nocebo effect**, that illustrates the complexities of informed consent and other ethical principles that we have just discussed.

Have you heard of the **placebo effect**? It's often found in medical studies that utilize a *treatment* group and a *control* or comparison group to test the effectiveness of a drug. While the treatment group receives the drug, the control group receives a placebo – a treatment that looks like the drug, but does not contain the drug's effective ingredients (e.g., they might receive a sugar pill). The placebo effect is when research participants in the control group experience some benefit or improved outcome after taking the placebo. Since the research participants *think* the placebo will offer them a benefit (as they believe the placebo is the drug), they begin to feel better, due to measurable neurological or physiological processes (for more discussion, see Miller, Colloca, Crouch, & Kaptchuk, 2013). Remarkably, placebos have been linked to 'real physiological responses, from changes in heart rate and blood pressure to chemical activity in the brain' (Feinberg, 2013).

Although the placebo effect has long interested researchers, a second, related phenomenon – the *nocebo effect* – has recently also gained attention (Robson, 2015a). The nocebo effect is a sinister twist on the placebo effect. Specifically, it is when an individual experiences undesirable outcomes or side effects after 'the administration of an inert substance or treatment believed by the receiver to be harmful' (Pollo & Benedetti, 2012, p. 332). In other words, an individual experiences negative consequences from a treatment that is actually harmless (e.g., a sugar pill). Like the placebo effect, the nocebo effect is also believed to result from psychological expectations, as an individual's belief that a treatment will have undesirable consequences actually causes that individual to experience undesirable consequences (Pollo & Benedetti, 2012, p. 332).

The nocebo effect illustrates the ethical complexities of informed consent. Ethical principles mean researchers must be forthright with research participants about all the potential side effects or undesirable consequences of a treatment. At the same time, ethical principles also require research participants to be protected from harm. The nocebo effect illustrates that these two goals may conflict, as explaining all potential side effects or undesirable consequences 'may itself induce adverse effects' (Wells, 2012, p. 22) – effects which the individual would not have experienced, if he had not been warned about them in advance. The nocebo effect, therefore, presents a significant ethics conundrum, not only for researchers but also for doctors prescribing drugs with rare side effects (Häuser, Hansen, & Enck, 2012, p. 459).

Researchers have proposed a variety of different strategies for responding to nocebo effects. Informing patients or research participants about the power of our expectations to affect our perception of a treatment's effects has been posited as a potential method for offsetting nocebo effects (Robson, 2015a). Such education efforts should commence before the actual treatment is administered, since 'it may be difficult to convince a patient that he is experiencing a nocebo effect once the side effect has occurred' (Doering & Rief, 2013, p. 261). Researchers and medical professionals can also endeavour to reduce patient worry about side effects by explaining that they are not serious and, seen in a more optimistic light, are 'an indicator that the drug is taking its effect' (Doering & Rief, 2013, p. 261). Other remedies call for a modification in current definitions of informed consent. Wells (2012, p. 22), for example, has argued for 'contextualized informed consent', a modified process that will allow 'providers to minimize nocebo responses while still maintaining patient autonomy' by considering, on a case-by-case basis, the 'possible side effects, the patient being treated, and the particular diagnosis involved'. One possible strategy for responding to the nocebo effect is to focus on 'the fact that the proposed treatment is usually well tolerated', and make this point salient in patients' minds (Häuser et al., 2012, p. 459).

The nocebo and placebo effects are just two of the many issues researchers often deal with when evaluating interventions using treatment and control groups. If this discussion of treatment and control groups interests you, then stay tuned for Chapter 4, where we will explore different types of experiments.

3.12.4 Replicability

In addition to anonymity and informed consent, a third key principle in research ethics is *replicability*. Scientific knowledge is distinguished from other kinds of knowledge (e.g., intuition) in part because of its emphasis on 'experimental replication', or repeatedly testing the validity of theories through experiments (Morgan & Morgan, 2009, p. 75). Replication is particularly important in social science research, since findings might not apply to other situations or groups of research participants, or may be due to chance or researcher error (Bauernfeind, 1968, p. 126). This focus on replication mirrors our discussion in Chapter 2 on *external validity*. As we saw in that discussion, external validity addresses whether the findings of a particular study apply more broadly to other groups, historical periods, or environments. One important method for promoting external validity is, of course, replication. By replicating a study in a different setting or with a different sample of research participants, you can see whether your original findings have broader application. Even if you are not currently able to undertake a replication of your study in a different setting, you can rigorously document each step of your research and analysis processes to aid future researchers' attempts to replicate your work (Mays & Pope, 1995, p. 110).

By documenting and clearly describing the methods used in your study, you will also increase your study's *descriptive validity*, another essential type of validity that we explored in Chapter 2 (Farrington, 2003, p. 61). Descriptive validity requires researchers to be specific about the characteristics of their sample and the limitations of their research methods, important information for future researchers interested in replicating the original study

(Gill, 2011, p. 203). (Additionally, greater descriptive validity can help other scholars assess more fairly the strengths and limitations of your methods, and is therefore a good ethical practice to adopt, even if you think it unlikely that future researchers will ever attempt to replicate your work.) Although no widespread consensus yet exists among social scientists regarding the *standards* for a sufficient replication, many scholars have expressed interest in developing such guidelines (Brandt et al., 2014).

stop and think

Why is descriptive validity so important for replication?

Whether replication gains greater prominence in social science research in the near future remains to be seen. However, at the moment, replication typically receives less attention from social science researchers and publication outlets than new, original research. For example, a review of highly cited educational journals revealed that only 0.13% of studies published in these journals were replications of previous studies (Makel & Plucker, 2014) – a finding that highlights larger trends. Of course, not all types of social science studies may be suitable for replication. For example, studies that focus on a very specific group of people or on non-repeatable events may not be replicable; other studies whose findings are not intended to be generalized beyond a specific setting may not be suitable for replication either. However, in studies with findings that *are* intended to be generalized, replication is an important concern.

3.12.5 Ethical codes

Although the principles we have discussed in this chapter broadly apply across the social sciences, different disciplinary organizations have established specific ethical codes. Given their discipline-specificity, these ethical codes can be particularly useful for young researchers to consult, as they may address specific situations that commonly arise in research from your discipline. For example, the British Society of Criminology's (2015) Statement of Ethics offers case studies of situations researchers might face and also includes links to numerous other resources, mainly aimed at criminologists and researchers from related fields, with some international coverage.

The American Sociological Association's (1999, p. 6) Code of Ethics focuses on five key principles: 'professional competence', 'integrity', 'professional and scientific responsibility', 'respect for people's rights, dignity, and diversity', and 'social responsibility'. These principles overlap in many ways with the general themes we have already discussed in this chapter.

The Australian Psychological Society's (2007) Code of Ethics focuses on principles that are important for psychologists to uphold both in conducting research and in their other daily work (pp. 3–4). Included within these principles are some of the themes we have already addressed in this chapter, including informed consent and the preservation of privacy, as well as other more specific themes related to the provision of psychological services.

In addition to these discipline-focused ethical codes, several broader international initiatives have also been launched to promote ethical research. Perhaps the best known of these initiatives is the Declaration of Helsinki, adopted by the World Medical Association in 1964 and periodically updated since then (see World Medical Association, 2015), which sets ethical standards for medical studies that use humans as research subjects.

A more recent international ethics initiative is the Singapore Statement on Research Integrity (2010). The Singapore Statement sets out important guidelines for ethical research, centred on four specific principles: 'honesty in all aspects of research'; 'accountability in the conduct of research'; 'professional courtesy and fairness in working with others'; and 'good stewardship of research on behalf of others'.

In this section we have explored codes of ethics from two broad international initiatives, and from three different social science disciplines (criminology, sociology, and psychology) in three different countries (the UK, the USA, and Australia). The breadth of these examples illustrates the importance of ethics across different research fields, as well as the range of specific ethical codes that exist for different professional organizations.

let's try this!

Which social science discipline most interests you? Public health? Politics? Criminology? Psychology? Sociology? Anthropology? Or something else entirely? See if you can find a professional organization that focuses on your discipline; ideally, try to find a professional organization that is located in your country, although this may not be possible. For example, if you are interested in politics and currently living in the USA, you might select the American Political Science Association; if you are interested in psychology and currently living in the UK, you might select the British Psychological Society. For the professional organization you select, investigate its website to see if it has a code of ethics. If so, what principles does its code of ethics focus on? In what ways are these principles similar to and different from those we have already discussed in this chapter?

Hopefully the exercise you've just completed has helped you familiarize yourself with the general ethical codes promoted in your discipline. It is also essential, however, to investigate the specific research ethics regulations at your university or institution. Many universities and other institutions have a formal research ethics committee, institutional review board (IRB), or research advisory board that must review all proposals for research with human subjects *before* any data is collected or analysed. Such bodies feature panels of experts specifically tasked with ensuring that the rights and interests of research participants are respected (Mayo Clinic, n.d.). If you are a university student, check to see whether your university has such a body in place, and familiarize yourself with its requirements, as you will need to seek approval from this body before conducting research on human subjects.

Concluding Thoughts

Sometimes the data analysis process can feel like an endless parade of decisions. You'll need to decide which research questions to examine, and then decide how to turn those questions into hypotheses. You'll have to decide which research methods to employ, and how you'll collect or obtain your data. You'll need to choose how to organize your data effectively and how to present your results. Each of these decisions is important, so it's worth spending a bit of time at the start thinking about the ultimate *aims* of your research project. What questions do you want to answer? What do you hope to gain from your research project? Thinking carefully about these decisions at the outset will save you significant time later on in the data analysis process.

The most important consideration at the outset of any research project, however, is ethics. How can you ensure that ethical principles are upheld in your work? In this chapter we've reviewed specific rules and norms that should guide any data analysis. However, conducting ethical research involves more than just 'following a set of rules'; it also requires you 'to make reasoned and thoughtful decisions' throughout the research process (Willis, Jost, & Nilakanta, 2007, p. 316). Conducting ethical research involves cultivating a broader sense of professional responsibility to your research participants, your fellow scholars, and the public at large. This theme of professional responsibility is central to the entire research process, and we will return to it throughout this textbook.

Summary

- Before beginning any research project, you need to think carefully about how you will obtain and organize the data you collect.
- You might choose to collect data yourself, or you might choose to analyse *secondary data* (which is data that has already been collected by other researchers).
- Sometimes valuable datasets can be found in unexpected places, as illustrated by the example of John Laub and Robert Sampson's (2003) criminological research.
- Initiating a research project usually involves conducting a thorough review of previous literature on the topic, as well as formulating a testable hypothesis.
- Before beginning your study, it may be helpful to formulate a research plan and conduct a pilot study.
- It may not be possible to study the entire population you are interested in. In such cases it may be necessary to select a sample from that population. This chapter described different strategies for selecting a sample, including: simple random sampling; stratified random sampling; systematic sampling; cluster sampling; deliberate sampling; snowball sampling; convenience sampling; and most- or least-similar case selection.
- Data analysts frequently encounter issues of non-response and missing data, and in this chapter we explored a variety of techniques for dealing with such problems.
- Research ethics is essential in every project, and the ethical principles discussed in this chapter included confidentiality and anonymity, informed consent, and replicability.

- Many professional organizations have adopted their own specific codes of ethics; additionally, several international initiatives have been launched to promote ethical research practices. Before beginning your research project or collecting/obtaining data, you should consult the relevant code of ethics for your discipline, as well as investigate the procedures for gaining ethical approval for your study at your university or institution.

Further Reading

One of the most popular types of social science research is survey research. Whether you hope to administer your own survey, or plan to use survey data already collected by other researchers, you may encounter more complex sampling and analysis challenges that extend beyond the scope of this book. For a more advanced overview of common complications in survey research, see:

Lee, E. S., & Forthofer, R. N. (2006). *Analyzing complex survey data* (2nd ed.). Thousand Oaks, CA: SAGE Publications.

One important question that survey researchers frequently encounter is how to deal with non-response. As we briefly noted in this chapter, one solution for handling non-response in data analyses is to use weighting adjustment. For more technical background about the process of weighting and non-response, take a look at the following academic article:

Kreuter, F., Olson, K., Wagner, J., Yan, T., Ezzati-Rice, T. M., Casas-Cordero, C., Lemay, M., Peytchev, A., Groves, R. M., & Raghunathan, T. E. (2010). Using proxy measures and other correlates of survey outcomes to adjust for non-response: Examples from multiple surveys. *Journal of the Royal Statistical Society, Series A, 173*(2), 389–407.

As a student, two practical concerns that you're likely to encounter in the early stages of a research project are *limited time* and *limited money*. A great resource with practical tips about how to handle challenges in low-budget, time-pressed research projects is:

Knight, P. T. (2002). *Small-scale research: Pragmatic inquiry in social science and the caring professions.* London: SAGE Publications.

Several different approaches exist for handling missing data. One approach that has received increasing attention in recent years is multiple imputation, an approach too complex to cover in detail in this chapter. If you want to learn more about this technique, consider exploring the following sources:

Carpenter, J. R., & Kenward, M. G. (2013). *Multiple imputation and its application.* Chichester: John Wiley & Sons.

This work is a relatively recent overview of advances in multiple imputation, and includes guidance on both introductory and more advanced elements related to the technique. A classic article that is older and offers a briefer (but still thorough) analysis of key concerns related to multiple imputation is:

Schafer, J. (1999). Multiple imputation: A primer. *Statistical Methods in Medical Research,* 8, 3–15.

One of the most important topics we explored in this chapter was research ethics. An excellent overview of ethical issues and descriptions of policies and issues in a range of different countries (including Australia, the USA, the UK, and Canada) can be found in the following book:

Israel, M., & Hay, I. (2006). *Research ethics for social scientists*. London: SAGE Publications.

However, note that this book is now a few years old, and official policies may change over time. An important aspect of research ethics which we were only able to briefly address in this chapter is how to ensure appropriate credit is given to different researchers who have worked on a project. Additionally, when different stakeholders are involved in a research project (such as senior academics, students, funding bodies, and other organizations), conflicts can arise regarding control over, and credit for, the research project. For more information about how to ethically handle these issues, take a look at:

Cryer, P. (2006). *The research student's guide to success* (3rd ed.). Maidenhead: Open University Press. See in particular the discussion on page 88.

As we discussed in this chapter, covert research can present particularly thorny ethical challenges for researchers. If you are considering conducting covert research, it is essential to first obtain thorough knowledge of these challenges. The following sources are a good first step for beginning to gain such knowledge:

Lee, R. M. (1993). *Doing research on sensitive topics*. London: SAGE Publications. This book contains a thorough discussion of issues related to covert research beginning on page 143.

Spicker, P. (2011). Ethical covert research. *Sociology, 45*(1), 118–133.

Holdaway, S. (1982). 'An inside job': A case study of covert research on the police. In M. Blumer (Ed.), *Social research ethics* (pp. 59–79). London: Macmillan.

This famous study used covert methods to research the police.

Discussion Questions

1 In this chapter we discussed the problem of non-response in surveys. Imagine that a researcher wants to survey university undergraduates about their attitudes to 'free trade'. He plans to mail paper copies of the surveys to students at their university addresses. The survey consists of 100 questions, 50 of which are multiple-choice and 50 of which are free-response. The researcher is concerned about potential non-response. What advice would you offer him about how to reduce non-response? Develop at least three specific suggestions.

2 In the formal context of research methods, explain the difference between *confidentiality* and *anonymity*.

3 Imagine that you have just been asked to be a research participant in a research project. The research project is exploring students' opinions on data analysis textbooks. You have been asked to take part in a 45-minute interview in which you will be asked questions on your experience of learning data analysis, and your feelings about this textbook. What concerns might you have about participating in this project? What questions would you want to ask the researcher before

deciding whether to participate? What rights or protections (e.g., the right to privacy) would you want to be upheld? Once you've considered these questions, take a moment to think about how, as a *researcher*, you might alleviate these concerns and uphold these rights/protections during the research process.

4 Look back at our discussion of the nocebo effect case study. Given what you've read in this chapter about informed consent and other ethical principles, what should researchers and doctors do in situations where there is a risk of a nocebo effect? Explain how your answer upholds the ethical principles we've discussed.

5 Do you think it is possible – or useful – to adopt a single code of ethics for all social science disciplines? Or do you think each discipline requires a specific code? Explain the reasons for your answer.

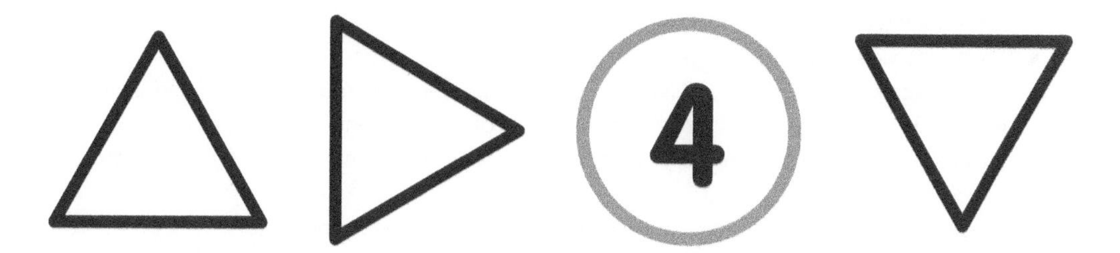

Introducing Quantitative Data Analysis

contents

Chapter Overview

In this chapter we will dive into the world of *quantitative* data analysis, introducing both key terms and basic mathematical operations that constitute the foundation of many quantitative methods. By the end of this chapter, you'll know how to:

- Identify, and briefly describe, key quantitative research methods including *experiments*, *evaluations*, *surveys*, and *secondary data analysis*
- Locate secondary datasets in key online repositories
- Differentiate between *independent* and *dependent* variables, and determine whether a variable is measured at the *nominal*, *ordinal*, *interval*, or *ratio* scale of measurement
- Identify the difference between *populations* and *samples*, and between *population parameters* and *sample statistics*
- Calculate the three main measures of central tendency: *mean*, *median*, and *mode*
- Calculate important statistics that describe the spread of a dataset: *variance*, *standard deviation*, and *range*
- Conceptualize the process of *significance testing* using *p-values*, a procedure that forms the foundation for the quantitative data analysis techniques we will explore in Chapter 5.

What is Quantitative Data Analysis?

Quantitative data are *numerical*, or represented by numbers. Quantitative data analysts use these numbers to understand relationships between variables, or explain social phenomena. Much, but not all, quantitative data analysis is rooted in the *positivist* tradition discussed in Chapter 2, in which researchers conduct rigorously controlled studies to uncover objective truths about the social world (Westerman, 2006). An essential element of this process is minimizing the influence of *confounders* – or alternative explanations for your results – so that you can isolate particular relationships or discover whether an observed effect is due to a particular cause (Wimmer & Dominick, 2014, p. 118).

Quantitative data analysts often use statistical methods to determine the likelihood that an observed relationship between variables is not due to chance. Such analysts typically endeavour to uncover findings that can be generalized beyond a single case or context. As we saw in Chapter 2, if a study's findings can be broadly applied to other environments, groups, or time periods then they have *external validity*. Achieving high external validity, therefore, is often an important goal of quantitative research, although it can be difficult to attain in practice since, for practical reasons, a quantitative study may have been conducted in just one particular setting or with one particular group or in one particular country. How can we be certain, for example, that the findings of a quantitative study conducted in the UK would also apply in the USA or in China? This complexity highlights a key challenge in much quantitative research: how to maximize different types of validity despite the real-world challenges of data collection and analysis.

4.3 Quantitative Data Analysis Approaches

Numerous specific approaches exist for collecting and analysing quantitative data. Although it is impossible to explore all of these specific methods in this chapter, this section offers an overview of the main research methods that produce quantitative data for us to analyse. Understanding how these methods operate is crucial in order to select a data analysis procedure that is appropriate for your project.

4.3.1 Experiments

Experiments are perhaps the best-known quantitative research method. Long a staple of the natural sciences, experiments have also received increased attention and scrutiny from many different types of social scientists in recent years. In an experiment, a researcher manipulates one variable to see how changes to it affect the value of another variable. (For more information on variables, see Section 4.6.) A well-designed experiment will give you confidence that any results you observe are not due to chance or to alternative, confounding variables, since a well-designed experiment minimizes these threats (Walker, 2005, p. 573).

In an experiment, research participants should be *randomly* selected for inclusion in either the *experimental* group or the *control* group. (The *randomness* of the selection process is the reason why the term **randomized controlled trial** (RCT) is often used to denote experiments in the social and medical sciences.) The research participants included in the experimental group receive the treatment or condition the researcher is interested in, while those research participants included in the control group do not receive the treatment or condition but may receive a placebo. (Can you recall what a *placebo* is? If not, take a look back at the case study in Section 3.12 now, where we discuss the placebo – and the fascinating 'placebo effect' – in detail.) The ability of rigorously conducted experiments to minimize confounding and isolate the effects of a particular independent variable contributes to their high *internal validity* (Walker, 2005, p. 574). However, the presence of high *internal* validity does not guarantee that *external* validity will be achieved, if a study's findings do not apply to other contexts, environments, or groups.

stop and think

What is *internal validity*? (If you can't remember, revisit the discussion of validity in Section 2.7 now.) Why is internal validity so important in data analysis?

4.3.2 Quasi-experiments

In the social sciences it is often impossible to conduct an RCT or a 'true' experiment with individuals randomly assigned to experimental and control groups. It may be unethical to randomly assign individuals to a control group with access only to a placebo rather than a potentially beneficial treatment (Glicken, 2003, p. 137). In such circumstances, quasi-experiments may be undertaken instead.

Like an experiment, a quasi-experiment also typically seeks to determine whether one variable (such as the imposition of a particular programme) affects another variable (such as performance at school), but research participants are not randomly assigned to the groups, or no control group is offered (Stommel & Wills, 2004, p. 92). Although quasi-experiments have value, you cannot assume their findings can be generalized to other contexts, or that all potential confounding variables have been eliminated. In other words, unlike in true experiments or RCTs, you cannot dismiss the possibility that other, confounding causal factors may actually be responsible for the effect you perceive in a quasi-experiment, since research participants are not randomly assigned to experimental and control groups (Weathington, Cunningham, & Pittenger, 2010, p. 493).

4.3.3 Evaluations

Evaluations, which are sometimes conducted using experimental or quasi-experimental methods, aim to answer questions about the effectiveness or impact 'of an established policy or planned intervention' (Clarke & Dawson, 1999, p. 3). Policy-makers and practitioners may be particularly interested in evaluations, as such studies can determine whether particular policies or programmes 'work' and represent a valuable use of public resources. Some evaluations focus not only on the results of a programme, but also on whether the programme has been correctly implemented (Dooley, 2001, p. 288). These evaluations, known as *process* or *implementation* evaluations, assess whether the programme or policy is actually functioning as intended. Many evaluations also include a cost–benefit analysis component, so that policy-makers and citizens alike can learn whether the benefits of a programme or policy exceed its costs (Morçöl, 2002). Evaluation research is of interest to many social scientists, and it forms a key component of *policy research*, which explores how public policies can be more effective and more useful for solving societal problems (Majchrzak & Markus, 2014, p. 2).

4.3.4 Surveys

Another popular and useful quantitative method is to collect **survey** data. Surveys typically feature an instrument or questionnaire which participants fill out by themselves or with a research worker present. If you are interested in conducting survey research, a major decision is whether you will develop your own instrument or questionnaire, or whether you will use one that has already been developed by other researchers. Both choices have advantages and disadvantages. If you choose to design your own survey, you will be able to ask the exact questions that you are interested in; however, since your questionnaire or instrument will be brand new, you will need to take significant care that your questions are not biased or leading. A common strategy to combat this risk is to *pilot* your questionnaire with a smaller group of research participants before conducting your large-scale survey. During the pilot, you can receive feedback from the participants about the question wording and general content of the survey, so that you can make appropriate revisions.

If you want to use an instrument that has already been developed by other researchers, you will need to ensure you have permission from those researchers to use it. An obvious disadvantage of this strategy is that you will be limited to the questions already contained in the survey, which may not exactly match your research questions. However, an advantage is that the questions will have been validated in previous studies, and the risk that they are biased or leading may therefore be lower. Nevertheless, if you are using the questionnaire with a population that is very different from the population studied by the original researchers (for example, you are conducting the survey in a different country or cultural context), you may still want to *pilot* the instrument before beginning your full study.

In addition to conducting your own survey or using an instrument developed by other researchers, it is important to remember that governments and organizations around the world regularly conduct large-scale surveys on various topics. The data collected in some of these surveys are publicly available, and present useful opportunities for analysis. The next subsection of this chapter, on secondary data analysis, presents suggestions of where to find these publicly available survey datasets.

Conducting surveys with large, diverse samples can enhance the external validity of your findings (or increase the likelihood that your findings about your sample apply to a broader population). Some of the potential pitfalls of quantitative surveys which may impact their internal validity include concerns about the accuracy of individuals' responses, particularly for questions about illegal behaviours and other sensitive topics (Harrison, 1997). Another limitation that can affect both internal and external validity is a low response rate to a survey, and a significant literature has developed regarding different tactics for improving participation in surveys (see discussion in Iarossi, 2006, pp. 149–155).

stop and think

Have you ever completed a survey? How did you feel about the experience?

(When designing a survey, try to keep the survey respondent in mind. Think carefully about how the respondent will feel when completing the survey. Will the respondent be able to understand all the questions? Will the survey hold the respondent's interest, or is the respondent likely to get bored or frustrated and give up?)

4.3.5 Secondary data analysis

As we saw in the previous chapter, secondary data analysis is when you analyse data collected by other, previous researchers. (In other words, you didn't collect the data yourself.) In recent years, as more large-scale datasets have become publicly available, secondary data analysis has become increasingly popular across many social science disciplines (Dale, Wathan, & Higgins, 2008). Advantages of using secondary data rather than primary data include access to a much larger sample than you might be able to recruit yourself, as well as reduced monetary and time costs, since the data has already been collected (Vartanian, 2011, pp. 10, 13). Additionally, since secondary datasets often span a long time, they can allow a researcher to track how variables, or relationships between variables, evolve across time (Chan & McGarey, 2012, p. 372).

Before moving on to the next section, take a look at Table 4.1, which summarizes the different types of quantitative data we've just discussed. Although this list is not exhaustive, it includes the forms of quantitative data that you're most likely to encounter. So it's helpful to briefly check: can you define each of these data types?

Table 4.1 Common sources of quantitative data

Name	Description
Experiments	A researcher manipulates one variable to see how these changes affect values of another variable Research participants are *randomly assigned* to the experimental group or the control group to minimize the risk that any observed differences between the groups are due to an alternative explanation than the manipulated variable
Quasi-experiments	A researcher manipulates one variable to see how these changes affect values of another variable Unlike an experiment, research participants are not randomly assigned to the groups, and a control group may not be present at all
Evaluations	Formal assessments that investigate whether a policy, programme, or intervention is meeting its stated goals May use experiments, quasi-experiments, other quantitative methods, or even qualitative methods In addition to appraising the results of a programme, some evaluations may also assess whether the programme has been implemented correctly, and whether the programme's benefits exceed its costs
Surveys	Research participants are asked to fill out a questionnaire (or answer a series of questions) either by themselves or with a research worker present
Secondary data	Data that has been collected by previous researchers May have been collected through any of the above methods (experiment, quasi-experiments, evaluations, or surveys) or any other quantitative or qualitative methods

Cross-Sectional and Longitudinal Data

When searching for secondary data, you may find datasets that are identified as either *cross-sectional* or *longitudinal*. **Cross-sectional data** is focused on a particular moment in time, while **longitudinal data** (sometimes called *panel data*) is about the same group of research participants at different points in time (see, for example, Institute for Work & Health, 2015). One clear advantage of longitudinal data is its ability to capture the order in which events happen and variables change; however, before making claims about causality (i.e., suggesting that the first event *caused* the second event), you need to think carefully about your results and whether theoretical explanations support your analysis (Taris, 2000, p. 4).

It can be particularly difficult to collect longitudinal data, given the vast time commitment and resources needed to follow up with the same research participants over a substantial time span. Indeed, for students, collecting longitudinal data for a thesis or dissertation is usually impossible. However, if you require longitudinal data to answer your research questions, consider whether any secondary datasets fit your needs. In recent years, substantial efforts by governments, international organizations, and other research bodies have vastly increased the number and scope of longitudinal datasets available globally (Hsiao, 2014, p. 3). Therefore, fortunately, it may be possible for you to obtain secondary data if you want to explore longitudinal questions.

stop and think

Why might a researcher prefer to use *longitudinal* data instead of *cross-sectional* data to answer a research question?

Advantages and Disadvantages of Secondary Data

Engaging in secondary data analysis can be a useful exploratory step before you begin to collect your own data. The findings of your secondary data analysis may help you generate hypotheses and research questions to probe in the data you collect yourself. However, secondary data analysis is also subject to limitations, as we hinted in Chapter 3. In particular, since you have not collected the data yourself, you may find that the dataset fails to include certain variables you are interested in – or that it defines concepts in slightly different ways (Bachman & Schutt, 2007, p. 403). Another issue that often arises when analysing secondary data is how to deal with observations that are 'missing', or simply have not been collected in a given year or for a particular variable. We explored the issue of missing data in detail in the previous chapter, and I urge you to revisit that discussion. When dealing specifically with secondary data, the question of how to handle missing data can be particularly tricky, since, unlike for data you've collected yourself, you may not immediately know *why* the data is missing. Exploring the extent of missingness, and the reasons for such missingness, is therefore important in secondary data analysis.

Despite these limitations, secondary data analysis still presents numerous advantages and opportunities for researchers. Key sources for obtaining such data include the Office for National Statistics for data about the UK (see http://www.ons.gov.uk/ons/index.html), the United States Bureau of the Census for data about the USA (see http://www.census.gov/), and UNdata, a special initiative of the United Nations Statistics Division (see http://data.un.org/). However, in addition to these sources, numerous other large-scale datasets have been collected by various national and local government agencies, non-profit organizations, and academic researchers. Knowing what datasets exist and are available for secondary data analysis can be a challenge, particularly for new researchers. Therefore it is usually a good idea to begin by searching large repositories of datasets. Such repositories may show you a range of datasets related to your topic or research questions, some of which may be suitable and available for your own secondary analysis. Even if such repositories do not carry a dataset that you can use, investigating available datasets can be a useful first step in determining where else you should search for data. Numerous data repositories exist; here are a few that might be particularly relevant for your own social science research:

- The Interuniversity Consortium for Political and Social Research (ICPSR) at the University of Michigan is a treasure trove of secondary datasets on topics of potential interest to social scientists. You can search by topic or variable to find datasets on the ICPSR's website. Many of the datasets are freely available to download, and your university may already be a member of the ICPSR. The ICPSR also offers workshops on topics related to data analysis during the summer. You can find out more on the organization's website: icpsr.umich.edu
- The UK Data Service is a fantastic resource that features a wide variety of both quantitative and qualitative datasets. Some of the datasets are UK-specific and some are international. The UK Data Service website contains guides about how to use and cite the available data, as well as more general information about different research methodologies. Finally, the website also features a calendar of upcoming methods-related workshops and events throughout the UK and sometimes overseas. It's worth checking whether any of these events will be held in your area. The UK Data Service also conducts regular webinars, so if you can't attend an event in person, you may still be able to participate remotely. You can access the website at: https://www.ukdataservice.ac.uk/
- The Harvard Dataverse Network is another useful repository, containing datasets from all over the world on a range of interesting topics. Visit the website here: https://thedata.harvard.edu/dvn/
- Several more discipline-specific data repositories are available, which may be of interest if you are working in a particular social science area. For example, researchers working on crime and criminal justice issues should take a look at the website of the National Archive of Criminal Justice Data (NACJD), which is hosted by the ICPSR and sponsored by the Bureau of Justice Statistics, the National Institute of Justice, and the Office for Juvenile Justice and Delinquency Prevention (all three of these agencies are part of the US Department of Justice). The NACJD contains a wealth of datasets on crime and criminal justice issues, and some of the available data may also be of interest to social scientists working in other areas. Visit the website here: http://www.icpsr.umich.edu/icpsrweb/NACJD/

let's try this!

Visit at least one of the databases described above and spend some time investigating the datasets that are available there. Do any of these datasets interest you? Could you use any of these datasets in a future thesis or paper?

4.6 What Is a Variable?

We have already come across the term *variable* several times in this book. You may already have some understanding of what a variable is. However, given the fundamental role of variables in quantitative data analysis – indeed, such analysis often involves the use of statistical methods to measure variables or quantify relationships between variables – it is important to step back and consider exactly *what* a variable is in more detail.

Put simply, a **variable** is any measurable characteristic, concept, cause, or set of items that you want to investigate through rigorous analysis. Examples of variables include age, temperature, height, or nationality. In our data analyses, we will encounter two main types of variables: *dependent variables* and *independent variables*. A **dependent variable** (which is also often called an *outcome variable*), is a variable representing the outcome you are interested in. It is the variable whose values you are attempting to predict or explain in your data analysis. An **independent variable** (known also as a *predictor variable*), is a variable that you believe might impact or predict the dependent variable that you're interested in. In Chapter 1 you considered the question of whether temperature affects crime rates. In that example, temperature would be the independent variable and the crime rate would be the dependent variable.

In order to include a variable in your data analysis, you must first *operationalize* the concept or phenomenon you are interested in. This process of *operationalization* involves turning the object or characteristic of interest into something that can be accurately measured and feasibly included in a data analysis as a variable. For example, we might operationalize the concept of 'temperature' as 'average daily temperature in degrees Celsius'. In a quantitative data analysis, you will typically operationalize your variables using numeric values (or categories that can be converted to numeric values), so that you can include those variables in statistical tests. (Interestingly, as we will see in Chapter 6, in a qualitative data analysis, you might undertake an analogous process to operationalize – or, more accurately, define – the concepts you are interested in, so that you can identify those concepts in your data or when conducting fieldwork. However, in a qualitative data analysis, you are unlikely to use the term 'variables' to refer to these concepts.)

When deciding how to best operationalize your variables in a quantitative data analysis, it is crucial to look first at previous research to understand whether and how that concept has been operationalized in previous studies. Drawing on past definitions means that you don't have to 'reinvent the wheel', or spend time and energy developing definitions that already exist. Moreover, even if you ultimately choose to operationalize your variables (or concepts) differently from previous researchers, it is important to recognize that different disciplines maintain specific conventions about how to most appropriately operationalize variables. You will need to acknowledge such conventions, regardless of whether your own work ultimately diverges from such conventions.

Variables are typically operationalized as either *discrete variables* or *continuous variables*. A **discrete variable** can only exhibit a few different values or categories, while a **continuous variable** can exhibit a wide variety of values (Howell, 2007, p. 4). Determining whether your independent and dependent variables are continuous or discrete is fundamental as this choice can affect the type of statistical analysis you ultimately undertake. Later in this book we will explore quantitative analysis techniques that you can employ for discrete and continuous variables.

The differences between discrete and continuous variables are summarized in Table 4.2.

Table 4.2 Discrete and continuous variables

Variable Type	Definition	Examples
Discrete variable	A variable that can only exhibit a limited number of different values or categories	Never married, married, divorced, widowed
Continuous variable	A variable that can exhibit a wide variety of different values	Individual's annual income

In addition to this broad categorization of discrete and continuous variables, a more specific, four-part scheme for classifying variables in quantitative data analysis was developed by Stevens (1951). This scheme classifies data as either *nominal, ordinal, interval*, or *ratio*. **Nominal** data is data arranged in categories that *are not* ranked or ordered in any way. For example, 'nationality' would be a nominal variable if one had a sample of people from different European countries. Each person in the sample would fall into a particular category such as 'Dutch', 'French', or 'Italian'. **Ordinal** data is data arranged in categories that *are* ranked or ordered in some way. For example, if we had a sample of people learning a new language, we could create the ordinal variable 'language ability' by assigning people to the categories 'beginner', 'intermediate', and 'advanced'. These categories have an innate order or rank.

Both **interval** and **ratio** data are continuous, with each case able to take on any value within a set range. However, unlike interval data, ratio data features an absolute zero, or a point at which there is complete absence of the quantity of interest; additionally, only ratio data allows researchers to express relationships between observations as consistent ratios. This means that, for ratio data, you can use statements such as 'twice as large as' or 'three times the distance of' or 'half as long as' to compare observations. For example, a plane flight that lasts 4 hours is *twice* as long as a plane flight that lasts 2 hours. Time, when measured in hours, is an example of ratio data, so a 4-hour flight really is twice as long as a 2-hour flight. However, imagine that a researcher has devised a scale, ranging from 1 to 100, to capture people's satisfaction with their current job. Since this scale does not have an absolute zero, one *could not* state that an individual with a score of 80 on the scale is twice as satisfied with their job as an individual with a score of 40. This scale would therefore be an example of interval data. In the real world it is often difficult to distinguish between interval and ratio variables, and many researchers do not formally distinguish interval and ratio data in their analyses (see, for example, Brain, 2000, p. 217). Fortunately, statistical tests and software packages rarely require researchers to make this distinction.

Nevertheless, understanding the differences among these types of variables is important, as nominal, ordinal, and interval/ratio data can require different statistical tests. When statistical tests are presented in subsequent chapters of this book, be sure to note whether the test is suitable for nominal, ordinal, or interval/ratio data, so that you can determine whether the test is appropriate for your dataset.

4.7 Populations, Samples, and Statistical Inference

Quantitative data analysts are often interested in a particular *population*. A population is the total set or collection of individuals, items, groups, societies, or other units that you are seeking to understand. In social science research, the population might be as large as all of humanity, or as small and specific as all qualified nurses in one neighbourhood of London. As we saw in Chapter 2, developing generalizable findings that apply to an entire population is an essential component of *external validity*. Quantitative data analysts therefore often want to uncover findings that apply to entire populations. However, it is typically impossible to study entire populations, given their substantial size; researchers can usually only gather data about a *sample*, or a smaller selection of individuals or units within the population. Researchers can then use information about the characteristics of that sample to make inferences about the characteristics of the population more generally (for example, we could use information about the average nightly hours of sleep for a sample of individuals to infer an estimate of the average nightly hours of sleep for a country's population). This process, known as *statistical inference*, is remarkable because it means we can use our humble sample of data to make much broader and bolder conclusions about the social world. Statistical inference is therefore a key element of quantitative data analysis. (Interestingly, the impact of statistical inference extends beyond social science and statistics. A similar process is also employed by computer science data specialists, who typically refer to it as 'learning' (Wasserman, 2004, p. 87).)

Our discussion thus far of statistical inference may have left you with a huge question: how we can be certain that our small sample accurately reflects the population as a whole? After all, if we want to use our sample to make conclusions about the population, then our sample should accurately reflect the population's characteristics. But what if our sample differs from the population in some way? For example, what if we want to draw conclusions about the average weight of 30-year-old men in the UK, but the men in our sample are all marathon runners? This is a serious concern, but we can reduce the potential for bias – and increase the likelihood of finding a sample that *is* representative of the population – by using *simple random sampling*, a technique in which every unit (i.e., each individual or organization or other entity you are interested in) has an exactly equal chance of being selected for the sample. (We discussed simple random sampling, and explained how it differs from other sampling approaches, in Section 3.7. If you don't recall this discussion, take a moment to review the relevant material now.) By using random sampling, we can employ known rules from probability theory to assess the likelihood that our predictions about the population are accurate (Panik, 2012, Section 1.3). In other words, although we can never eliminate the risk of error when using a sample to generalize about a population, using a *random* sample allows us to assess the likelihood that our generalization is *correct*. This property is the reason why – as we hinted in the previous chapter – random sampling is such an important concept in quantitative data analysis, and why so many statistical tests are designed to be used with random samples. Indeed, random sampling is what makes statistical inference possible; we can use a randomly drawn sample from a population to infer characteristics of that population.

4.7.1 Terminology for describing samples and populations

When moving between samples and populations, there's one more difference to be aware of: a difference in *terminology*. Researchers use the phrase **population parameter** to describe the particular characteristic of a population that they are interested in. For example, a researcher might want to estimate the average income of households in London. On the other hand, the term **sample statistic** refers to the estimate of that parameter that is found in a particular sample. (A sample, of course, is a smaller group of cases that have been taken from the larger population.) Since it may not be possible (or feasible) to obtain data on the income of every household in London, a researcher may instead collect data about the incomes of a sample of households. The average income of those households would be a sample statistic, and through statistical tests we will learn later in this book, we may derive an estimate of the population parameter (i.e., the average income for all households in London as a whole). Helpfully, data analysts typically differentiate between samples and populations by employing Greek letters (such as α or μ or σ) to denote population parameters, and Latin letters (such as a or b or s) to represent sample statistics.

4.7.2 What population are we interested in?

One of the most important questions that researchers must ask before embarking on a quantitative data analysis is: what *population* are we interested in? Precisely defining your population is essential for both practical and philosophical reasons. Practically speaking, the characteristics of your population can affect the type of statistical test you should select to analyse your data. Philosophically speaking, keeping in mind the population of interest will clarify your thinking, as well as the ultimate goals of your research. Determining whether you want to make conclusions about left-handed university students in France or about all human beings is not a trivial decision. How generalizable you want your findings to be is a particularly important philosophical question for social scientists, since we focus on *human* characteristics and phenomena, which can be quite diverse, changeable, and complex.

When defining your population, it is important to keep in mind that most well-known, classical tests of statistical inference assume that the population of interest is *infinite*. In keeping with the example above, such tests assume we are trying to generalize to all left-handed university students in all societies with economic and social characteristics identical to those of France (Kault, 2003, p. 229). However, if our population of interest is really just left-handed university students currently in France, our population is *finite* rather than *infinite*. Since most classical statistical tests of inference are predicated on infinite populations, we need to apply the *finite population correction* to slightly adjust the formulas for such statistical tests when our population is actually finite. In reality, application of the finite population correction is really only essential in cases where the sample is greater than 5–10% of the finite population of interest (Cochran, 1977, pp. 24–25). Since we rarely have such large samples in social science, consideration of the finite population correction rarely makes a substantial difference to our statistical conclusions, and most introductory textbooks do not address the question of whether populations are finite or infinite in any detail. However, this distinction is still an important philosophical issue, and reminds us of the importance of precisely defining our population of interest.

Descriptive Statistics

We have already described the process of *statistical inference*, in which we use data received from a sample to draw conclusions about a population. In addition to drawing such inferences, sometimes we also want to *describe* key features of our sample as well. What is the average value of our sample? How much variation do we detect in the sample's different scores or data points? *Descriptive statistics* are the statistics that can answer such questions. Descriptive statistics can give us an overall understanding of the characteristics of our sample data, and help us uncover any extreme values or atypical patterns in our data. Deriving descriptive statistics is often an important first step in the quantitative data analysis process, to gain greater insight into the features of one's sample before endeavouring to generalize from that sample to a population.

Measures of Central Tendency

One of the most common and useful types of descriptive statistics are those that measure the *central tendency* of samples. Measures of central tendency give a value for the 'centre' of a particular set of data. The three most common measures of central tendency are *mean*, *median*, and *mode*.

4.9.1 Mean

The first measure of central tendency, the **mean**, is simply the average of all the different values or observations in your sample. (In fact, when people refer to a dataset's 'average' value, they're often really referring to the mean.) The mean is calculated by adding all the different data points in the sample and dividing that total by the number of data points in the sample. The mean for a sample of data is typically represented by the symbol $\bar{x}$ (pronounced 'x-bar').

The mean for a population is typically represented by the Greek letter μ (pronounced 'mew'). The mean is the most important measure of central tendency because, as we will see throughout this book, it is employed more frequently in statistical tests than the other measures. However, one potential challenge in using the mean is that its value can be sharply affected by a few extreme data points, or cases with extremely high or extremely low values relative to the other data points. This sensitivity can make the mean less attractive to researchers.

The widespread use of the mean is thanks in part to the efforts of Adolphe Quetelet, the nineteenth-century Belgian statistician whose research on weather and crime we explored in Chapter 1. Quetelet examined numerous graphs of height and weight, finding that most of the measurements of these characteristics in populations would typically 'cluster around a central parameter' – the mean (Morabia, 2007, p. 19).

4.9.2 Median

The second measure of central tendency for us to explore is the **median**. For a sample containing an odd number of cases, the median is the value of the middle case, when the cases are arranged in numerical order. For example, let's say we have a sample that consists of seven individuals with the following ages: 24, 26, 26, 29, 33, 35, 35. The median age for this sample is 29, the middle value of this sequence. For samples that contain an even number of cases, the median is the average of the middle two values. For example, if our sample instead consisted of just six individuals with the following ages: 24, 26, 26, 29, 33, 35, the median age would be 27.5, or the average value of the two middle values (26 and 29).

The key advantage is that, relative to the mean, the median is less influenced by a small number of extreme values. On the other hand, the median lacks the special statistical properties we described in our discussion of the mean; as a result, the mean is more frequently employed in the statistical tests and formulas we will explore in this book.

stop and think

What are the key differences between the *mean* and the *median*?

4.9.3 Mode

The third measure of central tendency, the **mode**, is also used much less frequently than the mean, although it too can offer useful insight. The mode is the value that appears most often in your dataset. Sometimes a set of data has two values that appear most frequently and thus is said to be *bimodal*. This is true of the example discussed above, in which we considered a sample of seven individuals with the following ages: 24, 26, 26, 29, 33, 35, 35. This sample has two modes – 26 and 35 – and thus is bimodal.

One advantage of the mode is that, unlike the mean or the median, a score with its exact value is guaranteed to be found in the data. A second potential advantage of the mode is that it is not impacted at all by extreme values, but, unlike the mean or the median, the mode does not necessarily represent a dataset's middle or average. After all, the most frequently occurring value in a dataset could be at the edge of a dataset, rather than at its middle.

Since the mean, median, and mode are calculated in different ways, they will not necessarily be equal for a set of data. Although no single, universally accepted set of guidelines exists about when to use each measure of central tendency, in making this decision, it is important to consider what the goals of your research are, and how your goals align with the advantages of the three measures. A market researcher interested in determining which size television consumers prefer might be most interested in the mode, while a student who wants to perform certain statistical tests on her dataset might be most interested in the mean. A key consideration is whether many extreme values exist in your dataset, and how much influence you want these values to exert on the measure of central tendency. As described above, the mean can be sharply impacted by extreme values, while the median is much less impacted by extreme values. The mode is not impacted at all by extreme values.

let's try this!

Imagine that you've been given a dataset with the prices of all houses sold in England and Wales during the previous 12 months. To summarize this dataset for the general public, which measure of central tendency (*mean, median, or mode*) would you use? Why? Why wouldn't you use the other two measures?

4.10 Measures of Variability

In addition to these measures of central tendency, it is also useful to understand the *spread* or *variability* of one's data. Are all of the values highly clustered around the centre, or are the values spread out more thinly? To answer this question, we will explore three different measures of variability: *range, variance,* and *standard deviation.*

4.10.1 Range

The most straightforward method for measuring the variability of one's data is to examine its **range**. The range measures the distance between the highest value and the lowest value in a dataset. By taking into account the highest value and the lowest value, the range offers information about the full extent of variation in one's data. However, the range on its own cannot tell us much about the typical or average variation among data points.

4.10.2 Variance

Therefore, quantitative data analysts are also often interested in a dataset's **variance**, which is a more complex but often more useful method for measuring variability. The variance considers the average deviation (or difference) between each score in a dataset and the mean. However, since some scores are greater than the mean and some scores are less than the mean, we would get a value of 0 if we simply added up all the deviations and divided this total by the number of scores in the dataset. To prevent this, we need to first square each deviation before adding them up. Then we add up all the squared deviations and divide them by N, the number of cases or observations in the dataset.

We can express this process as a mathematical equation as follows:

$$\sigma^2 = \frac{\Sigma(X_i - \mu)^2}{N}. \tag{4.1}$$

In this formula, framed in terms of a population rather than a sample, σ^2 (where σ is the Greek letter sigma) is variance, while X_i is each case in the dataset, μ is the mean, N is the number of cases in the population, and Σ is the summation sign (indicating that we should add up all the squared deviations).

If we are interested in obtaining the variance for a sample from the population rather than for the population itself, the formula changes slightly:

$$s^2 = \frac{\Sigma(x_i - \bar{x})^2}{n-1}. \qquad (4.2)$$

When we move to a sample, we use Latin letters rather than Greek letters. Additionally, we now divide by $n - 1$ rather than N. (Lower-case n is the number of observations in the sample.) The '–1' needs to be included now due to the error incurred when using sample statistics to infer population parameters, as using the full value of n would underestimate the population variance. Although we can't delve into the mathematical reasons for the switch here, interested readers can explore Book (1979) for more information.

4.10.3 Standard deviation

Although the variance will be very useful to us in some of the statistical tests we will introduce later in this book, it is difficult to directly interpret. We need a more straightforward measure that can tell us about the variation in our data.

Such a measure is the **standard deviation**, denoted by σ in a population and s in a sample. The standard deviation is simply the square root of the variance measure described above. Although the standard deviation 'has no *intrinsic* meaning other than as the square root of the variance' (Mohr, 1990, p. 11), it does give us an understanding of the spread of our data that is easier to interpret than the raw measure of variance.

Given that the standard deviation is simply the square root of the variance, it is straightforward to modify formulas (4.1) and (4.2) to show how to calculate the standard deviation of a population:

$$\sigma = \sqrt{\frac{\Sigma(X_i - \mu)^2}{N}}. \qquad (4.3)$$

Similarly, if we are interested in calculating the standard deviation of a sample rather than a population, we use the following formula:

$$s = \sqrt{\frac{\Sigma(x_i - \bar{x})^2}{n-1}}. \qquad (4.4)$$

4.11 The Sampling Distribution

We've seen already that a key goal of much quantitative research is to determine whether findings or characteristics of a sample apply to the entire population from which the sample was drawn. In particular, we may have calculated a particular sample statistic for our sample, and want to know whether this sample statistic is a good approximation of the population parameter. To answer this question, we need to consider the **sampling distribution**. The sampling distribution portrays the different values of a sample statistic that you would find if you continually drew numerous random samples from the population, and calculated the sample statistic for each sample. For example, if the sample statistic we are interested in is the mean, we could draw numerous random samples (each containing the same number of observations) from the population and calculate the mean of each sample. If we graphed the distribution of all those different sample means, we would see that some values of the mean were more common than other values. The distribution of all these sample means would be the sampling distribution of the mean for our population.

There will, of course, be some variation between samples – not all samples will have the same mean – and the sampling distribution gives us an idea of *how much* variation we might expect to see, even if no mistakes in calculation have been made. Such information is fundamental to quantitative data analysis since it indicates whether the variability we see in the samples we collect is likely to be just random variation, or something more meaningful.

The standard deviation of the sampling distribution even has a special name – the **standard error**.

4.12 The Normal Distribution

Many people who are not familiar with statistics have a general idea of what the **normal distribution** is. It is a symmetrical, bell-shaped curve, as shown in Figure 4.1.

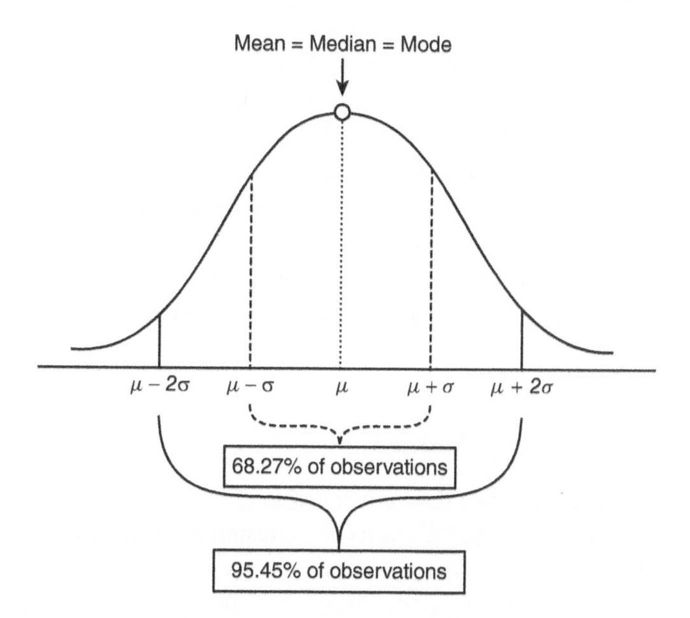

Figure 4.1 The normal distribution

Take a careful look at Figure 4.1, as you'll come across this distribution frequently. The normal distribution is so important in quantitative data analysis because it explains the distribution of many characteristics in the population, such as height, as well as many other continuous variables that social scientists want to study. Even more important, however, is the *consistency* of the normal distribution – the normal distribution *always* exhibits certain properties, and we can exploit these properties when analysing our data. Specifically, we can predict where the mean, median, and mode of our normal distribution will lie, and what percentage of observations will fall within certain distances from the mean. It sounds complicated, but will make more sense if you look at Figure 4.1. Since the distribution describes a population, and not a sample, we will use the Greek letter μ to refer to the mean and the Greek letter σ to refer to the standard deviation. In Figure 4.1, the mean, μ, is marked by the circle at the top of the dotted line in the middle of the distribution. Do you see it? Interestingly, this same point is also the median and the mode! In a normal distribution, the mean equals the median equals the mode. This characteristic makes sense if you think about the normal distribution's bell shape, since the most popular value (the mode), is also at the centre of the distribution (the median) and, given the symmetric nature of the distribution, is likely also to be the average value (the mean).

Now, let's take a look at the standard deviation (σ) of the normal distribution. The dashed lines in Figure 4.1 show the location of the point which is one standard deviation below the mean ($\mu - \sigma$) and the point which is one standard deviation above the mean ($\mu + \sigma$). As you can see, 68.27% of observations fall within 1 standard deviation from the mean, and 95.45% of observations fall within 2 standard deviations of the mean. The fact that the normal distribution consistently exhibits these characteristics – that we know exactly what percentage of observations should fall within each standard deviation of the mean – is important, and is a property we can exploit when conducting statistical tests.

The normal distribution describes the shape of many continuous numerical variables, such as the height of adults or the operational life of appliances. But of course not every variable is normally distributed. Remarkably, however, even for those variables that do not follow the normal distribution, the *sampling distribution* of the means will still follow a normal distribution if the samples are of a sufficient size – generally at least 30 cases (Norman & Streiner, 2008, p. 32). This insight has been mathematically proved via the central limit theorem (Newton & Rudestam, 2013, p. 72). Since many statistical tests depend on the normal distribution, this finding is important for quantitative data analysis, and allows us to use our data – and make use of the special properties of the normal distribution – in a wide variety of statistical tests.

Introducing *p*-Values

One of the appealing properties of the normal distribution is that it has consistent, known characteristics. In particular, due to the efforts of many previous generations of data analysts, we know what percentage of a variable's values should fall within each segment of the curve. Therefore, we can use our knowledge of the normal distribution to aid our process of hypothesis testing.

We discussed earlier how quantitative research typically involves the formation of a null hypothesis and an alternative hypothesis. (If you don't recall this discussion, take a moment to revisit Section 2.5.) Although we are usually most interested in the alternative hypothesis, research typically involves testing the null hypothesis. Hypothesis testing involves asking ourselves whether, based on the results we receive from our statistical tests, we reject the null hypothesis or we fail to reject the null hypothesis. We can make this decision by looking at the ***p*-value** we find in the results of our statistical test. The p-value tells us the likelihood that we would obtain results equivalent to, or more extreme than, the results we actually see in our data, if the null hypothesis were true. Although this definition may seem complex, the practical point to remember is that, by interpreting a p-value, we can decide whether to reject our null hypothesis. To interpret a p-value, you must consider what level of error you are willing to accept. At first glance, the answer to this question seems simple: we want our level of error to be as low as possible. However, in reality the answer is complicated by the fact that there are actually two types of error to consider: *Type I error* and *Type II error.*

Type I Error and Type II Error

The first type of error to consider, **Type I error**, occurs when we wrongly reject the null hypothesis when we should actually fail to reject it (i.e., we reject the null hypothesis when the null hypothesis is actually true). Type I error is typically denoted α, the Greek letter alpha. The second type of error, **Type II error**, occurs when we wrongly fail to reject the null hypothesis when we should in fact reject it (i.e., we fail to reject the null hypothesis when the null hypothesis is actually false). Type II error is denoted β, the Greek letter beta.

Let's consider a hypothetical example. A company decides to introduce new office chairs in an effort to reduce back pain in its employees. A company researcher is asked to evaluate the effectiveness of the new chairs. Her null hypothesis is that the new chairs *do not* have an impact on back pain. Her alternative hypothesis is that the new chairs *do* have an impact on back pain. Her evaluation would encounter Type I error if she concluded that the new chairs *did* have an impact on back pain when in fact the chairs *did not* have an impact. In other words, she *rejected* the null hypothesis when she should have *failed to reject* the null hypothesis. Her evaluation would encounter Type II error if she concluded that the new chairs *did not* have an impact, when in fact the chairs *did* have an impact. In other words, she *failed to reject* the null hypothesis when she should have *rejected* the null hypothesis.

Quantitative data analysts typically select an α-value of 5%, corresponding to $p < 0.05$, when testing hypotheses. This means they are willing to accept a 5% chance of making a Type I error. In other words, they are willing to accept that 5 times out of 100 they might wrongly reject a null hypothesis that they should in fact have failed to reject. For Type II error, on the other hand, no single β-value is typically used by most data analysts; instead, researchers typically 'aim for a Type II error between 10% and 20%' (Riegelman, 2005, p. 43; see also the discussion in Gravetter & Wallnau, 2009, pp. 243–244). This means that researchers are often willing to accept that 10 or 20 times out of 100, they will mistakenly fail to reject a null hypothesis when they should in fact have rejected it.

If a researcher wants to decrease the risk of making a Type I error, he may choose to employ a narrower boundary point, such as $p < 0.01$, but doing this would increase the chance of Type II error, or mistakenly failing to reject a null hypothesis when it should actually be rejected. Hypothesis testing therefore involves much deliberation on the part of the data analyst, and a careful weighing-up of the risks of Type I and Type II error. However, although the process of selecting an α-value involves judgement, it is important to stick with your predetermined value as you conduct your analysis. If you initially choose an α-value corresponding to $p < 0.05$, but find that $p = 0.06$ in your statistical analysis, do not suddenly change your α to 10%, or $p < 0.10$, to make your results look significant.

stop and think

Both Type I error and Type II error are concerning, but it is typically impossible to entirely eliminate both from a data analysis. Which of the two error types do you think is more serious? Why? Does your answer differ for different research questions or study designs?

4.15 One-Tailed Tests and Two-Tailed Tests

To test the null hypothesis, a researcher can choose to conduct either a *one-tailed statistical test* or a *two-tailed statistical test*. A **one-tailed test** is *directional* and requires you to propose a hypothesis specifying *in which direction* you expect the alternative hypothesis (H_1) to deviate from the null hypothesis (H_0). If your null hypothesis (H_0) is that there is no difference between the mean of sample A and the mean of sample B, then your alternative hypothesis (H_1) for a one-tailed test could be that the mean of sample A is greater than the mean of sample B. You will therefore fail to reject the null hypothesis if you discover that the mean of sample A is equal to the mean of sample B, *or* if you discover that the mean of sample B is greater than the mean of sample A.

In contrast, a **two-tailed test** does not require a researcher to specify a directional hypothesis. In this same example with an H_0 specifying no difference between the mean of sample A and the mean of sample B, an alternative hypothesis suitable for a two-tailed test would be that there is a difference between the mean of sample A and the mean of sample B (i.e., that the two means are not equal). As you can see, this alternative hypothesis does not specify a particular direction for the difference. You will therefore reject the null hypothesis if you find that the mean of sample A is greater than the mean of sample B, or if you find that the mean of sample B is greater than the mean of sample A.

Most social science research involves two-tailed tests. Why? Accurately predicting the relationship between variables can be difficult; many statistical analyses in the social sciences have uncovered unexpected findings in a different direction than was hypothesized. Therefore, even when you *do* expect an effect to fall in a particular direction, it's still prudent to perform a two-tailed test, in case your results unexpectedly fall in the other direction. Some experts feel that one-tailed tests should not be undertaken at all (see discussion in Heath, 1995, p. 128). I have only ever used two-tailed tests in my own quantitative research, which is fortunate as I have frequently uncovered effects in a different direction than I expected!

stop and think

Can you think of an example of when it would be appropriate to use a one-tailed test? What about a two-tailed test?

4.16 Beyond Significance Testing

Although the process of null hypothesis **significance testing**, as outlined here, has been a staple of social science research for more than a century, its limitations have received increasing scrutiny in more recent times (Gliner, Leech, & Morgan, 2002). Among the most important of these limitations is the inability of a significance test to offer any information about the *size* of any significant relationships or differences detected in your data, as a significance test can only reveal whether the relationships or differences you observe in your data were unlikely to be due to chance alone (Ziliak & McCloskey, 2008, pp. 4–5). Determining the magnitude of such relationships is critical since very large samples can produce 'statistically significant' results that are so small in terms of real-world magnitude that they are actually 'meaningless' (Sullivan & Feinn, 2012, pp. 279–280).

Given these limitations, more journals and professional associations in the social sciences (in particular, in psychology) have begun recommending that researchers report *effect sizes* in addition to significance tests (Vacha-Haase & Thompson, 2004; Fritz, Morris, & Richler, 2012). An **effect size** is exactly what it sounds like – the size of the effect that you uncover in your study. Effect size measures can be particularly useful in evaluation research, or research that assesses the effectiveness of programmes or treatments. By presenting effect size measures and clearly explaining the meaning of these measures, researchers can 'communicate evaluation findings in ways that might better assist stakeholders make more thoughtful judgments about the implications of evaluation findings for action' (Mark & Henry, 2006, p. 329). Although simply including a measure of effect size cannot overcome all of the limitations of significance testing, effect sizes can offer further context for interpreting one's findings. Their use will likely continue to grow across social science disciplines in years to come.

stop and think

What is an *effect size*? What new information does an *effect size* offer that cannot be gained from significance testing alone?

Concluding Thoughts

Clearly, quantitative data analysis is a diverse field, but many of the analysis techniques you'll encounter focus on *significance testing*. Researchers want to know whether their findings are *statistically significant*, or whether some pattern or relationship apparent in the data is unlikely to be due to chance. In Chapter 5 we will see how this process of significance testing undergirds many popular quantitative analysis procedures. Since you're now familiar with significance testing, you're already well on your way to becoming a fully fledged quantitative data analyst. We'll build on this knowledge in the next chapter and investigate concrete examples of how significance testing can work in practice.

Summary

- Quantitative data is *numerical*, or represented by numbers. Much, but not all, quantitative data analysis is rooted in the *positivist* tradition.
- Numerous specific approaches exist for collecting quantitative data, including: *experiments*, *quasi-experiments*, *evaluations*, and *surveys*. *Secondary data analysis*, which is the analysis of data that has been collected by previous researchers, has become increasingly popular in recent years thanks to the proliferation of large-scale surveys and publicly accessible data repositories.
- Variables can be either *discrete* or *continuous*. Additionally, Stevens (1951) developed a four-part scheme for classifying data as *nominal*, *ordinal*, *interval*, or *ratio*. Your choice of statistical test can depend on which of these categories your data belongs to.
- Quantitative data analysts are often interested in an entire *population*, but can often only obtain data about a *sample*. The process of using information about the characteristics of a sample to make inferences about the characteristics of the population as a whole is known as *statistical inference*, and is a key element of quantitative data analysis.
- Researchers often use different terminology when describing characteristics of populations and characteristics of samples. *Population parameters* are typically denoted by Greek letters, while *sample statistics* are usually represented by Latin letters.
- *Descriptive statistics* are an important part of quantitative data analysis, as they can give us an overall understanding of the characteristics of our sample data, and help us uncover any extreme values or atypical patterns in our data.
- Measures of central tendency give a value for the 'centre' of a particular set of data. Each of the three most common measures of central tendency – the *mean*, *median*, and *mode* – has its own particular advantages and limitations.
- In addition to central tendency, it is also useful to understand the *spread* or *variability* of one's data. Three key measures of variability are *range*, *variance*, and *standard deviation*. The standard deviation is simply the square root of the variance.
- When testing whether findings or characteristics of a sample apply to the entire population, it is important to consider the *sampling distribution*, a representation of the values of a given sample statistic that are obtained after repeatedly drawing numerous different samples at random from the population.

- *Type I error*, denoted α, occurs when we mistakenly reject the null hypothesis when the null hypothesis is actually true. *Type II error*, denoted β, occurs when we mistakenly fail to reject the null hypothesis when the null hypothesis is actually false.
- Quantitative data analysts typically select an α-value of 5%, corresponding to $p < 0.05$, when testing hypotheses. This means they are willing to accept a 5% chance of making a Type I error.
- To test the null hypothesis, a researcher can choose to conduct either a *one-tailed statistical test* or a *two-tailed statistical test*. One-tailed tests are directional, while two-tailed tests are non-directional. The vast majority of social science research studies use two-tailed tests.

Further Reading

In this chapter we briefly examined several key approaches for quantitative data, including experiments, quasi-experiments, evaluations, surveys and secondary data analysis. Each of these approaches is complex and deserves a textbook of its own; many other quantitative methods also exist which were not covered in this chapter. For more information about the methods discussed here – and additional methods that were not discussed – you can take a look at:

Crano, W. D., Brewer, M. B., & Lac, A. (2015). *Principles and methods of social research* (3rd ed.). New York: Routledge.

The distinction between nominal, ordinal, interval, and ratio data can be very important in helping you decide which statistical test to use with your data. Interested in learning more? Why not take a look at Stevens's (1951) original article, which pioneered this four-part distinction:

Stevens, S. S. (1951). Mathematics, measurement and psychophysics. In S. S. Stevens (Ed.), *Handbook of experimental psychology* (pp. 1–49). New York: Wiley.

Understanding the process of hypothesis testing and the need to balance concerns about Type I error and Type II error is one of the most fundamental issues in quantitative data analysis. For a comprehensive but engaging overview of this concept, refer to:

Mohr, L. B. (1990). *Understanding significance testing*. Thousand Oaks, CA: SAGE Publications.

Finally, in this chapter we reviewed numerous potentially useful sources of secondary data. Take a look back at the discussion of secondary data analysis in Section 4.3, as it contains descriptions of various websites and data repositories that might be useful for you.

Discussion Questions

1. What particular concerns might a researcher have when working with *secondary data* for quantitative data analysis rather than data she has collected herself?
2. What are descriptive statistics? Why are they so important in quantitative data analysis?
3. What are the advantages and disadvantages of each of the three measures of central tendency: *mean*, *median*, and *mode*? Which of these measures of central tendency would you use to study average family income in your country? Which measure would you use to study average reaction time among participants in a psychological test?

4 What are the advantages and disadvantages of selecting an α-value of 5%, corresponding to $p < 0.05$, rather than an α-value of 1% ($p < 0.01$) to test a hypothesis?
5 Some experts have argued that one-tailed tests should not be undertaken at all. Do you agree? Why or why not?

Applying Quantitative Data Analysis: Correlations, *t*-Tests, and Chi-Square Tests

contents

Chapter Overview

In the previous chapter, we explored how to analyse quantitative data – or data that consists of numbers – through basic methods such as finding measures of central tendency and conducting significance tests. In this chapter, we'll build upon that knowledge and explore three popular, more advanced statistical tests: *Pearson's correlation coefficient*; the *t-Test*; and the *chi-square test of association*. By the end of this chapter, for each of these three tests, you'll be able to answer the following questions:

- Will this statistical test allow me to address my research question?
- Does my data satisfy the assumptions of this statistical test?
- How can I actually conduct this statistical test on my data?
- How do I interpret my results?
- What are common problems I might encounter, and how might I overcome these problems?
- Do any alternative tests address similar research questions, and how can I learn more about such tests?

Introduction: Associations and Differences

If you've read Chapters 2 and 4 (and hopefully you have, as they contain information that we'll build on here!) then you've already completed some quantitative data analysis. In those chapters we explored how to use *measures of central tendency*, such as the *mean*, *median*, and *mode*, to uncover the average value of a sample of data. We also introduced the process of *significance testing*, in which *p-values* can determine whether the results obtained from a statistical test were unlikely to be due to chance. Significance testing is an integral component of many statistical techniques, including the three techniques we'll examine in detail in this chapter.

The three techniques can offer insight into two broad research questions: *Are two variables related in some way?* And *are groups in your dataset different from each other in some meaningful way?* These two questions have numerous applications in the social sciences. Let's look at some of these potential applications now.

1. *Are two variables related in some way?* This first question is one of the most basic – but also most important – questions we might want to ask about the social world. It's fundamental in many disciplines. An education researcher, for instance, might be interested in whether there is an *association* between class size and student achievement, or a psychologist might be interested in whether there is an *association* between time spent in front of computer or television screens and children's attention spans. Similarly, a criminologist might want to know whether there is an *association* between the unemployment rate and the crime rate. As the unemployment rate increases, does crime also increase? Or does crime stay the same – or even decline? Answering this question could have important policy implications.
2. *Are groups in your dataset different from each other in some meaningful way?* Numerous examples of this type of research question can also be found in the social sciences.

A public health researcher, for example, who is interested in the effects of a nutrition education initiative, might want to explore whether the initiative has different effects on men as opposed to women. A sociologist might want to examine whether individuals with a university degree are more likely to be employed than individuals without a university degree. An international development scholar might want to determine whether the introduction of a free school breakfast increases educational achievement among a group of children (in this example, the groups being compared are [1] the group of children before the introduction of the free breakfasts, and [2] the same group of children after the introduction of free breakfasts).

These examples illustrate the range of research questions that can be explored using the statistical tests described in this chapter. Although it won't be possible to investigate every potentially useful statistical test, by examining *correlations*, *t-tests*, and *chi-square tests*, we will develop a useful toolkit for investigating ***associations*** and ***differences*** within quantitative data. Suggestions for further reading will also be provided if you're interested in exploring alternative tests or more advanced issues. As we investigate each test, we'll examine the kinds of research questions it can answer, and the types of data with which it can be used.

5.3 Introducing Correlation

The first type of statistical test we will explore is **correlation**, which detects *associations* between different variables. Correlation is often represented by the Greek letter rho (ρ). (A Greek letter is used to describe the concept of correlation because, theoretically, we are interested in correlation in the entire population.) Correlation allows us to answer the research question: *Are two variables in my dataset related in some way?* In other words, as one variable increases in value, does the other variable also increase in value? Or, as one variable increases in value, does the other variable decrease in value? Or is there no consistent pattern?

let's try this!

In the previous section, we outlined several hypothetical examples of research questions that could be explored through correlation. For instance, we discussed how a criminologist might investigate whether there is a relationship between the unemployment rate and the crime rate. Now it's your turn. Think about an area of research that you're interested in. Are there two variables that you think might be related? Why do you think those variables might be related?

The type of correlation we'll investigate first, and in most detail, is **Pearson's correlation coefficient**, which is named after the mathematician Karl Pearson and is represented by an italicized lower-case r. (We use r rather than a Greek letter because our calculation is typically based on a sample, rather than the entire population.) This type of correlation is only appropriate if both of your variables are measured at the interval or ratio level of measurement (in other words, both variables are *continuous*, or exhibit a wide variety of values and are not limited to just a few distinct categories. Examples of continuous variables include height, income, and temperature.) If at least one of your variables is not continuous – if it is *ordinal* or *nominal* – then you will have to use an alternative statistical test to assess correlation. We'll discuss these alternative tests later in this chapter.

In addition to determining which type of correlation to use, we also need to specify our hypotheses. Think back to the example of the criminologist who is interested in whether the unemployment rate is related to the crime rate. As unemployment increases, does crime also increase? Or does crime stay the same, or even decrease? The criminologist's null hypothesis is that there is no relationship (or no correlation) between the unemployment rate and the crime rate, and the alternative hypothesis is that there is a relationship (or correlation). We can formally denote these hypotheses in the following manner:

H_0: There is no association between the unemployment rate and the crime rate ($\rho = 0$).

H_1: There is an association between the unemployment rate and the crime rate ($\rho \neq 0$).

As you can see, the criminologist has decided to use a *non-directional* alternative hypothesis (e.g., 'There is an association...') rather than a *directional* alternative hypothesis (e.g., 'There is a negative association...' or 'There is a positive association...'). Recall from Chapter 4 that social science researchers tend to use non-directional hypotheses, since research often uncovers unexpected findings in a different direction than was hypothesized. However, if you have a strong reason for adopting a directional hypothesis – perhaps previous research has indicated that unemployment is associated with higher crime rates only – then you could adopt a directional alternative hypothesis for your correlation. In practice, however, it's rare to see a directional hypothesis in an academic study.

In our hypotheses, we use the term 'associated'. On a general level, we know what this term means – that the two variables are related to each other in some way. But to conduct a statistical test, we need to be a bit more precise in our definition. How exactly are the variables meant to be related? In the context of correlation, what we're really testing is whether, when one variable moves away from its mean, the other variable also moves away from its mean. In this example, therefore, we're asking: *When the unemployment rate is particularly low, is the crime rate particularly low?* And the movement does not need to be in the same direction; we could just as readily ask: *When the unemployment rate is particularly low, is the crime rate particularly high?*

5.4 Understanding Covariance and Correlation

To understand how this line of thinking translates into a statistical equation, it's helpful to step back and recall our discussion of *variance* in Chapter 4. We saw then that variance captures the average deviation – or difference – between each value of a variable and that variable's mean. If all the values for a given variable are tightly clustered around the mean, then the variance is low; if all the values for a given variable are spread out quite far from the mean, then the variance is high. You'll recall that the formula for variance in a sample is:

$$s^2 = \frac{\Sigma(x_i - \bar{x})^2}{n-1}. \tag{4.2}$$

In this equation, s^2 is the variance of a sample of data, x_i represents each observation in the sample, $\bar{x}$ denotes the mean of the sample, and n denotes sample size. We can build on this equation to examine **covariance**, or the extent to which two variables deviate from their respective means in corresponding ways. Covariance is calculated using the following, similar formula:

$$\text{cov}(x,y) = \frac{\Sigma(x_i - \bar{x})(y_i - \bar{y})}{n-1}. \tag{5.1}$$

All we're doing is introducing a second variable, y, into the equation and exploring how it also deviates from its mean. To calculate Pearson's correlation coefficient, we simply insert the standard deviations of both variables (denoted by s_x and s_y) into the denominator (or the bottom half of the fraction), resulting in the following equation:

$$r = \frac{\text{cov}(x,y)}{s_x s_y} = \frac{\Sigma(x_i - \bar{x})(y_i - \bar{y})}{(n-1)s_x s_y}. \tag{5.2}$$

The reason for inserting the variables' standard deviations into the denominator is to *standardize* the measure of covariance, ensuring that its value is not impacted by the variables' different units of measurement. Variables may be measured in pounds, kilograms, miles, metres, inches, or numerous other units. Standardizing the measure of covariance allows us to make comparisons between different correlations, without worrying that the original variables may have been measured in very different units.

When studying statistical tests, it's often best to learn by doing! So let's use some fictional data to explore how to calculate and interpret Pearson's r. A university maintains a campus-wide bus service, but the number of passengers who use the service seems to fluctuate dramatically from day to day, particularly during the winter. The university wants to improve its estimates of passenger numbers, so that it can better predict how many buses to send out on a given day. A data analysis student who happens to work for the campus bus service thinks there might be a relationship between temperature and demand for buses during the winter. Perhaps this relationship is an *inverse* relationship; as the daily high temperature *decreases*, the number of students choosing to ride the bus *increases* as fewer students want to walk or cycle to class. Or perhaps this relationship is more straightforward; as the daily high temperature *decreases*, the number of students choosing to ride the bus *decreases* as fewer students want to get out of bed and go to class at all.

stop and think

What is the student's null hypothesis? What is the student's alternative hypothesis? See if you can write down H_0 and H_1 for the student's project before moving on to the next section.

To test the hypotheses you've just specified, the campus bus service collects data on the daily high temperature and the number of passengers who use the campus bus over a three-week period during the winter. The temperature readings are collected in degrees Fahrenheit, as the university is located in the USA. (Recall that 32 degrees Fahrenheit is equivalent to 0 degrees Celsius, the temperature at which water freezes.) Since the bus only runs on weekdays, weekends were excluded, resulting in 15 daily observations, as shown in Table 5.1.

Table 5.1 Temperature in Fahrenheit and campus bus passenger numbers over a 15-day period in winter

Day	Temperature (°F)	Campus bus passengers
1	43	498
2	41	528
3	28	533
4	32	528
5	27	601
6	33	578
7	33	569
8	29	612
9	32	596
10	26	603
11	29	591
12	29	583
13	32	584
14	34	570
15	45	534

The data analysis student wants to run a correlation to determine whether there is a significant association between temperature and passenger numbers. Since both variables appear to be continuous, we can use this data to calculate Pearson's r with formula (5.2). In this example, let's assume that temperature in Fahrenheit is our x variable and bus passenger numbers are our y variable. We can start by calculating the mean of both x and y. Can you remember how to calculate the mean? (If not, take a look back at Section 4.9.)

Given that we have 15 observations (so our $n = 15$), the mean temperature in Fahrenheit, $\bar{x}$, of our data is:

$$\bar{x} = \frac{43+41+28+32+27+33+33+29+32+26+29+29+32+34+45}{15}$$
$$= 32.87.$$

Similarly, the mean number of bus passengers, $\bar{y}$, of our data is:

$$\bar{y} = \frac{498+528+533+528+601+578+569+612+596+603+591+583+584+570+534}{15}$$
$$= 567.2.$$

In addition to the two means, we'll need the standard deviation of x (s_x) and y (s_y) to complete formula (5.2). Since we only have data from a sample of days rather than the entire population of days, we'll use the formula for standard deviations of samples, which we originally explored in Chapter 4 as formula (4.4). To refresh your memory, the formula looks like this:

$$s = \sqrt{\frac{\Sigma(x_i - \bar{x})^2}{n-1}}. \tag{4.4}$$

To calculate the standard deviation for temperature in Fahrenheit, s_x, we start by subtracting the mean temperature ($\bar{x}$ = 32.87) from each observed temperature reading (x_i). In Table 5.2, you can see this calculation in the column labelled 'Temperature – Mean'. We then square each of the resulting numbers. The results of this calculation are also visible in Table 5.2 in the column labelled '(Temperature – Mean)^2'.

Table 5.2 Calculating the standard deviation for the temperature in Fahrenheit variable (s_x)

Day	Temperature, x_i (°F)	Temperature – Mean $= x_i - \bar{x}$	(Temperature – Mean)^2 $= (x_i - \bar{x})^2$
1	43	43 – 32.87 = 10.13	10.13^2 = 102.68
2	41	41 – 32.87 = 8.13	8.13^2 = 66.15
3	28	28 – 32.87 = –4.87	$(-4.87)^2$ = 23.68
4	32	32 – 32.87 = –0.87	$(-0.87)^2$ = 0.75
5	27	27 – 32.87 = –5.87	$(-5.87)^2$ = 34.42
6	33	33 – 32.87 = 0.13	0.13^2 = 0.02
7	33	33 – 32.87 = 0.13	0.13^2 = 0.02
8	29	29 – 32.87 = –3.87	$(-3.87)^2$ = 14.95
9	32	32 – 32.87 = –0.87	$(-0.87)^2$ = 0.75
10	26	26 – 32.87 = –6.87	$(-6.87)^2$ = 47.15
11	29	29 – 32.87 = –3.87	$(-3.87)^2$ = 14.95
12	29	29 – 32.87 = –3.87	$(-3.87)^2$ = 14.95
13	32	32 – 32.87 = –0.87	$(-0.87)^2$ = 0.75
14	34	34 – 32.87 = 1.13	1.13^2 = 1.28
15	45	45 – 32.87 = 12.13	12.13^2 = 147.22

Finally, we need to sum all of the results from the '(Temperature – Mean)^2' column in Table 5.2. In other words, we must add up all the final numbers in this column. When we do this, the resulting sum is 469.73. According to formula (4.4), we must then divide this number by $n - 1$, where n is the number of observations in our sample. In this example $n = 15$, since we have temperature readings from 15 days, so $n - 1 = 14$. Therefore, 469.73/14 = 33.55.

Following formula (4.4), the final step is to calculate the square root of this result. Therefore,

$$s_x = \sqrt{33.55} = 5.79.$$

To find s_y, the standard deviation for bus passengers, we can repeat exactly the same process, as shown in Table 5.3.

Table 5.3 Calculating the standard deviation for the bus passengers variable (s_y)

Day	Campus bus passengers, y_i	Passengers – Mean number of passengers = $y_i - \bar{y}$	(Passengers – Mean number of passengers)^2 = $(y_i - \bar{y})^2$
1	498	498 – 567.2 = –69.2	$(-69.2)^2 = 4788.64$
2	528	528 – 567.2 = –39.2	$(-39.2)^2 = 1536.64$
3	533	533 – 567.2 = –34.2	$(-34.2)^2 = 1169.64$
4	528	528 – 567.2 = –39.2	$(-39.2)^2 = 1536.64$
5	601	601 – 567.2 = 33.8	$33.8^2 = 1142.44$
6	578	578 – 567.2 = 10.8	$10.8^2 = 116.64$
7	569	569 – 567.2 = 1.8	$1.8^2 = 3.24$
8	612	612 – 567.2 = 44.8	$44.8^2 = 2007.04$
9	596	596 – 567.2 = 28.8	$28.8^2 = 829.44$
10	603	603 – 567.2 = 35.8	$35.8^2 = 1281.64$
11	591	591 – 567.2 = 23.8	$23.8^2 = 566.44$
12	583	583 – 567.2 = 15.8	$15.8^2 = 249.64$
13	584	584 – 567.2 = 16.8	$16.8^2 = 282.24$
14	570	570 – 567.2 = 2.8	$2.8^2 = 7.84$
15	534	534 – 567.2 = –33.2	$(-33.2)^2 = 1102.24$

In this case, the sum of the '(Passengers – Mean number of passengers)^2' column in Table 5.3 is 16,620.4. Once again we divide this number by $n - 1 = 14$, which gives 16,620.4/14 = 1187.17.

Following formula (4.4), the final step is to calculate the square root of this result. Therefore,

$$s_y = \sqrt{1187.17} = 34.46.$$

Now that we have both standard deviations, and know that $n - 1 = 14$, the only missing component necessary to complete formula (5.2) is the numerator. So let's calculate $(x_i - \bar{x})(y_i - \bar{y})$. This task is much easier than it sounds, as all the values of $(x_i - \bar{x})$ are already listed in the third column of Table 5.2, and all the values of $(y_i - \bar{y})$ are already listed in the third column of Table 5.3.

So let's reprint those columns in a new table (Table 5.4). Then, for each row of the table (which represents a given day), we can calculate $(x_i - \bar{x})(y_i - \bar{y})$. This calculation is shown in the fourth column of Table 5.4. Make sure you understand how we obtained each of the numbers in Table 5.4 before moving on. (Depending on how you round your answers, be aware that the exact figures in your table might differ slightly.)

Table 5.4 Calculating Pearson's *r* for temperature in Fahrenheit and bus passengers

Day	Temperature – Mean = $x_i - \bar{x}$	Passengers – Mean number of passengers = $y_i - \bar{y}$	$(x_i - \bar{x})(y_i - \bar{y})$
1	43 – 32.87 = 10.13	498 – 567.2 =–69.2	10.13 × (–69.2) =–701.23
2	41 – 32.87 = 8.13	528 – 567.2 =–39.2	8.13 × (–39.2) =–318.83
3	28 – 32.87 =–4.87	533 – 567.2 =–34.2	–4.87 × (–34.2) = 166.44
4	32 – 32.87 =–0.87	528 – 567.2 =–39.2	–0.87 × (–39.2) = 33.97
5	27 – 32.87 =–5.87	601 – 567.2 = 33.8	–5.87 × 33.8 =–198.29
6	33 – 32.87 = 0.13	578 – 567.2 = 10.8	0.13 × 10.8 = 1.44
7	33 – 32.87 = 0.13	569 – 567.2 = 1.8	0.13 × 1.8 = 0.24
8	29 – 32.87 =–3.87	612 – 567.2 = 44.8	–3.87 × 44.8 =–173.23
9	32 – 32.87 =–0.87	596 – 567.2 = 28.8	–0.87 × 28.8 =–24.96
10	26 – 32.87 =–6.87	603 – 567.2 = 35.8	–6.87 × 35.8 =–245.83
11	29 – 32.87 =–3.87	591 – 567.2 = 23.8	–3.87 × 23.8 =–92.03
12	29 – 32.87 =–3.87	583 – 567.2 = 15.8	–3.87 × 15.8 =–61.09
13	32 – 32.87 =–0.87	584 – 567.2 = 16.8	–0.87 × 16.8 =–14.56
14	34 – 32.87 = 1.13	570 – 567.2 = 2.8	1.13 × 2.8 = 3.17
15	45 – 32.87 = 12.13	534 – 567.2 =–33.2	12.13 × (–33.2) =–402.83

The final step necessary to complete formula (5.2) is to calculate $\Sigma(x_i - \bar{x})(y_i - \bar{y})$ by summing up all the numbers in the fourth column of Table 5.4 above. So let's do this!

$$\begin{aligned}\Sigma(x_i-\bar{x})(y_i-\bar{y}) &= (-701.23)+(-318.83)+(166.44)+(33.97)+(-198.29)+(1.44)\\ &\quad+(0.24)+(-173.23)+(-24.96)+(-245.83)+(-92.03)+(-61.09)\\ &\quad+(-14.56)+(3.17)+(-402.83)\\ &= 2027.6.\end{aligned}$$

Now we've got all the numbers we need for formula (5.2). To confirm this, let's take another look at formula (5.2), so we can calculate Pearson's r for our own sample of data:

$$r=\frac{\text{cov}(x,y)}{s_x s_y}=\frac{\Sigma(x_i-\bar{x})(y_i-\bar{y})}{(n-1)s_x s_y}. \tag{5.2}$$

If we plug in all the numbers we just calculated into this formula, we obtain the following result:

$$\begin{aligned}r &= \frac{-2027.6}{14\times 5.79\times 34.46}\\ &= \frac{-2027.6}{2793.33}\\ &= -0.73.\end{aligned}$$

Great! So we've discovered that the correlation coefficient between temperature and bus passengers is –.73. But what does this mean? To answer this question, we'll first need to conduct a significance test.

5.5 Conducting a Significance Test

Before we can draw any firm conclusions about our results, we must first determine whether our results are significant. By conducting a *significance test*, we explore whether our value of r is statistically significant, or unlikely to be due to chance. Regardless of how interesting or persuasive our findings are, if they are just due to chance, then there's no point in using them to draw firm conclusions about our data. Significance testing is a central component of many statistical tests, and correlational tests are no exception. (For an overview of significance tests, take a look back at Chapter 4 now.) To conduct a significance test for our correlation coefficient, we need to start by selecting an α-value – a level of significance against which we will compare our results. In Chapter 4 we learned that quantitative data analysts typically select an α-value of 5%, or $p < 0.05$, when testing hypotheses. This α-value indicates we are willing to accept that 5 times out of 100 (i.e., up to 5% of the time) we will mistakenly reject a null hypothesis that is in fact true. (Another way of stating this fact is that we are willing to accept a 5% chance of making a Type I error. If you don't recall what a Type I error is, take a look back at Chapter 4 now.) In the context of correlation, our null hypothesis, H_0, is that $\rho = 0$. For example, the null hypothesis you might have developed earlier for our bus data could be:

H_0: There is no association between temperature and bus passenger numbers ($\rho = 0$).

So an α-value of 5%, or $p < 0.05$, indicates we are willing to accept a 5% chance of mistakenly concluding there *is* a significant association between the variables, when in fact there is *no* association. If you want to decrease the risk of mistakenly rejecting the null hypothesis, you could select a lower α-value, such as 1% ($p < 0.01$). However, as we discussed in Chapter 4, such a choice would increase the chance that you might mistakenly fail to reject a null hypothesis when it is in fact untrue.

In addition to our value of α, we need a second important piece of information to conduct a significance test: the *degrees of freedom*. Formally speaking, the **degrees of freedom** are the number of data points that can vary, or take on any value, in a statistical computation. Not all data points are free to vary in a statistical computation because a data analyst 'needs some solid (nonvarying) place to begin' (Jekel, Katz, Elmore, & Wild, 2007, p. 183). Informally, degrees of freedom play an important role in many statistical tests, including correlations, *t*-tests, and chi-square tests. Indeed, we will encounter degrees of freedom in all of the statistical tests we will explore in this chapter. Unfortunately, the formula used to calculate the degrees of freedom differs for each statistical test. For Pearson's *r*, the formula for calculating the degrees of freedom is $n - 2$, or the number of observations or cases you have minus 2. (In our bus example, we had 15 observations, so our degrees of freedom would be 13.) As we'll see later in this chapter, different formulas are used to calculate degrees of freedom for the *t*-test and the chi-square test. However, the degrees of freedom are an essential component of determining statistical significance in all these different tests.

Now that we know our values of α and the degrees of freedom, testing for significance is surprisingly simple! All we need to do is compare the value of Pearson's *r* that we obtained from our data to the critical values of Pearson's *r* given in Table 5.5. These critical values are the values that *r* must be higher than in order to reject the null hypothesis. Table 5.5 presents critical values for up to 100 *df* and for two common significance levels (0.05 and 0.01) using a two-tailed test. As we saw in Chapter 4, two-tailed tests are more commonly used and the significance level or α-level that researchers most commonly select is 0.05. However, if you want critical values for other significance levels or for one-tailed tests, or if you need critical values for more *df*, you can easily find tables that include these by searching the internet.

Table 5.5 Critical values of Pearson's *r*

Degrees of freedom (*df*)	α = 5% (0.05)	α = 1% (0.01)
1	0.997	0.9999
2	0.95	0.99
3	0.878	0.959
4	0.811	0.917
5	0.754	0.875
6	0.707	0.834

(Continued)

Table 5.5 (Continued)

Degrees of freedom (*df*)	**α = 5% (0.05)**	**α = 1% (0.01)**
7	0.666	0.798
8	0.632	0.765
9	0.602	0.735
10	0.576	0.708
11	0.553	0.684
12	0.532	0.661
13	0.514	0.641
14	0.497	0.623
15	0.482	0.606
20	0.423	0.537
25	0.381	0.487
30	0.349	0.449
35	0.325	0.418
40	0.304	0.393
45	0.288	0.372
50	0.273	0.354
60	0.250	0.325
70	0.232	0.302
80	0.217	0.283
90	0.205	0.267
100	0.195	0.254

In our example, our α is 5% or 0.05 and our *df* is 13. Therefore, we look at the cell in Table 5.5 that corresponds to these values. Check to see that you can find that cell. In that cell, the critical value of Pearson's *r* is 0.514. The value of *r* that we obtained from our statistical test was –0.73. It's important to note that, when comparing your *r* to the table, you can ignore the minus sign and instead consider the absolute value of *r*. Therefore, we can conclude that our *r* of 0.73 is higher than 0.514. This means that the Pearson's *r* obtained from our data is statistically significant at the 0.05 level, and we can state that the null hypothesis – that there is no association between our two variables – is unlikely to be true. More generally, if the value of Pearson's *r* obtained from the calculations is greater than the critical value found in the table, you can conclude that your value of *r* is statistically significant at the α-level you specified.

5.6 Interpreting Pearson's Correlation Coefficient

Now that we have our value of Pearson's *r* and know that our results are significant, there's just one final task to complete: we need to *interpret* our results. To interpret our value of *r*, we should first note that the value of Pearson's *r* varies from –1 to +1 (meaning it cannot be lower than −1 and cannot be higher than +1). Within this narrow range, the specific value of r offers information about both the *magnitude* of the relationship between the two variables of interest and the *direction* of the relationship.

Let's start with *magnitude*. If r is 0, then no association exists between the variables; values of r that are very close to 0 indicate a weak association. On the other hand, values of r that are close to either −1 or +1 indicate stronger correlations.

Now let's look at *direction*. Positive values of r indicate a positive association between the variables; this means that, as one variable increases in value, the other variable also *increases* in value. Correspondingly, as one variable declines in value, the other variable also declines in value. Negative values of r indicate a negative association between the variables; this means that, as one variable increases, the other variable *decreases*; and, as the first variable decreases, the other variable increases.

Since our r has a minus sign in front of it, the correlation is *negative*. This means that, as temperature decreases, the number of bus passengers increases. Additionally, as we saw in the previous section, the fact that our p-value is less than 0.05 means that our results are statistically significant. So we can report that a *significant* correlation exists between temperature and number of bus passengers. Therefore, bringing it all together, we can conclude that temperature is negatively correlated with the number of bus passengers ($r = -0.73$), and that this association is statistically significant ($p < 0.05$).

Before moving on, it's important to note one important conclusion that *can't* be drawn from our results. On the basis of a correlational test alone we can't conclude that one variable *caused* the other. The data analyst, for example, cannot claim with certainty that lower temperatures *caused* bus passengers to increase. Perhaps lower temperatures were more likely to occur on rainy or snowy days, and it was the precipitation rather than the temperature that *caused* passenger numbers to increase. This limitation reflects the key insight that *correlation does not necessarily mean causation*. All we can conclude is that the two variables are associated, and tend to move in concert with each other – which is a pretty interesting finding on its own! (If you're interested in learning more about causality and how we determine causation in social science research, take a look at the relevant sources listed in the 'Further Reading' section of this chapter.)

Checking Assumptions

Before concluding our discussion of Pearson's r, there is one final step we must undertake: checking assumptions. Does your data meet the assumptions of Pearson's r? If not, then this test is not an appropriate choice for your data.

In reality, checking assumptions is often the *first* step researchers complete, to know whether they should use Pearson's r or another alternative statistical test (and we'll explore some alternatives below). Pearson's r has five assumptions, and they're listed in Figure 5.1 below. As you can see, we've already discussed the first assumption: that both variables are continuous (or are measured at the interval or ratio level of measurement).

Assumption 1: The two variables are continuous. This means that both variables are measured at the interval or ratio levels of measurement (and are not nominal or ordinal). *Check this assumption by examining your data, and confirming how both variables were operationalized. If a variable can take on a wide range of values, then it's continuous. If, instead, it's limited to just a few distinct categories, then it's not continuous and your data does not meet this assumption.*

Assumption 2: Pearson's *r* is intended to be used with normally distributed variables only. Therefore, the distributions of both your variables should approximate the normal distribution. (This is one reason why the discussion of the normal distribution in Chapter 4 is so important!) If either of your variables deviates dramatically from the normal distribution, then Pearson's *r* is not an appropriate correlational measure for your data. *Check this assumption by inspecting the distributions of your variables. To inspect the distribution of a variable, construct a histogram. (Don't worry – we will investigate how to construct a histogram in Chapter 9. Feel free to skip ahead now if you want!)*

Assumption 3: The association between the variables is linear, or could be illustrated with a straight line. (Pearson's *r* is not designed to capture more complex relationships between variables, including associations that could be represented by curves or wavy lines.) *Check this assumption by constructing a scatterplot, with one variable featured on the x-axis of the scatterplot and the other variable featured on the y-axis. We will explore how to construct scatterplots in Chapter 9. If you see a clear nonlinear pattern in the* ***scatterplot****, your data may not meet this assumption.*

Assumption 4: Each observation in your dataset has values for both of the variables you are interested in. (Another way of stating this assumption is that both variables have exactly the same number of observations.) *Check this assumption by investigating whether there is any missing data in your dataset. If you are missing data for one variable for some observations in your dataset, then your data violates this assumption. For example, if there are a few days in your dataset where you recorded the temperature, but you did not record the number of bus passengers, then your data violates this assumption.*

Assumption 5: Each observation is independent. (Your data violates this assumption if some units are represented three or four times in the dataset and other units are represented only once.) *Check this assumption by looking at the observations in your dataset, and confirming the data collection procedures. In our campus bus example, if we found that multiple temperature readings from one day were included in our dataset but only one temperature reading from the other days was included, our data could violate this assumption, since the multiple temperature readings from one day would not be independent of each other.*

Figure 5.1 Assumptions of Pearson's *r*

If Your Data Does Not Meet the Assumptions of Pearson's *r*

What do we do if our data fails to meet one or more of the assumptions for Pearson's *r*? The answer to this question depends in part on *which* assumption your data fails to meet.

If your data violates Assumption 1, meaning that one or both of your variables is not continuous, then you need to consider alternative correlational tests. If both of your variables are nominal or ordinal, it may be appropriate to use a *chi-square test* instead. We'll explore the chi-square test in detail later in this chapter, so you can determine whether that alternative test is appropriate for your data. Alternatively, if one of your variables is a nominal variable with only two categories then you should consider either *biserial correlation* or *point-biserial* correlation (for information on the differences between these two tests, see Kline, 2005, p. 101).

If your data violates Assumption 2, as one or both of your variables are not normally distributed, then you should consider different, alternative correlational tests. The most popular alternative for non-normal data is *Spearman's rho*, which works by ranking the observations for each variable rather than using their true, non-normal values (Rees, 2001, p. 219).

If your data violates Assumption 3, as a scatterplot reveals a potentially nonlinear relationship, you should start by considering whether **outliers** are present and affecting the relationship between the variables. Outliers are data points that are far away from most data points in a dataset. You should scrutinize outliers in case they indicate mistakes during the data collection process. Of course, if the outliers are not due to errors in data collection, you can't simply delete them, as doing so would compromise the integrity of your analysis (Rees, 2001, pp. 217–218). In such cases, Pearson's r is not an appropriate test, and you need to consider more specialized alternatives. (Take a look at some of the more advanced resources listed in the 'Further Reading' section of this chapter for information about more specialized statistical tests.)

If your data violates Assumption 4, meaning that each observation does not have values for both variables, investigate the reasons for this missing data. Substantial amounts of missing data can indicate a more serious problem with your data collection procedures that would negatively impact any statistical tests, not just Pearson's r. Revisit our discussion in Chapter 3 about the different types of missing data and assess which type is present in your dataset. Consult the resources described in the previous chapter's discussion for more information about how to deal with the different types of missing data.

If your data violates Assumption 5, meaning that each observation is not independent, you should scrutinize the original data collection procedures. Why were some units or individuals represented several times in the dataset and other units or individuals represented only once? Since most alternatives to Pearson's r also specify that observations be independent, you may need to rethink the goals of your research project, and whether correlation is really the best type of statistical test to use.

The t-Test: An Overview

Instead of identifying *associations*, you might be more interested in *differences*. Are there differences between two groups in your dataset? And are those differences large enough to be 'statistically significant'? To answer these questions, you'll need to use another statistical test: the *t*-test. We'll now explore how to conduct a *t*-test by looking at a real-world example.

Imagine you work at a brewery. It's fun, but it's also hard work because you want to keep improving your product and stay competitive with other suppliers of beer. To keep improving your product, you need to be able to answer questions like: Will a new variety of hops improve the taste of your beer? Will a different type of barley yield more crop on the same amount of farmland?

These are important questions for you and your company, but answering them in a rigorous manner proves challenging because you have small samples. Because of the time and expense involved, you're only able to try out the new varieties of hops and barley a few times and, although the new varieties seem to be better than the older ones, how can you be sure that this difference is not just due to chance or *sampling error*? As we saw in Chapter 3, sampling error is the variation we tend to see in different samples drawn from the same population, even if those samples are drawn randomly and no mistakes or biases impact the sampling process. Inevitably, samples drawn at random will differ slightly from each other; they may have different means and standard deviations. Sampling error is an inevitable result of the sampling process itself and it is something we should be particularly wary of when samples are small. So how can we be sure that the differences we observed between the new variety of hops and the old variety of hops are not just a result of sampling error? How can we know whether those differences are real?

These are the kinds of questions that a real-life brewer, W. S. Gosset, faced while working at Dublin's famous Guinness Brewery in the early twentieth century (Box, 1987). In attempting to answer questions like these, Gosset developed some of the most widely used statistical tests, including the ***t*-test** (Ziliak & McCloskey, 2008, p. 3). (The *t*-test is also sometimes called *Student's t* since Gosset originally published his results under the pseudonym 'Student'; the brewery did not want its scientists to publish their findings in case competitors were interested. For more information on Gosset and the early history of statistics, see Salsburg, 2001.)

The *t*-test investigates whether two groups' mean values for some continuous variable are significantly different from each other. (Recall from Chapter 4 that the *mean* is the average of a sample of data.) Although you can instantly see whether the means of two groups differ, the *t*-test reveals whether this difference is large enough that it is unlikely to be due to chance or sampling error.

Formally speaking, there are three different types of *t*-test: the *one-sample t-test*; the *independent-samples t-test*; and the *dependent-samples t-test*. We will describe each of these three tests in more detail, and give an example of null and alternative hypotheses for each. First let's pretend you are an educational researcher evaluating a new reading programme that is being introduced into primary schools.

The **one-sample *t*-test** establishes whether the mean of your sample differs significantly from some established number that you specify. For our school reading programme example, we would use the one-sample *t*-test to determine whether the mean reading score for children who completed the programme (i.e., our sample) differs from the mean reading score of children nationwide (i.e., the population). Or, perhaps a researcher wants to determine whether the mean house price in a particular area significantly differs from the known national mean house price. This question could also be answered through a one-sample *t*-test.

The **independent-samples *t*-test**, sometimes called the *between-groups t-test* (Glicken, 2003, p. 204), explores whether the means of two independent samples or groups significantly differ from each other. For example, we could use the independent-samples *t*-test to determine whether the mean house price on a particular street differs from the mean house price on another street. Or, for the school reading programme example, we could compare whether the mean reading score of students given the programme (sample 1) differs from the mean reading score of students not given the programme (sample 2). This kind of experimental set-up, in which an experimental group (consisting of individuals who have been given the treatment you are interested in) and a control group (consisting of individuals who have not been given the treatment) are compared, is particularly appropriate for analysis with the independent-samples *t*-test. An independent-samples *t*-test is only appropriate if the groups consist of *different* individuals or cases – the same participant cannot be included in both groups, and a participant in one group should not be paired or matched with a participant in the other group (Sirkin, 2006, p. 272).

The **dependent-samples *t*-test**, also called the *paired-samples t-test* or the *within-groups t-test*, is used when just one group of participants is measured at two different points of time, such as before and after a programme or intervention is completed. We could therefore use the dependent-samples *t*-test to compare the mean house price for a sample of houses before and after the creation of a new park nearby. Or, for our reading programme example, we could use the dependent-samples *t*-test to compare the mean reading score for the same group of students *before* they completed the reading programme and *after* they completed the reading programme. Less commonly, the dependent-samples *t*-test can also be used when individuals in one group are paired or deliberately matched with individuals in the other group (i.e., the two groups are *not* truly independent and therefore *cannot* be compared through the independent-samples *t*-test) (Landau & Everitt, 2004, p. 30). For the reading programme example, the dependent-samples *t*-test would be appropriate if we had matched each student in the experimental group with another student in the control group who had an identical academic record. If no such matching had taken place, then the independent-samples *t*-test could be used instead. As you can see, both the independent-samples *t*-test and the dependent-samples *t*-test can be used to analyse data collected from experiments and evaluations – an important application across the social sciences.

Regardless of which type of *t*-test you select, a logical first step is to specify the null and alternative hypotheses. Let's explore example hypotheses for all three types of *t*-test, using the case of the school reading programme.

For the one-sample *t*-test, our null (H_0) and alternative (H_1) hypotheses could be:

H_0: There is no difference between the mean reading score of students who complete the reading programme and the national mean reading score of students,

H_1: There is a difference between the mean reading score of students who complete the reading programme and the national mean reading score of students.

Note that the alternative hypothesis is directionless; we do not specify whether we believe the mean reading score for programme completers will be higher or lower than the national average, only that it will be different. Since the hypothesis is directionless, we would employ a two-tailed significance test. If, on the other hand, our alternative hypothesis was directional (e.g., 'The mean reading score of students who complete the reading programme is *higher* than the national mean reading score of students'), then we would use a one-tailed significance test. However, as we have seen in our previous discussions of significance testing, a one-tailed test should only be employed if you have a well-founded reason (perhaps based on an extensive body of previous research) for believing that one group will have a higher mean value than the other group (Glicken, 2003, p. 204). Since two-tailed tests are more commonly used in the social sciences, we will focus on directionless hypotheses here.

For the independent-samples *t*-test, our null and alternative hypotheses could be:

H_0:There is no difference between the mean reading score of students who have been given the reading programme (i.e., the experimental group) and students who have not been given the reading programme (i.e., the control group).

H_1:There is a difference between the mean reading score of students who have been given the reading programme (i.e., the experimental group) and students who have not been given the reading programme (i.e., the control group).

For the dependent-samples *t*-test, our null and alternative hypotheses could be:

H_0:There is no difference between the mean reading score of the same group of students *before* they complete the reading programme and *after* they complete the reading programme.

H_1:There is a difference between the mean reading score of the same group of students *before* they complete the reading programme and *after* they complete the reading programme.

Formulas for the t-Test

Now that we've formulated our hypotheses, it's time to actually calculate our *t*-statistic. The formula we use to calculate the *t*-statistic differs depending on which type of *t*-test we've selected. For the one-sample *t*-test, the formula for calculating the *t*-statistic is:

$$t = \frac{\bar{x} - \mu_0}{s/\sqrt{n}}. \tag{5.3}$$

In the numerator of this formula, $\bar{x}$ is the mean of our sample and μ_0 is the known value (e.g., mean of a population) against which we are comparing our sample mean. In the denominator, *s* is the standard deviation of our sample and *n* is the sample size.

For the independent-samples *t*-test, the formula for calculating the *t*-statistic when you don't want to assume your samples have equal variances is:

$$t = \frac{\bar{x}_1 - \bar{x}_2}{\sqrt{s_1^2/n_1 + s_2^2/n_2}}. \tag{5.4}$$

In the numerator in this formula, $\bar{x}_1$ is the mean for the first group and $\bar{x}_2$ is the mean for the second group. The numerator therefore is the difference between the average value for each group. In the denominator in this formula, s_1^2/n_1 represents the variance for the first group divided by its sample size, while s_2^2/n_2 represents the variance for the second group divided by its sample size.

Keep in mind that this formula only applies when you *don't* want to assume that the two independent samples have equal variances. If you *do* believe the samples have equal variances (i.e., you think that the average difference between each score and the mean is the same in both samples), you'll need to use a different formula. (For the full details of this alternative formula, and information on whether to assume the variances are equal, see Kent State University Libraries, 2018a.)

Finally, for the dependent-samples *t*-test, the formula for calculating the *t*-statistic is:

$$t = \frac{\bar{d}}{s_d / \sqrt{n}}. \tag{5.5}$$

In the numerator, $\bar{d}$ is calculated by comparing each participant's value under the first condition with that participant's value under the second condition (e.g., subtract their value after treatment from their value before treatment). This calculation is made for each individual in the study, and $\bar{d}$ is simply the mean of the differences for all the participants in the sample. s_d is the standard deviation of the differences for all participants in the sample (in other words, it is the standard deviation of d). Finally, n is sample size.

Unlike Pearson's r, the *t*-statistic can take any value; it is not constrained to a narrow range of numbers. Positive values of t indicate that the mean of the first group entered into the formula is larger. Negative vales of t indicate that the mean of the second group entered into the formula is larger. If our *t*-statistic is large enough, we can reject the null hypothesis that there is no difference between our groups. As with Pearson's r, to determine whether our *t*-statistic is 'large enough' we compare the value of t we obtained from our data with the *t*-statistic's known distribution. To make the comparison, we must also first establish our α (or significance level) and the *degrees of freedom* (*df*) for our *t*-statistic. Once again we'll select an α-value of 5%, corresponding to $p < 0.05$.

We already encountered *degrees of freedom* in our discussion of Pearson's r. The *df* is important in the context of the *t*-test because it affects the shape of the *t-statistic*'s distribution. With a smaller *df*, the distribution is fatter, and with a larger *df*, the distribution is narrower. The formula for calculating degrees of freedom differs depending on which type of *t*-test you've conducted. For the one-sample *t*-test, the formula is:

$$df = n - 1. \tag{5.6}$$

For the dependent-samples *t*-test, the formula is:

$$df = n - 1. \tag{5.7}$$

For the independent-samples *t*-test, when you don't want to assume the variances of the two samples are equal, the formula is:

$$df = \frac{\left(\frac{s_1^2}{n_1} + \frac{s_2^2}{n_2}\right)^2}{\frac{1}{n_1 - 1}\left(\frac{s_1^2}{n_1}\right)^2 + \frac{1}{n_2 - 1}\left(\frac{s_2^2}{n_2}\right)^2}. \tag{5.8}$$

In the formulas above, n represents sample size. For the independent-samples formula, n_1 is the sample size of the first group and n_2 is the sample size of the second group, while s_1 is the standard deviation of the first group and s_2 is the standard deviation of the second group.

Let's try this!

To make sure we understand how to calculate the t-statistic, let's work through one example using fictional data. Imagine that a researcher was interested in helping people solve mathematics problems more quickly. She developed a series of engaging training exercises and wanted to know whether they reduce the time it takes for people to solve simple maths problems. To investigate this question, she recruited a sample of 34 adults and asked them to work on a simple maths problem. She recorded the number of seconds it took each participant to complete the problem, and then asked the participants to complete the series of training exercises. After completing the training exercises, the participants were asked to work on another maths problem of equivalent difficulty and the researcher recorded how long it took them to complete this second problem.

The researcher's null and alternative hypotheses were as follows:

H_0: There is no difference in length of time needed to complete the maths problem *before* completion of the training exercises and *after* completion of the exercises,

H_1: There is a difference in length of time needed to complete the maths problem *before* completion of the training exercises and *after* completion of the exercises.

After running the study, the researcher obtained the data shown in Table 5.6.

Table 5.6 Length of time needed to complete a maths problem before and after training exercises

Participant	Number of seconds needed to complete maths problem *before* exercises	Number of seconds needed to complete maths problem *after* exercises
1	84	81
2	67	71

Participant	Number of seconds needed to complete maths problem *before* exercises	Number of seconds needed to complete maths problem *after* exercises
3	82	73
4	71	52
5	66	34
6	91	82
7	35	37
8	56	52
9	79	77
10	87	46
11	82	71
12	54	38
13	67	68
14	98	82
15	76	66
16	87	82
17	79	58
18	77	75
19	92	85
20	58	62
21	91	76
22	77	75
23	86	80
24	46	33
25	91	87
26	78	69
27	76	74
28	62	67
29	90	81
30	88	72
31	87	73
32	99	90
33	56	44
34	83	78

stop and think

Based on the researcher's data and the goals of her study, should she use a one-sample *t*-test, an independent-samples *t*-test, or a dependent-samples *t*-test?

If, in response to the 'Stop and think' exercise above, you answered 'dependent-samples *t*-test', good work! A dependent-samples *t*-test would be appropriate since the researcher's data consists of the *same* group of 34 participants measured before and after completion of the training exercises.

Recall that the formula for calculating the dependent-samples *t*-statistic is:

$$t = \frac{\bar{d}}{s_d/\sqrt{n}}. \qquad (5.5)$$

As we discussed above, the first step in calculating the *t*-statistic is to calculate the difference between each participant's value under the first condition and under the second condition. In our example, we would need to calculate the difference between the number of seconds each person needed to complete a maths problem *before* the exercises and *after* the exercises. Once this calculation has been done for each participant in the study, $\bar{d}$ can be calculated by taking the *mean* of these values (i.e., the mean of the differences for each participant in the sample).

To show more clearly how $\bar{d}$ is calculated, Table 5.7 reproduces the data contained in Table 5.6, with additional columns added. Take a look first at the fourth column from the left, labelled 'Difference between number of seconds needed before and after exercises (*d*)'. This is the difference in the number of seconds each participant needed before the exercises compared with after the exercises.

Table 5.7 Calculating the *t*-statistic from our data

Participant	Number of seconds needed to complete maths problem *before* exercises	Number of seconds needed to complete maths problem *after* exercises	Difference between number of seconds needed before and after exercises (*d*)	$d_i - \bar{d}$	$(d_i - \bar{d})^2$
1	84	81	84 – 81 = 3	3 – 9.029 = –6.029	$(-6.029)^2 = 36.35$
2	67	71	67 – 71 = –4	–4 – 9.029 = –13.029	$(-13.029)^2 = 169.77$
3	82	73	82 – 73 = 9	9 – 9.029 = –0.029	$(-0.029)^2 = 0.001$
4	71	52	71 – 52 = 19	19 – 9.029 = 9.971	$9.971^2 = 99.41$
5	66	34	66 – 34 = 32	32 – 9.029 = 22.971	$22.971^2 = 527.65$
6	91	82	91 – 82 = 9	9 – 9.029 = –0.029	$(-0.029)^2 = 0.001$

Participant	Number of seconds needed to complete maths problem *before* exercises	Number of seconds needed to complete maths problem *after* exercises	Difference between number of seconds needed before and after exercises (*d*)	$d_i - \bar{d}$	$(d_i - \bar{d})^2$
7	35	37	35 – 37 = –2	–2 – 9.029 = –11.029	$(-11.029)^2 = 121.65$
8	56	52	56 – 52 = 4	4 – 9.029 = –5.029	$(-5.029)^2 = 25.29$
9	79	77	79 – 77 = 2	2 – 9.029 = –7.029	$(-7.029)^2 = 49.41$
10	87	46	87 – 46 = 41	41 – 9.029 = 31.971	$31.971^2 = 1022.12$
11	82	71	82 – 71 = 11	11 – 9.029 = 1.971	$1.971^2 = 3.88$
12	54	38	54 – 38 = 16	16 – 9.029 = 6.971	$6.971^2 = 48.59$
13	67	68	67 – 68 = –1	–1 – 9.029 = –10.029	$(-10.029)^2 = 100.59$
14	98	82	98 – 82 = 16	16 – 9.029 = 6.971	$6.971^2 = 48.59$
15	76	66	76 – 66 = 10	10 – 9.029 = 0.971	$0.971^2 = 0.94$
16	87	82	87 – 82 = 5	5 – 9.029 = –4.029	$(-4.029)^2 = 16.24$
17	79	58	79 – 58 = 21	21 – 9.029 = 11.971	$11.971^2 = 143.29$
18	77	75	77 – 75 = 2	2 – 9.029 = –7.029	$(-7.029)^2 = 49.41$
19	92	85	92 – 85 = 7	7 – 9.029 = –2.029	$(-2.029)^2 = 4.12$
20	58	62	58 – 62 = –4	–4 – 9.029 = –13.029	$(-13.029)^2 = 169.77$
21	91	76	91 – 76 = 15	15 – 9.029 = 5.971	$5.971^2 = 35.65$
22	77	75	77 – 75 = 2	2 – 9.029 = –7.029	$(-7.029)^2 = 49.41$
23	86	80	86 – 80 = 6	6 – 9.029 = –3.029	$(-3.029)^2 = 9.18$

(Continued)

Table 5.7 (Continued)

Participant	Number of seconds needed to complete maths problem *before* exercises	Number of seconds needed to complete maths problem *after* exercises	Difference between number of seconds needed before and after exercises (d)	$d_i - \bar{d}$	$(d_i - \bar{d})^2$
24	46	33	46 – 33 = 13	13 – 9.029 = 3.971	$3.971^2 = 15.77$
25	91	87	91 – 87 = 4	4 – 9.029 = –5.029	$(-5.029)^2 = 25.29$
26	78	69	78 – 69 = 9	9 – 9.029 = –0.029	$(-0.029)^2 = 0.001$
27	76	74	76 – 74 = 2	2 – 9.029 = –7.029	$(-7.029)^2 = 49.41$
28	62	67	62 – 67 = –5	–5 – 9.029 = –14.029	$(-14.029)^2 = 196.82$
29	90	81	90 – 81 = 9	9 – 9.029 = –0.029	$(-0.029)^2 = 0.001$
30	88	72	88 – 72 = 16	16 – 9.029 = 6.971	$6.971^2 = 48.59$
31	87	73	87 – 73 = 14	14 – 9.029 = 4.971	$4.971^2 = 24.71$
32	99	90	99 – 90 = 9	9 – 9.029 = –0.029	$(-0.029)^2 = 0.001$
33	56	44	56 – 44 = 12	12 – 9.029 = 2.971	$2.971^2 = 8.82$
34	83	78	83 – 78 = 5	5 – 9.029 = –4.029	$(-4.029)^2 = 16.24$
Mean				$\bar{d} = 9.029$	

Now that we've calculated the differences for each participant, we can calculate $\bar{d}$, the mean of all these differences:

$$\begin{aligned}\bar{d} &= (3 - 4 + 9 + 19 + 32 + 9 - 2 + 4 + 2 + 41 + 11 + 16 - 1 + 16 + 10 \\ &\quad + 5 + 21 + 2 + 7 - 4 + 15 + 2 + 6 + 13 + 4 + 9 + 2 - 5 + 9 + 16 \\ &\quad + 14 + 9 + 12 + 5) / 34 \\ &= 307 / 34 \\ &= 9.029.\end{aligned}$$

We record this value in the bottom row of Table 5.7 .

Looking back at formula (5.5), we can see that, in order to calculate t, we first need to calculate s_d, the standard deviation of the differences for all participants in the sample (in other words, the standard deviation of d).

stop and think

What is the formula for calculating standard deviation in a sample? Based on this formula, how would you go about calculating the standard deviation of d?

Hopefully you recall our discussion of standard deviation from Chapter 4. (If not, take a look back at Chapter 4 now!). We saw that the formula for calculating the standard deviation of a sample is:

$$s = \sqrt{\frac{\Sigma(x_i - \bar{x})^2}{n-1}}. \tag{4.4}$$

All we need to do is substitute d for x in formula (4.4). To calculate the numerator in formula (4.4), look at the $d_i - \bar{d}$ and $(d_i - \bar{d})^2$ columns in Table 5.7. We then need to sum all the values in the '$(d_i - \bar{d})^2$' column, as shown below:

$$\begin{aligned} d_i - \bar{d} = {} & 36.35 + 169.77 + 0.001 + 99.41 + 527.65 + 0.001 + 121.65 + 25.29 + 49.41 \\ & + 1022.12 + 3.88 + 48.59 + 100.59 + 48.59 + 0.94 + 16.24 + 143.29 + 49.41 \\ & + 4.12 + 169.77 + 35.65 + 49.41 + 9.18 + 15.77 + 25.29 + 0.001 + 49.41 \\ & + 196.82 + 0.001 + 48.59 + 24.71 + 0.001 + 8.82 + 16.24 \\ = {} & 3116.97. \end{aligned}$$

Finally, n is the sample size. In our example, the sample size, or number of participants, is 34. Therefore, our denominator in formula (4.4) would be 34 – 1 = 33. Substituting these values into formula (4.4), we obtain:

$$s_d = \sqrt{3116.97/33} = \sqrt{94.45} = 9.72.$$

Now, if we plug in our values for $\bar{d}$, s_d, and n into formula (5.5), we obtain the following value for t:

$$t = \frac{9.029}{9.72/\sqrt{34}} = \frac{9.029}{9.72/5.83} = \frac{9.029}{1.68} = 5.4.$$

(It's important to note that your value of t might vary by a few hundredths or even a few tenths depending on the amount of rounding you have included in your calculations. However, if your answer is off by more than that, take a moment to check your work.)

Now that we've found a value for *t*, we need to check whether our *t*-statistic is significant. As with Pearson's *r*, to conduct a significance test, we'll need to choose an α-value. In this example we will choose the most popular value for α: 5%, indicating that $p < 0.05$.

We will also need to calculate the degrees of freedom (*df*) for our *t*-statistic. The formula for calculating *df* for the dependent-samples *t*-test, as we saw earlier in this chapter, is:

$$df = n - 1. \tag{5.7}$$

So, in our example,

$$df = 34 - 1 = 33.$$

Keeping in mind our *df* and α, we compare our *t*-statistic to a table of critical values for the *t*-test. Table 5.8 presents critical values for a two-tailed *t*-test.

stop and think

How does a two-tailed test differ from a one-tailed test? Is it appropriate for us to use a two-tailed test in this example?

Since our hypothesis is non-directional, a two-tailed *t*-test would indeed be appropriate. In Table 5.8, we should look at the column 'α = 5%', as this is our chosen α value. Since our $df = 33$, we should look at that row of the table. Therefore, the relevant critical value of the *t*-statistic is 2.035. Do you see how that value was obtained from the table?

Table 5.8 Critical values of the *t*-statistic

Degrees of freedom (*df*)	**α = 5% (or $p < 0.05$)**	**α = 1% (or $p < 0.01$)**
1	12.706	63.657
2	4.303	9.925
3	3.182	5.841
4	2.776	4.604
5	2.571	4.032
6	2.447	3.707
7	2.365	3.499
8	2.306	3.355
9	2.262	3.250
10	2.228	3.169
11	2.201	3.106
12	2.179	3.055
13	2.160	3.012

Degrees of freedom (*df*)	α = 5% (or $p < 0.05$)	α = 1% (or $p < 0.01$)
14	2.145	2.977
15	2.131	2.947
16	2.120	2.921
17	2.110	2.898
18	2.101	2.878
19	2.093	2.861
20	2.086	2.845
21	2.080	2.831
22	2.074	2.819
23	2.069	2.807
24	2.064	2.797
25	2.060	2.787
26	2.056	2.779
27	2.052	2.771
28	2.048	2.763
29	2.045	2.756
30	2.042	2.750
31	2.040	2.744
32	2.037	2.738
33	2.035	2.733
34	2.032	2.728
35	2.030	2.724
40	2.021	2.704
45	2.014	2.690
50	2.009	2.678
55	2.004	2.668
60	2.000	2.660

(Note that Table 5.8 contains two columns of critical values for a two-tailed *t*-test: one for $\alpha = 5\%$, and one for $\alpha = 1\%$. If you need the critical values for other levels of α, or if you have a directional hypothesis and therefore need critical values for a one-tailed test, you can find a link to a more comprehensive table of critical values in the 'Further Reading' list at the end of this chapter.)

To determine whether the *t*-statistic obtained from our data is *significant*, we need to compare it to the relevant critical value given in the table. If the *t*-statistic obtained from the data is higher than the critical value given in the table, we can say that our *t*-statistic is significant at our α-level. Since the *t*-statistic obtained from our data is 5.4, it is higher than the critical value of 2.035; we can therefore say that our *t*-statistic is significant at the 0.05 level. So there is a statistically significant difference in the time needed for participants to complete maths problems *before* and *after* undergoing the training exercises! Since our *t*-statistic is positive, the mean of the first group is larger; in other words, the number of seconds needed to complete a maths problem was *lower* after the exercises. (A negative t-statistic would have indicated that the mean of the second group was larger.)

So, to bring together everything we've learned, we can state that, on average, the number of seconds needed to complete a maths problem was lower after completion of the training exercises, as our $t = 5.4$, and that this difference is statistically significant ($p < 0.05$).

Interpreting t-Test Results: A Cautionary Note

Although our results are exciting, as with correlation, we need to be careful about making *causal* claims. In other words, we can't be certain that the training exercises *caused* the decline in time, as some other factor might have also changed. It's therefore essential to still consider – and hopefully eliminate – alternative explanations for the results (such as the participants' greater familiarity with having to complete a maths problem while being timed). If we had instead conducted an independent-samples t-test in which participants were *randomly assigned* to undergo the training exercises or not, then we could be more confident that the exercises were responsible for the decline in time needed to complete the maths problem. Remember that random assignment – an underlying component of the randomized controlled trial that we discussed in Chapter 2 – helps data analysts make causal claims based on experimental data. In other words, it is not the use of the t-test that allows us to draw any firm conclusions about cause and effect, but rather the underlying design of the study (and whether the study employed randomization and other features of a true experiment).

Checking Assumptions

Like Pearson's r, the t-test also features certain assumptions, and it may not be appropriate to use the t-test with your data if your data does not meet these assumptions. The assumptions are listed in Figure 5.2.

Assumption 1: The variable you're interested in must be continuous – in other words, the variable must be measured at the interval or ratio level of measurement (see Freeman & Walters, 2010, p. 460). Variables that are ordinal but have five or more categories are typically considered to meet this assumption. An example of an ordinal variable with five or more categories would be a survey question with a Likert scale of answer options (e.g., strongly agree, agree, neither agree nor disagree, disagree, and strongly disagree). *Check this assumption by examining your data, and confirming how your variable of interest was operationalized.*

Assumption 2: The data is normally distributed. Like Pearson's r, the t-test also requires that your variables approximate the normal distribution, although if your sample size is very large, this assumption may be less important. *Check this assumption by constructing quick histograms of each of the variables you're interested in. (Details about how to construct a histogram are given in Chapter 9.)*

Assumption 3: There must be two groups that you are comparing. If you want to compare more than two groups, the *t*-test is not an appropriate choice (but we will discuss some more appropriate alternative statistical tests later in this chapter). *Check this assumption by examining your data, and confirming how the categories/groups were determined.*

Assumption 4 (only applies to independent-samples *t*-tests): To use an independent-samples *t*-test, the two groups you are comparing must truly be independent. This means that a participant cannot be counted in both groups, or paired with someone in the other group (Landau & Everitt, 2004, p. 29).

Figure 5.2 Assumptions of the ***t*-test**

Why is it important to check that your data meets the assumptions of the *t*-test?

5 13 If Your Data Does Not Meet the Assumptions of the t-Test

What do we do if our data fails to meet one or more of the assumptions for the *t*-test? As with Pearson's *r* and the chi-square test, the answer to this question depends in part on *which* assumption your data fails to meet.

If your data violates Assumption 1, meaning that the variable of interest is not continuous, then you need to consider alternative tests. For example, the chi-square test described in the next section might be appropriate if you're interested in categorical data.

If your data violates Assumption 2, meaning that your data is not normally distributed, consider how severe the deviation from normality is. If the deviation from normality seems relatively small, you may still be able to use the *t*-test, especially if your sample is big.

If your data violates Assumption 3, as you have *more* than two groups or categories that you want to compare, then analysis of variance (ANOVA) might be a more appropriate choice. (Unfortunately it is typically *not* appropriate to simply conduct multiple *t*-tests if you want to compare more than two groups. Conducting multiple *t*-tests increases the chance of making a Type I error, or mistakenly rejecting the null hypothesis when you should actually fail to reject it (Raudenbush, 2004, pp. 145–146). In other words, it increases the likelihood of finding a significant difference between the groups, when in fact there is no significant difference.) ANOVA is a distinct statistical procedure that builds on concepts related to the *t*-test but is designed for use with more than two groups. If you're interested in building upon your knowledge of the *t*-test and learning more about ANOVA, take a look at Cardinal and Aitken (2006) or Vik (2014).

If you are conducting an independent-samples *t*-test and your data violates Assumption 4 (meaning that the two groups you are comparing are not independent), consider whether your data is appropriate for a dependent-samples *t*-test instead. If a dependent-samples *t*-test is not appropriate either, you should scrutinize the original data collection procedures. Why are the observations *not* independent? Were some individuals accidentally included several times in the dataset and other individuals represented only once?

5.14 The Chi-Square Test of Association

The third type of statistical test that we'll investigate is the *chi-square test*. There are different types of chi-square tests, but the type we'll focus on is the **chi-square test of association** (which, confusingly, is also sometimes referred to as the *chi-square test for independence*; Smith, Gratz, & Bousquet, 2009, p. 420). The test explores whether membership in a specific category of one variable tends to be accompanied by membership in a specific category of some other variable. It's probably easiest to understand this definition by looking at a few examples of the kinds of questions we could answer with a chi-square test:

- *Is there a relationship between degree subject studied at university and employment status six months after graduation?* To answer this question with a chi-square test, the variable 'degree subject' would need to be broken down into several distinct categories (history, psychology, physics, anthropology, mathematics, etc.), and the variable employment status has two possible categories (employed, not employed). Through the chi-square test, we would explore whether membership in a particular category of one variable (e.g., choosing *physics* as a degree subject) was associated with membership in a particular category of the other variable (e.g., being *employed* six months after graduation).
- *Is there a relationship between marital status and self-reported life satisfaction?* The variable marital status has two possible categories (married, not married) and the variable life satisfaction would need to be broken down into discrete categories (e.g., high, medium, and low). Here the chi-square test would examine whether membership in one category of the 'marital status' variable (e.g., *married*) was associated with membership in one category of the 'life satisfaction' variable (e.g., *high* life satisfaction). If both variables were measured with more than two categories (e.g., if marital status was measured as never married, married, divorced, or widowed), a chi-square test could still be applied.

Formally speaking, the chi-square test involves calculating the chi-square statistic, denoted by χ^2, to explore associations between two *nominal* or *ordinal* variables. In other words, both variables *are not* continuous – instead, they should be limited to discrete categories. (If both variables *are* continuous, *Pearson's r*, which we explored at the beginning of this chapter, may be a better test to use.)

As with any data analysis, before jumping into our chi-square test, we should begin by specifying our null and alternative hypotheses. For the first example described above, our hypotheses would be:

H_0:There is no association between degree subject studied at university and employment status six months after graduation,

H_1:There is an association between degree subject studied at university and employment status six months after graduation.

You'll notice that both of our hypotheses include the word 'association'. We're interested in whether being a member of one category (e.g., choosing *physics* as a degree subject) is *associated* with being a member of another category (e.g., being *employed* six months after graduation). Or is membership in one category completely independent of (or, in other words, *not associated with*) membership in another category? If membership in the different categories is independent, then we would expect the number of observations in every combination of categories to be roughly similar, as the observations would be randomly distributed across categories.

The chi-square test examines whether the actual or *observed* number of observations in every combination of categories differs from the number we would *expect* to find, if the observations were distributed randomly (Sims, 2004, p. 29). To visualize this comparison, we can create a *contingency table* with columns representing one variable's different categories, and rows representing the other variable's different categories. We can then use the cells of the contingency table to evaluate whether the *observed frequency* of each combination of categories differs from the *expected frequency*, or the frequency you would expect if the observations were distributed randomly. Due to sampling error, we might see some small differences between observed and expected frequencies, but larger differences are less likely to be due to chance (Sirkin, 2006, p. 405).

Let's try building a contingency table from some hypothetical data. Imagine that a city is planning to build a new bicycle path. To encourage more commuters to use the path, city administrators have asked you to find out whether there is an association between age category and preference for cycling to work (over other commuting methods). You specify the following hypotheses:

H_0:There is no association between age category (*younger* or *older* commuters) and preference for cycling to work,

H_1:There is an association between age category (*younger* or *older* commuters) and preference for cycling to work.

You then conduct a survey of 135 employed adults in that city and obtain the results shown in Table 5.9.

Table 5.9 Observed frequencies for the commuting preference data

	Younger adults	**Older adults**
Prefer to cycle	46	19
Prefer not to cycle	14	34
Undecided	9	13

Table 5.9 reveals that 46 of the younger adults surveyed preferred to cycle and 14 of the younger adults preferred *not* to cycle. Just 9 of the younger adults were undecided on the issue. For the older adults, 19 preferred to cycle, 34 preferred *not* to cycle, and 13 were undecided. You can see these numbers by looking at the relevant cells in the table. Since these numbers indicate what you actually *observed* in your data, these numbers are called the *observed frequencies*.

Now let's calculate the *expected frequencies* and add them to the table to create the full contingency table we need. An *expected frequency* represents the number of observations that we would *expect* to see in each cell of the table, if the observations were distributed randomly. To make this calculation, we need to apply the following formula to each cell in the table:

$$\text{Expected frequency} = \frac{(\text{total no. of observations in row}) \times (\text{total no. of observations in column})}{n}. \quad (5.9)$$

In formula (5.9), n is the total number of observations in the table, which is also the total number of individuals or cases in your sample. By multiplying the total number of observations in a row by the total number of observations in a column and then dividing by n, we obtain the number of observations we would expect to see in that particular cell, if observations were spread randomly among the categories (and membership in one category was not associated with membership in another category). This is the expected frequency.

Since the formula for expected frequencies requires us to know total number of observations in each row and the total number of observations in each column, it can be helpful to first add these totals to our table. Let's start by calculating each row total. The total number of observations in the 'Prefer to cycle' row is 46 + 19 = 65. The total number of observations in the 'Prefer *not* to cycle' row is 14 + 34 = 48. The total number of observations in the 'Undecided' row is 9 + 13 = 22. If we add up all three row totals, we get 135, or the total number of respondents in our survey (65 + 48 + 22 = 135).

Now let's calculate each column total. The total number of observations in the 'Younger Adults' column is 46 + 14 + 9 = 69. The total number of observations in the 'Older Adults' column is 19 + 34 + 13 = 66. Once again, if we add up the two column totals, we get 135, the total number of respondents in our survey (69 + 66 = 135). See Table 5.10.

Looking at the column totals, it's clear that the numbers of younger adults and older adults in our sample were not equal; this sometimes happens and it is not a problem for the chi-square test.

Table 5.10 Observed frequencies with row and column totals

	Younger adults	**Older adults**	**Row totals**
Prefer to cycle	46	19	65
Prefer *not* to cycle	14	34	48
Undecided	9	13	22
Column totals	69	66	135

Now that we've added the row totals and column totals to our contingency table, we're ready to calculate the expected frequencies for this hypothetical dataset. Let's start with the cell at the upper left-hand corner, which represents younger adults who prefer to cycle. The total number of observations for this row is 65. The total number of observations in this column is 69. Take a look back at Table 5.10 to make sure you can spot where these numbers are coming from.

Since we included 135 people in total in our sample, our $n = 135$. Now we're ready to plug these numbers into formula (5.9). When we plug the numbers into the formula, we find that the expected frequency for younger adults who prefer to cycle is $(65 \times 69) / 135 = 33.222$. Make sure to multiply the two numbers on top first before dividing by n. We then repeat this process for the remaining five cells in the table (the cells that don't contain row or column totals). For example, for the cell that represents older adults who prefer to cycle, the total number of observations in this row is 65. The total number of observations in this column is 66. Our value of n remains the same, so $n = 135$. The expected frequency for older adults who prefer to cycle is $(65 \times 66) / 135 = 31.778$.

You can see this process repeated in Table 5.11, with the resulting expected frequency value displayed in **bold**. Look carefully at the table and make sure you understand how each value in the table was obtained. Since we don't calculate expected frequencies for the cells containing the row and column totals, we're now finished with this step!

Table 5.11 Calculating expected frequencies for the commuting preference data

	Younger adults	Older adults	Row totals
Prefer to cycle	(65 × 69) / 135 = **33.222**	(65 × 66) / 135 = **31.778**	65
Prefer *not* to cycle	(48 × 69) / 135 = **24.533**	(48 × 66) / 135 = **23.467**	48
Undecided	(22 × 69) / 135 = **11.244**	(22 × 66) / 135 = **10.756**	22
Column totals	69	66	135

The next step is to insert these expected frequencies into Table 5.10 to obtain the full contingency table. The full contingency table is shown as Table 5.12. The expected frequencies for each cell are given in parentheses. By showing us both the expected and observed frequencies, a contingency table allows us to compare, for each cell, the number of observations we observed with the number of observations we would expect to find, if the observations were distributed randomly across the categories.

Table 5.12 Contingency table for the commuting preference data

	Younger adults	Older adults	Row totals
Prefer to cycle	46 (33.222)	19 (31.778)	65
Prefer not to cycle	14 (24.533)	34 (23.467)	48
Undecided	9 (11.244)	13 (10.756)	22
Column totals	69	66	135

Table 5.12 suggests that the observed frequencies and expected frequencies for our hypothetical data are quite different. For example, the expected frequency for younger adults who prefer to cycle is 33.222, but the observed frequency is much higher, at 46. How do we know if these differences are actually *significant*? We would expect our observed and expected frequencies to diverge somewhat due to random variation across samples. But are the differences we see large enough that they are *not* likely due to random variation? The chi-square test allows us to answer this exact question. In other words, the chi-square test can tell us whether the differences between observed and expected frequencies are unlikely to be due to chance. The chi-square test does this by calculating the χ^2 statistic using the following formula:

$$\chi^2 = \Sigma \frac{(O-E)^2}{E}. \tag{5.10}$$

In this formula, O is the observed frequency and E is the expected frequency for a particular cell in our contingency table. Σ is the summation symbol, indicating that you need to sum (or add up) everything that follows the symbol. Therefore, for each cell in the contingency table, you need to subtract the expected value (E) from the observed value (O) and square this number; you then divide this result by the expected value (E). You apply this same process to every cell in the contingency table and then sum your results to obtain χ^2.

Let's try this with our data. If we take our observed and expected frequencies from Table 5.13 and plug them into formula 5.10, we obtain the following equation:

$$\begin{aligned}
\chi^2 &= \frac{(46-33.222)^2}{33.222} + \frac{(19-31.778)^2}{31.778} + \frac{(14-24.533)^2}{24.533} + \frac{(34-23.467)^2}{23.467} + \frac{(9-11.244)^2}{11.244} \\
&\quad + \frac{(13-10.756)^2}{10.756} \\
&= \frac{12.778^2}{33.222} + \frac{(-12.778)^2}{31.778} + \frac{(-10.533)^2}{24.533} + \frac{10.533^2}{23.467} + \frac{(-2.244)^2}{11.244} + \frac{2.244^2}{10.756} \\
&= \frac{163.277}{33.222} + \frac{163.277}{31.778} + \frac{110.944}{24.533} + \frac{110.944}{23.467} + \frac{5.036}{11.244} + \frac{5.036}{10.756} \\
&= 4.915 + 5.138 + 4.522 + 4.728 + 0.448 + 0.468 \\
&= 20.2.
\end{aligned}$$

Check that you can follow each step, and obtain the same results. (Once again, note that your results may differ slightly due to rounding discrepancies.) Our chi-square statistic is 20.2. The chi-square statistic can take on any value from 0 all the way up to $+\infty$, but in order to accurately interpret our χ^2, we need to compare it with the chi-square distribution. The chi-square distribution is a known distribution that statisticians have derived. In order to compare our χ^2 with this distribution, however, we must also consider two additional pieces of information: our α (or significance level) and the *degrees of freedom* for our χ^2 statistic. You'll recall that these are the same pieces of information we needed to assess the significance of Pearson's r and the t-statistic, so hopefully you're starting to recognize similarities among different statistical tests. In our previous examinations of significance testing, we've already explored the concept of α. We've seen that researchers typically employ an α-value of 5%, corresponding to $p < 0.05$ (although sometimes an α value of 1%, or $p < 0.01$, is used as an additional or alternative measure). Degrees of freedom for the chi-square test are associated with the size of the contingency table, with larger tables possessing higher numbers of degrees of freedom (Blaikie, 2003, p. 190).

The specific formula for calculating *df* for a chi-square statistic is:

$$df = (\text{no. of rows in contingency table} - 1) \times (\text{no. of columns in contingency table} - 1). \quad (5.11)$$

Any headings, row totals, or column totals in the table should not be counted in this calculation. Therefore, if we have two variables each with two categories, we can place these numbers into (5.11) and calculate *df* in the following manner:

$$df = (2 - 1) \times (2 - 1) = 1.$$

In our current example, in which we have two variables, one of which has three categories and the other of which has two categories, then we would calculate *df* this way:

$$df = (3 - 1) \times (2 - 1) = 2.$$

Now that we have our values for χ^2, α, and *df*, we can test for significance, and determine whether we can reject the null hypothesis that there is no association between membership in one category and membership in another category.

5.15 Determining Significance

As with Pearson's *r* and the *t*-test, testing for significance in the chi-square test is quite straightforward. All we need to do is compare the value of χ^2 that we obtained from our data to the critical values of χ^2 given in Table 5.13. These critical values are the values that χ^2 must be higher than in order to reject the null hypothesis. Table 5.13 presents critical values for up to 8 *df* and for three common significance levels (0.05, 0.01, and 0.001) using a two-tailed test. Since, as we saw in Chapter 4, two-tailed tests are more commonly used and the significance level is usually 0.05, this is the most common scenario. However, if you need critical values for more *df* or want critical values for other significance levels or for one-tailed tests, you can easily find tables that include these by searching the internet.

Table 5.13 Critical values of the chi-square statistic

	Significance level (α)		
Degrees of freedom (*df*)	**5% ($p < 0.05$)**	**1% ($p < 0.01$)**	**.1% ($p < 0.001$)**
1	3.84	6.63	10.83
2	5.99	9.21	13.82

(Continued)

Table 5.13 (Continued)

	Significance level (α)		
Degrees of freedom (*df*)	**5% ($p < 0.05$)**	**1% ($p < 0.01$)**	**.1% ($p < 0.001$)**
3	7.82	11.34	16.27
4	9.49	13.28	18.47
5	11.07	15.09	20.52
6	12.59	16.81	22.46
7	14.07	18.48	24.32
8	15.51	20.09	26.12

In our example, our α is 5% or 0.05, and our *df* is 2. Therefore, we look at the cell on Table 5.13 that corresponds to these values. Check to see that you can find that cell. In that cell, the critical value of χ^2 is 5.99. The value of χ^2 that we obtained from our statistical test was 20.2. If the value of χ^2 obtained in a chi-square test is greater than the relevant critical value found in the table, you can conclude that your χ^2 statistic is statistically significant at the α-level you specified. Since 20.2 is higher than 5.99, we can therefore conclude that our χ^2 statistic is statistically significant at the 0.05 level, and that the null hypothesis – that there is no association between our two variables – is unlikely to be true. In other words, we can state that there is a significant association between age category (younger adults versus older adults) and preference for cycling to work ($\chi^2 = 20.2$) and that this result is statistically significant ($p < 0.05$).

Testing Assumptions

Although the chi-square test *does not* assume the data is normally distributed, the test does require data to meet four other assumptions. These assumptions, and procedures for testing that your data does indeed meet these assumptions, are described in Figure 5.3. After we examine the assumptions, we will explore remedies and alternative procedures you can employ if your data *does not meet* these assumptions.

Assumption 1: Both variables are categorical, which means they are measured at the nominal or ordinal levels of measurement (Pett, 1997, p. 201). *Check this assumption by examining your data, and confirming how both variables were operationalized. If a variable is limited to just a few distinct categories, then it's categorical and meets this assumption. If, on the other hand, at least one of your variables can take on a wide range of values, then it's continuous and your data does not meet this assumption.*

Assumption 2: The categories are independent. This assumption means that 'each subject or object can only be represented once in the data' (Sheskin, 2004, pp. 494–495). For example, an individual cannot be counted in both the *unmarried* and *married* categories for the variable 'marital status'. If an individual is counted more than once in the dataset, then your data violates this assumption and the chi-square test of association is not an appropriate choice. *Check this assumption by looking at the observations in your dataset, and confirming the data collection procedures.*

Assumption 3: The number of cells in the contingency table with an expected frequency less than 5 should not exceed 20% of the total number of cells in the table (Cochran, 1952). *Check this assumption by calculating the expected frequency for each cell in your contingency table using formula (5.3).*

Assumption 4: The expected frequency for *every* cell in the contingency table must be greater than 1 (Chalmer, 1987, p. 274). *Check this assumption by calculating the expected frequency for each cell in your contingency table using formula (5.3).*

Figure 5.3 Assumptions of the chi-square test of association

5.17 If Your Data Does Not Meet the Assumptions of the Chi-Square Test of Association

What do we do if our data fails to meet one or more of the assumptions for the chi-square test? Once again, the answer to this question depends in part on *which* assumption your data fails to meet.

If your data violates Assumption 1, meaning that one or both of your variables is not categorical, then you need to consider alternative tests. If both of your variables are continuous, then Pearson's r (described in detail earlier in this chapter) might be appropriate. If, on the other hand, one of your variables is categorical and the other variable is continuous, then *biserial correlation* or *point-biserial correlation* might be appropriate alternatives. Both of these statistics are described in the discussion about the assumptions of Pearson's r earlier in this chapter.

If your data violates Assumption 2, meaning that each observation is not independent, you should scrutinize the original data collection procedures. Why were some individuals represented several times in the dataset and other individuals represented only once? Why are some individuals classified in multiple categories of a particular variable? (For example, if someone appears both as *married* and *unmarried*, there may have been an error during data collection.) If you have a dataset in which the same group of individuals was measured at two different points in time, one alternative test to consider is the *McNemar test*, although it is not frequently used by researchers (Morgan, Leech, Gloeckner, & Barrett, 2004, p. 148).

If your data violates Assumption 3 or Assumption 4, meaning that the expected frequency of one or more of the cells in your contingency table is too low, one possible remedy is to reduce the number of categories. Are there particular categories in your dataset that could be combined together? By reducing the number of categories, you'll be able to amalgamate different cells into one, and thereby boost the remaining cells' expected frequencies (Sheskin, 2004, pp. 494–495). If you have a 2 × 2 contingency table (meaning that both variables only have two categories) and you have a small overall sample size (fewer than 20 cases) or cells with fewer than 5 cases, then you should use Fisher's exact test rather than the chi-square test (Osborn, 2006, p. 262).

Concluding Thoughts

In this chapter we explored three very important statistical techniques: Pearson's *r*, the *t*-test, and the chi-square test. Although these techniques might be considered 'basic', don't underestimate their value. As we've seen in the examples we explored in this chapter, these techniques have great potential for answering fundamental questions about society, and are still widely used by researchers. Indeed, more complicated quantitative techniques are not necessarily 'better'; as Lacey and Luff (2007, p. 6) point out, many important research questions can be answered by relatively 'simple' statistical tests, and don't require more advanced quantitative analyses. Additionally – and interestingly – many advanced quantitative analyses also incorporate aspects of these basic tests. (You can see this for yourself if you consult the works about advanced statistical tests cited in the 'Further Reading' list at the end of this chapter.) Thus, regardless of your future data analysis goals, everything you've just learned will help you flourish as a data analyst.

Summary

- Pearson's *r*, the *t*-test, and the chi-square test are three of the most fundamental techniques in quantitative data analysis.
- *Pearson's correlation coefficient*, *r*, measures the association between two continuous variables. It ranges in value from –1 to +1, with values closer to –1 indicating stronger negative correlations and values closer to +1 indicating stronger positive correlations.
- It is only appropriate to calculate Pearson's *r* and a corresponding significance test if our data meets five assumptions: both variables are continuous; both variables are normally distributed; the relationship between the variables is thought to be linear; each observation has values for both of the variables you are interested in; and each observation is independent.
- We explored three different types of *t*-test: the one-sample *t*-test; the independent-samples *t*-test; and the dependent-samples *t*-test.
- The one-sample *t*-test establishes whether the mean of your sample of data is significantly different from some known value you specify (such as the mean of a population).
- The independent-samples *t*-test examines whether the means of two independent samples or groups are significantly different.
- The dependent-samples *t*-test is used when the same group of participants is measured at two different points of time, such as before and after a treatment is administered.
- The *t*-statistic can range from $-\infty$ to $+\infty$. Positive values of *t* indicate that the mean of the first group entered into the formula is larger. Negative vales of *t* indicate that the mean of the second group entered into the formula is larger.
- It is only appropriate to calculate the *t*-statistic if our data meets three assumptions: the variable of interest is continuous; the data is normally distributed; and there are two categories or groups to compare. For independent-samples *t*-tests, an additional assumption also must be met: the two groups you are comparing must truly be independent.
- The chi-square test, which yields our value of χ^2, explores whether membership in a particular category of one variable is associated with membership in a particular category of another variable.

- The chi-square test uses a contingency table to determine whether the actual or *observed* number of observations in every combination of categories differs from the number we would *expect* to find, if the observations were distributed randomly.
- It is only appropriate to calculate χ^2 if our data meets four assumptions: both variables are categorical; the categories are independent; the number of cells in the contingency table with an expected frequency less than 5 does not exceed 20% of the total number of cells in the table; and the expected frequency for each cell in the contingency table is greater than 1.

5.20 Further Reading

If you're interested in learning more about the early history of statistics and some of the pioneering scholars we mentioned in this chapter, including W. S. Gosset, take a look at the following absorbing account:

Salsburg, D. (2001). *The lady tasting tea: How statistics revolutionized science in the twentieth century.* New York: Henry Holt and Company.

For a more advanced overview of correlation, see:

Chen, P. Y., & Popovich, P. M. (2002). *Correlation: Parametric and nonparametric measures.* Thousand Oaks, CA: SAGE Publications.

In this chapter, we stressed the idea that correlation does not always mean causation. Are you interested in learning more about causation in the social sciences? This is a fundamental but complex issue, and the subject of renewed interest. A source you may want to look at is:

Steel, D. (2011). Causality, causal models, and social mechanisms. In I. C. Jarvie & J. Zamora-Bonilla (Eds.), *The SAGE handbook of the philosophy of social sciences* (pp. 288–304). London: SAGE Publications.

As you progress in statistics, you may want to use various statistical software packages to simplify your calculations. Two of the most popular software packages are the open-source program R (which is free to download!) and the program SPSS (which is not free, but which you may be able to access through your university's computer lab). Many excellent introductory textbooks exist for both of these programs, but two that I have found helpful are:

Crawley, M. J. (2015). *Statistics: An introduction using R* (2nd ed.). Chichester: John Wiley and Sons.

Field, A. (2009). *Discovering statistics using SPSS* (3rd ed.). London: SAGE Publications.

In our discussion of critical values for the *t*-statistic, we focused on Table 5.8, which included values for a two-tailed test at α = 5% (0.05) and α = 1% (0.01). If you need critical values for other levels of α, or if you have a directional hypothesis and therefore need critical values for a one-tailed test, you can find a link to a more comprehensive table of critical values for the *t*-statistic at the following Wikipedia link: https://en.wikipedia.org/wiki/Student%27s_t-distribution

Discussion Questions

1. What statistical test should you use if you want to look for *associations* between two variables, and your data is *categorical*? What statistical test should you use if you want to look for *differences between two groups*, and your data is *continuous*?
2. In your research, you've found that two variables are *negatively correlated*. How would you explain what a negative correlation means to someone who is not familiar with data analysis?
3. A researcher wants to compare the language skills of a group of students before and after they complete a Spanish language class. Should the researcher use a one-sample *t*-test, an independent-samples *t*-test, or a dependent-samples *t*-test? A different researcher wants to compare the language skills of a group of students who completed an in-person Spanish language class and a different group of students who completed an online Spanish language class. Should this researcher use a one-sample *t*-test, an independent-samples *t*-test, or a dependent-samples *t*-test? (*Hint*: If you're having trouble answering these questions, take a few minutes to review the *t*-test section of this chapter now.)
4. Can you think of a research question from your discipline that could be answered with a chi-square test? Explain *why* a chi-square test would be appropriate to answer this research question.

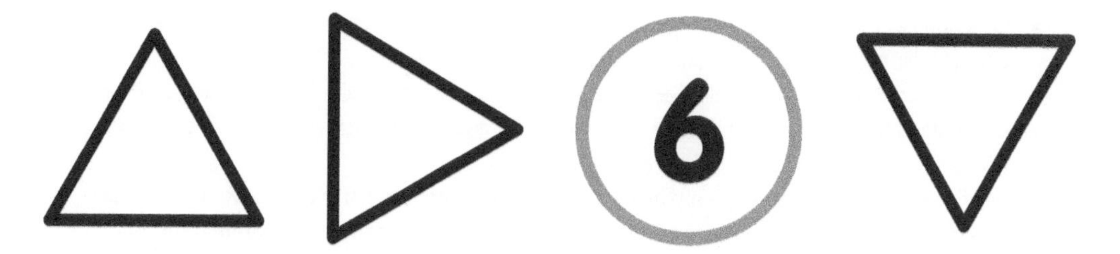

Introducing Qualitative Data Analysis

contents

Chapter Overview

It's time to shift gears and look at qualitative data, or data that is *not* primarily numeric in nature. As you'll see, qualitative data analysis procedures often differ dramatically from quantitative data analysis procedures; however, both methods also share important similarities. By the end of this chapter, you'll be able to:

- Describe key methods for obtaining qualitative data, including *interviews, life histories, surveys, ethnographic methods, document-based analysis*, and *visual methods*
- Identify sources for obtaining qualitative *secondary data*, and assess the challenges of analysing such data
- Understand the differences among key techniques for analysing qualitative data, such as *content analysis, discourse analysis*, and *narrative analysis*
- Define what *coding* is, and explain why it's a central component of many qualitative data analyses
- Describe two distinct case studies of real-world qualitative data analysis to illustrate both the benefits and challenges of such research.

What Makes Data 'Qualitative'?

There is no single form of qualitative data analysis. Instead, a diverse wealth of different techniques exist for collecting (or obtaining), organizing, analysing, interpreting, and describing qualitative data. As outlined in Chapter 2, qualitative data analysis typically focuses on textual or visual data; however, qualitative scholars have also analysed a wide range of other types of data, including behaviours, body language, landscapes, sounds, and more. Although this chapter cannot discuss methods to analyse *all* of these different types of data in detail, we will explore a range of key qualitative methods that are most likely to be of use to you. Such methods include interviews, life histories, surveys, ethnographic methods, and document-based analysis.

Despite their diversity, all qualitative methods share certain basic similarities; indeed, as Wolcott (1992, p. 19) has remarked, qualitative data collection typically involves some combination of *experiencing, enquiring,* or *examining* features of the social world. Even more broadly, one can argue that all qualitative data analyses feature, at their heart, the notion of *observation*, or using one's visual, auditory, and other senses to explore behaviours, attitudes, things, or phenomena – while also taking into account how one's own perspective or experiences might affect one's analysis (Kassebaum, 1970, p. 129). Qualitative research is often a process of collecting data, identifying key themes and patterns, and then exploring relationships among those themes. However, as Maxwell (2013, p. 2) has observed, in qualitative research, numerous activities often take place at the same time, with 'each influencing all of the others' – in other words, you may start to identify patterns at the same time that you are still conducting further observations and beginning to explore relationships between different themes. You may feel it is appropriate to wait until you have collected all your data to begin the analysis process – or you may feel ready to begin the analysis process as you start to collect the data. Some qualitative research follows a similar process to quantitative research (as described in Chapter 4), with the formulation and testing of hypotheses and the ultimate aim of generalizing one's results beyond the dataset at hand. Other qualitative research, however, does not feature the formal process of hypothesis testing. As we discussed in Chapter 2, some research that does not involve hypothesis testing instead seeks to develop theories from raw data; such research is said to follow the *grounded theory* approach (Glaser & Strauss, 1965, 1967). Similarly, not all qualitative researchers wish to generalize their results beyond their single dataset. Instead, they endeavour 'to develop a rich understanding of the local context' rather than 'generalizable laws' (Willis et al., 2007, p. 291). Thus a deep, comprehensive investigation of the context or phenomenon of interest is an essential component of qualitative inquiry.

Regardless of whether qualitative research seeks to test hypotheses or generalize to other contexts, much (but by no means all) qualitative research adopts an *interpretivist* perspective, asserting that there is no single objective reality, as all knowledge is 'socially constructed' (Morçöl, 2002, p. 225). As we saw in Chapter 2, interpretivist researchers assert that individuals maintain different perspectives and understandings of the social world, and that no single 'true' understanding of the world exists. The goal of interpretivist research, therefore, is often to uncover these disparate realities by illuminating the perspectives of the research participants (Gratton & Jones, 2010, p. 28).

Given this emphasis on interpretivism, one might assume that qualitative research is more fluid and personal than quantitative research. However, rigour and validity are just as important in qualitative data analysis as they are in quantitative data analysis. For example, it can be helpful to ask another researcher or independent reviewer to also examine your qualitative data analysis, and thus aid in the *triangulation* of your findings (Reid, Flowers, & Larkin, 2005, p. 23). (Can't remember what triangulation is? Take a look at the discussion in Section 2.8.) Similarly, regardless of which specific qualitative method you select, it is essential to keep detailed records of your data collection and analysis processes; not only will such records facilitate your own research process but, as noted in the discussion of validity in Section 2.7, such records can enhance the external validity of your analysis (Mays & Pope, 1995, p. 110).

What skills must a researcher possess in order to undertake a thorough qualitative analysis? Strauss and Corbin (1990, p. 18) have argued that a qualitative researcher must be ready 'to step back and critically analyze situations, to recognize and avoid bias, to obtain valid and reliable data, and to think abstractly'. Additionally, a qualitative researcher must be willing to think deeply about the act of research itself, and should consider how her own experiences and perspectives shape her reactions to the social world she is studying (Rossman & Rallis, 2003). A thoughtful researcher must endeavour to accurately present the views or opinions of research participants, but also be willing to critically analyse these views and 'reinterpret them in a wider context' (Scott & Garner, 2013, p. 70). As we explore different qualitative approaches in this chapter, think about how these skills might be applied to those methods.

6.3 Qualitative Data Analysis Approaches

6.3.1 Interviews

One of the most popular types of qualitative research methods is the **interview**. An interview is a spoken interaction between a researcher (the *interviewer*) and a research participant (the *interviewee*) that has a particular research purpose. The researcher asks the research participant questions and the researcher records or somehow makes a note of the research participant's answers. Interviews can be used as either the primary research method in a project, or as a supplementary method to other research techniques. For example, interviews can be used as a supplementary method in evaluation research to help a researcher understand *why* a particular programme or treatment produced particular results, and to confirm that 'no event other than the program has occurred that could plausibly explain' the observed results (Mark & Henry, 2006, p. 327). Since interviews allow a researcher to hear directly from research participants, this method can offer important and unique insights.

An interview can be **structured**, which means it follows a precise list of questions with little deviation; **semi-structured**, which means it features a set list of questions or topics that must be covered, but permits the researcher and participant to explore topics in greater depth; or **unstructured**, which means it is open-ended and without a predetermined plan or list of questions (Gill, Stewart, Treasure, & Chadwick, 2008). In addition to these three general interview types, other interview types also exist, such as the *ethnographic* interview, which is a more 'informal, spontaneous' type of interview and usually takes place 'while the investigator is busy hanging out with the people being studied' in the place of interest (Lindlof & Taylor, 2011, p. 176). Each of these interview types has advantages and disadvantages. Structured interviews can make it easier to compare respondents' answers, since you can be certain that all respondents are asked the same questions. Unstructured interviews, on the other hand, can help your research participants feel more involved in the research process, since they can have the opportunity to 'tell their stories or reflect on specific issues' and thereby learn about themselves during the interview process (Simons, 2014, p. 462).

Regardless of which type of interview you choose to conduct, it is helpful to consider Berg's (1995, p. 49) description of the interviewer's work as 'a *self-conscious performance*', with 'lines, roles, and routines ... prepared and rehearsed in advance'. This means that conducting an interview can be a complex task requiring preparation – and even rehearsal – on the part of the interviewer. Like an actor, you need to think about, and prepare for, your role. The interview itself can also require significant energy from the interviewer, since during the conversation the interviewer must remain focused and mentally alert, and consistently ready to interpret 'the cues, clues, and encoded messages offered by the interviewee' (Berg, 1995, p. 51). Conducting productive interviews is both a rigorous science and a creative art form, requiring preparation and focus alongside a willingness to improvise.

Researchers often produce *transcripts* of their interviews, or written records of the questions the interviewer asked and the exact responses of the interviewee. As we will see in the next chapter, researchers often analyse these transcripts in great detail, looking for the key themes that emerge in the interviewee's words. Yet, although transcripts might consume the bulk of a data analyst's attention, other, non-verbal aspects of an interview also merit consideration. An interviewee's facial expressions, body language, gestures, and even pauses in speech might also offer important insights. As Gibson and Brown (2009, p. 172) have observed, gestures are actually 'a distinct communicative mode', and researchers who focus only on an interviewee's words may miss the impact that such gestures can have on the communication process.

The moments of silence within an interview also deserve consideration, as an interviewee's silence about a particular issue can have multiple meanings. Specifically, silence may indicate that an interviewee failed to understand a particular question, or is reluctant to discuss an 'embarrassing' or 'taboo' topic, or believes that a particular issue deserves special emphasis or respect, or is frightened of speaking openly about something (Fontes, 2008, pp. 170–171). The meaning of a particular silence, then, can have significant implications and can offer additional insight into a researcher's key questions.

Since non-verbal elements of interviews typically do not appear in transcripts, it's important that the researcher document these elements in some other way. Specifically, to ensure that such thoughts are not forgotten, interviewers may write brief 'observational notes' or 'memos' that can be analysed later alongside the transcript of the interview itself (Polkinghorne, 2005, pp. 143–144). In the next chapter we will discuss memos in more detail and investigate different techniques for analysing them.

6.3.2 Life histories

A particular type of qualitative interview is the life history interview, which aims to uncover 'a narrator's biography', addressing issues as diverse as relationships, educational or work histories, daily routines, and historical experiences (Shopes, 2011, p. 452). Although different researchers define the term *life history* in diverse ways, **life history research** is typically focused on uncovering how individuals interact with their environments, and how experiences and historical or societal forces shape individuals' life trajectories (Cole & Knowles, 2001, pp. 11–12). In this way, life histories are often closely related to sociological, historical, and other forms of analysis. Indeed, historical methods and life history methods can often overlap when researchers 'seek external corroborating pieces of evidence' to enrich their broader analysis (Berg, 1995, p. 164).

6.3.3 Surveys

In Chapter 4 we explored the use of surveys in quantitative research. Yet surveys can also yield *qualitative* data if they include more open-ended or free-response questions. Indeed, much of our discussion of key issues in survey research, including the question of whether to design your own survey questionnaire or use one that has already been designed by previous researchers, also applies to qualitative surveys. So be sure to go back and review that material if you are interested in conducting qualitative surveys.

Yet qualitative surveys also differ from quantitative surveys in several important ways. While quantitative surveys typically aim to uncover the number of respondents who fall into the same category or who give the same responses to questions, qualitative surveys often probe 'the meaningful variation' among respondents (Jansen, 2010, para. 6). Additionally, quantitative surveys typically aim for larger samples and cover a wider variety of issues, but qualitative surveys may only be interested in a smaller, more specialized sample, and ask fewer questions with more detailed responses (Fink, 2003, p. 68). Sometimes qualitative surveys are used as an 'exploratory method' to help a researcher gain a more thorough understanding of a topic before launching a larger-scale survey or other research project (Lindlof & Taylor, 2011, p. 108).

stop and think

How do *qualitative* surveys differ from *quantitative* surveys?

6.3.4 Ethnographic methods

Ethnographic methods involve a researcher conducting extensive research in the field, and observing or participating in activities or daily life routines within an area, organization, society, or group of interest. As we discussed in Chapter 1, such research methods have a long history, as they were employed by Alexis de Tocqueville in *Democracy in America*, his classic study of the USA in the 1830s. However, the formal roots of **ethnography** can be traced to early twentieth-century anthropology and sociology, as many anthropologists during this period engaged in extensive fieldwork in societies in different areas of the world, while some sociologists (including scholars from the Chicago School) utilized ethnographies to understand the perspectives of marginalized urban residents within the USA to foster 'political leverage' for these groups (Neyland, 2008, pp. 3–5).

An ethnographer focuses on portraying his own interpretation or experience of a place, phenomenon, or society, rather than on presenting one universally accepted 'truthful account of reality' (Pink, 2007, p. 22). Indeed, the perspective of the researcher is an integral part of an ethnography, since a researcher's representation of a community is often shaped not only by her personal experiences, but also her role as an ethnographer, which may encourage her to employ particular vocabulary or interpretations when assessing her findings (Wolcott, 2008, p. 145). For example, think back to our discussion in Chapter 1 about how de Tocqueville's experiences as a foreign observer shaped his analysis of American customs.

The perspective of the *community* that is being studied can also be crucial to shaping the ethnography. Indeed, in a particular type of ethnography, the *collaborative ethnography*, researchers and volunteers from the community that is being researched work together to collect data and make sense of findings (Campbell & Lassiter, 2010, p. 370). The collaborative ethnography structure therefore breaks down barriers between researcher and research participants, to ensure that participants play an active role in the research process.

Ethnographic research can also present particular challenges, as researchers must maintain a delicate balance between developing detailed, close analysis of a phenomenon or society while still maintaining sufficient professional distance (Hine, 2000, p. 5). Becoming too close or familiar with the setting or group of interest is a particular hazard, and, after spending some time in the field, an ethnographer may need to take a break 'to refresh their perspective' before returning to the field with renewed curiosity (Neyland, 2008, p. 101). Another difficulty is that a researcher's ability to communicate with, and gain the respect of, different societies can be affected by factors beyond her control, 'such as nationality, gender, age, religion, race, or ethnic background', all of which 'may present additional challenges to developing trust and gaining access to communities' (Norman, 2009, p. 83). Nevertheless, ethnography remains a popular form of qualitative research, in part for the unique richness and detailed insights it can offer into communities. This richness is in part due to the ability of ethnographies to understand individuals' behaviour 'from a socially oriented perspective [rather] than from an individual or psychologically oriented one' (Wolcott, 2008, p. 279). In other words, ethnographies can offer unique insights into how individuals' actions and attitudes are shaped by their communities and societies.

A research method that is related to, and sometimes overlaps with, ethnography is **participant observation**, which formed the basis of many of de Tocqueville's insights (as we saw in Chapter 1). In participant observation, a researcher does not stand back as an objective, impartial witness, but instead wholeheartedly participates in the phenomenon, organization, or culture they are studying. Through participant observation research, a researcher can gain first-hand insight into what it is like to be a member of a specific group or engage in particular activities. An advantage of participant observation is that it can help a researcher forge 'emotional trust' with the individuals or communities she is interested in, and can therefore facilitate her efforts to gain 'access' to these individuals or communities (Norman, 2009, p. 82). On the other hand, as with ethnographies, researchers conducting participant observation studies must also take care not to become so close to or familiar with their research setting that they lose the ability to analyse and write about the phenomena of interest.

6.3.5 Document-based analysis

Sometimes qualitative research includes the analysis of documents that have been created by others. For example, historians conducting qualitative research may spend significant time analysing written records obtained from archives; media scholars may want to analyse newspaper or magazine articles; and political scientists may study the text of new laws or proposed legislative bills. One advantage of conducting document-based analysis is that it can be completed 'without disturbing the setting in any way', so a researcher does not need to worry that her presence has somehow altered the events or group dynamics that are of interest to her (Marshall & Rossman, 1995, p. 86). However, it is important to take a proactive role in scrutinizing the documents used to build your analysis, as such scrutiny will enhance the *validity* of your results. Specifically, you should ask the following questions of every document used in your study: 'Where was it located? What information supports the accuracy or authenticity of the material? What corroboration, if any, can be or has been located?' (Berg, 1995, p. 167).

Document-based analysis can yield valuable insight into 'the array of objects, symbols, and meanings that make up social reality shared by members of a society', since documents are produced by human beings and thus reflect the values, ideas, and culture of those human beings (Altheide, 1996, p. 2). Such reflexivity is important for all qualitative data analysts to consider when exploring both historical and more recent documents.

let's try this!

As a thought exercise, turn randomly to a different page of this book. Treat that page as if it were a document you wanted to include in a document-based analysis. Read that page like a qualitative researcher. Ask yourself the questions specified in the previous section to probe the meaning and the context of this document. What key themes emerge from the document? What can this document tell us about current society? How might this document be used as a data source in a qualitative study? What research questions could it help us answer? Although it might seem strange at first to consider a textbook page from the very different perspective of a researcher, this thought exercise can help you cultivate the kind of critical, inquiring mindset that a document-based researcher should bring to textual data.

6.3.6 Visual methods

The qualitative methods we've discussed so far – interviews, life histories, surveys, ethnographic methods, and document-based analysis – all revolve around *words*. A researcher who conducts an interview often produces a transcript of the interview to analyse later. A researcher who conducts an ethnography often produces written notes to analyse later. Yet words – or, more formally, textual data – are not the only kind of data that can be analysed with qualitative methods. Qualitative methods are also frequently employed to analyse **visual** data, or data that consists of images. Such image-based data may include photographs, paintings, buildings and geographic areas, and films and videos (i.e., moving images). Although visual media have long been analysed by art historians and cultural critics, social scientists (in particular, sociologists and anthropologists, but also members of other disciplines) have increasingly probed the themes and cultural implications of such images. Given images' unique power and social meaning, analysing such products might produce 'sociological insight that is not accessible by any other means' (Banks, 2007, p. 4).

Social science researchers have used a variety of different methods to analyse visual data. Perhaps the most popular approach is to focus on particular images or video segments, analyse the key features or themes present in those images/segments, and then apply codes to represent those features or themes (Bell, 2001, p. 15). (This approach to visual data mirrors the approach to document-based data described in the previous subsection.) A researcher also needs to think deeply about the particular *context* in which an image was created. Who created the image? What was the purpose or aim of the image? Does the image reflect a particular perspective or point of view? Images – even news photographs and documentary film footage – should never be assumed to be unbiased, comprehensive portrayals of 'reality'. Instead, a qualitative data analyst should always ask: To what extent does this image reflect the values and aims of the individuals or the society that created it?

In addition to analysing visual data created by others, researchers might also *create* visual data as part of the research process. An ethnographer, for example, might take photographs to illustrate the area or society she has investigated. However, keep in mind that even these visual images reflect a particular point of view (i.e., your own perspective as a researcher), even though you make every effort to portray your data honestly and without overt bias

(Gibson & Brown, 2009). Indeed, you can ask yourself the same question specified above: to what extent does the image you created reflect *your* values and aims, and the values and aims of your society?

A researcher might also wish to use **data visualization** techniques to visually represent the data analysed through other methods. You're probably already familiar with many specific data visualization techniques, including graphs, charts, maps, and other types of figures. Both quantitative and qualitative data can be presented with data visualization techniques, and we will explore such techniques in detail in Chapter 9.

6.3.7 Secondary data analysis

In Chapter 4 we saw how secondary data analysis – the analysis of data that has been collected by other researchers – is a popular technique in quantitative data analysis. Although less common in qualitative research, opportunities for secondary data analysis are also available. Given the expansive, wide-ranging nature of many qualitative datasets, it's certainly possible that you might find an accessible secondary dataset that can be used to answer your research questions.

However, before embarking on the secondary analysis of a qualitative dataset, it's important to recognize that you will not benefit from the same nuanced, personal knowledge of context that the original data collector enjoyed (Seale, 2011, p. 347). Therefore, before starting to analyse the data, you'll need to reflect on whether contextual knowledge is essential for understanding the phenomenon or society you are interested in. Despite this caveat, a growing interest in secondary analysis of qualitative data means that more resources are available to interested researchers (although not as many resources as are available for secondary analysis of quantitative data). If you are interested in exploring secondary analysis of qualitative data, here are some archives and databases you may want to check out:

- In the UK, the UK Data Service features a wealth of both qualitative and quantitative data. The service can be found online at: https://www.ukdataservice.ac.uk/
- Within the UK Data Service, users can directly search for data from qualitative surveys and interviews via the QualiBank database, which is located at: https://discover.ukdataservice.ac.uk/QualiBank
- In the USA, the Qualitative Data Repository at Syracuse University's Center for Qualitative and Multi-Method Inquiry is a developing initiative to archive and offer broader access to qualitative data and to facilitate secondary analysis. The repository's website is: https://qdr.syr.edu/discover
- The Henry A. Murray Research Archive at the Institute for Quantitative Social Science at Harvard University also seeks to preserve qualitative data, and researchers can search the archive's website for deposited data that focuses on different themes. The depository can be accessed at: https://murray.harvard.edu/dataverse
- Many more qualitative data archives also exist which may be more directly relevant to your specific areas of interest. If you are interested in a broader overview of different data repositories and archives (for both qualitative and quantitative data), take a look at the Registry of Research Data Repositories, which is available at: https://re3data.org

Analytical Strategies

Once you have collected data, you will need to analyse it. Numerous specific approaches exist for analysing qualitative data, including *content analysis, discourse analysis, narrative analysis,* and other focused approaches. Although each of these techniques will be introduced separately in this section, keep in mind that qualitative researchers often combine multiple techniques when analysing qualitative data. For example, both narrative analysis and discourse analysis can present unique advantages and challenges when used in the same research project (e.g., Court, 2004). Indeed, as we discussed in Chapter 2, employing multiple analytical strategies can facilitate *triangulation*, as you can explore whether different strategies produce the same results. However, if you want to employ a combination of different analytical strategies, you should ensure that each of those separate strategies is appropriate and theoretically sound for your study's particular type of data and specific research questions. This section will help you determine whether some of the more popular analytical strategies might be appropriate for your study. If none of these approaches seems appropriate, take a look at the 'Further Reading' section at the end of this chapter, as it lists sources you can consult to find information about additional analytical strategies.

6.4.1 Content analysis

The first analytical strategy we will consider, **content analysis**, is most often used in document-based analysis, but can be employed in any qualitative project that generates textual data – for example, it could be used on a written transcript from an interview (Berg, 1995, p. 59). Content analysis typically involves a researcher looking for 'patterns in the data' (Gläser & Laudel, 2013, para. 90; see also Marshall & Rossman, 1995, p. 85), or, more specifically, comprehensively assessing whether certain themes tend to appear frequently in a given text, and whether certain words are likely to be used together (Luker, 2008, p. 187). Qualitative researchers who employ content analysis often seek to investigate texts and search for 'cultural meanings and insights' that such texts provide (Noaks & Wincup, 2004, p. 127). This focus on meaning, nuance, or interpretation distinguishes *qualitative* content analysis from *quantitative* content analysis – since, in the latter approach, a researcher usually counts or makes numerical comparisons about the number of times different words or categories appear in texts (Mayring, 2004, p. 266). Even within qualitative content analysis, however, different specific approaches exist, with researchers disagreeing about whether content analysts should only consider those themes or values that are clearly evident and stated in the data, or whether researchers should also try to interpret 'symbolism' buried within the text itself (Berg, 1995, p. 176). Such debate highlights the variety of specific outlooks researchers can adopt, illustrating that there is no single, ideal form of qualitative content analysis that is appropriate for every project.

Regardless of which specific approach content analysts adopt, it can be helpful to start with a given list of potentially relevant themes or categories that have been identified in previous, similar studies. These predetermined themes or categories can assist the researcher in his initial attempts to identify patterns or categories in his own data. This use of predetermined categories, which differs significantly from the grounded theory approach discussed in Chapter 2, requires researchers to watch out for any 'temptation to force concepts on data' (Gläser & Laudel, 2013, para. 91). One useful remedy for avoiding this temptation - and for improving the overall triangulation of one's research findings - is to arrange for other experienced qualitative researchers to separately examine the qualitative data and compare how their coding compares to your own (Mays & Pope, 1995, p. 110). Significant divergences in the results obtained by the original researchers and by the additional researchers may be cause for concern, as such divergences could indicate inappropriate categorizations or biased interpretations. It is particularly important to engage in such triangulation efforts when using techniques that involve subjective judgement, such as qualitative content analysis.

6.4.2 Discourse analysis

Like content analysis, **discourse analysis**, the second analytical strategy we will explore, is also focused on texts and language. However, discourse analysts are particularly interested in the customs and standards that govern how language is employed in discourse, and how the language we use can affect how our ideas are interpreted (Tonkiss, 2004, p. 373). In other words, discourse analysts focus both on the practical conventions and patterns of discourse as well as on the effects of discourse on human thought patterns. Indeed, such analysts tend to view words and phrases 'as acts or performances to be interpreted' (Vogt, 2005, p. 92). Discourse analysts are interested in how individuals use language to create their own social worlds (Schreier, 2012, p. 47), focusing in particular on how the linguistic rules and conventions for communication reflect and shape social power dynamics (Lupton, 1992, p. 145).

Discourse analysis has been employed in a wide variety of social science disciplines, and discourse analysts have drawn upon a range of more specific theories to guide their work (Gee, Michaels, & O'Connor, 1992, p. 228). Despite this diversity, discourse analysts all tend to hold the view that language has broader meanings beyond just 'communicating information', as it reveals how individuals formulate knowledge about the world around them (Tonkiss, 2004, p. 373). This emphasis on the revelatory potential of language and communication is a hallmark of the discourse analysis approach.

6.4.3 Narrative analysis

Narrative analysis, the third analytical strategy we will explore, was pioneered by literary theorists to explore the stories and plots of texts (Patterson & Monroe, 1998). In recent decades, however, this technique has become increasingly popular among social scientists, as it offers significant potential for illuminating aspects of social life (Riessman, 2004). Narratives occupy a central role in individuals' lives and societies' dealings. Think about the last time a friend told you a funny anecdote, or the last time you heard an inspiring story about an athlete or other high-achiever. Narratives help human beings make sense of an often nonsensical world, and function as 'the principal way in which our species organizes its understanding of time' (Abbott, 2008, p. 3).

Therefore, by undertaking narrative analysis, you can shed significant light on the thought processes of your research participants. Narrative analysis can also help you gain insight into how individuals communicate with each other, since the act of constructing a narrative itself is often 'a form of social interaction' between a narrator and listeners or readers (Redwood, 1999, p. 674). Narrative analysis is frequently applied to interview transcripts, but it can also be used to analyse historical documents, written descriptions of events, and numerous other sources of text. Social scientists have used narrative analysis to probe a wide variety of different types of stories – including, for example, the stories told by policy-makers and other decision-makers to support their political positions (Hukkinen, Roe, & Rochlin, 1990). The next section will discuss how narrative analysis can be used in practice to illuminate the narratives contained in documents.

Table 6.1 Popular analytical approaches for qualitative data

Analytical approach	Description
Content analysis	By focusing on patterns and prominent themes, we can make sense of a complex qualitative dataset. We should look at how frequently different themes or words appear in the data, and whether particular themes or words tend to appear together.
Discourse analysis	By examining the linguistic nuances and conventions present in human discourse, we can gain insight into how individuals use language to create their own social worlds. We can also better understand how communication reflects and shapes social power dynamics.
Narrative analysis	By probing the narrative elements of textual data, we can illuminate the stories told by individuals and societies. Such stories can offer significant insight into how individuals understand their own lives and decisions, and how societies view their values.

This section discussed three popular analytical strategies – content analysis, discourse analysis, and narrative analysis – which are summarized in Table 6.1. However, it's important to recognize that these are not the only analytical strategies available to qualitative researchers. A wide variety of additional approaches can also be employed, and if you are interested in learning more about these additional strategies – or if none of the approaches discussed in this section seems appropriate for your data – take a look at the 'Further Reading' section at the end of this chapter. This list includes sources you can consult to find information about additional analytical strategies.

6.5 Coding: A Preview

Regardless of which specific analytical strategy you select, your qualitative analysis process will likely include some form of **coding** data. Although not all qualitative projects feature coding, most text- and image-based analyses rely on this process, and coding is therefore introduced in this section. However, this discussion of coding is just a preview. Chapter 7 offers a much more thorough overview of the coding process for readers interested in using coding in their data analysis work.

What is coding? Simply put, coding is the process of applying descriptive labels to a qualitative dataset to identify key themes present within that dataset. Coding helps a researcher 'distinguish raw data from "noise"' in the textual or visual sources he has assembled and, like content analysis, coding can also help suggest directions for more detailed and targeted explorations of the data (Gläser & Laudel, 2013, para. 90). Coding facilitates analysis since the process of generating codes and applying them to data forces a researcher to identify categories and significant themes, and trace the appearance of those themes and categories throughout his dataset. These themes or categories – referred to as *codes* – can thus 'serve as "signposts"' to help a researcher recognise important pieces of text that should be analysed in more detail (Kelle, 2004, p. 454; see also Seidel & Kelle, 1995).

A researcher typically considers his overall analytical strategy when selecting which specific coding method to use in a given research project. For example, researchers who adopt a narrative analysis strategy can use a *narrative coding* approach to assess documents (Saldaña, 2016). A narrative coding approach requires that a researcher code the plot- and character-based elements of the varied stories presented in documents (Riessman, 1993). Based upon an analysis of these codes, the researcher can then begin to put together the narratives contained in the documents. On the other hand, a researcher who selects discourse analysis as her overall analytical strategy would likely *not* choose a narrative coding approach but would instead employ another coding method that highlights grammatical and rhetorical elements of discourse. A researcher who wishes to bring a grounded theory approach to her analysis would employ a coding method that *does not* draw upon theory or previous research, but is instead 'theory-free', to allow themes to freely emerge from the data (Gläser & Laudel, 2013, para. 91). These coding methods represent just a small selection of the full range of methods that qualitative researchers can draw upon. More detailed information about many specific coding methods is given in Chapter 7.

For the moment, however, it is important to recognize that a researcher does not need to limit herself to just one coding method. A researcher interested in *both* narrative analysis and discourse analysis, for example, would likely want to engage in *both* narrative coding and coding that focuses on discourse. On the other hand, employing multiple coding methods is not *universally* better than employing just one method. As Saldaña (2016, p. 69) has warned, one should be 'cautious of muddying the analytic waters ... by employing too many methods for one study ... or integrating incompatible methods'. Indeed, the choice of which – and how many – methods to use must be made on a case-by-case basis, with a researcher carefully considering the characteristics of her data and her ultimate research questions.

Finally, a concern that many qualitative researchers share is recognizing when to 'stop' the coding and interpretation process. Indeed, many researchers – especially those new to coding or to qualitative data analysis more generally – worry about engaging in *too much* interpretation or analysis of their data. Although practical constraints mean that no researcher can spend an infinite amount of time analysing a particular dataset, new qualitative analysts should not be overly concerned about engaging in *too much* interpretation and analysis. Indeed, Gee et al. (1992, p. 233) have argued that 'to err on the side of overinterpretation is wiser' since the texts that individuals generate are often complicated, multilayered, and indicative of their unique cultural experiences. Given these complexities, it is not surprising that coding is often a time-consuming process, which requires researchers to engage in substantial amounts of interpretation.

let's try this!

Imagine you are a researcher in the field of education. You have recently begun a study driven by the following research question: 'How do contemporary data analysis textbooks define and conceptualize "data"?' Part of your study will involve a document-based analysis of several textbooks. Based upon your own knowledge of key themes in data analysis, think about some of the codes you would want to explore in your document-based analysis. What themes might emerge in your data? What codes might be important? Draw up a short list of codes to start with.

By completing the above exercise, you've gained first-hand experience of what the coding process is like for qualitative researchers. If you found the exercise difficult or still don't think you have a clear sense of what coding involves, don't worry. In the next chapter we will revisit the coding process in much more detail.

6.6 Examples of Qualitative Studies

This chapter has introduced numerous different research approaches, analytical strategies, and coding methods that all fall under the general umbrella of qualitative data analysis. Hopefully at least some of these approaches or techniques will prove useful to you in your own work. However, before you actually apply any of these approaches to your own data, you need to consider how practical concerns and real-world challenges can affect your efforts to perfectly implement these approaches. How can you actually apply these 'textbook' methods to real-world research situations? To begin to answer this question, we will investigate two examples of qualitative research projects that have faced significant hurdles – and yet still yielded fascinating findings.

The first example is the Mass Observation Project, which was launched in the UK in 1937, and is one of the most ambitious research projects ever undertaken (Storey, 2014). The goal of the project was to produce an 'anthropology of ourselves' by investigating the day-to-day experiences of people, originally through both diaries and qualitative surveys, as well as participant observation by a team of researchers (Mass Observation, n.d.). This participant observation work included researchers observing ordinary people in 'meetings, religious occasions, sporting and leisure activities, in the street and at work' and documenting their actions and speech (Mass Observation, n.d.). The project's unparalleled ambition also posed significant challenges, since developing a comprehensive understanding of people's experiences using only a limited team of researchers was no simple task. However, the Mass Observation Project developed an inspired solution to this problem; instead of just relying on a limited team of researchers, the project also empowered 'ordinary people throughout Britain' to observe and examine their own lives and communities (Sheridan, Street, & Bloome, 2013, p. 346). By involving a wider range of individuals in the project – beyond just professional researchers – the Mass Observation Project was able to develop a richer portrait of people's lives, and also prompt individuals to think critically about their own experiences.

stop and think

Why was the Mass Observation Project such a landmark piece of social science research?

The second example of real-world qualitative research for us to consider is Richard T. Wright and Scott Decker's (1994) *Burglars on the Job: Streetlife and Residential Break-ins*. Like the Mass Observation Project researchers, Wright and Decker also faced the challenge of trying to understand people's experiences in depth. Yet, unlike those researchers, Wright and Decker could not simply involve the general public in their efforts, since they were only interested in the experiences of a very particular subset of society: currently offending burglars. Therefore, to find potential burglars to interview, Wright and Decker (1994, p. 16) employed a snowball sampling strategy in which they asked interviewees to help them locate additional potential interviewees. They also *did not* ask law enforcement or other criminal justice system officials to help them find interviewees, as they did not want potential interviewees to think the project was really a police sting operation (pp. 16–17). These tactics helped Wright and Decker gain credibility and locate 105 interviewees willing to share detailed and deeply personal insights into their lives. Although the project was not without its challenges, the researchers' careful consideration of how to most effectively recruit interview participants allowed them to collect rich qualitative data – and ultimately produce landmark findings about the decision-making processes of burglars.

6.7 How to Select a Qualitative Approach

The two examples discussed in the previous section, the Mass Observation Project and Wright and Decker's (1994) study of burglars, show how different qualitative methods have been successfully used to investigate the social world. If you are embarking on a qualitative study for the first time, it is unlikely that you will be able to conduct a study as large in scope or as varied in methodology as the Mass Observation Project. Instead, it is more likely that you will need to choose one or two particular qualitative methods to use, and a limited selection of analytical strategies or coding methods to analyse your data. At first, making these choices might seem like a daunting task. How can you determine which specific qualitative research method is most appropriate for exploring your research questions? How can you establish which analytical strategy is best suited for your analysis, or which coding method is apposite for your type of data? Remember, though, that you can seek guidance in answering these questions from previous researchers, investigate which methods other studies have used to explore the questions you are interested in, and assess the advantages and limitations of these methods. Think carefully about your own expertise and working patterns as well, as you will want to select an analytical strategy that fits with your skills and inclinations.

Even after you have chosen your analytical techniques, you should continue to revisit your choices throughout the analysis process to ensure the techniques are still suitable for the data you have collected, and you should not be surprised if 'the main points of thematic interest and related analysis' may shift slightly as the data collection process proceeds (Noaks & Wincup, 2004, pp. 125, 123). This revision of strategies and main themes is a common part of many qualitative data analyses.

If multiple analytical techniques seem most appropriate for your data, consider using multiple techniques! You don't have to limit yourself to just one analytical approach or one coding method, although using different strategies together can pose additional challenges. Yet using multiple techniques together can also allow a researcher to develop a richer analysis of the phenomena of interest, and also can illuminate how her own background or choice of a single theoretical approach impacts her interpretation of the data (Frost et al., 2010).

This second point – that a researcher's own background or theoretical approach might impact her interpretation of the data – is essential to consider even in cases in which a researcher only employs a single analytical method. As discussed in Chapter 2, all human beings – including data analysts! – are fallible, and we cannot help but bring our own perspectives and biases to our interpretation of the data. Acknowledging such reflexivity or subjectivity is a key component of many qualitative data analyses. For example, when documenting their research methods, many researchers offer a 'reflexive account', which details 'their conceptual journey through the research', and may feature personal memos reflecting on the research process (Lacey & Luff, 2007, p. 28). Other qualitative researchers discuss the personal reasons for choosing their topic, so that readers are fully aware of 'the initial biases, values, and theoretical orientations' that the researcher brought to the research project (Berg, 1995, p. 92). Examples of real-world efforts to acknowledge reflexivity can be found in the Mass Observation Project: interestingly, the Mass Observation Project included 'analytic commentary by the writers themselves on their own lives', and the writers of such accounts often were transformed into 'researchers themselves by commenting on (and theorising) their own writing practices' (Sheridan et al., 2013, p. 351). By considering researchers' perspectives and experiences, this landmark qualitative project was able to acknowledge the key role of reflexivity in qualitative data analysis.

Acknowledging such reflexivity and subjectivity does not imply that validity is any less important in qualitative data analysis than in quantitative data analysis. On the contrary, validity is a preeminent concern in qualitative research, and even though 'multiple "truths"' may exist, 'validity will be judged by the extent to which an account seems to fairly and accurately represent the data collected' in a qualitative analysis (Lacey & Luff, 2007, p. 27). Therefore, it's worth keeping in mind: *Validity is central to all data analysis, including qualitative data analysis.*

Concluding Thoughts

It's exciting to consider the variety of opportunities available to the qualitative researcher. Interviews, ethnographies, documents, and all the other data sources described in this chapter present a wealth of unique possibilities for understanding and describing the social world. Of course, qualitative methods present challenges as well and it's essential to anticipate and respond to these challenges, just as we endeavoured to do in the previous section. As we investigate qualitative methods in more depth in the next chapter, you'll gain greater insight into these challenges, and into the specific advantages that these different qualitative methods offer. As you proceed through Chapter 7, take time to reflect on how the benefits and challenges of qualitative methods are similar to, and different from, the benefits and challenges of quantitative methods.

Summary

- Qualitative data analysis is the analysis of data that is not primarily quantitative in nature (i.e., data that is not made up of numbers). Typically, qualitative data analysis focuses on textual or visual data.
- Many (but not all) qualitative data analysts adopt an *interpretivist* perspective, asserting that there is no single objective reality, and that the goal of research is to uncover the numerous realities that exist for different individuals.
- Many different research methods exist for collecting qualitative data, including interviews, life histories, surveys, ethnographic methods, document-based analysis, and visual methods.
- Qualitative researchers have used numerous specific approaches to analyse qualitative data after it has been collected. These approaches include content analysis, discourse analysis, and narrative analysis. Each of these approaches has its own strengths and limitations, and sometimes qualitative researchers choose to combine multiple techniques in one study.
- Regardless of the specific qualitative approach one chooses, qualitative data analysis often features the 'coding' of data, or the act of categorizing qualitative data to reveal its essential themes or elements. Coding allows a researcher to trace the appearance of key themes and categories throughout a dataset.
- It is important for a researcher to acknowledge the ways in which her own background or theoretical approach might impact her interpretation of qualitative data.

Further Reading

We've seen already in this textbook that researchers adhere to different theoretical paradigms or research traditions (such as the *positivist* or *interpretivist* paradigms we discussed in Chapter 2), and these traditions can shape the analysis process. If you're interested in learning more about how different theoretical traditions approach the analysis of qualitative data, take a look at Chapters 1–5 of:

Willis, J. W., Jost, M., & Nilakanta, R. (2007). *Foundations of qualitative research: Interpretive and critical approaches*. Thousand Oaks, CA: SAGE Publications.

You can find out more about the history of the Mass Observation Project, and learn about how to access the project's data archives (currently held at the University of Sussex in Brighton), by visiting the following website: http://www.massobs.org.uk/about/history-of-mo

Wright and Decker's study of burglars' motivations and decision-making processes is an interesting example of qualitative data analysis in action, and an altogether fascinating read! Here is the book's full citation:

Wright, R. T., & Decker, S. (1994). *Burglars on the job: Streetlife and residential break-ins*. Boston: Northeastern University Press.

If you are interested in conducting secondary analysis of qualitative data, here are some data depositories that you might want to check out:

The UK Data Service, which features a wealth of both qualitative and quantitative data, can be found at: https://www.ukdataservice.ac.uk/

Within the UK Data Service, QualiBank (which allows users to directly search for data from qualitative surveys and interviews) can be located at: https://discover.ukdataservice.ac.uk/QualiBank

In the USA, the Qualitative Data Repository at Syracuse University can be accessed via: https://qdr.syr.edu/discover

The Henry A. Murray Research Archive at the Institute for Quantitative Social Science at Harvard University, which seeks to preserve qualitative data, can be accessed at: murray.harvard.edu/dataverse

The Registry of Research Data Repositories, which presents an overview of different data repositories and archives (for both qualitative and quantitative data), is available at: re3data.org

This chapter outlined some of the most popular strategies for analysing qualitative data, including content analysis and discourse analysis. These strategies are not the only techniques available for analysing qualitative data, however. For more information about additional potential analytical techniques, take a look at any (or all!) of the following books:

Cresswell, J. W. (2013). *Qualitative inquiry & research design: Choosing among five approaches* (3rd ed.). Thousand Oaks, CA: SAGE Publications.

Flick, U. (2007b). *Designing qualitative research*. London: SAGE Publications.

Warren, C. A. B., & Karner, T. X. (2014). *Discovering qualitative methods: Ethnography, interviews, documents, and images* (3rd ed.). New York: Oxford University Press.

Finally, for a more comprehensive guide to the various stages of the qualitative research process, you may want to consult:

Auerbach, C. F., & Silverstein, L. B. (2003). *Qualitative data: An introduction to coding and analysis*. New York: New York University Press.

Discussion Questions

1. How does qualitative data differ from quantitative data?
2. What questions or concerns should a researcher consider before deciding whether to use quantitative methods or qualitative methods?
3. Think about a research question relevant to your specific field of study. Would it be possible to answer that question through a qualitative study? Why or why not?
4. Define each of the following terms in three sentences or fewer: *content analysis*; *discourse analysis*; and *narrative analysis*. How are these techniques similar and different?
5. What was the Mass Observation Project? What lessons does it offer about how to conduct successful qualitative research projects?
6. What is *reflexivity*? Why is it important to acknowledge in qualitative data analysis?

Applying Qualitative Data Analysis

contents

Chapter Overview

In Chapter 6 we introduced *coding*, a process that is central to many qualitative data analyses. In this chapter, we'll explore coding in more detail, examining how you can use different coding strategies to analyse your own qualitative data. By the end of this chapter, you will be able to:

- Discuss the challenges inherent in analysing different qualitative data sources, including interview transcripts, documents, ethnographic observations, and non-textual data
- Offer a detailed definition of what *coding* is, and how it can be used to analyse qualitative data
- Explain how *codes* can be derived from previous studies or theories, or emerge directly from your data
- Describe the differences among different coding strategies, and how these coding strategies can be applied to real data
- Define what *theoretical memos* are, and explain how they can facilitate the qualitative data analysis process
- Explain what the acronym CAQDAS stands for, and outline the benefits and limitations of using CAQDAS to code qualitative data
- Understand conventions for presenting qualitative findings in academic articles and papers.

7.2 Analysing Qualitative Data: An Overview

Qualitative data is incredibly diverse, encompassing all data that is not primarily numerical or statistical in nature. Much qualitative data is *textual* data, or data that consists of written words; example sources for such data include the transcripts of interviews, responses to open-ended questions on surveys, and notes about ethnographic observations. However, as we saw in the previous chapter, qualitative data can also include a much broader range of sources, including visual images, buildings, films, household objects, and numerous other items. In this chapter we'll explore analytical strategies that can be applied to many different types of qualitative data, as well as examine the unique characteristics of each of these data types.

If you're new to qualitative research, it's possible you may feel a bit overwhelmed, and even unwilling to move forward, when you consider the *magnitude* of the analysis task facing you. Qualitative data is often lengthy and large and the analysis of such data requires deep, detailed thought; indeed, as Polkinghorne (2005, p. 141) has observed, a qualitative researcher is expected to 'dig below the surface' to uncover deeper and more complex insights. Ultimately, however, a researcher must also make these deep and complex insights *intelligible* to readers and describe the core findings in a clear and coherent manner. Sometimes, then, qualitative data analysis can feel like a multi-part balancing act, in which a researcher must navigate seemingly contradictory goals! If you find yourself challenged in this way, don't worry – this feeling is common, particularly for early-stage researchers. So be patient with yourself, and stay focused on your ultimate goals of finishing your project and answering the questions that interest you. The goal of this chapter is to give you the knowledge and skills necessary to guide you through these challenges.

7.3 What Are You Going to Analyse?

Regardless of which type of qualitative data you've obtained or collected, you'll need to precisely identify what elements or aspects of that data you will analyse. If you're interested in analysing textual data, for instance, you will need to decide whether you will focus on individual words, or sentences, or only paragraphs. If you're interested in analysing films, you'll need to consider whether you will focus on the images displayed on screen, or transcripts of dialogue, or artistic and technical elements such as cinematography and music. If you're interested in analysing online advertisements, you'll need to consider whether you will focus solely on the advertisements themselves, or consider them within the contexts of the websites on which they appear.

Given the diversity of qualitative data types, it's useful to consider the strengths, limitations, and unique features of the types you are most likely to encounter. In the next section, we'll discuss interview transcripts, documents, ethnographic observations, theoretical memos, and non-textual data sources in depth, to illustrate some of the challenges that can arise when researchers try to analyse these different data types.

7.4 Data Types

7.4.1 Interview transcripts

As we saw in Chapter 6, interviews are one of the most popular qualitative research methods. Given this popularity, it's important to think about how to most effectively analyse an interview transcript. An interview *transcript* is a verbatim written record of an interview, featuring both the researcher's questions and the respondent's answers. Interviews are typically transcribed to facilitate analysis; such analysis can be undertaken with the techniques we'll explore later in this chapter.

In addition to the actual words spoken by the researcher and respondent, an interview transcript might also include 'pauses and gross changes of volume and emphasis' to help readers gain a sense of the interview's full content (Wetherell & Potter, 1992, p. 100). Significant body language or other important visual elements of the interview that cannot be captured on audio recordings should be noted down by the researcher as soon as possible (Gibbs, 2007, p. 3). (As we saw in the previous chapter, such unspoken elements of an interview can actually contain significant information.) During the analysis process, these notes can then be assessed alongside the interview transcript itself, as visual elements of the interview might hold important insights.

Transcribing interview recordings can be a lengthy process; indeed, a typical estimate is that it takes around 10 hours to accurately transcribe one hour of a recorded interview (Baker & Charvat, 2008, p. 272). Although it's possible to engage a professional transcription service to complete this task, some scholars argue that qualitative researchers should transcribe their own interview recordings to gain a greater familiarity with their data (see, for example,

Klenke, 2008, p. 137). According to this perspective, transcribing interviews yourself 'forc[es] you to think about the data' and to develop an immediate fluency with your interviewee's words, jump-starting the analysis process (O'Dwyer, 2008, p. 395). However, given the time commitment transcription requires, it may not be practically possible to undertake this task on your own.

Whether you decide to transcribe the interviews yourself or hire someone else, as you inspect the interview transcript, be sure to make a note of any particularly revealing or important quotations; you may want to highlight these in your ultimate analysis to let your readers 'hear' your interviewees' voices and perspectives at first hand (Baker & Charvat, 2008, p. 273). Additionally, during your initial exploration of the interview transcript, keep in mind that, as we described in Chapter 6, interviews are 'social interactions' between interviewers and interviewees (Klenke, 2008, p. 137). Therefore even at this early stage of analysis it's essential to think about how social context – which includes factors like the interview's location, the interviewer's attitude, and the rapport between interviewer and interviewee – may have shaped the interview. As we will see throughout this chapter, contextual factors are important to consider in any analysis of qualitative data. However, such factors are particularly relevant to interview data, given interviews' social characteristics, and such factors should be considered even in preliminary phases of analysis.

7.4.2 Documents

Documents constitute a second prominent source of qualitative data. In the previous chapter we explored the advantages and pitfalls of analysing documents. An additional advantage to note now is that documents can be analysed with the same methods that are applied to interview transcripts, since interview transcripts are just 'another form of document' (Love, 2003, p. 91). Therefore, the coding techniques that we will discuss later in this chapter can be applied equally to documents or interview transcripts, as long as you take into account the unique features of these sources (e.g., the social and interactional elements of an interview, or the historical context of a document). Sometimes researchers collect interview data *and* document data as part of one research project, perhaps to triangulate findings. (Do you remember what *triangulation* is? If not, take a look back at the discussion of this concept in Chapter 2.) In such cases, the same codes 'used for interview transcript analysis can be used for documents', allowing the researcher to easily assess similarities and differences among the data sources (Love, 2003, p. 91). By highlighting findings common to both data sources, a researcher can 'integrate data gathered by different methods' and thus develop a richer portrait of the phenomenon of interest (Bowen, 2009, p. 32). As with interview transcripts and all forms of qualitative data, it is necessary to bring a thoughtful, savvy perspective to the analysis of documents. Think about the documents' potential biases, and be willing to question their authenticity (if such questions are warranted). Such thoughtfulness is essential for ensuring the validity of your eventual data analysis.

7.4.3 Ethnographic field notes

To conduct ethnographic research, a researcher typically undertakes extensive research in the field, observing or participating in activities or daily life routines within the area, organization, society, or group of interest. Usually, the researcher makes extensive notes about her observations and experiences, which she can subsequently analyse. These notes, called **field notes**, constitute the fundamental ingredients of an ethnographer's analysis, and can be analysed like other texts (Fetterman, 2010, p. 116). As with interview or document-based data, the analysis of ethnographic field notes involves 'searching for patterns' across different scenarios, statements, or events (Flick, 2007a, p. xiii). This emphasis on looking for patterns and commonalities means that the coding approaches we will explore later in this chapter can be applied to the analysis of ethnographic data.

However, field notes are also distinguished from other data sources by not being 'raw' data; instead, they are 'partially cooked', or shaped by the researcher's earlier choices about which events or interactions should be noted down and which can be ignored (Madden, 2010, p. 140). This means that field notes already reflect elements of the researcher's own perspective and judgement – a fact that highlights the particular importance of maintaining reflexivity in the analysis of ethnographic data. Indeed, as we discussed in the previous chapter, reflexivity is central to ethnographic research, since a researcher's representation of a community, area, or phenomenon is shaped by her personal experiences, as well as by her professional role as an ethnographer (Wolcott, 2008, p. 145).

From a practical perspective, it's often a good idea to start conducting some analysis as you're collecting data (rather than waiting until all the data is collected) so you can start to develop your findings before you forget specific details and can no longer decipher your own extensive field notes (Murchison, 2010, p. 116). Don't be afraid, therefore, to jump-start your analysis even before you've finished your data collection.

stop and think

What are *ethnographic field notes*? How does the analysis of ethnographic field notes differ from the analysis of other kinds of qualitative, textual data?

7.5 Non-Textual Analysis

Although textual data is the *most common* type of qualitative data that social science researchers encounter, it is not the *only* type. As we saw in the previous chapter, qualitative data can also be visual, consisting of items such as photographs or other images, films or television programmes (which are really moving images), objects, landscapes, and more. Sometimes visual data may be considered alongside textual data within the same research project; for example, a media studies scholar might examine the portrayal of female crime victims in newspapers by analysing both the text of articles and the images in their accompanying photographs. (Indeed, an entire discipline of *visual ethnography* has emerged, which emphasizes the use of visual materials – such as film or photographic methods – in ethnographic research, and often draws upon ideas from visual anthropology and media studies. If you're interested in learning more about this discipline, see, for example, Pink, 2007.) Similarly, interviews can be analysed through both textual methods (using transcripts, as we discussed above) *and* visual methods (using videos of the interviews). Since 'video data preserves some of the visual aspects of the data that are often lost when conversations are transcribed' (Gibbs, 2007, p. 3), analysing the video recordings of interviews can yield additional insights that may not be evident from analysing interview transcripts alone.

Like texts, images can also benefit from 'close reading' (Mitchell, 2012, p. 292), or a deep consideration of their components and meanings. The process of coding – which we introduced briefly in the previous chapter – can facilitate this task. Although most traditional coding techniques were designed for textual data, many of these techniques can be equally applied to images and other non-textual types of data as well. To offer just one real-world example, Parkin (2014) used coding to insightfully analyse visual images of harm reduction. Later in this chapter we will explore specific suggestions for applying coding techniques to non-textual data.

In addition to coding, a second similarity between textual data and non-textual data is the importance of considering *context*. As we discussed in the previous section, when analysing interview transcripts and ethnographic field notes, it is essential to explore the social and situational contexts in which these texts were produced. Similarly, when assessing images or other non-textual data sources, a researcher must reflect on 'contextual information' about the environment in which an image was produced, and the goals of the producer of the image – tasks that art historians have engaged in when looking at paintings (Rose, 2007, p. 36). Relatedly, researchers must also recognize that, like interview transcripts or ethnographic field notes, images are not necessarily 'true' portrayals of particular events or phenomena; instead, 'a photograph or film "constructs" the reality that it depicts', with the image-maker's choices affecting how the image might be interpreted (Chambliss & Schutt, 2010, p. 270). In recent decades, more attention has been given to the previously under-researched topic of 'audiencing', or thinking about how the audience for visual materials – whether that audience be cinemagoers, television viewers at home, or visitors to a gallery – are themselves 'meaning-makers' whose interpretation of the work might differ from the intended interpretation (Rose, 2007, p. 197). Thus, both the creator and the viewer can shape how an image or film is interpreted.

7.6 Beginning Your Analysis

Regardless of which type of qualitative data you've collected, you'll need to eventually begin the analysis process itself. It's common for researchers to wait until they've collected all their data to begin analysis. However, this is not always the case, and sometimes analysis can begin before data collection has finished. With ethnographic field notes, for example, as we noted earlier, it might be essential to start analysis in the midst of data collection so that you don't forget the meaning of your field notes. For methods other than ethnography you may still find yourself eager to dive into analysis, particularly as you start to organize your data during the collection process. Indeed, organizing data into a more manageable form can involve some analysis; O'Dwyer (2008, p. 401) has observed of qualitative research that 'as you organise, you analyse', since decisions about how to organize your data involve some analytical consideration. Feel free to also note down any insights that occur to you as you collect the data. Such insights or observations might help you during the formal coding process, which we will explore in the next section.

7.7 Launching the Coding Process

Coding is the process of categorizing data to uncover underlying themes or elements. (This is the definition of coding that we proposed in the previous chapter. If you missed that discussion, take a moment now to review Section 6.5.) Coding can 'make the job of analysis easier by being able to focus it on relevant issues' (Wetherell & Potter, 1992, p. 100) – in other words, it can help you focus on the most important insights contained within an expansive dataset. Coding is a way of organizing and making sense of a large body of data; with modifications it can be applied to textual, visual, and other types of qualitative data.

The general process of coding is straightforward. A researcher identifies a code – a single word or series of words – that encapsulates a key theme or finding present in a particular portion of the overall dataset (Kelle, 2004; Seidel & Kelle, 1995). By 'portion', I mean, for example, a few lines of text from an interview transcript, or even just a single phrase; alternatively, for visual data, a 'portion' could be part of an image, or an entire photograph or illustration. (The unit of analysis depends upon the characteristics of the data, as well as the researcher's best judgement.) The researcher then goes through the entire set of collected data, identifying different codes and applying them to relevant sections of data. In so doing, a researcher will likely discover themes that may not be immediately evident but are undoubtedly important (Monette, Sullivan, DeJong, & Hilton, 2014). A researcher will likely also discover connections between different pieces of raw data, as the same code might be relevant to different documents or different respondents' statements (Gläser & Laudel, 2013, para. 27). By reflecting on the various codes, a researcher can also assess his data more holistically, as he can focus on 'conceptual labels' (i.e., the codes) rather than the plethora of detailed, original data (Strauss & Corbin, 1990, p. 65). Through such holistic reflection, broader patterns may also be identified.

7.8 Predetermined and Spontaneous Codes

Codes can originate from two sources: they can be predetermined by the researcher, or they can emerge spontaneously from the data itself (Gläser & Laudel, 2013, para. 27). To use *predetermined* codes, a researcher specifies a list of codes before beginning the analysis process; these codes are typically based on previous research or guiding theoretical frameworks. The researcher then applies these codes to relevant portions of the data. To use *spontaneous* codes, a researcher must be more flexible, and allow codes to jump out spontaneously as she considers the collected data. Often researchers employ a combination of predetermined and spontaneous codes to generate a variety of potentially useful findings. Your approach will depend on the goals of your research project. While predetermined codes are particularly useful for identifying similarities across different datasets (Bowen, 2009, p. 32) and exploring specific concepts identified in previous theoretical work, spontaneous codes can account for unexpected findings. (And, in the social sciences, unexpected findings often occur!)

Your choice of codes may also depend on your specific analytical strategy. In the previous chapter we explored different analytical strategies, including *content analysis, discourse analysis, narrative analysis*, and even the *grounded theory* perspective. A researcher who adopts a narrative analysis strategy, for example, will likely employ some predetermined codes that capture plot-, character-, and story-based elements of the data (Saldaña, 2016). Alternatively, a researcher who adopts a grounded theory approach will likely emphasize spontaneous codes that *do not* draw upon theory or previous research (Gläser & Laudel, 2013, para. 91).

Regardless of which analytical strategy you select, your coding process will likely feature several stages. Although you may need to adapt these stages to meet the specific goals of your research or your particular analytical strategy, it is common for the initial stages of coding to be broad and flexible, allowing a researcher to experiment with different codes and themes of interest; the later stages of coding, however, are usually more focused and analytical, so a researcher can narrow down the list of potential codes to focus in greater depth on just a few key themes. In the next few sections we will explore the coding process in more detail, using terms popular in both grounded theory and other analytical perspectives to denote its constituent stages. Be aware that you may encounter different terms for these stages in other sources; however, even when different terms are used, the basic concept of moving from more flexible coding practices to more narrowly focused coding practices tends to remain consistent.

7.8.1 Open coding (or beginning the coding process)

The earliest phase of coding, which grounded theorists call **open coding**, is distinguished by its open, flexible, and even creative orientation (e.g., Strauss & Corbin, 1990, p. 62). In this phase, a researcher typically focuses on broader, simpler, or more 'generic' codes, while leaving deeper and more complex themes for later rounds of coding (Madden, 2010, p. 144). A researcher should feel free to be a little creative and open to new possibilities during this early stage, as such openness might produce unexpected insights. For example, even if you plan to emphasize predetermined codes (rather than grounded theory's spontaneous codes) in your overall analysis, don't be afraid to note – and assign codes to – additional themes that also jump out at you during this initial phase. At a later point, as we'll see in a moment, you'll have the opportunity to jettison any codes that turn out to be less germane.

During open coding, you should also focus on fairly and adequately representing the raw data through your codes (Monette, Sullivan, DeJong, & Hilton, 2014, p. 434), to ensure that no important themes are overlooked. Even if a theme does not neatly line up with your research questions, it might turn out to be a fruitful avenue for further exploration. Make sure that, in addition to noting the striking and unique elements of your data, you also give adequate attention to the 'commonplace and ordinary' elements, as these elements might also spur important conclusions (Gibbs, 2007, p. 41). Finally, during open coding you can also deploy codes as helpful 'signposts' in your data, to highlight particular segments of text that you want to return to for more analysis and reflection (Kelle, 2004, p. 454). Taking the time to complete such organizational work early on can save you significant time during later phases of your analysis.

To summarize: when you begin the coding process, don't be afraid to explore unexpected themes or to generate a very long list of codes. In later stages of coding, you will have the opportunity to streamline your analysis and reduce or refine your lists of codes. For the moment, you can be creative and 'open' to exploring a diversity of codes and themes. Get to know your dataset, have fun, and be curious!

let's try this!

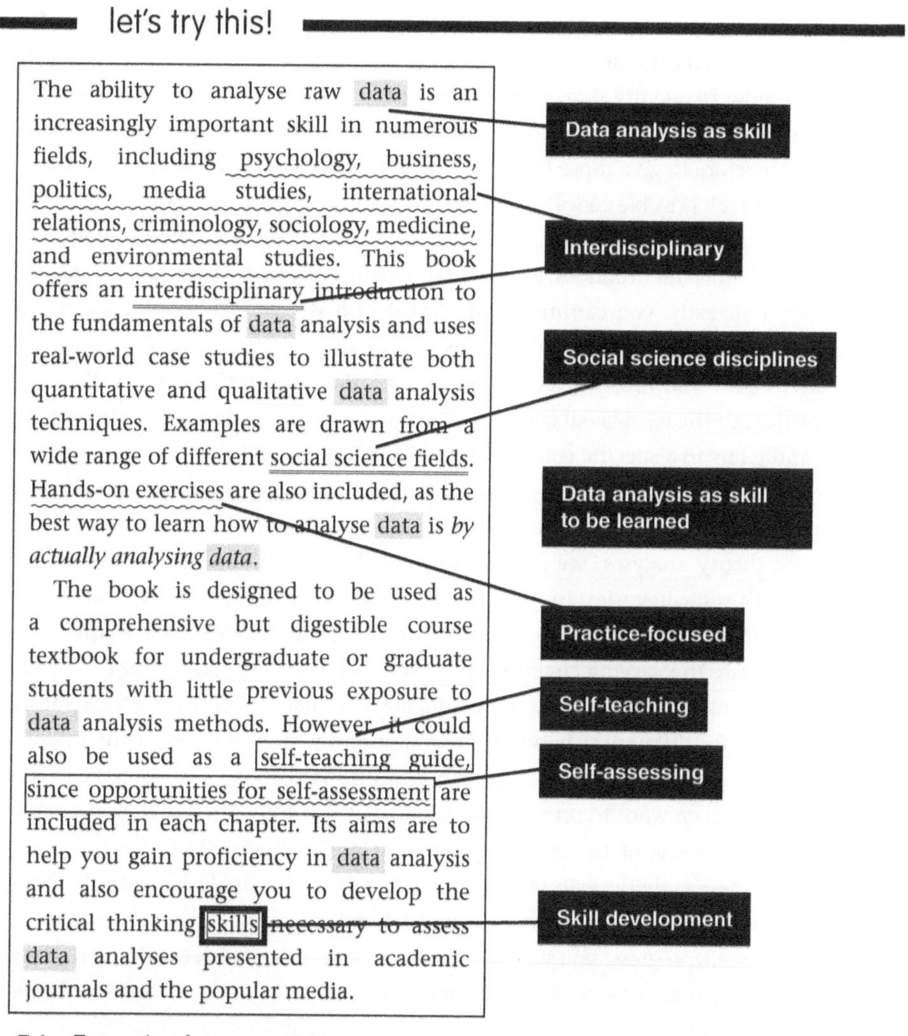

Figure 7.1 Example of open coding

(Continued)

What does open coding look like in practice? Figure 7.1 illustrates how open coding could be applied to a sample of text you're already familiar with: the opening paragraphs of the preface of this very book. Note that particular words and sentences are highlighted, and text boxes are used to emphasize particular themes. I didn't use any predetermined codes, as I had no previous research or theories to draw upon. Instead, all of the codes were spontaneous.

As you look at Figure 7.1, ask yourself whether you would code the text in the same way. What would your open coding efforts look like? (Remember that, although Figure 7.1 is printed in black and white, you could use different colours and highlights to further draw attention to important themes or language in the text.)

7.8.2 Axial coding (or continuing the coding process)

After a certain period of time, as you move through the data and generate a wide variety of different codes, you'll probably reach a point at which you want to start narrowing your focus and examining a few select themes in more detail. Perhaps you'll find that you've applied certain codes much more frequently than other codes, and you want to focus on these codes. Maybe some of your findings will seem particularly striking and relevant to your research questions, and you'll want therefore to give those findings more attention. Or, alternatively, you may feel that you've exhausted all possible codes and are ready to conclude the open coding process. Try to let this transition happen naturally; don't force yourself to move forward. However, you also need to be cognizant of time and deadlines, as you can't remain stuck in the open coding stage for ever.

Once you feel ready, you can move into **axial coding**, a stage in which you can begin to establish connections between the codes you've already identified, and collapse smaller or narrower codes into broader categories or codes (Strauss, 1987; Noaks & Wincup, 2004, p. 131). (Although the term 'axial coding' was originally developed in the context of grounded theory – and refers to a specific coding phase within a grounded theory analysis – note that I am applying the term more broadly here to include analyses conducted from other theoretical perspectives. For more information about how axial coding can specifically contribute to grounded theory analyses, see Strauss, 1987, p. 32.) In axial coding, your goal is to link 'categories with sub-categories' to probe how themes and findings in your data 'are related' (Charmaz, 2015, p. 71). You can also think about which codes appear most frequently in your data, and compare the varying circumstances under which those codes appear. (If you're having trouble starting this process of comparison, you can first try comparing 'extremes' in your dataset, looking for differences between the oldest and youngest respondents in your study, for example, before moving on to more subtle contrasts (Gibbs, 2007, p. 51)). During axial coding, you may even want to propose additional codes to show the full richness and breadth that exists within some of the codes you've already identified (Chambliss & Schutt, 2010, p. 273). All of these activities will set the foundations for your analysis, and will allow you to streamline your codes to focus on the themes that will constitute your final results.

To facilitate your progress, you will likely want to assemble a **codebook** – a well-organized written document that presents all your codes, explains how you've defined each code, and your criteria for applying each code to your data. The description should specify 'the boundaries of the code', giving information about 'what it includes' as well as 'what it doesn't include' (Bazeley, 2013, p. 230). A codebook helps the researcher recall the precise meaning of each code, a particularly important task for projects that involve a large amount of codes and that take place over a long period of time. A codebook can also instil greater consistency in the analysis process, ensuring that codes are defined and applied in the same way throughout the dataset.

let's try this!

What does axial coding look like in practice? Figure 7.2 uses the same sample of text examined in Figure 7.1: the opening paragraphs of the preface of this very book. After completing open coding, I moved on to axial coding. Figure 7.2 demonstrates how, during axial coding, codes can be combined, eliminated, or refined, and additional codes can be added. Identify how Figure 7.2 differs from Figure 7.1. What do these differences reveal about the differences between open coding and axial coding?

One key difference between Figure 7.1 and Figure 7.2 is the identification of additional themes, such as 'Undergraduate or graduate students'. During axial coding, you can take a second, in-depth look at your

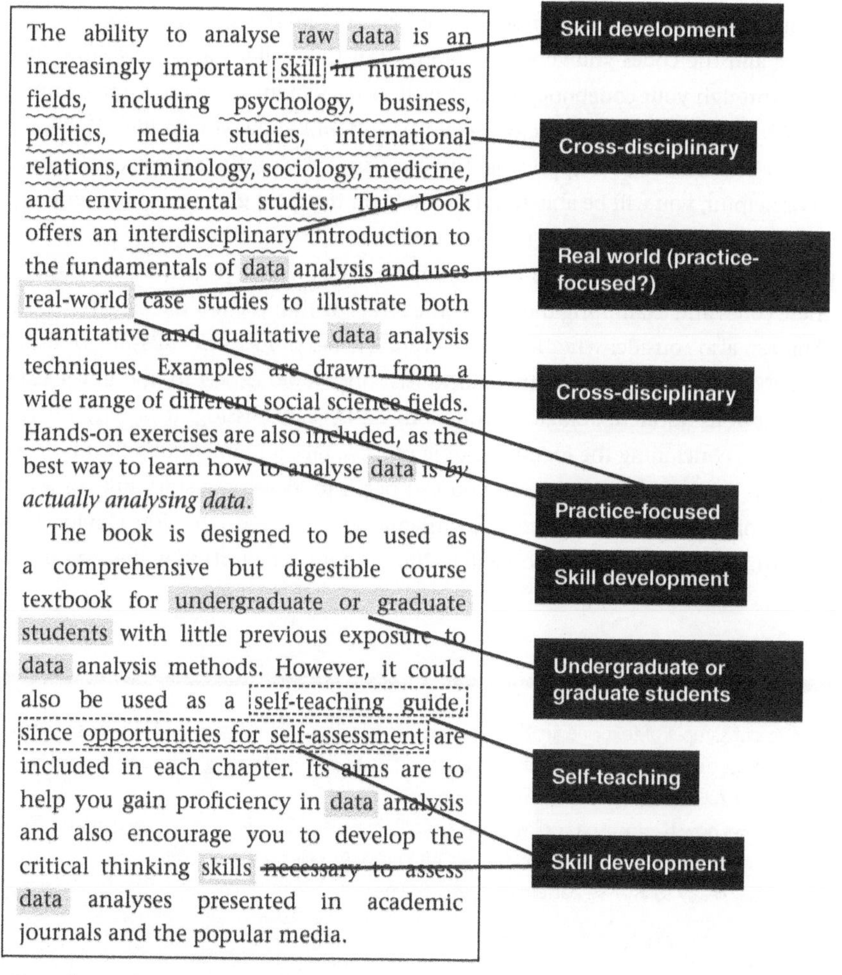

Figure 7.2 Example of axial coding

(Continued)

raw data, and may indeed identify additional themes not seen during the open coding process. A second key difference between the two figures is that some of the codes from Figure 7.1 have been renamed in Figure 7.2. For example, the codes 'Interdisciplinary' and 'Social science disciplines' in Figure 7.1 have both been renamed 'Cross-disciplinary' in Figure 7.2. This process of streamlining codes – identifying potential duplicate codes and establishing more uniformity in the names employed for your codes – is an important task as you progress through the coding process.

7.8.3 Focused coding (or concluding the coding process)

The final stage of the coding process has been given different names by researchers, including *theoretical coding* (Thornberg, 2012, p. 89) and *selective coding* (Strauss & Corbin, 1998).[1] We'll use the term **focused coding** here, since this stage involves narrowing the scope of analysis to focus on several key themes. Focused coding typically involves a close examination of your textual data and the codes you've already applied in the earlier stages of coding. (Be sure to take a look through your codebook again as well, since you may need to update your descriptions of each of your codes.) This close examination will allow you to identify which codes are the most useful and most applicable to your dataset. By culling those codes that are less relevant or helpful, you will be able to focus solely on the most germane codes (and, by extension, themes and findings) in your research (Marvasti, 2004, p. 87).

As you narrow your focus to the most germane codes, you can spend more time thinking about these codes and examining them in context (i.e., within the raw data itself) (Jensen, 1989, p. 99). You can also consider whether any relevant themes or ideas are 'missing' or 'invisible' in the data (Parkin, 2014, p. 102). Are there ideas that one would expect to find in the data (based on theory, previous research, or logical deduction), and yet are missing? If so, why are these ideas missing? Before concluding the focused coding process, take a moment to reflect holistically on your findings. Through such reflection you can begin to 'develop a story line' or an 'analytic thread that unites and integrates the major themes' in your research effort (Taylor, Bogdan, & DeVault, 2016, p. 181). Such reflection will facilitate your later efforts to write up your findings.

let's try this!

Let's return to our sample of text one final time to explore focused coding. Figure 7.3 illustrates how focused coding could be used to build upon our efforts during the open and axial coding phases. Compare Figure 7.3 to Figures 7.1 and 7.2. What's different in Figure 7.3?

Figure 7.3 shows how the focused coding phase typically includes a further streamlining of codes. Duplicate codes can be combined, and irrelevant codes can be culled. A well-executed focused coding process will leave a researcher ready to analyse patterns and key themes.

---

[1]Alternatively, focused coding and selective coding may also be viewed as separate processes, with selective coding understood as a more intense version of focused coding (for more information, see Monette et al., 2014, p. 434).

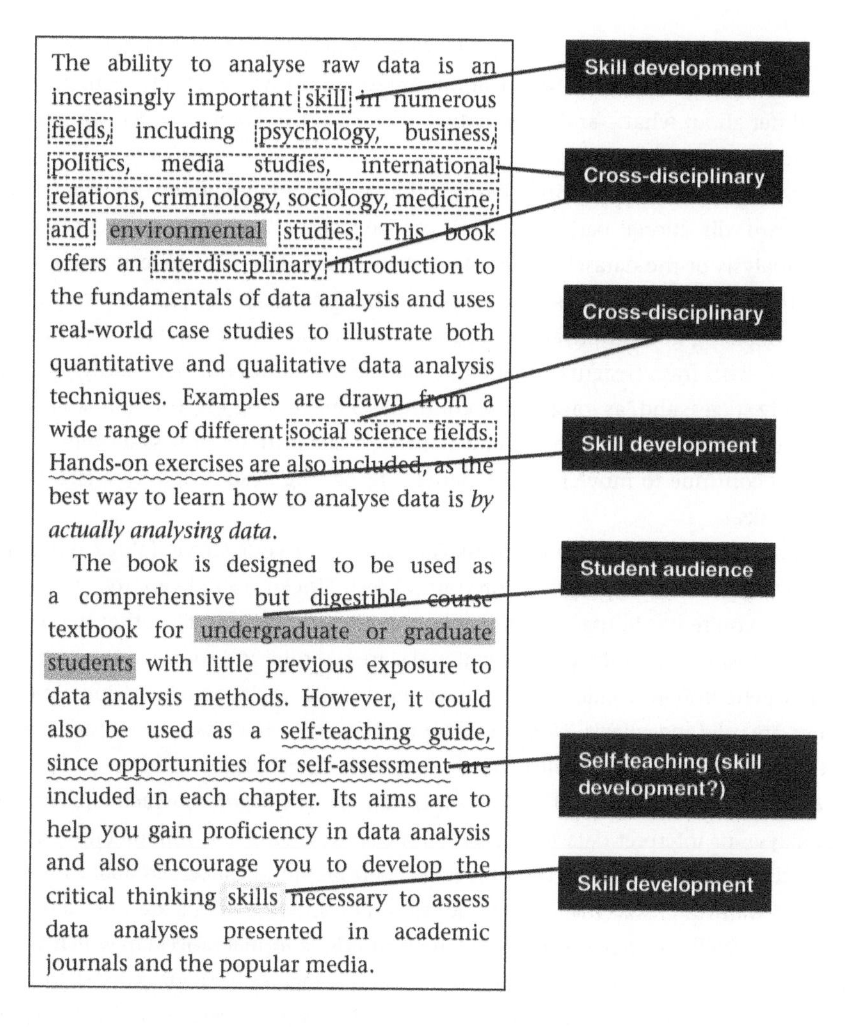

The ability to analyse raw data is an increasingly important skill in numerous fields, including psychology, business, politics, media studies, international relations, criminology, sociology, medicine, and environmental studies. This book offers an interdisciplinary introduction to the fundamentals of data analysis and uses real-world case studies to illustrate both quantitative and qualitative data analysis techniques. Examples are drawn from a wide range of different social science fields. Hands-on exercises are also included, as the best way to learn how to analyse data is *by actually analysing data*.

The book is designed to be used as a comprehensive but digestible course textbook for undergraduate or graduate students with little previous exposure to data analysis methods. However, it could also be used as a self-teaching guide, since opportunities for self-assessment are included in each chapter. Its aims are to help you gain proficiency in data analysis and also encourage you to develop the critical thinking skills necessary to assess data analyses presented in academic journals and the popular media.

Figure 7.3 Example of focused coding

7.9 Complexities in the Coding Process

Although the coding process typically moves through stages – we've identified the stages here as open, axial, and focused – it's important to keep in mind that these different stages can also 'blend together in a fluid process rather than into neatly separated activities' (Brower & Jeong, 2008, p. 828; see also Strauss and Corbin, 1998). In other words, it's not always clear where open coding ends and axial coding begins, or where axial coding ends and focused coding begins. You may begin the focused coding process, but then decide that you need to return to axial coding to identify more connections between your codes. Or you may make a preliminary identification of important themes during the open coding process, which you later return to. Such modifications to the three-stage coding process are all perfectly acceptable, as long as the reasons for the modifications are sound. As we've already seen, qualitative researchers differ about what – and how many – stages exist in coding, which illustrates the fluidity of the coding process.

It's also important to keep in mind that qualitative data analysis does not always follow a straightforward, directional path; instead, it can be 'cyclical', with the collection, organization, and analysis of the dataset taking place at the same time, and reflection continuing throughout the research process (Boeije, 2010, p. 89). Therefore, don't be concerned if you find yourself engaging in multiple activities at once, or if you sometimes revisit earlier stages of your analysis with fresh insights. Qualitative data analysis does not necessarily proceed in distinct, orderly stages, and, as long as you continue to make progress, this is not a cause for concern. (Of course, you need to be careful not to get stuck in an endless loop of analysis. Make sure you continue to move forward, perhaps by setting deadlines for yourself to complete certain tasks.)

Overall, the lesson here seems to be: think carefully about your methodological decisions, and make choices that are appropriate for your project. Since no single approach is suitable for all analyses, you're not limited by inflexible, constricting rules; on the other hand, you're responsible for ensuring that the choices you make are rigorous and sound.

Finally, researchers often wonder how to determine whether their coding decisions, and resultant findings, are *valid* and *reliable*. We saw in Chapter 2 that data analysts are interested in several different types of validity and reliability. One type is *inter-rater reliability* (Armstrong et al., 1997) or *inter-coder reliability* (Lombard et al., 2002), which captures the degree to which different scholars code, analyse, or interpret data in the same way. Since coding and interpretation are both deeply subjective activities, some qualitative researchers are quite concerned about inter-coder reliability, and want to ensure their coding decisions and interpretations are not idiosyncratic or overly unique. Such researchers can engage in *peer debrief*, a formal process in which a second qualitative data analyst separately examines the data and compares her coding decisions or findings with those of the original researcher (Burnard, Gill, Stewart, Treasure, & Chadwick, 2008, p. 431). Even if it's not feasible to ask another researcher to analyse *all* your data, it can still be worthwhile to ask another researcher to code a very small sample of your data, and then discuss coding choices and difficulties with you (Bazeley, 2013, p. 151). Such a discussion can prompt new discoveries and allow you to reflect further on your own coding process. If you're coding data for a thesis or dissertation, why not team up with another student who's also completing such coding work? By swapping small samples of your data, you can provide mini peer debriefs for each other (just make sure it's ethically acceptable to share your raw data).

7.10 Theoretical Memos

At every stage of the coding process, it can be helpful to create *theoretical memos*, or short, insightful notes about 'codes and relationships between codes, as well as questions' that deserve further attention (Thornberg, 2012, p. 89). Memos can serve an analytical purpose by allowing you to note ideas for codes that you may want to add later, and they can also serve a reflective purpose by allowing you to think about the overall progression of your coding and 'how the process of inquiry is taking shape' (Saldaña, 2016, p. 41). By creating memos, you can reflect on your own role within the research process and your own more informal reactions to the data you've collected. For collaborative projects, memos can facilitate communication among the different researchers (Taylor et al., 2016, p. 180). For solo projects, memos can help ensure that you don't forget any important insights.

Like coding, the memoing process can also evolve over the course of your research work. In the beginning stages of analysis, your memos might be broader and more exploratory, dealing with a wide range of ideas; in the later stages of analysis, your memos might 'take on a more focused character', bringing together 'previously separate pieces of data and analytic points' (Emerson, Fretz, & Shaw, 1995, p. 143). Such memos can help guide you as you formally write up your findings after you've completed your analysis. After all, as Richards (2005, p. 170) has observed, 'Writing is a way of running with an idea and trying it out'. Writing memos therefore allows you to reflect on, and clarify, your conclusions before you complete your coding efforts.

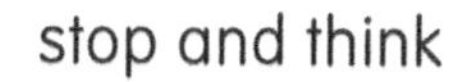

What are *theoretical memos*? How might a qualitative researcher use such memos during the coding process?

7.11 Coding with CAQDAS

Technological advances have substantially impacted qualitative data analysis, most notably by increasing the range of options available for completing the coding process. In the past, researchers could only code by hand. Data would need to be printed out or otherwise made available in paper form, and researchers would have to apply codes to the data with pen or pencil. Today, researchers can still choose to code by hand, or they can choose to use *computer-assisted qualitative data analysis software* (known by the cumbersome acronym **CAQDAS**). In certain cases, CAQDAS can greatly facilitate the analysis of qualitative data, saving a researcher much time and aggravation. In other cases, it might be more appropriate or easier to use the traditional method of coding by hand.

What are some of the specific advantages of CAQDAS? One advantage is that a researcher doesn't have to worry about arranging, organizing, and transporting a large number of paper documents, since all these documents can be uploaded into the software package and coding can be performed directly on the computer (Bhattacharya, 2015, p. 14). For datasets that consist of many sources, this can be an important practical benefit. A second advantage of CAQDAS is the ability to electronically search for particular words or excerpts of text to which the same code has been assigned (Chambliss & Schutt, 2010, p. 271). Although researchers can also perform such searches by hand, executing such searches electronically saves time and helps ensure accuracy. A third potential advantage is the ability to type out theoretical memos while coding, which can be saved and linked to relevant sections of the raw data (Tracy, 2013; Noble & Smith, 2014, p. 2). This feature can help the researcher recall the connections between the original data and his ideas or interpretations.

What are some disadvantages of CAQDAS? Perhaps the most prominent drawback of CAQDAS is that it can take a lot of time and effort to learn a new software package (Angrosino, 2007, p. 75). A researcher must be willing and able to fully commit to this learning process, as using a CAQDAS package you are not comfortable with can be counterproductive. Although not necessarily a disadvantage, it's also essential to recognize that CAQDAS is just a tool to facilitate your own analysis efforts; CAQDAS cannot conduct the analysis for you. Only a researcher can unpack the specific contextual and social meanings of language (Jensen, 1989, p. 99) and identify how findings uphold or contradict key theories. In other words, the most challenging parts of analysis – interpreting the data and assessing the significance of the results – can only be accomplished by a human brain. So although CAQDAS might make the analysis process easier, in the end, a given software package is only 'as good or as bad as the researcher using [it]' (Burnard et al., 2008, p. 430).

7.11.1 Selecting a CAQDAS package

If you do decide to use CAQDAS, think carefully about which software package you want to select. It's worth investigating the range of packages available to you before you start coding, so that you don't waste time and effort (and possibly money!) learning to use a package that doesn't suit your needs. A wide range of different CAQDAS packages exist, and each has its own advantages and disadvantages. Some are available free of charge, while others charge fees for different kinds of licences. To help you sort through the wide range of different CAQDAS packages out there (both free and not so free), Table 7.1 describes key features of many of the popular programs, based on the most up-to-date version of each program available at the time of writing. Many of these programs are updated regularly; before starting your project, it's a good idea to check whether any additional features have been added to the program you're interested in.

As Table 7.1 indicates, many different CAQDAS packages exist, and this list is by no means exhaustive. Although CAQDAS programs often incorporate similar features, each CAQDAS package has unique characteristics. To help you make a decision about which program best fits your research needs, it can be helpful to step back and consult some general sources about CAQDAS options. The University of Surrey (n.d.) maintains an excellent repository of reviews of popular CAQDAS packages, as well as guidance about using CAQDAS more generally.

Table 7.1 Characteristics of popular CAQDAS packages

Name	Characteristics	Find out more
ATLAS.ti 8	In addition to text (saved as .txt, .rtf, .doc, or .docx files), also supports PDFs, images, videos, and audio files 'Auto coding' feature can speed up the coding process by automatically applying particular codes to your data Lots of support is available to help you understand how to use the program, and can be accessed here: http://atlasti.com/support/ Not free, but your university may have access to it and discounted student licences are also available	Find out more at: http://atlasti.com/ Useful tutorials are also available at: http://guides.library.illinois.edu/c.php?g=347981&p=2345708
Coding Analysis Toolkit (CAT)	Free! Based entirely online, so no need to download new software (it works like a web browser) The web-based nature of the program makes it easy to collaborate remotely on projects, but may not be appropriate for data with enhanced security/privacy requirements Tutorials are available to help you understand how to use the program. Take a look at: http://www.screencast.com/t/pvzmAaz2 Currently only supports data files uploaded in the following formats: plain text; HTML; CAT XML; and merged ATLAS.ti coding	Find out more at: http://cat.texifter.com/ For more about the history of CAT and its development at the Qualitative Data Analysis Program at the University of Massachusetts Amherst, see: http://www.umass.edu/qdap/
Dedoose	Not free, but offers monthly pricing plans for individuals and groups Cloud-based, which facilitates collaboration, as multiple researchers can work on the same project at the same time Allows you to access your project on different devices Additional privacy and encryption services are available for projects that require enhanced data security Resources to help you familiarize yourself with the program include videos, a blog, and a user guide In addition to text, can also accomodate PDFs, videos, and audio files, as well as text in different languages	Find out more at: http://www.dedoose.com
f4analyse	Not free, but discounted 6-month licences available for students Webinars available to help you learn how to use the program Also works on iPad and Android Program's creators offer f4transkript, a tool to facilitate the transcription of interview data. See more information at: https://www.audiotranskription.de/english/f4.htm At the time of writing, not able to handle PDFs, audio files, or videos	Find out more at: https://www.audiotranskription.de/english/f4-analyse

(Continued)

Table 7.1 (Continued)

Name	Characteristics	Find out more
MAXQDA	Not free, but your university may have access to it, and discounted student licences are available for 6- or 24-month periods Can analyse text, as well as PDFs, audio files, and videos An app is available for iOS and Android Can analyse text in a wide variety of languages (in addition to English), including Spanish, Italian, Japanese, Russian, Turkish, and Czech Webinars and workshops available Researchers who do not have a MAXQDA licence can still view projects using the free MAXQDAReader program	Find out more at: http://www.maxqda.com/
NVivo	Can analyse text in several different languages (in addition to English), including Spanish, French, and Japanese Can analyse PDFs, videos, and audio files, in addition to text files Not free, but your university may have access to it, and discounted student licences are available Offers an internet browser plug-in that allows you to obtain (and then analyse) data from the internet In addition to free online training resources, webinars are also offered to help you familiarize yourself with the software, as described here: http://www.qsrinternational.com/nvivo-learning/free-nvivo-webinars	Find out more at: http://www.qsrinternational.com/ Kent State University Libraries (2018b) maintains a very informative webpage about NVivo, with numerous useful links to further information: http://libguides.library.kent.edu/statconsulting/NVivo
RQDA	In the 'Further Reading' section at the end of Chapter 5, we learned about R, an open source (i.e., free) software program widely used for advanced quantitative data analysis. RQDA is a package that can be added to analyse text-based data Like R, RQDA is free! Currently only able to analyse plain text files, but can analyse text in languages other than English Since the program is part of R, it's easy to switch back and forth between qualitative and quantitative analysis Instructional videos available on YouTube if you search for 'RQDA', or follow this link: https://www.youtube.com/watch?v=mLsyGH3ztYY	Find out more at: http://rqda.r-forge.r-project.org/

If you're currently enrolled at a university, investigate whether any CAQDAS programs are available in student computing labs. Some universities and departments even offer free or discounted software packages for students to use on their own laptops, so it may also be worth checking whether this option is available to you. If you're not able to access university resources and/or cannot afford to pay for software, don't worry – a number of free software options are also available. In addition to the free packages described in Table 7.1, a more extensive list of popular free CAQDAS packages has been compiled by the library at the University of Illinois at Urbana-Champaign (2015).

Finally, you may decide that none of these CAQDAS packages is right – and that CAQDAS in general is not appropriate for your project. That's absolutely fine! If you choose not to use CAQDAS and opt instead to code by hand, there are still practical measures you can take to facilitate or speed up your analysis. For example, if possible, print out textual data on paper with 'wide margins in which to record codes' and be sure to 'keep a clean copy of the original data, as a backup resource' (Bazeley, 2013, p. 133). The latter tip – keeping an extra copy of the unanalysed data – really applies to any data analysis effort, including quantitative projects.

7 12 Presenting Findings

Once you've completed the different phases of coding, you'll need to start writing up your results so you can finish your project! But how do you know if you're ready to move on? Hopefully, after several rounds of coding, you'll reach a point at which you've 'exhausted the themes/insights in the data and found that few new insights [are] emerging' (O'Dwyer, 2008, p. 401). For example, you may find yourself returning to the same text, but unable to add new codes. This moment should arrive naturally – you shouldn't have to push yourself to reach it – and, once you arrive at this point, it's appropriate to move on to the writing-up phase. But if this moment does not seem to arrive, or you feel unwilling to move on, assess the reasons for your reluctance. If you're reluctant because you think there's an additional theme or question that needs to be investigated, it may make sense to delay until you've completed that investigation. However, if you're reluctant because of a 'fear of failure' or concerns that your writing won't do justice to the richness of your analysis (Ely, Vinz, Anzul, & Downing, 1997, p. 12), then you do need to press through these fears and move on. Many researchers – even researchers with many years of experience – can feel uncertainty or self-doubt. Writing communicates your ideas to others, and thus exposes them to public critique. It's understandable, then, that many researchers can become reticent when confronted with the reality of putting their ideas down on paper. However, the best way to overcome this feeling is to ignore it and jump straight into the writing process. Remind yourself that there is no need to express yourself perfectly the first time; there will be plenty of opportunities for revision later. The most important task is to start writing.

And, if you think about it, you've probably started writing already! As Wolcott (2009, p. 9) has observed, 'The moment you generate sentences that *might* appear in your completed account, you have begun your writing'. So look back at memos and other notes you made during the data collection and analysis phases. Can any of this writing be adapted for inclusion in your first full draft? As we saw earlier in this chapter, memoing throughout the research process has many advantages; one advantage is that it can jump-start your formal writing efforts later on. Writing down your thoughts can help you unpack these thoughts and appreciate their complexities, allowing you to more easily shape them into coherent arguments as you move forward in the research process.

One of the most difficult aspects of writing up qualitative research is deciding which findings to report. Qualitative projects often produce a wealth of findings that far exceed the limited word counts allocated to journal articles or even dissertations. A researcher must therefore sift through his wide assortment of findings to focus only on those results that are most prominent, interesting, and relevant to his research questions. Although it's important to address unexpected findings, if new research questions occur to you now, think carefully about whether it's feasible to address them in your current project. If not, they might be the perfect starting point for a future study. (If you talk to a veteran researcher in your field, you'll probably discover that they do this all the time – construct plans for future studies based on ideas or questions they couldn't fully address in a past study.)

Once you've determined which findings are most essential to present, you'll need to consider how to best *interpret* these findings. Interpretation is a skill, an art, and a science combined into one, and is therefore rarely straightforward. As Feldman (1995, p. 2) has eloquently observed, 'Starting to create an interpretation is like trying to start a jigsaw puzzle that has a million indeterminate pieces' and 'no unique solution'. This does not mean that all solutions are equally accurate or helpful; you'll need to spend time thinking about your data and research questions to determine how to best interpret your findings. But there is rarely one 'perfect' interpretation, and it may be difficult to decide which interpretation is 'best'.

Remember, of course, that the most important goal is to truthfully represent the data, or accurately portray research participants' views (Noble & Smith, 2014, p. 2). After accuracy is achieved, however, there are further goals to also strive for. In particular, a qualitative researcher should develop 'coherent descriptions and explanations that still include all of the gaps, inconsistencies, and contradictions inherent in personal and social life' (Miles, Huberman, & Saldaña, 2014, p. 10). In other words, a researcher must present the findings in a clear and comprehensible manner without oversimplifying. This task will likely involve making generalizations, or identifying models that 'capture the key features of a given phenomenon' without getting lost in the phenomenon's nuances (Coffey & Atkinson, 1996, p. 143). But determining exactly how much generalization you should include can still be difficult and project-specific.

One strategy for jump-starting the interpretation and writing-up processes is to focus on certain important and thought-provoking codes. Are there any codes that are particularly prevalent in your data, or seem particularly important? As you review all your codes, ask yourself: Why did I choose to include this particular code? What's interesting about this code? What do I think about when I see this word, or this phrase, in context in my data? An insightful code can serve as the centrepiece for a narrative that can weave together the overall discussion of your results.

At this stage it can also be helpful to identify compelling cases, stories, or examples from your data that illustrate broader themes or findings (see discussion in Tracy, 2013). Searching for illustrative cases or stories can help you synthesize your results and develop a coherent understanding of your raw data. It's particularly important to identify such cases and stories if you're unable to recollect the *details* of different interviews, events, or documents (Richards, 2005, p. 172). By briefly narrowing your focus, you can regain your knowledge of these details and be more precise in your examination of your data.

There's no one correct method for reporting qualitative findings – which is perhaps not surprising given the diversity of qualitative analysis methods (O'Dwyer, 2008, p. 403). For example, while some qualitative researchers follow the quantitative practice of constructing separate Results and Discussion sections, other qualitative researchers effectively combine their Results and Discussion sections, to both report and analyse results at the same time (Burnard et al., 2008, p. 431). Qualitative articles that use textual data often feature numerous direct quotations from that data; on the other hand, tables, graphs, or other 'summary illustrations' are less common in qualitative articles, although they can certainly be included (Richards, 2005, p. 187). In Chapter 9 we'll explore visualization techniques that can be used with qualitative data.

Although we've focused on clearly and accurately presenting *findings*, it's equally important to clearly and accurately describe your *methods*. Readers need to understand exactly how you obtained, analysed, and interpreted your raw data. You must also be completely 'transparent' about your methods' limitations; such transparency is a central principle in research ethics (Noble & Smith, 2014, p. 2). No study is perfect, and acknowledging your study's limitations and weaknesses will strengthen – not diminish – your arguments.

Be transparent as well about your own role in the research process: what preconceptions, biases, or motivations did you bring to the data? When writing up qualitative research, feel free to acknowledge your part in the collection and interpretation of your data. Don't think that you need to write up your findings 'in the voice of the detached, objective researcher' (Hatch, 2002, p. 221). Qualitative papers don't need to mimic the impersonal, scientific style of quantitative papers. You can often use 'I' and the first-person voice. This acknowledgement is really a form of *reflexivity*, or an opportunity for you to consider how your own 'identity' has influenced the data collection and analysis processes (Banks, 2014, p. 296). In Chapter 3 we discussed the importance of maintaining a *reflexive* perspective in qualitative research, and the writing-up phase can be an opportunity to emphasize such reflexivity.

7.13 Concluding Thoughts

In this chapter we've covered many of the most fundamental activities of qualitative data analysis, including coding, memoing, and, ultimately, presenting your results. However, it's important to remember that 'thinking' may be the most important activity of all, as it's essential to continually reflect on your data, your codes, and your analysis (Boeije, 2010, p. 89). Don't underestimate the amount of time and mental energy you will need to devote to this process of reflection. Such reflection should take place throughout the data collection and analysis processes. Even after you've begun to write up your findings, you may still derive new insights by reflecting on your data.

Not surprisingly, this reflection – undertaken in parallel with your coding, analysis, and writing-up tasks – requires much mental energy. By the time you reach the writing-up stage, you will have been working, and reflecting, on your project for so long that it's essential to remember to take mental breaks. Even if deadlines are approaching, breaks are important – not only for your own good, but also for the good of the project. As Bazeley (2007, p. 179) has asserted, going for walks, talking to friends, or engaging in other relaxing endeavours 'will allow your brain to process the information that you've been absorbing' and even help you make new discoveries that you can investigate in more detail later. Taking breaks, and maintaining a full and active life outside of your research, will help you maintain a critical distance from your work and keep you from feeling overwhelmed in the intense final stages of the research process. Be kind to yourself!

One final point. If you're new to qualitative data analysis and you've just finished reading this chapter, don't worry if you feel a bit overwhelmed. We've covered a lot of ground, and qualitative data analysis, like many difficult skills, will get easier with practice. Indeed, as James (2012, p. 575) has observed, qualitative interpretation and analysis can't simply be taught; it's something you can only truly learn through first-hand experience. So don't be afraid to get started.

Summary

- Qualitative data is diverse, and interviews, documents, ethnographic field notes, and non-textual data each present their own analytical challenges.
- Codes can originate from two sources: they can be predetermined by the researcher (and based on theories, previous research, or hypotheses), or they can emerge spontaneously from the data itself.
- The coding process typically moves through several stages, with the researcher progressing from more flexible coding practices early on to more narrowly focused coding practices later.
- Coding – and qualitative data analysis more generally – does not necessarily proceed in distinct, orderly stages, and, as long as you continue to make progress, this is not a cause for concern.
- Theoretical memos allow the researcher to make notes about important questions or themes that emerge during the analysis process, and these memos can be revisited later to jump-start the writing process, and ensure that important insights are not forgotten.
- CAQDAS, or computer-assisted qualitative data analysis software, can facilitate the coding process, but may not be appropriate for all projects, and cannot conduct the analysis on its own.

- When writing up your findings, remember that the most important goal is to truthfully represent the data, and accurately describe your methods (and their limitations).
- Since qualitative research is diverse, there is no universal model for presenting qualitative findings. However, don't be afraid to be reflexive and acknowledge your own role in the research process.

Further Reading

A thorough overview of useful theories and techniques for conducting any analysis of document-based qualitative data, not just documents that come from the media, can be found in:

Altheide, D. L. (1996). *Qualitative media analysis*. Thousand Oaks, CA: SAGE Publications.

For a good overview of data collection and analysis issues for different types of qualitative research, as well as an examination of how different theoretical and historical traditions still impact current practices, see:

Scott, G., & Garner, R. (2013). *Doing qualitative research: Designs, methods, and techniques*. Boston: Pearson Education.

Saldaña, J. (2016). *The coding manual for qualitative researchers* (3rd ed.). Thousand Oaks, CA: SAGE Publications.

This provides a thorough introduction to different types of coding methods, and when to use them, with useful examples.

For an example of how coding can be used to analyse visual material in social science research, take a look at:

Parkin, S. (2014). *An applied visual sociology: Picturing harm reduction*. Farnham: Ashgate.

For a thorough exploration of the writing-up stage, see:

Wolcott, H. F. (2009). *Writing up qualitative research* (3rd ed.). Thousand Oaks, CA: SAGE Publications.

7.16 Discussion Questions

1 Define *open coding* in one or two sentences. Explain how *focused coding* differs from *open coding*.
2 In Section 7.8, we used a sample of text to try out *open coding*, *axial coding*, and *focused coding*. If you don't remember this discussion, take a look back at Figures 7.1–7.3. Now it's your turn: here

are some more samples of text from the preface to this textbook. As we did in Section 7.8, see if you can begin by open coding this text. Once you've done that, move on to axial coding and then focused coding. (If you own this book, feel free to mark the text directly; if you've borrowed or rented this book, make a paper copy of this text on a photocopier and code that paper instead.) The best way to learn how to code is to actually try the code for yourself!

Although quantitative data often seems to garner greater media attention, both quantitative and qualitative data analysis techniques are indispensable for understanding individuals and societies. Qualitative analysis can uncover nuances and complexities that could not be ascertained through quantitative techniques alone; similarly, quantitative analysis can detect patterns and relationships undetected in qualitative work. Although data analysts typically specialize in just one of these approaches, a working knowledge of both is required to fully engage with current developments in one's discipline. This book therefore explores quantitative approaches, qualitative approaches, and mixed-methods approaches (or approaches that draw upon both quantitative and qualitative methods). The theoretical background driving each of these approaches is discussed, and practical guidance is offered on when and how to implement these approaches. Finally, the limitations of quantitative, qualitative, and mixed-methods approaches are also each explored, since overconfidence in one's findings is a particularly alluring and dangerous temptation for many data analysts.

Any book of this kind must make a trade-off between breadth and depth. When dealing with a topic as expansive as data analysis, the implications of this trade-off are acute. For the textbook to remain manageable (and affordable!) for students, not all relevant material could be included. To decide which material to focus on, quantitative and qualitative breadth was privileged, with priority given to providing students with in-depth experience of actually *doing* data analysis. After reading this textbook, students should be able to interpret and critically evaluate the data analysis they encounter in everyday life, whether that be in the media, politicians' speeches, or the arguments of their lecturers. Students should also be able to embark on their own data analysis projects, using the basic and intermediate techniques for which detailed practical instruction is provided in the text. Students can then build on the knowledge acquired in this introduction for more advanced exploration of these and other techniques – a task facilitated by the further reading given at the end of each chapter. A key tenet of this book is that data analysis involves a particular way of thinking, a *rigorous attitude* that advances a rational and methodological approach to beliefs and questions about the world. Thus, although every specific data analysis technique cannot be covered in detail in this book, developing this *rigorous attitude* will equip students to more effectively explore additional data analysis methods on their own or in a more advanced course.

Data, in some form, is essential to all academic disciplines; acquiring data analysis skills has become an increasingly important component of university courses in a range of subjects. Since data analysis methods are often cross-disciplinary, this textbook is not aimed at a single discipline or subject-matter area. Indeed, advances in data analysis that are made in one discipline are often usefully applied to research in another discipline. The cross-disciplinary perspective of this book honours this intellectual cooperation and complements the recent rise of cross-disciplinarity in universities. In keeping with this approach, examples and case studies discussed in this text are taken from a diverse range of fields, particularly in the social sciences, and were chosen to interest a broad, general audience. Finally, it is important to note that, although the fundamentals of data analysis are not discipline-specific, each discipline does maintain unique conventions and customs – particularly regarding the selection of analytic techniques and the reporting of findings – which cannot always be discussed in detail in this book. Readers are therefore advised to seek out further information from colleagues in their discipline.

Figure 7.4 Open coding exercise

3. What are *theoretical memos*? Describe two ways in which writing theoretical memos can help a researcher.
4. What does the acronym CAQDAS stand for? What is one benefit of using CAQDAS to analyse qualitative data? What is one limitation of using CAQDAS to analyse qualitative data?
5. Imagine you want to use different coding techniques to analyse the photographs that appear on the front page of ten different national newspapers over the course of seven days. Think of at least three predetermined codes you think you might use. What criteria would you use for determining whether these codes apply to a particular image?
6. Find an article published in a leading academic journal in your field that uses qualitative methods. Compare that article to an article that uses quantitative methods. What differences in structure and style do you notice? What similarities do you notice?

Introducing Mixed Methods: How to Synthesize Quantitative and Qualitative Data Analysis Techniques

contents

 Chapter Overview

By the end of this chapter, you will be able to:

- Define what *mixed-methods* research is, and identify how it differs from exclusively quantitative and exclusively qualitative research approaches
- Appreciate how mixed-methods research can illuminate different features of a complex phenomenon, as shown by the real-world example of excess winter mortality
- Explain key rationales for using mixed methods, including *triangulation*, *illumination*, and *diversification*
- Discuss three popular approaches for applying mixed methods: the *parallel* approach; the *consecutive* approach; and the *mixed* approach
- Identify key limitations of using mixed methods, and why mixed methods may not be appropriate for all studies.

 What is Mixed-Methods Research?

As we've seen throughout this textbook, quantitative and qualitative methods each have their own advantages. One question that may have crossed your mind is whether it's possible to combine quantitative and qualitative techniques to take advantage of each technique's strengths. The short answer to this question is: yes! Research that uses both quantitative and qualitative methods is known as **mixed-methods research**, and it will be the focus of this chapter. We'll explore both the benefits and challenges of using mixed methods to collect and analyse data.

We discussed quantitative and qualitative methods in separate chapters in this textbook, emphasizing how these approaches differ from each other. Dividing quantitative methods from qualitative methods is the convention in many research methods courses and textbooks, and it reflects a larger methodological split that exists in every social science discipline. You've probably already encountered researchers in your field who *solely* utilize quantitative methods or *solely* utilize qualitative methods, or academic journals that specialize in just one type of methodology. The separation of data analysis techniques into quantitative methods and qualitative methods is a useful way of organizing a body of knowledge into something digestible, but separating the methods could further entrench opposition between quantitative and qualitative researchers (Silverman, 2010). This opposition means that, even today, some researchers presume that quantitative and qualitative methods cannot be harmoniously combined (Howe, 1988). As Duckett (2011, p. 173) has explained, a 'bifurcation' has arisen between quantitative and qualitative methods, and these two paradigms are often seen as competing theoretical and methodological paradigms. Yet, as we will see in this chapter, with careful consideration, these two methods can often be adroitly synthesized. Both quantitative and qualitative methods have advantages, and, by using mixed methods, a researcher can benefit from these advantages and bridge the quantitative–qualitative divide (Johnson & Onwuegbuzie, 2004, pp. 23–24).

Although traditionally not as popular as quantitative research or qualitative research, mixed-methods research has gained increasing prominence in the social sciences in recent decades, and is now widely recognized as a separate and equally important methodological paradigm (see the discussion in Teddlie & Tashakkori, 2009). In this chapter we will examine key rationales for using mixed methods, as well as real-world examples of how mixed-methods approaches have been used by other researchers. We will also outline some disadvantages of using mixed methods, and the practical issues that can arise when you try to synthesize quantitative and qualitative methods or findings.

The growing popularity of mixed methods means that, even if you don't anticipate using this approach in your own research, you'll likely come across mixed-methods studies conducted by other researchers. To assess the quality of these studies, it's essential to become familiar with this approach.

8.3 Why Use Both Quantitative and Qualitative Methods? The Example of Excess Winter Mortality

Let's start with the most basic question: why might a researcher want to use both quantitative and qualitative techniques? To answer this question, we can look at an example of a real-life research topic that has been explored through both quantitative and qualitative research: the problem of excess winter mortality. Excess winter mortality is often seen in countries with seasonal climates, and refers to the fact that more people die in the winter than in the summer (Carter, 2014). In England and Wales, for example, during the winter of 2014–2015, there were more than 43,000 'excess winter deaths', calculated by comparing how many deaths occurred during December–March against other time periods (Siddique, 2015). Similarly, in Northern Ireland, 'the number of deaths during December and January is 10% higher than the annualised daily figure' (Carter, 2014). Given such scale, it's clear that finding ways to reduce this excess mortality would have substantial benefits for society. But what strategies might be most effective? To answer this question, we need to investigate what factors *cause* and *exacerbate* (or worsen) the phenomenon.

stop and think

What factors do you think *cause* and *exacerbate* excess winter mortality? Convert your answer into a testable hypothesis. How might you test that hypothesis in a quantitative study? How might you explore that hypothesis in a qualitative study?

To identify the cause of excess winter mortality, it's helpful to first explore the phenomenon in more detail. For example, we should ask: are all groups in the population equally affected by this phenomenon, or are certain groups more affected than others? Not surprisingly, older age groups are disproportionately affected. As Pin et al.'s (2012) analysis of French data from 1998–2007 illustrates, the relationship between age and excess winter mortality can be detected through correlation, a statistical technique we introduced in Chapter 5. In particular, they found that individuals aged 76 and older were more likely to be affected by the phenomenon than younger people (Pin et al., 2012, p. 309.e4).

Knowing that the phenomenon primarily affects older people might lead us to suspect that *cold temperatures* are the cause of excess winter mortality, since cold temperatures are known to be associated with negative health consequences in this age group (see the discussion in Tod et al., 2012). However, the relationship between *consistently* cold temperatures and excess winter mortality may not be straightforward, since, on the whole, UK data reveals 'no overall correlation between a cold winter and a rise in excess winter mortality' (Carter, 2014). Instead, shorter periods of particularly cold temperatures might be more important, as demonstrated by another quantitative study of Shanghai. Ma et al. (2013) compared mortality rates during a period of cold temperatures with a similar period that did not feature cold temperatures; they found that the period of cold temperatures triggered 'a short-term increase in total mortality of 13%', and specifically a significant increase in deaths from cardiovascular-related causes. As one would expect, they found age to be significant, with individuals over the age of 65 most affected. Therefore it's important to consider the impact of *particularly cold periods* during the winter, in addition to the overall impact of the winter.

An additional question that may have occurred to you is: what about regional variations? Some areas of the world experience mild winters; other areas don't experience 'winter' at all. How do these climatic differences affect excess winter mortality rates? Healy (2003) explored this very question by examining data from a range of European countries using regression, a statistical technique related to correlation. Surprisingly, Healy found that the country with the greatest rate of winter mortality in his sample was Portugal, even though Portugal is a southern European country that experiences less severe winters than many northern European countries. At first glance, this finding seems to contradict our hypothesis that cold temperatures cause the excess mortality. However, Healy's analysis reveals a further interesting nuance: greater thermal efficiency in houses was associated with *lower* winter mortality. (Alternatively, one could state that thermal efficiency and winter mortality were *negatively correlated*. Recall from our discussion of correlation in Chapter 5 that a negative relationship between two variables means that as one variable increases, the other variable decreases.) So comparatively warmer countries, where residents have less need to adopt thermal efficiencies, can still be affected by cold temperatures and excess mortality.

Other studies have revealed the relationship between excess winter mortality and economic concerns. One study used a survey questionnaire and temperature monitoring in 50 disadvantaged households in Athens during the winter; the study found that many households were not able to maintain adequate heating (Santamouris et al., 2014). In Wales, researchers conducted semi-structured qualitative interviews with women in their 60s, 70s, and 80s (O'Neill, Jinks, & Squire, 2006). These interviews identified key themes, including the relationship between economic concerns and fuel poverty (or a lack of funds to heat one's residence). The same researchers then compared these qualitative results to findings from quantitative research, and showed how both research methods had discovered that older people sometimes sacrificed food consumption to pay for heating (O'Neill et al., 2006, p. 102). Another set of qualitative interviews conducted with older people in the UK found that the cost of heating was an important barrier, but surprisingly, other concerns were also important, including a lack of understanding about how heating systems functioned or how much heating actually cost (Allmark & Tod, 2013, pp. 112–113). As expected, the same interview-based study found that older individuals were often at elevated risk of winter mortality; however, some younger individuals (aged 50–60 years) were also found to be at increased risk, particularly if they were economically disadvantaged, suffered from physical or psychological challenges, lacked adequate information about relevant services, or 'were fiercely protective of their privacy' (Tod et al., 2012, p. 9). Once again, the use of a different research method (in-depth interviewing) allowed researchers to uncover more nuanced insight into this phenomenon.

Thus far we've focused on the role of cold temperatures in producing excess winter mortality. But is temperature the only potential cause of this phenomenon? Data analysts should never rush to a conclusion, but should instead carefully consider alternative explanations. (And now that you've made it to Chapter 8, you're obviously already starting to think like a data analyst!) So what alternative explanations, besides cold temperatures, could account for excess winter mortality? One possible explanation is seasonal influenza, which tends to peak during the winter months (Foster, 2014). Sadly, flu can sometimes be very dangerous and even deadly – particularly for elderly individuals or individuals with weakened immune systems. Around the world, at least 250,000 people die every year from the flu (Robson, 2015b). It's not surprising, then, that quantitative research has identified a link between seasonal flu and excess winter mortality. One study used statistical models to calculate the impact of particularly severe seasonal flu outbreaks on overall mortality rates in the USA, and found that just six flu epidemics during the 1970s and early 1980s produced 200,000 excess deaths, with upwards of 80% of these excess deaths occurring in individuals aged 65 and over (Lui & Kendal, 1987). Although vaccines against seasonal flu are available, their effectiveness can vary from year to year depending upon which specific strains of flu predominate; not surprisingly, less effective vaccines are associated with higher excess winter mortality (see, for example, Siddique, 2015). These findings about the seasonal flu highlight the difficulties of isolating *specific* causes of social phenomena; sometimes multiple causes might play a role.

Given these complexities, it's not surprising that researchers have used a range of different approaches to explore excess winter mortality. As the examples above illustrate, both quantitative and qualitative methods have been employed to identify the causes and characteristics of this phenomenon. Interestingly, quantitative methods have uncovered findings not apparent from qualitative methods, and qualitative methods have uncovered findings not apparent from quantitative methods. Although the vast majority of the studies we reviewed here were not, on their own, mixed-methods studies – in other words, they employed solely quantitative or solely qualitative methods – taken together, they demonstrate the power of using different methods to examine similar research questions. If an enterprising researcher *had* used mixed methods to explore excess winter mortality, that researcher might well have uncovered a broader range of findings than a researcher using one method alone.

Rationales for Using Mixed Methods

The excess winter mortality example illustrates the value of utilizing both quantitative and qualitative methods to examine the same phenomenon. However, to have such value, mixed-methods research should be a thoughtful, premeditated *synthesis* of qualitative and quantitative approaches rather than a hasty mishmash of different methods. In this section, we'll explore this theme in more detail, and look at three specific reasons why researchers might choose mixed methods. These reasons are: *triangulation*, *illumination*, and *diversification*. In this section we'll define what each of these terms means and explain how it relates to mixed-methods research.

8.4.1 Triangulation

The first popular reason for using mixed methods is *triangulation*, or exploring whether you obtain similar findings from both methods, to bring greater credence to those results. In other words, you want to ask yourself: do the results obtained from quantitative methods match the results from qualitative methods? In Chapter 2 we discussed the importance of triangulation to ensure the validity of your data analysis conclusions. If you end up uncovering similar findings in the quantitative and qualitative components of your analysis, this can help lend additional support to those findings; on the other hand, if your quantitative and qualitative results don't match, 'alternative, and likely more complex, explanations are generated' that may reveal previously hidden nuances of the phenomenon you are examining (Jick, 1979, p. 608). This phenomenon – a divergence or even contradiction between the findings of quantitative and qualitative research – is known as *discordance* (Fetters, Curry, & Creswell, 2013, p. 2144). Discordance is not necessarily a problem, or an indication of flaws in your methodology. However, if you encounter discordance in your own research, you should check once again that there are no errors in your methods or analysis. Assuming you don't find any errors, think carefully about other potential explanations for this discordance. What theories might explain these divergences? Social phenomena are complex and, as we saw with the example of excess winter mortality, they can feature multiple causes and characteristics. Discordance may simply be a sign that the phenomenon or society you are studying is multifaceted or characterized by contradictory forces.

Keep in mind that mixed methods is just one of many strategies for achieving triangulation. Depending on the features of your dataset and the goals of your study, you may also want to take additional steps to further increase triangulation. Other strategies for promoting triangulation include inviting additional researchers to analyse parts of your data, or employing multiple theoretical perspectives to analyse the same dataset (Noaks & Wincup, 2004, p. 8). Within a mixed-methods study, the triangulation of the qualitative component could be promoted by comparing your final conclusions against the initial conclusions present in your field notes, or by showing your final conclusions to your interviewees (or other research participants) to receive their input (e.g., Zammar et al., 2010, p. 2). Therefore, although one clear rationale for using mixed methods is to increase triangulation, don't assume that mixed methods is the only strategy for achieving this goal.

8.4.2 Illumination

A second key reason for employing mixed methods is **illumination**. What do I mean by illumination? Simply that a researcher can use findings obtained from qualitative research to inform (or illuminate) questions or themes to investigate in subsequent quantitative research, or vice versa. For example, through quantitative research, a data analyst might identify puzzling results or incongruities that can be explored in greater depth with qualitative methods (Hesse-Biber, 2010, p. 466). Alternatively, a researcher who has collected qualitative text-based data can apply codes to her dataset, and these codes can then be quantified (i.e., the researcher can count the frequency with which particular codes were applied during the coding process). Quantitative, statistical methods can then be used to analyse these counts, allowing the researcher to uncover broader, underlying patterns in the data (see, for example, Hodson, Chamberlain, Crowley, & Tope, 2011). The two examples discussed in this paragraph reveal that illumination can flow both ways: quantitative results can prompt new questions to consider with qualitative methods, and qualitative results can stimulate new ideas to test with quantitative methods.

Harrison and Reilly's (2011, p. 15) extensive review of mixed-methods studies in marketing research revealed the importance of illumination, finding that qualitative methods were often employed to inform future quantitative methodological choices, such as decisions about which variables to test in statistical models, which questions to ask in surveys, or which categories/classifications to apply to numerical data. Illumination has long been cited as a goal for mixed-methods research, with Greene, Caracelli, and Graham (1989) noting three decades ago that the results obtained through one method can help a researcher refine his use of the other method to examine the same issue.

8.4.3 Diversification

A final reason for utilizing mixed methods is to achieve **diversification**. By using both quantitative and qualitative methods, a researcher may uncover a broader and more diverse set of findings than could be found with one method type alone. Qualitative methods, for example, can be used to probe the nuances and ambiguities present in quantitative data, and thus convey a more comprehensive portrait of the phenomenon under consideration (Hesse-Biber, 2010, p. 466). In-depth qualitative analyses of particular cases within a quantitative dataset can also be used to explore the effects of different treatments, programmes, or variables (Mark & Henry, 2006, p. 327). A qualitative case study, in other words, can illustrate in more specific terms the broader findings revealed in a statistical analysis. On the other hand, quantitative methods (such as surveys) can be used to test whether the findings obtained from a focus group or interview-based study can be generalized to a larger population (see the example studies reviewed in Wisdom, Cavaleri, Onwuegbuzie, & Green, 2012). Since it can be difficult to study a large sample in in-depth qualitative research, quantitative research can be used to see whether similar findings are present in a larger or different sample. Additionally, quantitative research, with its emphasis on random samples, can also be used to make more definitive conclusions about cause-and-effect relationships that are hinted at in qualitative research (Powell, Mihalas, Onwuegbuzie, Suldo, & Daley, 2008, p. 305). In other words, the lack of randomization in many qualitative studies can impede efforts to *definitively* establish the causes of a particular phenomenon, but this shortcoming could potentially be overcome by conducting additional quantitative research on randomized samples. These are just a few specific suggestions of how quantitative and qualitative methods can be synthesized in practice to achieve the goal of diversification.

As we saw in the example of excess winter mortality, using a variety of quantitative and qualitative approaches can allow researchers to gain broader insight into a complex phenomenon. Quantitative and qualitative methods each have their own limitations, which we explored in previous chapters of this book. Using mixed methods, however, ensures that your analysis is not circumscribed by the limitations of one method. Instead, you can offset the drawbacks of one particular method with the benefits of the other method (Axinn & Pearce, 2006, p. 185); thus, through mixed methods, you can benefit from each method's respective advantages. (This ideal outcome can sometimes be difficult to achieve in practice, however, as we will see in Section 8.6.)

Table 8.1 Rationales for conducting mixed-methods research

Rationale	Definition	Hypothetical examples
Triangulation	A researcher employs mixed methods to confirm whether the findings obtained from different methods are similar, which would lend credence to the researcher's conclusions	Through qualitative research on a small sample, a researcher identifies particular themes. The researcher then administers a quantitative survey to a much larger sample to see if similar themes emerge, thereby reaffirming the original findings
Illumination	A researcher wants to use findings obtained from qualitative research to illuminate questions or approaches to use in subsequent quantitative research, or vice versa	Through quantitative research, a data analyst identifies particular themes or incongruities to be explored in greater depth with qualitative methods A researcher who has collected qualitative text-based data applies codes to her dataset. The frequency with which codes appear is quantified, and analysed with quantitative methods
Diversification	By using mixed methods, the researcher hopes to uncover a broader and more diverse set of findings than could be found with one method type alone	A researcher performs an in-depth qualitative analysis of particular cases or variables that were only broadly explored in a larger quantitative analysis A researcher identifies potentially interesting variables through qualitative research, and then uses quantitative methods on randomized samples to make cause-and-effect conclusions

stop and think

What is *diversification?* How does *diversification* differ from *triangulation?*

Table 8.1 presents a summary of the three rationales for using mixed methods that we've just explored. However, this list only includes the rationales that are most frequently described by mixed-methods researchers. Are there any additional rationales for using mixed methods that you can think of?

Types of Mixed-Methods Research

Once a researcher has decided to use mixed methods, she must then consider *how* exactly quantitative and qualitative methods should be combined in practice. There is no one answer to this question, and the best approach will, of course, depend on the researcher's goals and the characteristics of her data. The most popular approach in mixed-methods research is *parallel mixed data analysis*, in which a researcher conducts separate but parallel quantitative and qualitative investigations, with the findings of both investigations later synthesized and compared to draw broader conclusions (Teddlie & Tashakkori, 2009, p. 266). Parallel mixed data analysis can allow a researcher to meet the goals of *triangulation* and *diversification*, although *illumination* may prove more difficult to achieve since both methods are employed at the same time.

A second specific approach for combining qualitative and quantitative methods is to use each method *consecutively*. Rather than conducting the quantitative and qualitative analyses at the same time, one method is used first, and the results of that method are used to inform the application of the second method. For example, quantitative methods can be employed first to generate broad findings about a dataset; qualitative methods can then be used to follow up, or gain deeper insight into, themes or cases uncovered in the quantitative results (Harrison & Reilly, 2011, p. 16). One way of selecting cases for qualitative analysis is to identify 'extreme cases' in the quantitative results that feature particularly interesting or unexpected characteristics (Caracelli & Greene, 1993). Regardless of which specific methodological choices you make, this general methodological structure – in which each method is employed *consecutively* – would be particularly apt for achieving the goal of *illumination*. Employing the methods consecutively means that you can use the findings from the first method to encourage and shape your application of the second method.

A third specific approach to mixed-methods research is *inherently mixed data analysis* in which a researcher converts quantitative data into a qualitative format (or converts qualitative data to a quantitative format), so that both quantitative and qualitative data analysis techniques can be performed on the same set of data (Teddlie & Tashakkori, 2009, p. 273). For example, as described in our discussion of illumination in the previous section, the codes from a qualitative study can be quantified based upon the frequency with which they appear in the data; these frequencies can then be analysed with quantitative,

Table 8.2 Approaches to mixed-methods research

Name of approach	Description
Parallel approach	A researcher conducts separate but parallel quantitative and qualitative investigations, with the findings of both investigations later synthesized and compared to draw broader conclusions
Consecutive approach	Rather than conducting the quantitative and qualitative analyses at the same time, a researcher uses one method first, and the results of that method are used to inform the application of the second method
Mixed approach	A researcher converts quantitative data into a qualitative format (or converts qualitative data into a quantitative format), so that both quantitative and qualitative data analysis techniques can be performed on the same set of data

statistical methods (see, for example, Hodson et al., 2011; see also Caracelli & Greene, 1993). However, in practice, this process of quantifying a qualitative analysis can consume substantial time and money, and may even produce the perverse result that researchers 'reduce sample sizes or limit the time spent interviewing' to meet time or cost constraints (Driscoll, Appiah-Yeboah, Salib, & Rupert, 2007, p. 26). So be aware of these potential pitfalls if you select this approach.

The three general approaches outlined above – *parallel, consecutive*, and *mixed* – encompass the majority of mixed-methods designs that you are likely to come across (see Table 8.2 for a summary). However, beyond these broad suggestions, there are endless specific permutations of how quantitative and qualitative methods can be combined. If you want to use mixed methods, you will need to think carefully about the order in which you will conduct your analyses (will you conduct both analyses at the same time, or will you conduct one analysis first?) and whether you will give more attention and weight to one of the methods (or will you emphasize both methods equally?); see Powell et al. (2008, Table 1, p. 296) for a variety of options for prioritizing and ordering your quantitative and qualitative components. Ultimately, there is no one right answer to the question of how to best combine quantitative and qualitative approaches; instead, you will need to find the solution that best fits your dataset and research goals.

8.6 The Challenges of Crossing the Methodological Divide

In this chapter we've identified numerous advantages of mixed-methods research. So, by this point, you may be wondering: why don't all researchers use mixed methods? Why are so many studies still mono-method (i.e., based on either quantitative *or* qualitative methods)? These are sensible questions, and they don't have one single answer. However, some of the most prominent answers to these questions include: mixed-methods studies are not appropriate in all circumstances; mixed-methods studies have their own disadvantages and limitations; and mixed-methods studies can sometimes be difficult to conduct due to practical barriers. We'll explore each of these answers in this section to better understand why mixed methods may not always be the right choice.

stop and think

We've explored a range of rationales for using mixed methods. But can you think of an example in which it would *not* be appropriate to use mixed methods? Consider this question for a moment before moving on to the next paragraph.

The idea that mixed methods are not appropriate in all circumstances seems obvious: some datasets can only be explored with one method (quantitative *or* qualitative), and some research questions can only be explored through one theoretical framework. As we learned in Chapter 2, the most prominent theoretical paradigms in social science research are the *positivist* perspective and the *interpretivist* perspective. (Just to refresh your memory: while the positivist perspective holds that a physical, discoverable reality exists and can be investigated through thorough empirical research, the interpretivist perspective posits that numerous individualized realities exist and the aim of research should be to probe different individuals' interpretations of reality. If you can't recall these definitions, or want to know about these two perspectives, it's worth revisiting Chapter 2 now.) Although both theoretical frameworks have been used in quantitative and qualitative research, positivist perspectives have been more frequently applied to *quantitative* data and interpretivist perspectives have been more frequently applied to *qualitative* data (Merriman, 2009, p. 8; Gratton & Jones, 2010, p. 29–30). If you want to employ *both* quantitative and qualitative methods in your study, you need to think carefully about which theoretical framework you want your research to follow. Since the positivist and interpretivist theoretical perspectives spring from different philosophical orientations, don't assume you can seamlessly combine the approaches. Indeed, heedlessly throwing together different research methods that reflect incompatible theoretical paradigms can be problematic (Sale, Lohfeld, & Brazil, 2002), particularly if you fail to acknowledge differences between their associated positivist and interpretivist theoretical frameworks.

A second explanation for the limited use of mixed methods is that the mixed-methods approach has important limitations, despite its many strengths. One intriguing limitation is the possible *loss* of nuanced information that can occur when you employ both quantitative and qualitative methods. (I use the word 'intriguing' here because, as we've already seen, one potential benefit of using mixed methods is to uncover more nuanced findings that could not be found through one method alone. So, paradoxically, mixed methods can both increase and decrease your chances of discovering more nuanced findings! Data analysis is never easy, is it?) So why might the application of mixed methods cause you to *lose* nuanced information? As we saw earlier in this chapter, one of the most common ways of applying mixed methods is to *quantify* data obtained through *qualitative* methods, and apply statistical methods to this quantified data. (For example, a researcher might count the number of times a particular theme appeared in interview transcripts.) However, as critics of this approach have observed, 'reducing rich qualitative data to dichotomous variables renders them single dimensional' (Driscoll et al., 2007, p. 25). In other words, the important complexities of qualitative data can be lost in the drive to quantify such data for mixed-methods research. For instance, trying to quantify a concept like 'happiness' or 'well-being' might not fully capture the diversity and complexity of either of these concepts; such diversity and complexity might only emerge in qualitative analysis. Of course, a potential remedy for this problem might be to apply *both* quantitative and qualitative methods to that same sample of qualitative data to ensure that the nuances lost to quantification are still discovered. However, such a remedy would pose additional difficulties, as quantitative and qualitative methods often rely on different *kinds* of samples. Quantitative studies typically employ larger samples than qualitative studies, as it would be impossible to perform detailed, thorough qualitative research on a very large sample; additionally, while *random* samples are necessary for many quantitative studies, many qualitative studies do not feature fully random samples (Morse & Niehaus, 2009, p. 119). Therefore, although the use of the same sample for both quantitative and qualitative analyses might increase the triangulation of one's findings, such an approach may not always be appropriate.

A third and final reason why researchers might not use mixed-methods studies is the presence of *practical barriers*. To complete a mixed-methods study, a data analyst must obtain diverse methodological knowledge. As we've seen in previous chapters, quantitative and qualitative methods each require different kinds of skills and expertise. Developing knowledge and experience about *one* method is difficult enough; developing such knowledge about *both* methods is even more challenging. As Hollstein (2014, p. 21) has observed, producing high-quality mixed-methods studies requires substantial skill and dedication, since a researcher must 'apply both approaches at equally high levels of sophistication' and synthesize those approaches into a set of coherent results. For example, suppose a mixed-methods researcher is interested in examining the attitudes and motivations of newly qualified science teachers. He plans to conduct a large-scale quantitative survey and in-depth qualitative interviews with a smaller sample of teachers. In order to conduct this study, he needs to develop methodological expertise in both qualitative interviewing and in quantitative survey design and analysis. Both of these skills require a significant time investment. However, even after mastering both of these skills, the researcher must then cultivate the additional skill of *synthesizing* – and making sense of – the results discovered through both methods. Unfortunately, many researchers do not have the time or ability to develop all of these skills. Therefore, this simple, practical barrier – lack of knowledge about both methods and the ability to integrate results – has likely impeded the growth of mixed methods in the social sciences.

However, don't let this discussion of the difficulties of mixed methods discourage you, if you're interested in using such methods in your own work. The fact that you've arrived at this point in the book means you've already developed substantial knowledge about *both* quantitative and qualitative methods. So you're well on your way to acquiring the skills necessary for mixed-methods work.

A dearth of knowledge is not the only practical barrier that has impeded the use of mixed methods. A lack of time or funding can also make it difficult to apply mixed methods. Due to their complexity and multiple components, mixed-methods studies can demand more time and money from researchers than single-method projects (Hollstein, 2014, p. 21). Due to time or funding constraints, some researchers may only be able to use one method, even if they have the skills to use both methods.

Other practical barriers can arise when mixed-methods researchers try to communicate or publish their findings. As Wisdom et al. (2012) have noted, it can be challenging for a mixed-methods researcher to convey her findings to an audience that is solely versed in either quantitative or qualitative techniques, and it may even be difficult to locate 'appropriate publishing outlets with reviewers who have expertise in mixed methods research techniques'. Although interest in mixed-methods social science research has grown substantially in recent years, familiarity with mixed-methods approaches still varies across subdisciplines, and some academic journals specialize in publishing studies using one type of method (i.e., quantitative *or* qualitative) rather than studies using the other type of method or mixed-methods studies. Since decisions about which methods to use are influenced by a range of factors – including individual preferences, disciplinary norms, and 'the influence of peers' (Denscombe, 2008, p. 279) – these practical barriers may also impede the use of mixed methods. However, as we saw at the beginning of this chapter, mixed methods have gained increasing recognition in recent years, so *don't let these practical barriers discourage you.* Many leading social science journals regularly publish mixed-methods work, and some journals even specialize in mixed-methods studies. (For more information about one of these journals, take a look at the 'Further Reading' section at the end of this chapter.) So, if you decide that it is theoretically appropriate and methodologically feasible to use mixed methods in your own work, don't let concerns about publishing your work deter you.

8.7 Examples from Across the Disciplines

Now that we've assessed the potential benefits and limitations of mixed-methods research, it's time to look at some real-world examples of recent mixed-methods work. How have researchers actually combined quantitative and qualitative methods in practice? What can we learn from their experiences?

We'll explore four different mixed-methods studies, all published in 2017, from four different disciplines: public health, criminology/law, labour and economics, and development studies. The studies also focus on four different countries – the UK, Hong Kong, South Africa, and Pakistan – further highlighting the broad applicability of mixed methods.

8.7.1 Example study 1: Alcohol regulations in England and Scotland

Li et al. (2017) investigated public attitudes towards alcohol regulations in Scotland and England. The quantitative component of their study consisted of a telephone survey of 3477 respondents. The qualitative component of their study included discussions with 16 different focus groups (featuring 89 participants in total). The results of the survey were analysed with statistical methods, and these results informed the themes to be explored in the focus groups. While the surveys found that women, older respondents, and more moderate drinkers were more likely to support alcohol regulations, the focus groups revealed the importance of whether a respondent thought a policy would be *effective* at reducing harms related to alcohol.

What can we learn about mixed methods from Li et al.'s work? First, their study reinforces the same theme we first identified at the very beginning of this chapter in our exploration of excess winter mortality: mixed methods can reveal more complex or nuanced findings that could not be uncovered through the use of one method on its own. This advantage can be particularly important when you are exploring a complex concept like public attitudes. Li et al.'s work also follows the traditional pattern of utilizing a larger sample for the quantitative component but exploring a smaller sample in greater depth in the qualitative component. The study also reveals the importance of *illumination* as a rationale for using mixed methods, since findings from the study's quantitative component were used to inform the qualitative component.

Full citation of study: Li, J., Lovatt, M., Eadie, D., Dobbie, F., Meier, P., Holmes, J., Hastings, G., & MacKintosh, A. M. (2017). Public attitudes towards alcohol control policies in Scotland and England: Results from a mixed-methods study. *Social Science & Medicine*, *177*, 177–189.

let's try this!

Take a moment to search for Li et al.'s (2017) article online. (At the time of writing, the article was open access, or freely available on the internet.) After reading through the article, do you think it uses a *parallel* approach, a *consecutive* approach, or a *mixed* approach to mixed methods? Why? (If you can't remember the differences among the three approaches, take a moment to revisit Section 8.5 above.)

8.7.2 Example study 2: Young offenders in Hong Kong

Chui and Cheng (2017) were interested in young offenders' attitudes to their legal representation in Hong Kong's justice system. Did young offenders feel their lawyers treated them fairly and respectfully? In the quantitative component of their study, Chui and Cheng administered a survey to a sample of 168 young offenders. After conducting statistical analyses on the results of their survey, Chui and Cheng were able to conclude that juvenile offenders with privately hired lawyers expressed greater satisfaction with their treatment than juvenile offenders with publicly provided lawyers. In the qualitative component of their study, Chui and Cheng undertook in-depth interviews with 30 young offenders. These interviews revealed that publicly provided lawyers' time constraints could explain some of the dissatisfaction expressed by the survey respondents.

As with example study 1, Chui and Cheng's work also highlights the ability of mixed methods to reveal findings that could not be discovered through the use of just one method. The study is also an example of how the same sample – or a subset of the same sample – can be used in both quantitative and qualitative analyses, as the interviewees for the qualitative component of Chui and Cheng's (2017, p. 276) work were chosen from among the quantitative survey respondents, with 'purposive sampling' employed to make certain 'that youths who had hired private lawyers and those who had used public lawyers would both be represented' among the interviewees, since the quantitative survey indicated differences in the attitudes of the two groups. Their work also demonstrates the importance of carefully considering sampling strategies to ensure that you select the strategy most appropriate for your research goals.

Full citation of study: Chui, W. H., & Cheng, K. K.-Y. (2017). Perceptions of fairness and satisfaction in lawyer–client interactions among young offenders in Hong Kong. *Journal of Mixed Methods Research, 11*(2), 266–285.

stop and think

Based on the summary of Chui and Cheng's (2017) article given above, why do you think the researchers decided to use mixed methods? Does this study reflect any of the three rationales – triangulation, illumination, or diversification – that we discussed earlier in this chapter?

8.7.3 Example study 3: Unemployment in South Africa

Wilkinson et al. (2017) explored unemployment among young adults (aged 18–24) in rural South Africa. As with example studies 1 and 2, once again the quantitative component of this study consisted of a survey (featuring 187 respondents). Survey results indicated that men were more likely to be employed than women, and that manual labour was the most common type of employment. Wilkinson et al. (2017) then conducted interviews with 14 of the survey respondents; the interviews revealed the interesting finding that women were often seen as 'more suitable for formal employment', but, since formal employment opportunities were 'scarce', counterintuitively, 'women were more likely to pursue further education and yet less likely to be employed' (p. 17). This study is an excellent example of a theme we discussed at the beginning of this chapter: how mixed methods can result in *diversification* – obtaining a broader understanding of a phenomenon's different components.

Full citation of study: Wilkinson, A., Pettifor, A., Rosenberg, M., Halpern, C. T., Thirumurthy, H., Collinson, M. A., & Kahn, K. (2017). The employment environment for youth in rural South Africa: A mixed-methods study. *Development Southern Africa, 34*(1), 17–32.

stop and think

Based on the summary of Wilkinson et al.'s (2017) study given above, would you say the study uses a *parallel* approach, a *consecutive* approach, or a *mixed* approach to mixed methods? Why?

8.7.4 Example study 4: Child nutrition in Pakistan

Kureishy et al. (2017) isn't a completed study; instead, it's a study protocol, or a thorough description of the methods the researchers are planning to use to conduct a study in the near future. Kureishy et al. are interested in how most effectively to reduce malnutrition in children in several geographical districts in Pakistan. They will conduct surveys, a randomized controlled trial (or experiment), interviews, and focus group meetings. This combination shows that many different types of quantitative and qualitative methods can be used together; however, studies with so many different components can require significant time and resources. Kureishy et al.'s (2017) article is an example of a large-scale, multi-year, team-based, mixed-methods research project to explore a critical issue.

Full citation of study: Kureishy, S., Khan, G. N., Arrif, S., Ashraf, K., Cespedes, A., Habib, M. A., Hussain, I., Ullah, A., Turab, A., Ahmed, I., Zaidi, S., & Soofi, S. B. (2017). A mixed methods study to assess the effectiveness of food-based interventions to prevent stunting among children under-five years in Districts Thatta and Sujawal, Sindh Province, Pakistan: Study protocol. *BMC Public Health, 17*, 24. DOI 10.1186/s12889-016-3976-y

let's try this!

Take a moment to search for Kureishy et al.'s (2017) article online. (At the time of writing, the article was open access, or freely available on the internet.) After reading through the article, imagine that you have been asked to review this proposal. What challenges do you think the researchers are likely to encounter as they complete their mixed-methods study?

8.8 Concluding Thoughts

In this chapter we've explored the value of mixed-methods research in the social sciences. As Kelle (2006, p. 293) has argued, such research can promote 'the mutual validation of data and findings' as well as reveal a more comprehensive and intricate portrait of a phenomenon than quantitative or qualitative research on its own. However, mixed-methods work also has important limitations, as we've discussed, and it would be a mistake to assume that it is *always* richer than mono-method research, or that a solely quantitative or solely qualitative study is somehow incomplete (Sandelowski, 2000, p. 254). Similarly, a researcher shouldn't presume that the strengths of a second method automatically offset or compensate for deficiencies present in the first method (Jick, 1979, p. 604). In other words, a mixed-methods approach will not allow you to conceal deficiencies in your quantitative or qualitative methods. Indeed, the quality of a mixed-methods study is entirely dependent upon the underlying rigour of its quantitative and qualitative components.

If you decide to use mixed methods, it's important to carefully consider your reasons for doing so, and to articulate these reasons clearly. Shockingly, in an analysis of over 230 social science journal articles that used mixed methods, Bryman (2006, p. 107) found that authors *did not* articulate a rationale for using mixed methods in a quarter of the articles! In addition to always articulating your own reasons for using mixed methods, Bryman (2006, p. 98) also advises thinking carefully about other researchers' rationales for using mixed methods whenever you read or review mixed-methods studies. Such reflection will help you assess the methodological soundness and rigour of other work in your discipline.

The present is an exciting time for mixed-methods researchers. As mixed methods have gained increasing prominence, such research is no longer viewed 'as a clumsy stitching together of two incompatible systems but as a genesis of a "third paradigm"' (Duckett, 2011, p. 173). Although not suitable for every study or research question, as a savvy data analyst, it's advantageous to add knowledge of this approach to your methodological toolkit.

8.9 Summary

- Mixed-methods research, which draws on quantitative and qualitative methods, has many advantages, and key reasons for employing mixed methods in the social sciences include *triangulation* (using the results from one method to confirm the results from the other method), *illumination* (using the results from one method to inspire new questions to investigate with the other method), and *diversification* (using one method to investigate additional aspects of a phenomenon that cannot be investigated using the other method alone).
- A *parallel* approach is perhaps the most common mixed-methods design, and involves a researcher conducting separate but parallel quantitative and qualitative investigations, with the findings of both investigations later synthesized.
- A *consecutive* approach to mixed-methods research involves a researcher using one method first, and then applying the results of that method to inform the application of the second method.
- A *mixed* approach involves a researcher converting quantitative data into a qualitative format (or converting qualitative data into a quantitative format), so that both quantitative and qualitative data analysis techniques can be performed on the same set of data.
- Researchers may decide *not* to use mixed methods for a number of reasons, including: mixed-methods studies are not appropriate in all circumstances; mixed-methods studies have their own disadvantages and limitations; and mixed-methods studies can sometimes be difficult to conduct due to practical barriers.
- When conducting mixed-methods research, think carefully about your *reasons* for using mixed methods and articulate these reasons clearly in your paper/article/dissertation. When reading mixed-methods studies by other researchers, reflect on their rationales for employing this method.

8.10 Further Reading

For an informative general overview of mixed-methods research and its potential benefits, see:

Johnson, R. B., & Onwuegbuzie, A. J. (2004). Mixed methods research: A research paradigm whose time has come. *Educational Researcher, 33*(7), 14–26.

For a more detailed exploration of the different types of mixed-methods approaches and how to effectively bring together quantitative and qualitative methods, see:

Teddlie, C., & Tashakkori, A. (2009). *Foundations of mixed methods research: Integrating quantitative and qualitative approaches in the social and behavioral sciences.* Thousand Oaks, CA: SAGE Publications.

The Library at the University of California San Francisco maintains a helpful website with links to various mixed-methods resources. It's a great place to start a deeper investigation of this research tradition. The address is: http://guides.ucsf.edu/c.php?g=100971&p=655231

We saw in this chapter that some social science academic journals have begun to specialize in mixed-methods research. The most prominent of such journals is the *Journal of Mixed Methods Research*, and it's worth taking a look at some sample issues of this journal to gain insight into current issues and trends in mixed-methods research. (However, remember that, if you produce a mixed-methods study, you don't *have* to submit it to a journal that specializes in mixed methods. Many generalist academic journals are increasingly willing to publish mixed-methods studies, so you have wide options.)

Finally, see if you can find at least one or two of the example articles discussed above for guidance about how mixed methods can be used in practice.

Discussion Questions

1. Describe the *parallel* approach to mixed-methods research, and explain in one or two sentences how it differs from the *consecutive* approach.
2. What is one limitation or disadvantage of using a mixed-methods approach?
3. In this chapter we discussed Bryman's (2006, p. 107) review of over 230 social science journal articles that used mixed methods. Surprisingly, Bryman found that, in a quarter of the articles, authors *did not* articulate a rationale for using mixed methods. Why might this be?
4. Take a look at the summaries of the four example studies we discussed in Section 8.7. What similarities do you notice among the studies' research methods? What differences do you notice?
5. Revisit the discussion of *excess winter mortality* in Section 8.3. Imagine that you've been asked to construct a mixed-methods study into excess winter mortality in your home country. What kind(s) of quantitative and qualitative methods would you use? Take a few minutes to briefly summarize the components of your hypothetical study, following the format of the summaries of the four mixed-methods example studies given in Section 8.7.

Communicating Findings and Visualizing Data

contents

Chapter Overview

By the end of this chapter, you will be able to:

- Identify essential principles to follow when communicating your findings
- Discuss the importance of thinking about your *audience* when deciding how to present your results
- Describe numerous methods for visualizing data, including *tables*, *bar charts*, *word clouds*, and *network maps*
- Assess the strengths and limitations of these different data visualization methods, and outline the particular types of data that are most appropriate for each method
- Identify key guidelines for creating data visualizations, such as presenting data and findings *clearly* and being *ethical* in your visualization efforts
- Explain what future developments in the field of data visualization might look like
- Describe two key examples of real-world interactive data displays.

Wait... We're Not Done Yet?

Congratulations! You've formulated your research questions, identified hypotheses, considered ethical issues, collected your data, analysed your data, and interpreted your findings. In other words, you've completed all the difficult steps. But there's still one important (and maybe even fun?) step left: sharing your findings with the world.

You've invested your time and energy in your research project, and your findings merit attention. They deserve to be noticed by other researchers, policy-makers, and even the public at large. But in order to ensure that your findings *do* receive attention, you'll need to think about how to *communicate* them. In making this decision, you'll have to consider how to *accurately* represent your findings in a way that your *audience will understand*.

This task – how to effectively communicate your results to other scholars and to the broader public – is the focus of this chapter. We'll take a look at the different challenges that can arise when reporting quantitative, qualitative, and mixed-methods findings. We'll explore the ever-growing field of 'data visualization', and look in detail at different techniques for visually displaying your results in graphs, charts, word clouds, maps, and other forms of imagery. We'll discuss how to present results in academic outlets such as journals or dissertations, as well as in more popular outlets such as talks for the general public. We'll also identify key questions that you should ask when examining – and critiquing – other researchers' findings. So let's get started!

Communicating Findings: General Principles

Before we investigate the specific challenges that can emerge when communicating quantitative, qualitative, and mixed-methods findings, it's helpful to first explore some general principles that apply across the board. Some of these principles seem obvious, but a surprisingly large number of studies overlook at least one of these principles. So it's worth considering each of them in detail.

The first principle, of course, is to present your results *accurately*. Don't exaggerate your findings or misrepresent what you've found. Accurately and transparently reporting your results is a key component of ethical research practice.

The second principle is to make sure your audience can *understand* your findings. Are your results presented in a clear and straightforward manner? Do you use a vocabulary that is appropriate for your particular audience? To achieve this principle, you will need to think carefully about the characteristics of your audience. Is your audience composed solely of scholars from your specific subfield, or do you intend to present your results to policy-makers and the general public? Depending on how you answer this question, you will need to use different language to communicate your results. Don't assume that 'sophisticated' academic language always sounds better; expert vocabulary may not be appropriate if readers are not experts. Later in this chapter we will return to this principle and will explore some specific recommendations for interacting with different kinds of audiences.

A third principle to keep in mind is to make sure that you don't *overstate* your results, or force your conclusions to fit into an inappropriate theoretical framework. This principle is related to the first principle we discussed – the need to present results accurately – but is not identical. While deliberately misrepresenting one's results involves *intent*, making overly ambitious conclusions or applying inappropriate theoretical frameworks can be *accidental*. You may not realize you are doing it, and that's why it's so important to be cognizant of this principle. Asking a fellow student or mentor to review your writing can be helpful for many reasons; one reason is to get confirmation from another scholar that your arguments and conclusions are supported by your data.

A fourth principle is to recognize, and fully describe, the limitations of your methods, to help readers appreciate your results. Throughout this book we've seen how this principle is central to upholding research ethics, and becoming a responsible, professional data analyst. Every research project has limitations, and recognizing those limitations will increase – not decrease – other researchers' respect for your work.

In order to describe your limitations, you will also need to thoroughly describe your methods. This fifth and final principle – the need to include a complete description of methods – is known as *descriptive validity* (Perry, 2010). (As we saw in Chapter 2, *descriptive validity* is gaining increasing attention among data analysts and is now considered by some researchers to be one of the most important determinants of a study's rigour and quality (Farrington, 2003, p. 61).) Descriptive validity encompasses more than just accurately describing the steps in one's research process; it also requires a researcher to acknowledge a study's methodological limitations *and* describe the population/sample studied in the research (Gill, 2011, p. 203). All of this information is essential for other researchers to determine the value and applicability of your findings.

let's try this!

In Chapter 8, we explored Li et al.'s (2017) mixed-methods study of public opinion about alcohol regulations in England and Wales. If you didn't already look up that study, take a moment to do so now.

(Continued)

Look closely at how the study's authors describe their research methods. Do you think their description is thorough, or do you think further details should have been included? Do you feel that enough information was provided to allow other researchers to replicate the study's methods? Based on your answers to these questions, do you think the study exhibits adequate *descriptive validity*?

9.4 Think about Your Audience(s)

Thinking about your intended audience is one of the most important principles in data communication (Balnaves & Caputi, 2001, p. 235). Specifically, you'll need to ask yourself questions like: Is your audience just your professor, or are you writing for a larger pool of potential readers? Are your readers experts in your field, or are you writing for policy-makers or for the general public? Are your readers familiar with the jargon – or specialized vocabulary – in your discipline?

As you write up your findings, reflect on whether a reader would judge your writing to be 'organized, concise, and interesting' (Speight, 2012, p. 88). Although no one expects academic writing to be as gripping or as eloquent as the writing in a best-selling, prize-winning novel, a reader will expect – and, indeed, deserves to see – writing that is clear, focused, and engaging. One way to make your writing more engaging for a broader, non-specialist audience is to show why your findings are relevant to the 'everyday experience' of your audience members (Huff, 2009, p. 202).

To illustrate such relevance, you could use 'stories, anecdotes, case studies, and other methods', all of which would make your results seem more 'concrete and personal' rather than 'esoteric and abstract' (Welch-Ross & Fasig, 2007, p. 419). For many people, stories and narratives have an intuitive appeal; therefore, employing a particular story or example to convey larger themes can help you connect with diverse audiences. As Russell (2010, p. 85) has explained, to achieve 'real value in a public policy or consumer context, scientific knowledge has to be re-framed to engage audiences in terms specific to their culture and understanding'. In other words, you need to think about how cultural and situational factors might impact the audience's understanding of your work. You also need to think about language, and whether – or to what extent – technical vocabulary can be employed. When communicating with broader, non-specialist audiences, it's fine to include some jargon, but be careful 'of introducing technical terms too abruptly', as such tactics could 'drive away ... the public that you are trying to reach' (Gastel, 1983, p. 11). Table 9.1 offers a list of questions you may want to ask yourself about the intended audience for your results, and some specific suggestions for targeting different kinds of audiences.

Despite its challenges, communicating with broad audiences is a rewarding task and can help you grow as a writer and thinker. Indeed, it can bring 'a crispness and timeliness' to your writing that can benefit your future academic projects (Hirsh-Pasek & Golinkoff, 2007, p. 189). For more guidance on how to communicate with diverse audiences, why not look at other magazine articles, blog posts, podcasts, and documentaries that have resonated with the public (Gastel, 1983, p. 6)? If you examine those pieces of writing closely and think about why they were successful, you may learn some important skills that you can apply in your own work.

Table 9.1 Thinking about your intended audience

Question	Potential response
Will my intended audience contain individuals with similar disciplinary backgrounds and levels of expertise, or individuals with very different backgrounds and expertise?	If your audience will contain individuals with diverse levels of expertise, you will need to make sure you take this diversity into account when communicating your findings. You will need to appeal to readers/viewers with differing levels of knowledge and interest in the discipline, without alienating other readers/viewers. One method for accomplishing this task is to include a more detailed appendix at the end of your written article, which discusses more advanced or technical elements of your data analysis in more detail. (If you are presenting your results at a conference, you could print out copies of the appendix for interested conference participants.)
Will my intended audience be familiar with specialist vocabulary from my discipline?	If your audience will not be familiar with specialist vocabulary, try to limit your use of jargon. When you do employ specialist vocabulary, make sure to clearly define each term.
Will my intended audience be familiar with the specific data analysis techniques I intend to employ?	If the data analysis techniques you intend to employ are advanced or obscure, and your audience is unlikely to be familiar with them, then you will need to explain the steps of your analysis in particular detail. If, on the other hand, the techniques are well known (e.g., *t*-tests), and your audience is likely to already be familiar with them, then it may not be essential to give as much detail.
What aspects of my findings will most interest my audience? What implications of my findings will be most relevant for my audience?	Although academic writing will never be as attention-grabbing as a popular novel, you do want your readers to be *interested* in your findings and to recognize their importance. You should therefore clearly articulate the value of your research efforts. Make sure your readers appreciate your work's contribution to your discipline.
Will my intended audience benefit from seeing visual representations of my data (e.g., graphs or other charts)?	In the second half of this chapter, we'll explore how data visualization techniques can facilitate the communication of your findings. Both expert and broader, non-expert audiences can benefit from data visualizations. However, as we will see in Section 9.6, it's important to think about your audience when designing data visualizations.

stop and think

Why might it be beneficial for a data analyst to communicate findings with broader audiences, such as the general public?

9.5 Different Venues for Communicating Findings

So far we've discussed general advice for communicating findings, regardless of the venue in which you intend to present those findings. Your intended venue could be a thesis or dissertation, an article for an academic journal, a conference presentation, a conference poster, or another more informal outlet. Each of these venues has its own unique characteristics, and you'll need to tailor your presentation strategy accordingly. It's time to look in detail at these different venues, and discuss more targeted tips for communicating data. The easiest, and clearest, way to do this is through a table. So take a close look at Table 9.2 for specific tips to keep in mind for each of these venues.

Table 9.2 Different venues for communicating findings

Venue	Key considerations
Dissertation or thesis	Make sure you're aware about your university's guidelines for formatting and preparing your document. See if you can access past theses/dissertations that students from your department have successfully submitted. Consider setting up a 'writing group' with other students in your programme. You can meet weekly or monthly to discuss challenges you've encountered and offer encouragement during the thesis writing process. Theses and dissertations often include longer and more detailed literature reviews and research methods descriptions than academic journal articles. So be prepared to offer more details about past studies and your own methods.
Academic article	The word count for academic articles is typically limited, and much shorter than that for theses or dissertations. Therefore, be prepared to be ruthless with your editing, as any less relevant content will need to be excised. Investigate whether it's possible to submit data visualizations or additional materials such as an online appendix to your article, as more journals are now allowing such innovations. Data visualizations can help readers grasp your findings, and appendices with more information about your methods or analyses can help readers gain a more comprehensive picture of your work. Take a look at the specific formatting requirements for the journal you've chosen. Make sure you're aware of the required citation style and word count for submissions. Think about the journal's audience. Some journals are targeted at a very specific subfield, while other journals accept submissions from a range of social science disciplines. As we discussed in the previous section, the vocabulary and tone you adopt may differ depending on whether you are writing for a specialist or generalist audience.
Conference presentation	Investigate the guidelines for presentations at this particular conference. What is the maximum time allotted for a presentation? Will a projector be available to allow you to present visual slides? Unless you've been invited to give a longer, keynote address, it's likely that you'll have to be very economical in your presentation of your literature review and methods. Make sure you don't waste precious time discussing more minute issues of methodology or past research, as conference participants will likely be most interested in your own findings. So leave enough time to adequately present your results. If you want to include tables in your presentation, think carefully about how you will present them. It can be difficult for audience members to read expansive tables presented on a projector screen, so you may need to abbreviate your tables or prepare a printed handout that shows the full tables for interested viewers. If this is your first conference presentation, try to practise the presentation while timing yourself. Ideally, ask a friend or fellow student to watch you practise and offer feedback.
Conference poster	Check with the conference organizer about whether there is a maximum or recommended size for posters. Investigate which software package you want to use to design the poster, and how you will print the poster. Some universities actually offer poster printing services for students; alternatively, numerous shops offer different poster printing services. Visualization techniques are of prime importance in conference posters. Think carefully about how you can present your findings (and perhaps even the methods and theories you used) using graphs, charts, or other visualization techniques. (We will explore visualization techniques in the next section of this chapter.)

Venue	Key considerations
	Be careful not to include too much text on the poster, as text is not as attention-grabbing as visualizations. If you do include text, make sure the font is large enough that viewers will be able to read it from several feet away. Focus on the most important and noteworthy aspects of your findings. Make sure your contact details are visible on the poster in case viewers want to get in touch later. If possible, bring some business cards to facilitate networking. (Some universities offer business cards to employees and students; alternatively, it's not difficult to print out personal business cards on your own.)
Elevator pitch	An 'elevator pitch' is a short, straightforward, attention-grabbing summary of your research project. It's useful to develop an elevator pitch for your thesis/dissertation, or other research project you're working on. Many people – other students, professors from other departments, family members, friends, and researchers you meet at conferences – will ask you about what you're working on. Giving an engaging answer will make your life easier. More importantly, having an elevator pitch ready will help you get instant, informal feedback about your research questions and topic. You never know whom you might randomly meet; perhaps a casual acquaintance will ask a very perceptive question that forces you to consider your topic in a new way, or will be able to introduce you to important contacts with expertise in your field.

stop and think

One venue that is not mentioned in Table 9.2 is a classroom presentation. However, data analysis students are often asked to prepare a presentation for their classmates. (You might even need to do this one day!) If 'classroom presentation' were to be listed in Table 9.2, what points would you list in the 'key considerations' column?

9.6 Data Visualization

Now that we've explored data communication in general, let's look at one form of data communication in more detail: the *visual* communication of research results. The visual communication of research results – or, more simply, data visualization – has received increased attention in recent years and is an increasingly essential element of data analysis.

Most people are inherently visual learners and respond more strongly to visual displays of data – graphs, charts, pictures, or other images – than to streams of numbers or lists of words. Therefore it's important to think about how you might use different visual tools to communicate your results to different audiences. Perhaps you're thinking of including some tables or graphs in a report, thesis, or dissertation? Or maybe you want to include a map in an academic article you're writing with other students and lecturers? Or you've signed up for a poster session at an upcoming conference and want to design an eye-catching display that grabs the attention of busy conference participants? Regardless of your goals and current circumstances, developing data visualization skills is imperative – both for communicating the results of your research and for furthering your own career. Public interest in visual displays of data has exploded, and both academic and popular publication outlets are increasingly eager to publish visual displays of data. Cultivating your own data visualization skills is therefore crucial not only for academic research fields, but also for business, consulting, marketing, public relations, and numerous other industries.

Through data visualization tactics, you can help others understand your findings, detect underlying relationships in your data, and perceive the importance or meaning of your discoveries (Gohil, 2015, p. 1). A good data visualization should be targeted at its audience, and mindful of the average audience member's level of knowledge about the topic; a good data visualization should also be clear (so that viewers can correctly interpret the results) and should present 'a story' that will grab viewers' attention and help them recognize the most important elements of the data (Stikeleather, 2013).

Data visualization is closely related to the field of *information design*, the discipline that explores how to most effectively choose, arrange, and convey information to different audiences; such communication should be both efficient and, of course, accurate and objective (Wildbur & Burke, 1998, p. 6). Although the field of information design encompasses a broader range of tasks that exceeds the purview of social scientists – such as presenting information related to health and safety, or producing navigation-related signage – its findings about how to capture viewers' attention and convey knowledge are very relevant, and we will draw upon some of these findings throughout this chapter. (If you're interested in learning more about information design, take a look at the 'Further Reading' section at the end of this chapter, which includes information about a useful primer.)

Many data visualization methods can be equally applied to quantitative, qualitative, and mixed-methods data. Some methods may be *most* relevant for one type of data (quantitative *or* qualitative *or* mixed-methods), a point that will be noted as we explore each visualization method in more detail. When deciding which visualization method to use, you should consider the *specific characteristics* of your data. For example, if you have quantitative data, is that data *continuous* or *categorical*? (If you can't remember the difference between these two terms, take a look back at Chapter 5.) As we will learn, some visualization methods work best with data that exhibits specific characteristics. Additionally, you should also consider the particular *aims* of your research. What are your goals? What information do you hope to communicate through visual methods? Finally, you need to think about *visual appeal*. Does your visualization capture the attention of viewers? Here's your chance to sharpen your artistic skills, and bring some creativity to your scientific work.

With these concerns in mind, we'll now look in depth at different visualization options. Let's start with the most basic method for visualizing data – a table.

9.6.1 Tables

Tables are a common tool for presenting data, findings, or other information in an straightforward and organized fashion. If you've ever conducted quantitative research, you're probably very familiar with tables; many statistical software packages automatically generate tables as they produce results. These automatically generated tables are usually edited and reformatted before being included in a paper, thesis, or journal article. You can also create your own tables in the word-processing program of your choice. Table 9.3 illustrates how quantitative data can be effectively communicated in tabular format.

Table 9.3 Calculating the standard deviation for the bus passengers variable (s_y)

Day	Campus bus passengers, y_i	Passengers – Mean number of passengers = $y_i - \bar{y}$	(Passengers – Mean number of passengers)² = $(y_i - \bar{y})^2$
1	498	498 – 567.2 = –69.2	$(-69.2)^2 = 4788.64$
2	528	528 – 567.2 = –39.2	$(-39.2)^2 = 1536.64$
3	533	533 – 567.2 = –34.2	$(-34.2)^2 = 1169.64$
4	528	528 – 567.2 = –39.2	$(-39.2)^2 = 1536.64$
5	601	601 – 567.2 = 33.8	$33.8^2 = 1142.44$
6	578	578 – 567.2 = 10.8	$10.8^2 = 116.64$
7	569	569 – 567.2 = 1.8	$1.8^2 = 3.24$
8	612	612 – 567.2 = 44.8	$44.8^2 = 2007.04$
9	596	596 – 567.2 = 28.8	$28.8^2 = 829.44$
10	603	603 – 567.2 = 35.8	$35.8^2 = 1281.64$
11	591	591 – 567.2 = 23.8	$23.8^2 = 566.44$
12	583	583 – 567.2 = 15.8	$15.8^2 = 249.64$
13	584	584 – 567.2 = 16.8	$16.8^2 = 282.24$
14	570	570 – 567.2 = 2.8	$2.8^2 = 7.84$
15	534	534 – 567.2 = –33.2	$(-33.2)^2 = 1102.24$

Do you recognize Table 9.3? We've seen it before! It's actually a copy of Table 5.3 from the discussion of correlation in Chapter 5. The table displays the calculations necessary for computing the standard deviation of a variable. Take a moment to look at the table before moving on to the 'Stop and think' exercise below.

stop and think

How easy is it to interpret Table 9.3? What conclusions can you draw about the variable based on this table?

The first conclusion we can draw from Table 9.3 is that the title clearly identifies the table's content. We can also see that the table has been given a number, which makes it easier to refer specifically to this table in the text. The table has four columns and numerous rows. Note the headings presented in bold at the top of the table. The headings indicate what data will be presented in each column. Therefore, even presented out of context, the structure of a table can still communicate important insights, which illustrates the value of using tables to clearly and efficiently convey results.

Although tables are most commonly used to present the results of quantitative research (as in Table 9.3), tables may also be helpful for presenting the results of *some* qualitative methods as well. For example, the codes or categories used in the coding process could be efficiently summarized in a table (Kumar, 2010, pp. 103–104). If you think that a table could help clarify or organize your qualitative findings, feel free to include one.

Finally, in addition to presenting results, tables can also be employed to succinctly present important details about the research methods used in either quantitative or qualitative work. For example, instead of writing up a long, wordy account describing the age or gender breakdown of the participants in your study, you could efficiently display this information in a table. Or you could use a table to clarify other aspects of your models. An example of this kind of informational table is shown as Table 9.4.

Table 9.4 Popular analytical approaches for qualitative data

Analytical approach	Description
Content analysis	By focusing on patterns and prominent themes, we can make sense of a complex qualitative dataset. We should look at how frequently different themes or words appear in the data, and whether particular themes or words tend to appear together.
Discourse analysis	By examining the linguistic nuances and conventions present in human discourse, we can gain insight into how individuals use language to create their own social worlds. We can also better understand how communication reflects and shapes social power dynamics.
Narrative analysis	By probing the narrative elements of textual data, we can illuminate the stories told by individuals and societies. Such stories can offer significant insight into how individuals understand their own lives and decisions, and how societies view their values.

Hopefully you recognize this table as well, as it's a copy of Table 6.1, which we first encountered in Chapter 6. The table has a straightforward title which identifies the table's aim: to instruct viewers about popular analytical approaches for qualitative data. The table features two columns with clear headers. In contrast to a wordy description in the text – which might confuse a reader trying to distinguish the different analytical strategies – the table communicates this information in an organized, efficient manner.

Regardless of which type of table you plan to use – i.e., a quantitative data table, or a qualitative data table, or simply an informational table – there are some important guidelines to keep in mind. First, make sure you always refer to each table at least once in the text of your paper/thesis/article/dissertation. If a table is never referenced in the text, a reader may wonder what the table's purpose is, and how it relates to your findings or arguments. On the other hand, don't feel that you need to repeat *all* the details contained in a table in the text of your paper/thesis/article/dissertation. If your tables are designed clearly enough, readers should be able to interpret them without excessive description in the text.

Another important guideline to keep in mind applies primarily to quantitative tables. As mentioned earlier, many statistical and quantitative software packages automatically produce tables as part of their results output. However, don't succumb to the temptation to simply copy and paste those tables into the write-up of your results. Automatically produced tables may not include all essential information, or they may include *too much* information, a portion of which can be cut. Some of the automatically produced tables may not be needed at all, so think carefully about which tables are most relevant – and which pieces of information on those tables are most relevant – to present in your final write-up (Munro, 2005, p. 15).

When making this decision, take a moment to also consider the *formatting* of your final tables. The tables that are automatically produced by a software package may not be in an appropriate font or style or size to be included in your final write-up. Similarly, if you're producing qualitative or informational tables yourself, you need to make sure the style and appearance of these tables is appropriate. For example, if you're intending to submit your findings to an academic journal, be sure to look at past issues of that journal, consult the author guidelines produced by the journal, and use tables from past issues as models for the format and style of your own tables. If you're producing a thesis or dissertation, check whether your department or university has formatting guidelines for tables, and, if so, that your tables match these guidelines.

Hopefully it's clear by now that well-produced tables can clarify and communicate research findings. However, tables also possess an important limitation: they're rarely visually striking and, even with careful attention to formatting issues, it's rare that tables will capture viewers' attention (Smyth, 2004, p. 185). Therefore, to engage viewers and further explore your findings, it can be helpful to include different kinds of visual displays. In the next few subsections we'll discuss various types of graphs and figures that data analysts frequently use.

9.6.2 Bar charts

One of the most popular ways to visually display data is to use a **bar chart**. As its name suggests, a bar chart uses bars to represent the prevalence of different categories in your dataset. Figure 9.1 shows a typical bar chart.

Like the table we examined in the previous subsection, this bar chart is numbered (it is 'Figure 9.1'), and it contains a clear, descriptive title. Based on its title, we can conclude that the bar chart reveals the number of US states that had the death penalty in 2015. With its wide, distinctive bars, the bar chart has an intuitive appeal which helps us immediately conclude that more states had the death penalty than not. However, it's difficult to ascertain the *exact* number of states in each category. For example, it's clear that the number of states with the death penalty was between 30 and 35, and was probably closer to 30; however, unlike in a table, the exact number takes some effort to detect. (It was 32 states.)

As this example illustrates, bar charts are typically used to present nominal or categorical data. Nominal or categorical data *cannot* take on any numeric value, but is instead restricted to a few specific categories such as 'with death penalty' and 'without death penalty'. The horizontal axis (or *x*-axis) of the bar chart typically displays the categories of interest, while the

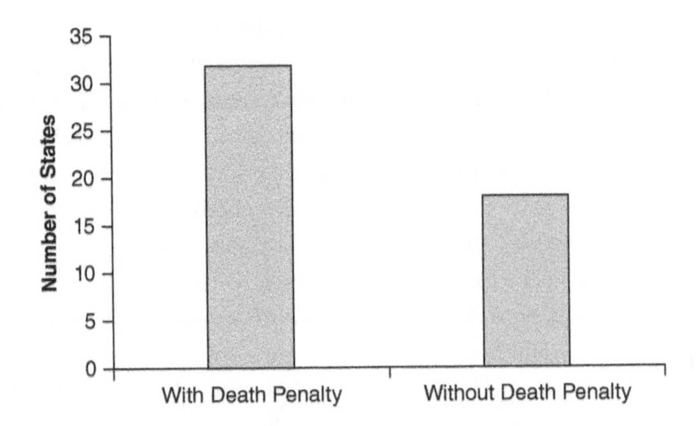

Figure 9.1 Number of US states with and without the death penalty, 2015. Data from: Death Penalty Information Center (2017). States with and without the death penalty. Retrieved from http://www.deathpenaltyinfo.org/states-and-without-death-penalty

vertical axis (or *y*-axis) show how many (or what percentage of) cases fall into each category. (Although it's possible to flip the axes around and put the categories on the vertical axis and the number or percentage on the horizontal axis, this design is less common and therefore may be more difficult for viewers to interpret (Hofmann, 2010, p. 197).) The categories with the most observations have the longest bars; the categories with the fewest observations have the shortest bars. Because the categories are distinct – in other words, there is no intersection between them, since a state cannot both have the death penalty and not have the death penalty – there should always be blank space between different bars (Christopher, 2017, pp. 60–61). Although the bars are, of course, of different heights, their widths should be identical, to ensure your presentation is not lopsided or misleading (Hofmann, 2010, p. 197). Be particularly careful when designing the *y*-axis; make sure that the numbering and size of the *y*-axis are not skewed in any way that will mislead viewers. Designing fair, accurate axes for graphs is an important element of all data visualizations and of ethical research practice in general.

In the example in Figure 9.1, only two categories were included on the bar chart. However, bar charts can feature more than just two categories – in fact, theoretically speaking, an unlimited number of bars can be included. Practically speaking, however, it's wise to limit the number of bars you include to help readers make sense of your findings. I'd suggest limiting yourself to a maximum of 6–10 bars per chart; however, this rule-of-thumb is not firm or universal, and the appropriate maximum for your chart depends on your own 'eyeball' judgement.

Figure 9.1 illustrates the most straightforward kind of bar chart: a single comparison between just two different categories. However, several more complex alternatives exist, including *stacked bar charts*, in which the bars are stacked atop each other to highlight the relative size of each category (Hanneman, Kposowa, & Riddle, 2013, p. 37), and *grouped bar charts*, in which the bars representing multiple categories are grouped together so that you can easily compare many different categories at once (Wallgren, Wallgren, Persson, Jorner, & Haaland, 1996, p. 26). For an overview of stacked bar charts and numerous tips about how to improve visual display of data, see Kirk (2016, in particular pp. 177–178).

9.6.3 Histograms

Since bar charts are appropriate for categorical or nominal data, what should you do if your data is *continuous*? (Recall that continuous data is data that can take on a wide range of numeric values and is not restricted to a few particular categories. Continuous data is also known as *interval* or *ratio* data.) Is there a way to visualize such data that is analogous to the bar chart?

Yes, there is! It's called the **histogram**. A histogram divides your continuous variable into equal-sized 'bins', or categories, which represent a range of values. For example, the bins for a particular histogram might feature the following ranges: 0–4, 5–9, 10–14, and 15–19. A case that has a value of 1.3 would be placed in the first bin, while a case that has a value of 12.3 would be placed in the third bin. Like a bar chart, the histogram uses bars to indicate how many cases in the dataset fall into each bin (or category), allowing you to immediately visualize the spread or *distribution* of a continuous variable. (Do you remember the term *distribution* from Chapter 4? It refers to the overall spread of a variable's values.) Take a look at the example histogram in Figure 9.2, which illustrates unemployment rates in US states in 2015. What can you conclude about the distribution of unemployment rates based on the histogram?

From the histogram, it appears that the distribution of unemployment rates is most concentrated around 5–6%. A few states have very low rates (lower than 4%) and no state has a rate higher than 7%. Although it would also be possible to obtain this information from a table or written description, a histogram allows the information to be communicated more efficiently. (As an aside, it's worth noting that, as we saw with the bar chart earlier, it's difficult to detect *exact* values in a histogram. Therefore it can still be important to report *exact* statistics in the

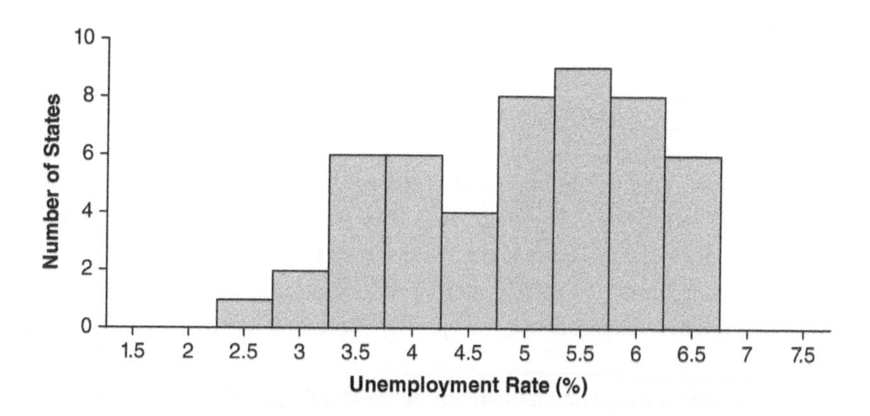

Figure 9.2 Unemployment rate in US states, 2015. Data from: United States Department of Labor, Bureau of Labor Statistics (2017), local area unemployment statistics, annual average series

text of your Results section (Smyth, 2004, p. 185). The real benefit of the histogram is its ability to communicate the overall pattern or shape of your data.)

One key difference between our histogram and the bar chart we examined earlier is that the histogram's bars touch each other, unlike the bar chart's bars which were separated from each other by blank spaces (Tu, 2008, p. 69). How might we explain this difference? A bar chart, if you recall, presented data in distinct categories; the blank spaces between the bars indicated that the categories could not intersect or overlap. However, because a histogram presents continuous data (i.e., the variable can theoretically take on any value), there is no 'space' between the categories (Manikandan, 2011).

How wide should the bins in your histogram be? They should be of an identical width to ensure your histogram isn't misleading (McNabb, 2002, p. 177). But what width should you choose? Bins with a narrower width will include fewer values; bins with a wider width will encompass more values. If you opt for narrower bins, then your histogram will feature more bars and more closely follow each oscillation in the distribution; however, if there are lots of 'random fluctuations' in your distribution, this close mirroring could produce a histogram that is 'bumpy' and difficult to interpret (Jacoby, 1997, p. 17). If you opt for wider bins, your histogram will appear 'smoother' – and may therefore be easier to interpret – but you may miss potentially important nuances in the distribution (Jacoby, 1997, p. 17). The choice is therefore a kind of balancing act in which you must weigh these trade-offs. It's worth experimenting with different bin sizes and comparing the resultant histograms to see if they offer you new insights into the distribution of the variable you are interested in. Finally, in Figure 9.2, the values on the *x*-axis represent the midpoint of each bin. However, you could label the upper and lower bounds of each bin instead if you prefer.

stop and think

What are the key differences between a *histogram* and a *bar chart*?

9.6.4 Frequency tables

A popular alternative to the histogram is the **frequency table**. Like the histogram, the frequency table captures the overall spread of your data and indicates how many observations fall into different categories. By summarizing a dataset in this manner, a frequency table may reveal patterns that might not be visible when you look at each data point individually. (In other words, a frequency table can help you see the 'forest' of your dataset without getting distracted by all the 'trees'.)

As with a histogram, a frequency table requires a researcher to divide up a dataset into different *bins* or *intervals*. Deciding *how many* intervals to include – and, correspondingly, *how large* these intervals should be – requires some thought. In general, the intervals in a single frequency table should all be the same size; if you want to compare multiple frequency tables to each other, it's also a good idea to employ the same size intervals in the different tables (Dunn & Clark, 2009, pp. 38–39). The key difference between a histogram and a frequency table is that the former is really a graph while the latter is – spoiler alert! – a table. So let's examine how the same dataset displayed in Figure 9.2 as a histogram would look in a frequency table.

Table 9.5 Frequency table of unemployment rates in US states, 2015

Unemployment rate (%)	Frequency
2.25–2.74	1
2.75–3.24	2
3.25–3.74	6
3.75–4.24	6
4.25–4.74	4
4.75–5.24	8
5.25–5.74	9
5.75–6.24	8
6.25–6.74	6

In Table 9.5 the first column presents different intervals, and the second column shows how many states had an unemployment rate within that interval. In other words, we can see that 4 states had an unemployment rate between 4.25% and 4.74%, and that 6 states had an unemployment rate between 6.25% and 6.74%. Table 9.5 presents the simplest kind of frequency table, which consists solely of the intervals and the frequency count of observations that fall into each interval. However, you could also expand the table to include additional information such as the percentage or proportion of observations that fall into each interval.

stop and think

Take a moment to compare the histogram (Figure 9.2) to the frequency table (Table 9.5). What is one advantage of using the histogram to display this dataset? What is one advantage of using the frequency table to display this dataset?

9.6.5 Pie charts

Pie charts are not only the best-named data visualization method – they're also one of the most intuitive to understand. Because they're shaped like pies, with each slice of the pie representing a different category or group in your dataset, pie charts have a unique visual appeal. Interpreting pie charts is also simple, since even viewers unfamiliar with your study or field will recognize the idea of taking slices from a pie (Kumar, 2010, p. 113).

The size of each slice represents the size of a particular category or group relative to the other categories/groups, with larger slices indicating larger categories/groups. Typically, the largest slice of the pie is placed at the top of the chart, with the other slices arranged in a clockwise fashion, in order of descending size (Hofmann, 2010, p. 197). This structure is visible in Figure 9.3, which displays public health mortality data from England and Wales. Specifically, the chart presents the causes of death for females in 2013. According to the chart, what was the leading cause of death?

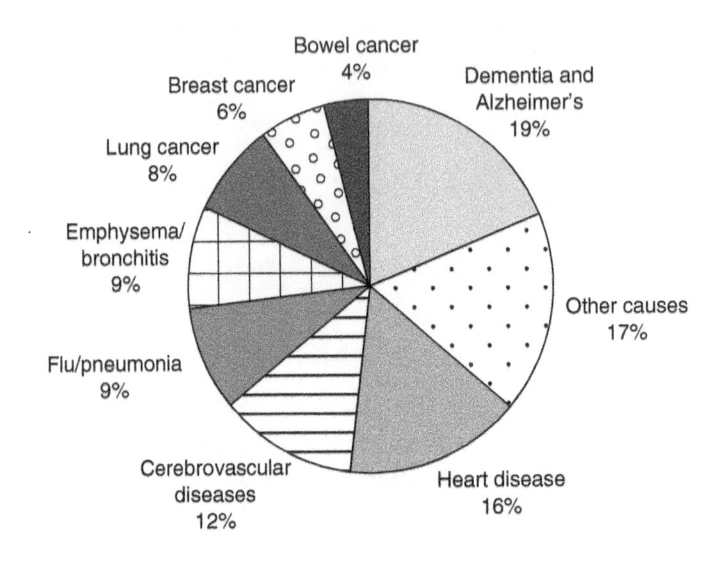

Figure 9.3 Causes of death for females in England and Wales, 2013. Data from: Office for National Statistics (2015)

The most common cause of death, accounting for 19% of deaths among women in England and Wales in 2013, was dementia and Alzheimer's disease. Since this is the largest slice of the pie, it begins at the 12 o'clock position. The use of different shadings and the clear identification of each slice both facilitate interpretation of the pie chart. Although this pie chart is in greyscale, you could also employ multiple colours to further help viewers distinguish the different slices of your pie. Whether or not you use different colours (or patterns or shadings) to differentiate the slices, make certain that you clearly identify which group or category is represented by each slice. In Figure 9.3, you can see that a label is provided for each slice; additionally, the exact percentage in each category is listed next to the label. Providing exact percentages on the pie chart is not essential, but it can be helpful.

Although pie charts are typically easy to interpret, this advantage disappears if *too many* slices are included. An overabundance of slices can confuse viewers and make it difficult to distinguish among the categories. So how many slices is *too many*? What's the maximum number of slices that should be included in a pie chart? Torres, Preskill, and Piontek (2005, p. 318) recommend including a maximum of six slices, while Kumar (2010, p. 113) suggests that up to ten slices can be displayed. So clearly there's no one firm rule about the appropriate number of slices; instead, you'll need to consider whether your specific pie chart – given its size, colours or shadings, and intended audience – is clear and not too crowded. Figure 9.3 features nine slices. Do you think the slices are still legible, or does the pie look overcrowded?

If you feel that a pie chart is overcrowded, what can you do to reduce the number of slices? One popular approach is to *collapse* two or more similar categories into just one category. For example, to simplify Figure 9.3 and reduce the number of slices in the pie, a data analyst could combine similar causes of death. Specifically, the categories representing different kinds of cancer could be collapsed into a single category, as long as this combination was noted in the chart's legend. This technique of combining categories can help unclutter a pie chart and improve its clarity; however, keep in mind that this technique can also make it more difficult to identify nuanced differences. For instance, if we did combine the different types of cancer into a single category, we would lose the ability to differentiate between these different types. This loss of nuance would be particularly concerning if your research seeks to compare different types of cancer.

As with bar charts and histograms, an additional advantage of pie charts is that they are easy to produce in many popular software programs, including Excel, SPSS, Stata, and R (Kumar, 2010, p. 113). However, just because it's simple to produce a pie chart doesn't mean that *no thinking* is required. Thinking is absolutely essential; as we've seen, you'll need to carefully consider how many slices to include, how to differentiate the slices, and how to ensure that your viewers understand your findings. When designing a pie chart with software, you'll also need to assess the formatting options offered by the software. For example, many software packages feature the option to create either a two-dimensional or three-dimensional pie chart. Figure 9.3 contains a two-dimensional pie chart; the pie looks flat and without any depth. In contrast, Figure 9.4 presents exactly the same data in a three-dimensional pie chart.

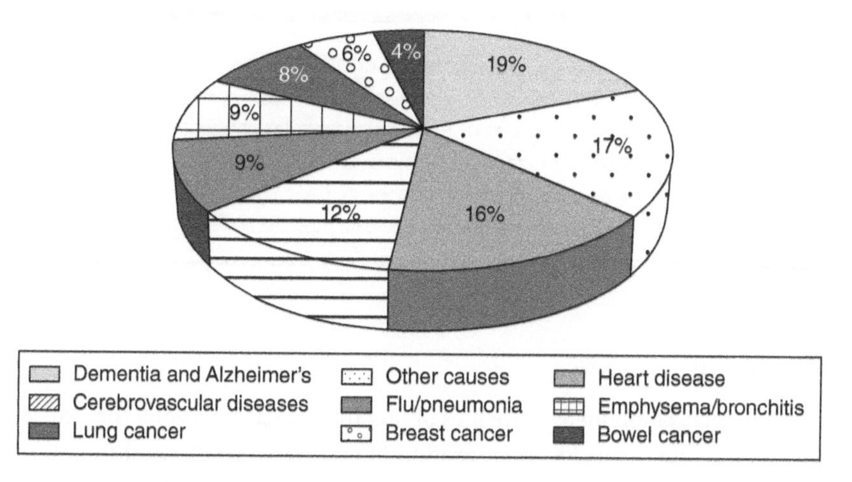

Figure 9.4 Causes of death for females in England and Wales, 2013 (Alternative version). Data from: Office for National Statistics (2015)

At first glance, the three-dimensional pie chart seems more eye-catching, doesn't it? To my eyes at least, the sense of depth provided by the third dimension seems to offer more professional luster to the figure, in contrast to the more staid two-dimensional chart. However, look closely at the slice in the lower right-hand corner which represents 'heart disease'. Although this slice represents 16% of deaths, it looks bigger than the slice in the upper right-hand corner for 'dementia and Alzheimer's', which represents 19% of deaths! Such 'distortions' are common in three-dimensional pie charts since 'the slices that seem closest to the viewer will be deemed the most important ones' (Torres et al., 2005, p. 318). Therefore, before you decide to use a three-dimensional pie chart, consider whether it presents your data in a fair, accurate, and precise manner. Of course, this advice applies to all types of data visualization, not just pie charts. When designing and formatting charts and figures, don't simply rely on the default options provided by software packages without first considering whether these choices are appropriate and present the data accurately. Even in a world of ever escalating technology, there's no substitute for a researcher's logic and sound judgement.

Let's take one last look at Figure 9.4 before moving on. Is there anything else about the figure that strikes you as problematic? One problem that stands out to me is the difficulty of distinguishing each slice. Since the pie chart is in grey scale (rather than colour) it's not easy to differentiate the different grey slices from each other. It's much easier to differentiate the slices in Figure 9.3, where they are clearly labelled. The use of a legend (or key) in Figure 9.4 to identify each slice is not necessarily problematic – it could work well if used for a multicoloured pie chart, in which bright colours clearly distinguish each slice. Figure 9.4 therefore illustrates that one single approach is not appropriate for all pie charts; instead, you'll need to tailor your approach to fit the characteristics of your data, the goals of your analysis, and the formatting options available to you.

let's try this!

You've probably encountered a lot of pie charts in the past – they're certainly one of the most popular data visualization techniques. Take a few minutes now to search for pie charts on the internet. Try to stick to reputable sources, such as government websites or research reports. Find at least three different pie charts and look through them carefully. Which of these three pie charts has the most visual appeal (or seems most attractive to the eye)? Why is this particular pie chart so appealing (i.e., colour scheme, layout, choice of fonts, etc.)? Of the three pie charts you found, which presents the data most accurately or fairly?

9.6.6 Scatterplots

The next data visualization method we'll examine, the scatterplot, is one that we've already briefly discussed in our discussion of correlation in Chapter 5. You'll recall from that discussion that scatterplots graphically illustrate the association (or lack of association) between two continuous variables. (Remember that a *continuous* variable can take on a wide range of numeric values. If, instead of continuous data, you have *categorical* data, go back and take a look at the *bar chart* or *pie chart* discussed earlier, as these options may be a better choice.)

In a scatterplot, one variable is placed along the horizontal axis (or *x*-axis) and one variable is placed along the vertical axis (or *y*-axis). If you've already hypothesized that a particular variable is your *independent* variable, then that variable should be placed on the x-axis, while the hypothesized *dependent* variable should be placed along the y-axis (LeGates, 2005, p. 183). However, if you're just exploring your data and aren't sure which variables might be independent or dependent, then the axis doesn't matter. Figure 9.5 shows an example scatterplot of the relationship (or lack of relationship?) between the unemployment rate and the level of property crime in US states. (The level of property crime is measured as the number of property crimes reported to the police for every 100,000 state residents (United States Department of Justice, 2016).) This scatterplot is just exploratory – neither variable has been designated as the independent or dependent variable. Nevertheless, do you detect any relationship here?

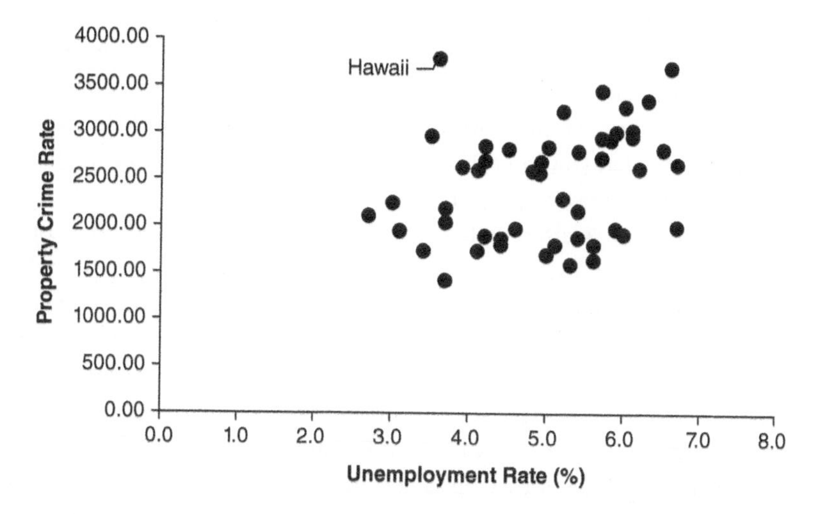

Figure 9.5 Relationship between unemployment and property crime in US states, 2015. Data from: United States Department of Labor, Bureau of Labor Statistics (2017), local area unemployment statistics, annual average series; United States Department of Justice (2016)

Each dot on the graph represents a particular observation, and the dot's position indicates that observation's values for the independent and dependent variables. Therefore, in Figure 9.5, each dot represents a particular state's values of unemployment and property crime. If you see a line of dots extending from the bottom left-hand corner to the upper right-hand corner of the graph, this means that as one variable increases, the other variable increases as well. In other words, a *positive* relationship exists between the two variables. If, on the other hand, you see a line of dots extending from the upper left-hand corner to the bottom right-hand corner of the graph, this means that as the independent variable increases, the dependent variable *decreases*; this indicates that a *negative* relationship exists between the variables. If there seems to be no such pattern, then you have neither a positive or negative relationship. However, it's possible that a more complicated relationship might exist, so don't conclude that *no* relationship exists until you examine your data in more detail. (For example, there might be a positive relationship for low values of one variable, but at higher values of the variable the relationship becomes negative. These kinds of complicated relationships are difficult to spot in scatterplots.)

What do you think – is there any evidence of a positive or negative relationship in Figure 9.5?

In general, the dots within a scatterplot are *not* labelled, as listing a name for every single dot would make the figure difficult to decipher. Also, the aim of a scatterplot is to illustrate the overall relationship (or lack of relationship) between the variables, so providing identifying information for each dot is not essential. However, it may make sense to identify and label a few specific points, if there is a particular case that you want to highlight (see discussion in Jacoby, 1997, pp. 59–61). For example, in Figure 9.5, the dot representing Hawaii is labelled, as it appears to be an *outlier* – or a data point located far away from the other data points. It appears that Hawaii had a relatively low unemployment rate in 2015, compared to other states, but its level of property crime was relatively high. What might explain these values? Could Hawaii's high level of tourism increase the risk of property crime, as well as decrease the unemployment rate? Or are there other potential explanations that you can think of? Perhaps you're already starting to formulate a hypothesis for a future research project!

If you conclude from your scatterplot that a positive or negative relationship exists between your variables, you can also use your scatterplot to estimate how strong that relationship might be; specifically, dots clustered tightly together indicate a stronger relationship, while dots that are spread further apart indicate a weaker relationship (Smyth, 2004, p. 193). Even if you find a very strong relationship between your variables, however, don't assume that increases in one variable *cause* increases or decreases in the other variable (LeGates, 2005, p. 183). All you can conclude from a scatterplot is that a potentially interesting association exists between two variables and that this association deserves further investigation. (Such further investigation can be conducted with *correlation*, a statistical technique we explored in Chapter 5. If you're interested in learning more, why not revisit Chapter 5 now?) The ability of scatterplots to hint at potentially interesting associations means that they can be helpful in the early stages of your data analysis efforts. Even if you don't plan to include a scatterplot in the final write-up of your results, you can create scatterplots for yourself for more exploratory purposes, such as investigating whether a potential relationship exists between *any* two variables, before you perform your more formal analyses (Mitchell, Jolley, & O'Shea, 2004, p. 66).

9.6.7 Line charts

The next visualization method we will explore – the **line chart** – shares some similarities with a scatterplot, as it also features different data points arranged around *x*- and *y*-axes and is also most appropriate for *continuous* data (Kumar, 2005). However, a key difference is that, unsurprisingly, the points in a line chart are connected by a line. Line charts are particularly helpful for displaying trends in individual variables (McNabb, 2002, p. 179). Indeed, if you have time series data – or data on a particular variable that is collected at regular time intervals, such as every month, every week, or every year – it may be helpful to present such data on a line chart. By placing time on the x-axis and the variable you are interested in on the y-axis, you can look for any patterns in the past data and consider whether such patterns might continue into the future (Mendenhall, Beaver, & Beaver, 2013, p. 19; Christopher, 2017, p. 70).

Figure 9.6 offers an example of a time-series line chart. Here, a single variable – the unemployment rate in California – is shown over the period 1998–2015. Do you detect any trends over time?

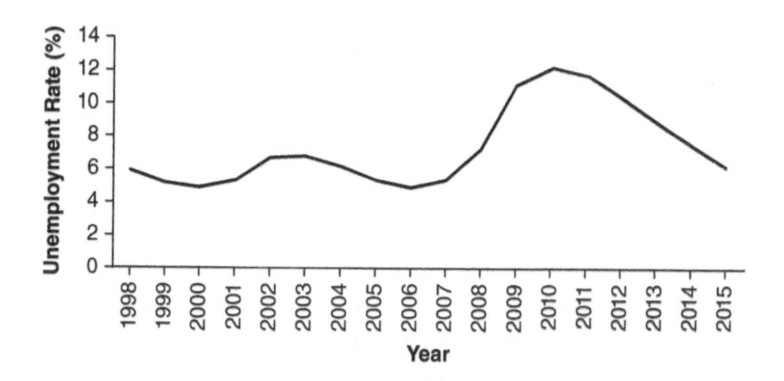

Figure 9.6 Unemployment rate in California, 1998-2015. Data from: United States Department of Labor, Bureau of Labor Statistics (2017), local area unemployment statistics, annual average series

From Figure 9.6 it's easy to see that the unemployment rate dramatically increased around 2009. This finding makes sense, given the collapse of the housing bubble and the subsequent economic recession that took place around that time. Although presenting the annual unemployment rates in a table could also communicate this information, a table would not present this information in such an efficient and visually striking manner. You can emphasize particular points on a line chart by adding dots or other symbols to the line; alternatively, if you prefer to use smoother lines (as in Figure 9.6), you can forgo such symbols and instead discuss any important years or data points in your write-up.

If you want to model more than one variable over time, you can include multiple lines on a line chart, although it's helpful if the variables are all measured on the same scale so that the position of both lines relative to the y-axis has the same meaning. For example, an appropriate second line to add to Figure 9.6 might be the unemployment rate in another US state, since it is measured on the same scale, and would make an interesting comparison with California. A chart with more than one line is known as a *multiline chart* (LeGates, 2005, p. 182). In a multiline chart, it's perfectly fine if the different lines intersect, just make sure that your graph is still easy to read, and that you clearly distinguish the different lines by employing different colours, shadings, or thicknesses (Hofmann, 2010, p. 197). However, as with the bar chart, be wary of including *too many* lines on a line chart. Smyth (2004, p. 201) has recommended including a maximum of four lines on a single line chart, as more than this number can produce an overly crowded graph that may be difficult for viewers to decipher.

9.6.8 Boxplots

Another method for displaying different quantitative data points is the **boxplot**. The boxplot, devised by legendary statistician John Tukey (1977), summarizes *continuous* data by representing just five of its key features: the minimum data point, the point representing the lowest 25% of observations (or the *first quartile* of the dataset), the median (or the midpoint of the dataset), the point representing the lowest 75% of observations (or the *third quartile* of the dataset), and the maximum data point (Gonzalez, 2009, p. 138). A box is then drawn around the edges of the first and third quartiles, with a line demarcating the median (Healey & Prus, 2010, p. 103). Whiskers – or additional vertical lines – are drawn outward from the bottom and top edges of the box to the maximum and minimum data point. *Outliers*, or data points that are much higher or much lower than most points in the dataset, may be excluded from the whiskers and instead presented as separate, additional points.

These instructions sound confusing when expressed in words, but are easier to understand when viewing an example. Figure 9.7 contains three different boxplots. These boxplots illustrate the gross domestic product (GDP) per capita for 162 different countries in 2000, 2010, and 2016, respectively. The dataset, obtained from the World Bank's (2017) International Comparison Program database, reflects purchasing power parity (PPP). (PPP estimates of GDP take into account differences in purchasing power and the cost of living between countries, to facilitate cross-country comparisons (see the discussion in Pulsipher & Pulsipher, 2006, pp. 35–36).)

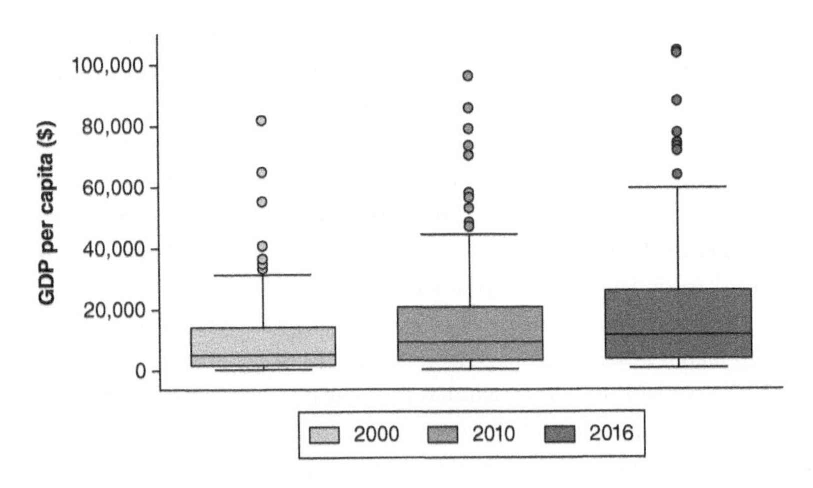

Figure 9.7 Boxplot of GDP per capita for 162 countries. Data from: World Bank (2017)

Figure 9.7 allows us to instantly see the overall distribution of countries' GDP per capita values, and to compare how this distribution changed between 2000, 2010, and 2016. Can you see the median (or horizontal line) within each of the boxes? It looks like it increased slightly from 2000 to 2016. Now take a look at the vertical lines emanating from the top and bottom of each box, which form the shape of a capital letter 'I' around the box. The vertical line at the top of each box is longer than the vertical line emanating from the bottom of each box. In fact, the vertical line emanating from the bottom of each box is so short it is almost imperceptible. This difference indicates that the data points above the third quartile of each distribution are more spread out than the data points below the first quartile. Finally, in all three years a number of outliers – shown as circular points – are present above the top whisker. These outliers indicate that a few countries with very high values of GDP per capita are present in each year's dataset.

This example illustrates the main advantage of boxplots: they clearly illustrate how spread out a dataset's observations are. Additionally, by creating multiple boxplots for different datasets, you can efficiently compare whether the observations in one dataset are more spread out than in the other dataset (as we did for the 2000, 2010, and 2016 data above). However, since boxplots rely on only five key pieces of information, some details of a dataset's shape and distribution will inevitably be lost. If you want more nuanced information about the exact shape and distribution of your dataset, it might be better to make a histogram; however, if you're only interested in broad knowledge about a dataset's spread, a boxplot could be a better choice (Wallgren et al., 1996, p. 52).

9.6.9 Word clouds

Theoretically, all of the visualization methods we have discussed so far – bar charts, histograms, pie charts, scatterplots, and line charts – could be used with qualitative, textual data. However, some quantification of the data would be necessary. For example, you'd need to count up the number of times different words appeared in the text, or the number of times different codes were applied in your own analysis. However, what if you want to present the results of a text-based analysis visually without losing the fundamental, *textual* nature of the data? In such cases, a **word cloud** might be appropriate.

A word cloud uses words, not numbers, to indicate how frequently particular words are used in a sample of text; words that appear more frequently in a text are displayed in a larger font than words that appear less frequently (Dudeney, Hockly, & Pegrum, 2014, p. 178). The simplicity of word clouds is compelling; they allow a viewer to instantly gain an understanding of the most prominent terms and ideas in what may be a very long and complex text. To see how intuitive word clouds are, take a look at Figure 9.8, which presents a word cloud I created using the full text of Chapter 2 of this book. We can use the word cloud to identify the most prominent themes and concepts in Chapter 2.

Not surprisingly, the words 'research', 'data', and 'analysis' were prominent in Chapter 2. What's most surprising is that 'validity' also appears to have been a prominent theme. Even though I'm very familiar with Chapter 2, I didn't realize 'validity' was such an important concept in that text. This unexpected finding illustrates the ability of word clouds to reveal previously unknown patterns and features in your data.

The ability of word clouds to quickly identify prominent themes means that, in addition to communicating results after a research project has been completed, a word cloud can also

Figure 9.8 Word cloud of text from Chapter 2
Word cloud created with Wordle (http://www.wordle.net/)

be used *early on* in the research process to explore a dataset. Word clouds can be particularly helpful in suggesting *codes* that should be applied during the coding process (Beebe, 2014, p. 157; Bhattacharya, 2015, p. 15).

Word clouds can be easily created in many popular CAQDAS programs. (Recall from our discussion in Chapter 7 that CAQDAS stands for 'computer-assisted qualitative data analysis software'. For more information about different CAQDAS programs, and the advantages and disadvantages of using CAQDAS in qualitative research, take a look at Chapter 7 now.) Conveniently, programs that create word clouds typically exclude commonly used words like 'the' or 'is' to allow a researcher to focus instead on more meaningful terms (Dudeney et al., 2014, p. 178). In addition to the general CAQDAS programs discussed in Chapter 7, a free online program called Wordle can be used to create word clouds. In fact, the word cloud in Figure 9.8 was created with this program. Wordle was constructed by Jonathan Feinberg and is available at: http://www.wordle.net/

let's try this!

If you're able to, take a moment to access the Wordle website now (http://www.wordle.net/). Create a word cloud of your own by typing some random text into the box. After you've created the word cloud, experiment with different font, colour, and layout options available on the website.

9.6.10 Network maps

In addition to visualizing numeric and word data, you may also want to visualize *relationship* data. Perhaps you want to illustrate how different interviewees are related to each other, or how different organizations are connected within a hierarchy. A **network map** can accomplish these goals. A network map is typically composed of *nodes*, which are the units or individuals you are interested in, which are typically illustrated with circles, triangles, or other shapes (Lima, 2011, p. 86). A network map also features *links* or *edges*, which are the relationships and connections between those units or individuals, and are illustrated with 'connecting lines' (Lanum, 2017, p. 4). This use of shapes and lines allows a network's overall structure to be easily communicated to interested viewers. A network map can also reveal the position of a particular actor within a larger system of relationships, and help a researcher recognize whether any important actors have been excluded from the analysis (Häussling, 2014, p. 114).

Although network maps can be used to represent *any* kind of network – including networks of organizations or governments that interact with each other – they are most frequently used to represent *social networks*, or networks of individuals who share relationships or interactions. Such networks are the focus of the exciting and ever-growing field of *social network analysis*, which probes 'social dynamics within groups' and seeks to identify the 'key players' within networks (Lanum, 2017, p. 22).

To understand how network maps are made, and how they facilitate social network analysis, let's explore an example study of social networks and health issues. The study was conducted by Fyrand, Moum, Finset, and Glennås (2003) and is also discussed by Biordi and Nicholson (2013, p. 123). The study explored how to help mobilize a patient's social network when that patient faced health issues. As part of the study, 'the researchers mapped the participant's present social network', a task that not only 'helped the participants to obtain a deeper analysis of the makeup of their social networks' but also helped the researchers identify the important individuals within each participant's network (Fyrand et al., 2003, p. 71). This example shows not only how social network analysis can work in practice, but also how social network analysis can help researchers (and research participants) make sense of complex social data.

It's important to note that, despite its name, social network analysis is not limited to the study of friendships or other social relationships; it can also examine professional relationships to understand an industry or particular sector. For example, Deschaux-Beaume (2013, p. 137) explored how key stakeholders in France and Germany conceptualized and presented defence policy options. Constructing a network map of the stakeholders was central to this analysis, as the map highlighted connections and interactions among the experts that could not be easily conveyed through text alone. This real-world example of social network analysis illustrates how network maps can be used not only to *communicate* findings but also to *explore and organize* findings during the research process.

9.6.11 Geographic methods

Instead of a network map, perhaps you're more interested in creating a 'traditional' geographic map (i.e., a map of physical space). Maybe there are spatial or geographic patterns in your dataset that you want to explore further, or maybe you're interested in comparing the characteristics of different regions. Technological advances have revolutionized the process of creating geographic maps, and researchers use the term *geographic information system* (**GIS**) to denote 'the computer hardware and software used to store, query, display, manipulate, and analyse geographic information' (Montello & Sutton, 2013, p. 284). GIS programs can be particularly useful for social scientists as they allow a researcher to explore 'multiple layers of information' and detect whether characteristics or variables are spread randomly throughout an area, or follow some geographic pattern (LeGates, 2005, p. 39). In other words, GIS programs can allow a researcher to perceive patterns and differences in the spread of different variables across regions. Through GIS programs, a researcher can also perform 'overlay analysis' to probe whether 'two or more features tend to exist in the same location' – for example, are higher unemployment rates present in the same areas that voted more strongly for Brexit? – a phenomenon known as 'spatial coincidence' (LeGates, 2005, p. 39). For more information, take a look at the 'Further Reading' section at the end of this chapter.

9.7 Recommendations for Data Visualization

At the beginning of this chapter we explored some *general* guidelines to follow when presenting the results of quantitative, qualitative, and mixed-methods data analyses. Now we'll look at more specific recommendations for creating *visualizations* of your data or results. Regardless of which type of data visualization method you select – whether you choose to create tables, bar charts, histograms, pie charts, scatterplots, line charts, word clouds, network maps, geographic methods, or other graphs or figures – these recommendations are helpful to keep in mind.

9.7.1 Think about the viewer

The first recommendation is to always keep the viewer of your data visualization at the forefront of your mind as you design your visualization. This recommendation is similar to the idea we described at the beginning of this chapter that you should think carefully about your intended audience and employ an appropriate vocabulary and style when *presenting* your findings. Analogously, when *visualizing* your findings, you should think about your intended viewers' level of knowledge and methodological background. Are your intended viewers all experts in your specific field, or are your viewers from a wider variety of backgrounds? Viewers who lack expertise in your field may need more guidance to interpret your visualizations; such guidance could include more detailed labels in the figures (Lanum, 2017, p. 82). As Kostelnick and Roberts (2011, p. 270) explained, 'what you choose to emphasize depends on the rhetorical situation – the readers, the display's purpose, and how readers use it'.

9.7.2 Present your data and findings *clearly*

This second recommendation is easy to understand but surprisingly difficult to put into practice! How do you make sure your figures/graphs are *clear*, or straightforward for viewers to understand?

Clarity has multiple components, including the design and layout of your graphs/figures, the fonts you employ, the colours you select, and the presence of a key or legend (Kostelnick & Roberts, 2011, p. 17). (This last point – including a helpful key or legend – is a critical but often overlooked element of clarity, as viewers need to be able to easily decipher the intricate meaning of each figure you include.) Additionally, although the information in a figure should not be wholly repeated in the write-up of your results, make sure to at least refer to each figure in the text of your thesis/dissertation/article/essay. If a figure appears without any introduction or discussion in the text, it will likely only confuse readers.

This recommendation builds upon the first recommendation ('Think about the viewer') since, to determine whether your visualization is clear and understandable, you'll need to consider how your audience is likely to *interpret* your visualization. Even if *you* think a graph or figure is clear and easy to understand, you should ask colleagues or friends for second, third, and even fourth opinions. In the end, what *you* think about your visualization is irrelevant; what matters is whether your audience thinks a graph is straightforward and understandable (Cleveland, 1994, p. 20).

9.7.3 Take time to think about your visual choices

In order to present your findings clearly, you'll have to scrutinize your visual choices. Such choices include the decision about which type of visualization to create (e.g., is a bar chart more appropriate for your data, or would a line chart be better?), as well as more minute – but still important – design decisions (such as what colours and fonts to use). In making these decisions, it's helpful to think about the fundamental design principle known as the 'pop-out effect', in which a particular object grabs a viewer's attention by differing dramatically from the other objects around it, or from the background (Ware, 2008, p. 29). If there are particular lines, shapes, or data points that you want to highlight, think about how to exploit contrasts in 'color, orientation, size, motion, and stereoscopic depth' to take advantage of the pop-out effect (Ware, 2008, p. 29).

9.7.4 Be ethical and responsible in your visualization efforts

It's essential to recognize that, by creating tables, graphs, and figures, you gain 'enormous power to control which data – and which relationships among the data – to emphasize or deemphasize' (Kostelnick & Roberts, 2011, p. 268). In other words, you acquire the ability to shape viewers' interpretations of your data to a degree not possible through text or numbers alone. You must therefore be careful and ethical when exercising this power, and remember that your primary aim is always to *accurately* present your data/results; accuracy always takes precedence over all other goals, including clarity and aesthetic appeal.

9.8 The Future of Data Visualization

In this chapter we've explored many of the most prominent visualization methods that are in use today. However, it's important to remember that data visualization is a rapidly evolving field, and technological advances will continue to expand the techniques and options available to researchers. As Wildbur and Burke (1998, p. 17) have argued, traditional visualization methods such as bar charts still have an important role to play, but newer methods that draw on 'the moving image' and 'interactive media' have also gained increasing prominence. Therefore, to effectively communicate findings in the future, researchers will need to expand their visualization repertoire to also include 'typography, graphics, the moving image, sound and music' (Wildbur & Burke, 1998, p. 17).

This emphasis on engaging more fully with viewers is reflected in another recent trend: the growth of *interactive* data displays. Interactive data displays allow viewers to customize their visual experience. For example, instead of merely presenting the averages from a dataset, an interactive data display allows viewers to select subsamples within the dataset (such as respondents of a particular gender or age group) and explore averages for those specific groups (Viegas & Wattenberg, 2011). More generally, interactive displays can permit viewers 'to navigate and query data', as well as 'zoom in on items of interest, filter out uninteresting data, select an item', or perform similar activities (Kitchin, 2014, p. 106). As technologies develop and more online venues for presenting visualizations become available, the opportunities for creating interactive elements will likely increase.

stop and think

Do you agree with these predictions about the future of data visualization? Are there any other trends or developments that you can foresee?

9.9 Examples of Innovative Data Visualizations

Visualization techniques can illuminate key features and relationships within a dataset; adding interactive features to such visualizations can grab viewers' attention and allow them to more fully engage with your findings. Technological advances have made it easier for data analysts to create such displays, and have increased the popular visibility of such displays. To show how such interactivity can work in practice, let's explore two real-world examples of interactive data visualizations. These two examples focus on very different kinds of data and adopt different visualization approaches, illustrating the diversity of interactive displays.

The first example is the CrimeMAPS website, which presents data from the San Francisco Police Department (City and County of San Francisco (n.d.) (https://data.sfgov.org/Public-Safety/SF-Crime-Heat-Map/q6gg-sa2p/data)). Interested members of the public can use the website to find data and even produce maps of crime incidents reported to police. Specifically, at the time of writing, viewers are able to search CrimeMAPS for particular types of offences: data is available for homicide, forcible rape, robbery, aggravated assault, arson, burglary, larceny (theft), vehicle theft, vandalism, and drug offences. Viewers can also search based on the location of the offence within San Francisco, or the date on which the offence occurred (with data available for the previous 90 days). The website allows individuals to gain greater awareness of an important issue – crime – in their community. From a data analyst's perspective, the website is a striking example of how geographic methods can be used to illuminate patterns and features within a dataset.

The second example is Column Five's entertaining visualization of the value of different sports franchises around the world (Column Five (n.d.) http://bit.ly/2IXnb9O). The visualization allows viewers to compare the number of championships, years in existence, and estimated financial value of franchises in different sports. The visualization is a kind of sophisticated scatterplot, as dots representing various sports franchises are situated along two axes. The visualization invites viewers to interact with it, since, by moving a computer cursor over each dot, one can see information about each team. The visualization is also distinguished by its use of bright, appealing colours, and its ability to clearly present comparative financial information. Given these attributes, it's not surprising that this visualization received significant popular media attention, as described on Column Five's website.

Concluding Thoughts

As a researcher, it's tempting to believe that your results will 'speak for themselves' – that, once you've conducted your analyses, your job is done. But this belief is only partly true. Yes, a data analyst's *most important* task is to conduct rigorous and ethical research. But this isn't your *only* task. You also need to appropriately and effectively communicate your findings. Indeed, as we've seen in this chapter, the ability to clearly and compellingly present research results is a skill that, increasingly, data analysts *must* possess.

How can a data analyst communicate findings effectively? First and foremost, by *thinking* about the audience. Audiences have varying interests and levels of knowledge, and different presentation venues (e.g., dissertations, books, journal articles, and conference presentations) require targeted approaches. Always keep in mind that, when presenting research results, one size does not fit all. Instead, think carefully about how you can target your presentation strategy to your audience's interests and needs.

Another key theme in this chapter was the value of *visually* presenting research findings. A wide range of different visual presentation techniques exist, and we've discussed how each of these techniques possesses its own advantages and limitations. There is no one 'correct' visual presentation style that will work for all projects. Instead, you'll need to consider the unique goals and features of your own data analysis work. This pervasive need to tailor your presentation approach – rather than simply follow a set of presentation 'rules' that work in all instances – might seem overwhelming. How can you predict what approaches will work best in different circumstances? It's understandable that this question might seem overwhelming, but don't let such feelings stop you from moving forward. Presenting data analysis findings effectively is a skill; like all worthwhile skills, it will take time and attention to master. Over time, as you gain more experience, presenting findings will get easier, although even seasoned data analysts can sometimes find this task challenging. Challenging – but worth doing right.

Summary

- When communicating the findings of your data analysis, make sure your paper/presentation/thesis/dissertation exhibits high *descriptive validity* (which means that your research methods, and the limitations of those methods, are described in detail).
- Additionally, when communicating findings, think about your *audience*. The vocabulary and tone you employ should take into account your audience's knowledge and expertise regarding your topic and research methods.
- Data visualization – which explores how different visual strategies can accurately and engagingly communicate a dataset's features – is a rapidly growing field. The most popular methods for visualizing data include tables, bar charts, histograms, pie charts, scatterplots, line charts, word clouds, network maps, and geographic methods.
- When creating data visualizations, some important guidelines to keep in mind are: to think about the viewer; to present your data and findings clearly; to take time to think about your visual choices; and to be ethical and responsible in your visualization efforts.
- Future developments in the field of data visualization will likely include more technological sophistication, a greater diversity of visualization options available to researchers, and an emphasis on interactivity with viewers.
- Examples of real-world interactive data displays include San Francisco's CrimeMAPS website and Column Five's visualization of sports franchises. Both of these examples illustrate how appealing visual methods and interactivity can help viewers engage with data.

9.12 Further Reading

For a useful primer on many basic data visualization methods, including histograms and scatterplots, take a look at:

Jacoby, W. G. (1997). *Statistical graphics for univariate and bivariate data*. Thousand Oaks, CA: SAGE Publications.

A broader, general overview of data visualization methods can be found in:

Tufte, E. R. (2001). *The visual display of quantitative information* (2nd ed.). Cheshire, CT: Graphics Press.

At the beginning of the chapter, we described the emerging discipline of *information design*, which explores how information can most effectively and accurately be communicated to viewers. For an excellent, visually stunning introduction to this discipline, see:

Wildbur, P., & Burke, M. (1998). *Information graphics: Innovative solutions in contemporary design*. New York: Thames and Hudson.

Another striking overview of different visualization methods is:

Lima, M. (2011). *Visual complexity: Mapping patterns of information*. New York: Princeton Architectural Press.

For a creative and inspiring overview of the many ways that data can be visualized, visit the *Information is Beautiful* website, created by David McCandless. The website showcases numerous innovative examples of visualizations, and is updated regularly. The website's address is: http://www.informationisbeautiful.net/

In this chapter we also briefly explored how GIS software can be employed to explore spatial or geographic data. However, such a short discussion could not do justice to this expansive topic. To start to learn more about this software and how it can be used to visualize data, take a look at:

LeGates, R. (2005). *Think globally, act regionally: GIS and data visualization for social science and public policy research*. Redlands, CA: ESRI Press.

Discussion Questions

1 What is *descriptive validity*? Why is descriptive validity important when communicating the findings of a data analysis?

2 It's essential to *consider your audience* when you present your results. If, for example, your audience is broad and consists of non-specialists, you should minimize your use of jargon and employ different communication strategies, such as metaphors or stories, to convey more complex ideas. To explore how real-world data analysts communicate with their audiences, let's revisit two studies we explored in Chapter 8: Chui and Cheng's (2017) study of young offenders in Hong Kong's justice system, and Wilkinson et al.'s (2017) study of unemployment among young adults in rural South Africa.

   Take a moment to look through both of these studies again. (If you're unable to read the full articles, then just re-read the abstracts.) Based upon the language and structure of Chui and Cheng's (2017) article, *who* do you think is the intended audience for their work? The general public? Policy-makers? Social scientists in general? Lawyers and legal scholars? Or just lawyers and legal scholars who specialize in Hong Kong's criminal justice system? What clues can you identify in the text of the article to support your conclusion?

   Then consider Wilkinson et al.'s study. Based upon the language and structure of this article, *who* do you think is the intended audience? What clues can you identify in the text of the article that support your conclusion?

3 What are two main advantages of using a table to present data? What are two main limitations of using a table to present data?

4 In the field of data visualization, what does the acronym GIS stand for? What kinds of data are most appropriate to explore with GIS?

5 What is the 'pop-out effect'? Why is it important to consider this effect when producing a data visualization?

6 In this chapter we explored two real-world examples of interactive data visualizations: the CrimeMAPS website from San Francisco and Column Five's visualization of sports franchises. Choose one of these examples and spend a few minutes exploring the visualization. Once you become familiar with the visualization, reflect upon your experience as a viewer. Is the visualization easy or difficult to interpret? What do you like about the visualization? What is one recommendation you would make to improve the design or operation of the visualization?

Conclusion: Becoming a Data Analyst

contents

10.1 Chapter Overview

By the end of this chapter, you will be able to:

- Understand the importance of constructing 'good' research questions to guide social science data analysis
- Explain why maintaining ethical standards is a crucial component of data analysis, and outline how such standards can be upheld
- Clarify what responsible *data management* entails, and why, in appropriate circumstances, *data sharing* can benefit researchers
- Offer advice for selecting an appropriate analytical method
- Discuss the fundamental limitations of data analysis, and explain why identifying limitations is so important
- Clarify why *now* is an exciting time to study data analysis, and describe the potential benefits and challenges posed by 'big data' and other new developments in this field.

Becoming a Data Analyst: Key Principles

You've done it – you've finally made it to the end of the book! It's been a long journey, and over the course of the previous nine chapters we've examined the quintessential ideas underlying all forms of data analysis, as well as specific guidelines for completing quantitative, qualitative, and mixed-methods studies. We've explored numerous real-world examples of data analysis, and discovered how lessons from these examples can be applied to your own work. We've covered an almost overwhelming amount of material; therefore, it's time, in this chapter, to slow down and reflect on what we've learned.

To clarify the book's most important conclusions, let's focus on the key principles that you should keep in mind as you continue your data analysis journey. The key principles we'll review here are: *thinking carefully about your research questions; maintaining ethical standards; selecting appropriate analytical methods*; and *recognizing limitations*. These guidelines apply regardless of the type of data analysis you undertake and are the most fundamental, general data analysis lessons to be gleaned from this textbook.

10.2.1 Think carefully about your research questions

The first principle to remember is that data analysis is driven by *questions*. Learning to ask 'good' questions is perhaps the most important – and most underrated – research skill. But what makes a particular question a 'good' question for a research project? The most important criterion is that the question is interesting and important *to you*. Data analysis takes substantial time and effort, but knowing that your research questions are interesting and important can help you stay motivated. If your research project is a dissertation or thesis, you may spend years exploring your research questions, and you can't simply switch questions later on if you get bored! So it's worth spending time at the outset to develop intriguing, relevant, and weighty questions. Even if you don't have full control over your research questions – perhaps the questions are dictated by an advisor or your research group or even a funding body – there may still be ways to *tailor* the questions to match your interests. Are there particular aspects of the questions that appeal to you and that you can focus on? Will answering these questions have real-world impacts? Thinking about the practical, meaningful implications of your research questions can help you remain engaged in your work.

stop and think

What do you think are the key characteristics of a 'good' research question?

Since well-thought-out research questions can help you narrow your focus, select research methods, and decide what kinds of data to focus on, these questions should be in place before you even begin to collect data. Research questions should also inspire your hypotheses, if you're planning on testing hypotheses in your work. (What's a *hypothesis*? It's a belief or argument about the social world that's based on experience, intuition, or the findings of previous research. If you can't recall this definition, or if you can't remember how hypotheses are used in social science research, it's worth revisiting Chapter 2 now.) As we saw in Chapter 2, researchers typically develop hypotheses and then collect and analyse real-world data to test whether data supports, or contradicts, their hypotheses. This process, *hypothesis testing*, is the cornerstone of most forms of data analysis. (The key exception, of course, is research based on *grounded theory* in which researchers collect data first, and then build theories from the data (Glaser & Strauss, 1967).) Formulating reasonable, compelling research questions can greatly facilitate the process of hypotheses testing – and data analysis overall (Balnaves & Caputi, 2001, p. 45).

How can a researcher formulate 'good' research questions? Where do research questions come from? Since your own research will build upon the work of previous scholars, it's essential to investigate the findings of past research on your topic of interest. Before collecting data, researchers typically perform a thorough *literature review* to determine relevant findings or theories from past research. Compiling a literature review involves a rigorous search of relevant research databases and library catalogues. The types of sources researchers look for include books, academic articles, government reports, and reports by non-profit or research organizations. For guidance about how to compile a literature review, visit your university or town library and speak to a librarian. Many university libraries employ librarians who are subject-matter experts, and can help you access relevant databases and library catalogues to find previous relevant research on your topic.

10.2.2 Maintaining ethical standards

As we saw in Chapter 3, principles such as *informed consent* are fundamental for ensuring the integrity of the research process. Other important ethical principles, as delineated in the cross-disciplinary Singapore Statement on Research Integrity (2010), include 'honesty', 'accountability', 'professional courtesy' and 'good stewardship'. Before collecting or analysing any data, you need to think carefully about how you will uphold these principles. As we saw in Chapter 3, the *cumulative* nature of research (i.e., the fact that all researchers build upon the work of previous scholars) means that unethical practices by one researcher can have serious cascading consequences for entire social science disciplines (Israel & Hay, 2006, p. 5).

Maintaining ethical standards is not simply a matter of following a given list of rules, however. It also involves cultivating a broader sense of professional responsibility, in which you reflect upon your own role as a researcher and the ways in which your beliefs and experiences might influence your perspective on your data (Lambert, Jomeen, & McSherry, 2010, p. 322). A researcher must always think carefully about how their own 'life history' and chosen research methods 'shape and structure' the data collection and analysis processes (Banks, 2014, p. 296). This reflection must include reflection on ethical issues.

In addition, this reflection should include an acknowledgement of your own power as a researcher. You possess tremendous sway over how your viewers/readers *respond* to your data and findings. In the previous chapter, for example, we discussed how the use of different visualization methods (such as tables, graphs, and figures) can shape viewers' interpretations of your results. Researchers must be cautious in exercising this power; Kostelnick and Roberts's (2011, p. 268) admonition to 'be wary about using emphasis strategies that might deceive' the audience applies not only to visualization methods but also to the presentation of your results more broadly. Tricks such as altering your hypothesis after you've analysed your data to better 'fit' your results are unethical and unacceptable in professional research.

stop and think

Why is it unethical to alter your hypothesis after you've analysed your data to better 'fit' your results? What would be the consequences of making such an alteration?

10.2.3 Selecting appropriate analytical methods

Data analysis is an incredibly diverse field. In this book we've seen this diversity at first hand. Quantitative, qualitative, and mixed-methods approaches are very different – but each of these methods has its own value. Moreover, as we've learned, a wide range of more specific procedures exist within each of these categories. So how does a researcher choose which method to use? While the proliferation of research methods helpfully increases a researcher's options, this abundance can also feel overwhelming. With so many choices, how can a researcher be sure that their chosen method is the best choice? Unfortunately, the pressure to select the perfect research method can be counterproductive, resulting in extra stress that delays the commencement of the actual research project. Don't let this pressure impede your own progress. Instead, recognize that, for many research projects, there is no one 'perfect' research method; since every method has its own advantages and limitations, multiple methods might be equally effective for achieving your project's goals.

To make the decision about which method to use, you should first consider your research questions. (One reason why it's important to think carefully about your research questions is that they should dictate the methods you ultimately employ.) What methods could most comprehensively answer your research questions? What kind of data would you need to fully explore those questions? If, for example, your research questions could only be answered with qualitative data then of course you'd want to select a qualitative method for your project.

The most important consideration should be your research questions, but you can consider additional factors when making the decision about which methods to use. For example, you can learn from the efforts of past researchers. Take a look at your literature review; what methods did the studies cited in your literature review use? What methods have previous studies used to explore similar research questions? Of course you don't have to use the same methods that previous researchers employed, but previous studies can provide helpful guidance about what methods *might* be appropriate. You can evaluate the strengths and limitations of the methods employed in previous studies to help you determine whether you want to use the same methods, or try new techniques.

Sometimes practical constraints can also affect your choice of methods. A lack of resources or time can limit the methodological choices available to you – particularly if you're a student – and it's essential to acknowledge this reality. Additionally, as we discussed in Chapter 6, one's methodological knowledge and ability to execute particular methods (e.g., your access to particular software packages) can impact decisions about which methods to use. It's only natural to want to use methods for which you have expertise. On the other hand, however, don't shy away from learning new methods. To grow as a data analyst, you'll need to keep pushing yourself. Don't solely rely on the basic methods gleaned from this book or from your course or from your supervisor/advisor. If there's a more sophisticated method that you think might be appropriate for your data, why not try to learn more about that method? Numerous resources are available to help data analysts learn new techniques, including specialized textbooks, short courses, and free online tutorials. Take a look at the 'Further Reading' lists at the end of all the chapters in this textbook, in case any of those sources seem useful. Becoming a data analyst is really a process of continuous learning, and even experienced data analysts (including myself) are constantly challenging themselves to learn new techniques.

10.2.4 Considering data management issues

An often overlooked – but critically important – aspect of data analysis is the *management* of data. Thinking about how you will organize, preserve, and, if appropriate, share your data are all essential tasks. In recent years, the concept of *research data management*, which includes all 'activities undertaken in relation to the collection, processing, preservation and sharing of' data, has received increasing attention in social science research (Research & Enterprise Services, University of Reading, n.d.). Engaging in responsible research data management will help you preserve the 'reliability and integrity of your data', and allow you to easily open your methods and data to outside scrutiny – thereby promoting the rigour of your data analysis (Research & Enterprise Services, University of Reading, n.d.).

A key element of responsible research data management is the creation of useful *metadata*. Metadata 'is descriptive information about a project, the experiments, the equipment used, the researchers, and the data themselves' to help other researchers understand, and work with, the data (Data Services, University of Tennessee Knoxville, 2017). Metadata can include descriptive names for computer files, *codebooks* identifying each variable and how it was collected, and other guidance notes for future scholars interested in your dataset. There are a number of steps you can take during the data collection and analysis processes to facilitate the construction of metadata. For example, you should take careful notes about how you collected the data and any changes you made to the variables (as it can be surprisingly easy to forget what you did later on); additionally, be sure to leave clear notes about the labelling scheme you used, as other researchers may not be familiar with the abbreviations or names you employed (Data Management Services, Massachusetts Institute of Technology (MIT) Libraries, n.d.a). Naming your files may seem like a simple task, but it does require some thought to ensure your file names could be easily deciphered by other researchers. It's worth spending a bit of time at the beginning of the data collection or organization process to establish some formal rules for naming files, to ensure that you don't lose track of the most recent version of a file, and that research collaborators (or future researchers, if you plan to share your data) could easily work with your data (Data Management Services, Massachusetts Institute of Technology (MIT) Libraries, n.d.b). Even if you don't plan to collect your own data, it's still helpful to become familiar with the concept of metadata, since you'll encounter the metadata *other researchers* have produced when you use their secondary datasets. If you're interested in learning more about the best practices for creating metadata, take a look at the helpful advice of Data Services, University of Tennessee Knoxville (2017).

In addition to creating useful metadata, a second essential component of responsible research data management is ensuring that data is properly *stored*. Throughout this book, we've emphasized the importance of *research ethics*, and such ethical responsibilities extend into data management and storage. Indeed, as a researcher, you are obliged not only to *collect* and *analyse* data in an ethical manner, but also to *protect* and *preserve* that data in an ethical manner. Storing data in an ethical manner means that you adequately protect the security of that data, and ensure that the data is not modified or altered in a misleading manner. The precise security precautions you must employ will vary depending on a dataset's particular characteristics (e.g., datasets containing more sensitive information will of course require more intense precautions), laws in your jurisdiction, and the requirements of your institution or funding body. However, there are also a number of sensible precautions that should *always* be followed by researchers. Such precautions include regularly changing your computer and email passwords, updating your anti-virus programs, and keeping your computer hardware safe from theft (Edinburgh Napier University, 2017a). Certain types of sensitive data, like health information, might require you to take *specific* enhanced security procedures, and it is worth investigating what these procedures are before you decide to conduct research using such data. If you plan to *collect* identifiable data, it may be necessary to inform your research participants about how the data will be *stored* as part of your 'informed consent procedures' (Van den Eynden, Corti, Woollard, Bishop, & Horton, 2011, p. 20). (Do you remember what *informed consent* is? For a quick refresher, take another look at Chapter 3 now.). In other words, potential research participants will need to be informed about how their data will be stored *before* they make their decision about whether to participate in your study.

We've just discussed the importance of preserving the *privacy* and *security* of data. However, when ethically permissible and appropriate, the *sharing* of data can have substantial benefits – both for you as a researcher, and for social science research more broadly. Benefits of sharing data include increasing public awareness of your research, and thereby expanding the potential for your research and data to have real-world impacts (Edinburgh Napier University, 2017b). An additional benefit of sharing your data with other researchers is that you can facilitate *triangulation* by allowing these researchers to *replicate* your work. (Do you remember what *triangulation* is? If not, take a moment to read over our discussion in Chapter 2 now.) Allowing other researchers to replicate your work lends credence to your findings (i.e., if other researchers reach similar conclusions, critics will be more likely to accept your findings), and may even be required by some research funders (Sieber, 1991). For all these reasons, it's not surprising that interest in replicability and data sharing has exploded in recent years in a range of social science disciplines, although impediments to data sharing still exist; see Curty, Yoon, Jeng, & Qin, 2016). Of course, before sharing your data, you must ensure that such a task is ethically permissible and would not violate the privacy of your research participants (Data Management Services, Massachusetts Institute of Technology (MIT) Libraries, n.d.c).

This section has offered *general* advice about data management; however, many universities and academic departments offer more *precise* institutional or discipline-specific guidelines. Many universities have specific policies for data management that their researchers must follow, and many universities require researchers to develop a formal plan for managing their data to ensure that ethical and quality standards are met (e.g., Research & Enterprise Services, University of Reading, n.d.; Edinburgh Napier University, 2015). Before beginning your research project, it's a good idea to check whether any more specific guidance on data management is available to you. Ultimately, although data management may not receive as much attention as data collection or analysis, it is a critically important element of the research process. Managing your data responsibly and thoughtfully will greatly facilitate your analytical efforts.

10.2.5 Recognizing limitations

Throughout this book we've explored the great potential of data analysis to offer insight into the social world. We've seen that both quantitative and qualitative data analysis methods can shed light on some of the most fundamental questions we face in social life. But each of these methods also has limitations. Quantitative methods, for example, have been criticized for only being able to assess 'abstracted variables' which may not offer a full, in-depth 'feel' for the cases or units a researcher is interested in (Bryman, 1989, p. 115). Qualitative methods, on the other hand, have been criticized for being 'strongly subject to researcher bias', and not reproducible or generalizable to other settings or populations (see the discussion in Mays &

Pope, 1995, p. 109). Of course, these critiques don't apply to all quantitative and qualitative studies, and specific forms of quantitative and qualitative research exhibit more unique limitations as well. It is your job as a responsible researcher to think critically about the limitations of your own methods, and be thorough and forthright in acknowledging these limitations when writing up your findings. Acknowledging such limitations does not diminish the value of your work; on the contrary, it underscores your professionalism.

10.3 Concluding Thoughts: The Future of Data Analysis

It's an exciting time to learn data analysis, as technological advances have increased both the amount of data available to analyse, and the methods that can be used to analyse that data. In particular, the so-called 'democratization of data', or the wider availability of large datasets and software packages, will increase the opportunities available to data analysts, and allow social science research to influence policy and practice in new, positive ways (National Research Council, 2012, p. 99). This idea connects to another exciting development that we've already explored: the *big data* phenomenon, or the broader range and larger scale of data that is now available due to technological advances. As we discussed in Chapter 1, the growth of big data has dramatically affected many areas of the economy and social life, and its impacts will likely only increase in future (Liebowitz, 2013; Doering, 2014). Although exciting, this development also poses new challenges: for example, the emergence of larger datasets and more sophisticated technological data analysis techniques increases the likelihood of uncovering relationships between unrelated variables, or patterns that are illusory (Fletcher, 2014; Taleb, 2013). (The epidemiologist John Ioannidis's (2005) thought-provoking analysis 'Why most published research findings are false' describes how, when researchers look for numerous correlations between variables in large datasets, the chance of finding some significant results due to chance alone can be troublingly high.)

These technological transformations mean that *right now* is a fascinating time to explore data analysis; indeed, the opportunities and needs for competent data analysis skills will likely only continue to grow (Mayer-Schönberger & Cukier, 2013). By studying this book, you've already begun to prepare yourself for the job market. I wish you every success in your data analysis journey, and hope that this is just the beginning of what might become a lifelong learning process.

10.4 Summary

- At the outset of every research project, it's essential to think carefully about your research questions. Choose questions that interest you and that can adeptly guide your subsequent data analysis.
- Maintaining ethical standards is critical in each phase of data collection and analysis. More than merely following a given list of rules, maintaining ethical standards also means cultivating a

broader sense of professional responsibility to your research participants, fellow scholars, and future readers of your work.

- Choose an analysis method that is appropriate for your research questions and data. However, don't get stuck worrying over whether your chosen method is 'perfect', as every method has advantages and limitations.
- Acknowledge the limitations of your data analysis methods, and be completely honest and open with your future readers about these limitations.
- Technological changes and other recent changes mean that *right now* is an opportune time to study data analysis, with more exciting developments likely to emerge in the future.

10.5 Further Reading

Now that we've reached the end of this textbook, it's worth reflecting on the data analysis process and its advantages, limitations, and challenges. Two other excellent textbooks that present a thoughtful, reflective perspective on data analysis are:

Bentz, V. M., & Shapiro, J. J. (1998). *Mindful inquiry in social research.* Thousand Oaks, CA: SAGE Publications.

Luker, K. (2008). *Salsa dancing into the social sciences: Research in an age of info-glut.* Cambridge, MA: Harvard University Press.

Each of these books highlights important issues in social science data analysis, and will force you to reflect on your own understandings of the discipline.

In addition to further general sources about data analysis, you're probably also interested in finding more advanced, in-depth sources about *specific* data analysis methods, such as correlation. If you're interested in learning more about a particular quantitative method, investigate whether that method has been covered in a SAGE 'little green book'. These books, which form the Quantitative Applications in the Social Sciences (QASS) series, are short but detailed introductions to many key quantitative techniques, and are available in many university libraries. You can find out more about the topics covered in the books here:

https://us.sagepub.com/en-us/nam/qass

If you're interested in qualitative methods, a great place to start learning about more advanced methods is a website maintained by the University of Leicester. The website features useful links to further sources about different qualitative methods and software packages. You can access the website at: http://www2.le.ac.uk/offices/red/rd/research-methods-and-methodologies/qualitative-methods

Finally, near the end of this chapter, we discussed data management issues, such as the importance of protecting privacy when sharing data. For a very thorough but readable guide to these issues, take a look at:

Van den Eynden, V., Corti, L., Woollard, M., Bishop, L., & Horton, L. (2011). *Managing and sharing data* (3rd ed.). Colchester: University of Essex, UK Data Archive. (At the time of writing, the guide was freely available online, so try doing an internet search for the title.)

10.6 Discussion Questions

1. What do you think is the most important lesson of this book?
2. What does the term 'democratization of data' mean (National Research Council, 2012, p. 99)? Do you think this phenomenon will continue to grow in the future? Why or why not?
3. Toward the end of the chapter, I mentioned John Ioannidis's (2005) thought-provoking analysis 'Why most published research findings are false'. Take a few minutes to locate and read this important paper. (At the time of writing, the paper was freely available online.) What are your reactions to the paper? Do you agree with Ioannidis's arguments? Are there any limitations or gaps in logic in his arguments? How, if at all, does the paper change your thoughts about data analysis?

Glossary

action research: An approach to social science research in which the goal of research is to generate action

alternative hypothesis: A hypothesis that there *is* a relationship or a difference that the researcher is interested in

anonymity: When identifying information is not to be disclosed to others

axial coding: Originally developed in the context of grounded theory, an intermediate stage of the qualitative coding process in which a researcher begins to identify links between codes and to combine or excise particular coding categories

bar chart: A graph in which bars are used to represent the prevalence of different categories in a dataset

big data: The broader range and larger scale of data that is now available due to technological advances

boxplot: A method for visualizing continuous data by representing its minimum data point, first quartile, median, third quartile, and maximum data point

CAQDAS: Computer-assisted qualitative data analysis software, or software that assists a researcher with the coding of qualitative data

case-study research: A form of qualitative research in which the researcher explores a few specific cases in detail rather than one large sample

chi-square test of association: Also known as the chi-square test for independence, a statistical test that explores whether membership in a particular category of one variable is associated with membership in a particular category of another variable

cluster sampling: A sampling strategy in which a population is first divided into clusters such as geographic areas or schools, and clusters are randomly selected for inclusion in the sample

codebook: A document identifying all of the variables included in a quantitative dataset, or a document describing the codes applied to a qualitative dataset

coding: The act of categorizing qualitative data to reveal the essential themes or elements of the data, without worrying about counting or quantifying the categories

confidentiality: When information is not to be divulged or disclosed to others

construct validity: A measure of how well the variables or measures included in a study actually reflect the constructs or concepts they are intended to represent

content analysis: A form of data analysis that explores the frequency with which certain themes and patterns appear in a dataset

continuous variable: A variable that can exhibit a wide variety of values

convenience sampling: A sampling strategy in which a researcher simply includes in the sample those units that are easiest to access

correlation: A measure of the association between two variables

covariance: The extent to which two variables deviate from their respective means in corresponding ways

covert research: A type of research in which participants are not informed that they are participating in a research project

critical research: An approach to social science research that scrutinizes and contests the existing social order, illuminating inequalities within a society

cross-sectional data: Data that captures conditions at a particular moment in time

data: Quantitative or qualitative information about ourselves, society, or the universe

data visualization: The use of visual techniques to communicate features of a dataset or the results of a data analysis

degrees of freedom: Formally, degrees of freedom are the number of data points that can vary, or take on any value, in a statistical computation. Informally, degrees of freedom play an important role in many statistical tests, including correlations, *t*-tests, and chi-square tests

deliberate sampling: A sampling strategy in which only cases that exhibit certain characteristics are purposively chosen from a population

dependent-samples *t*-test: A *t*-test that examines whether the means of the same group of participants measured at two different points in time – such as before and after a treatment is administered – are significantly different

dependent variable: A variable embodying the outcome you are interested in

descriptive validity: The degree to which a study's data collection and analysis procedures have been accurately and comprehensively described

discourse analysis: A form of qualitative data analysis that probes the linguistic nuances and conventions present in human discourse to gain insight into how communication reflects and shapes social power dynamics

discrete variable: A variable that can only exhibit a few different values or categories

diversification: A rationale for using mixed methods, in which the goal is to uncover a broader and more diverse set of findings than could be found with one method type alone

effect size: A standardized measure of the magnitude of the effect observed in a particular study

ethnography: An in-depth qualitative investigation of a particular area, community, or phenomenon through extensive fieldwork and observation

experiment: A research method in which a researcher manipulates one variable to see how these changes affect the values of another variable

external validity: The extent to which the findings of a particular study can be generalized to other settings, time periods, or groups

field notes: Notes taken by a researcher while conducting an ethnography or other fieldwork-based study, which can subsequently be analysed

focused coding: A later stage of the qualitative coding process in which the researcher culls less important codes and thinks about how to coherently report the overall findings

frequency table: A table that illustrates the overall spread of a dataset and indicates how many observations fall into different categories or intervals

GIS: Geographic information system, or a general term encompassing the various computer programs designed to store, analyse, and present geographic data

grounded theory: An approach to social science data analysis that emphasizes developing theories from data, rather than using data to test hypotheses

histogram: A data visualization technique in which a continuous variable is divided into equal-sized 'bins', or categories, which represent a range of values

hypothesis: A belief or argument about the social world based on experience, intuition, or the findings of previous research

hypothesis testing: A formal process of examining whether a hypothesis actually matches data collected in the real world. Based on these findings, you then reject, fail to reject, or revise your original hypothesis. This process is a central component of data analysis

illumination: A rationale for using mixed methods in which a researcher aims to use findings obtained from qualitative research to inform (or illuminate) questions or themes to investigate in subsequent quantitative research, or vice versa

independent-samples *t*-test: A *t*-test that examines whether the means of two independent samples or groups are significantly different

independent variable: A variable that might potentially affect or explain values of the dependent variable, or might cause the effect you are interested in

informed consent: The important ethical principle that research participants should be provided with information about the research project to competently decide whether they want to take part in the project

internal validity: A measure of how well a researcher's data analysis actually reflects the relationship or effect the researcher is interested in

interpretivist tradition: A theoretical framework in social science data analysis which posits that no single objective reality exists, so researchers should instead focus on uncovering different individuals' interpretations of reality, rather than trying to isolate the effects of particular variables

interval data: Continuous data that does not feature an absolute zero, or a point at which there is complete absence of the quantity of interest

interview: A conversation between researcher and research participant that has a particular research purpose

life history research: Research that focuses on uncovering how experiences shape individuals' life trajectories

line chart: A data visualization technique for continuous data in which data points are connected by a line

literature review: A written description of past research findings on a particular topic that often appears at the beginning of a research paper, thesis, or academic article

longitudinal data: Data about the same group of research participants or units collected at different points in time

mean: The popular understanding of 'average', calculated by adding all the different data points in the sample and dividing that total by the number of data points in the sample

median: The middle value of a sample or population of data

mixed-methods research: Research that employs both quantitative and qualitative methods

mode: The value that appears most frequently in a sample or population

narrative analysis: An approach to qualitative data analysis that focuses on probing the narrative elements of textual data to illuminate the stories told by individuals and societies

network map: A visual representation of the relationships or links between particular individuals or organizations

nocebo effect: A phenomenon in which an individual experiences undesirable outcomes or side effects after being exposed to a harmless treatment that the individual *thinks* might have undesirable effects

nominal data: Data arranged in categories that *are not* ranked or ordered in any way

normal distribution: A symmetrical, bell-shaped curve that explains the distribution of many characteristics in the population, such as height

null hypothesis: A hypothesis that there is *no* relationship or difference of interest

one-sample *t*-test: A *t*-test that examines whether the mean of a sample of data is significantly different from some known amount specified by the researcher

one-tailed test: A statistical test for a directional hypothesis

open coding: An early phase of the coding process distinguished by its open, flexible, and even creative orientation

ordinal data: Data that is arranged in categories that *are* ranked or ordered in some way

outlier: A data point located far away from the other data points in a dataset

participant observation: A type of qualitative research in which a researcher actively participates in the phenomenon, organization, or culture he is researching, and does not attempt to maintain neutral, objective distance

Pearson's correlation coefficient: A measure of the correlation (or association) between two continuous variables

pie chart: A data visualization technique in which each pie slice represents the size of a particular category or group in a dataset relative to the other categories or groups in the dataset

pilot study: A preliminary, smaller-scale study that allows a researcher to test and refine research methodologies before conducting the actual, larger study

placebo effect: A phenomenon in which research participants in the control group experience some benefit or improved outcome after only taking a placebo (in other words, after not receiving any experimental treatment)

population: The totality of objects, individuals, countries, or other elements that a researcher is interested in studying

population parameter: The particular characteristic of a population that a researcher is interested in

positivist tradition: A theoretical framework in social science data analysis which posits that an objective reality exists which researchers can uncover and that, by establishing rigorously controlled conditions, a researcher can isolate the effects of a particular variable or set of variables

primary data: Data that a researcher has directly collected (in contrast to *secondary data*)

***p*-value**: The likelihood that we would obtain results equivalent to, or more extreme than, the results we actually see in our data, if the null hypothesis were true. Practically speaking, a *p*-value helps a researcher to determine whether the null hypothesis can be rejected

qualitative data: Data that consists of texts or images or other non-numerical content

quantitative data: Data that is numerical or seeks to quantitatively represent social phenomena

randomized controlled trial: A type of experimental research in which participants are randomly assigned to receive, or not receive, the treatment or condition the researcher is interested in

range: The distance between the highest and lowest values in a sample or population

ratio data: Continuous data that features an absolute zero, or a point at which there is complete absence of the quantity of interest

sample: A selection of cases drawn from a population, which a researcher uses to make inferences about a population

sample statistic: An estimate of a population parameter that is found in a particular sample

sampling distribution: A distribution of the values of a sample statistic that are obtained after repeatedly drawing numerous different samples at random from the population

sampling error: The random variation we see across samples in the values of their sample statistics such as means and standard deviations, even when samples are drawn randomly and no errors in measurement occur

sampling frame: The source from which a researcher draws her sample

scatterplot: A visual illustration of the association (or lack of association) between two continuous variables

secondary data: Data that has been collected by previous researchers (in contrast to *primary data*)

semi-structured interview: An interview that features a set list of questions or topics that must be covered, but permits the researcher and participant to explore topics in greater depth

significance testing: A formal procedure for determining whether the results achieved in a statistical test are unlikely to be due to chance

simple random sampling: A sampling strategy in which every unit – i.e., each individual or organization or other entity a researcher is interested in – has an equal probability of being selected for the sample

snowball sampling: A sampling strategy in which individuals who agree to participate in a study are asked for the names of more individuals to take part in the study, allowing a researcher's sample to grow like a rolling snowball

standard deviation: The square root of the variance and a common measure of the spread of a dataset

standard error: The standard deviation of the sampling distribution

stratified random sampling: A sampling strategy in which a population is split into different categories (such as males and females, or different age brackets) and the researcher then chooses units at random from those different categories

structured interview: An interview that follows a precise list of questions with little deviation

survey: A quantitative or qualitative research method in which participants are asked to fill out a questionnaire (or answer a series of questions) either by themselves or with a research worker present

systematic sampling: A sampling strategy in which a researcher selects cases at regular intervals from address directories, informational databases, or other similar sources

triangulation: The use of multiple data sources, data collection approaches, and data analysis methods to study the same issue or research question

***t*-test**: A statistical test examining whether the means of two groups on some continuous variable are significantly different

two-tailed test: A statistical test for a non-directional hypothesis

Type I error: Mistakenly rejecting the null hypothesis when the null hypothesis is actually true

Type II error: Mistakenly failing to reject the null hypothesis when we should actually reject it because it is false

unstructured interview: An open-ended interview without a predetermined plan or list of questions

variable: A measurable characteristic, concept, cause, or set of items that a researcher wants to investigate through rigorous analysis

variance: A measure of the average difference between each observation in a dataset and the mean

visual methods: Research methods used to analyse data that consists of images (such as photographs or videos)

word cloud: A visual representation of the frequency with which particular words appear in a sample of text; words that appear more frequently in a text are displayed in a larger font than words that appear less frequently

References

Abbott, H. P. (2008). *The Cambridge introduction to narrative* (2nd ed.). Cambridge: Cambridge University Press.

Aguinis, H., & Henle, C. A. (2002). Ethics in research. In S. G. Rogelberg (Ed.), *Handbook of research methods in industrial and organizational psychology* (pp. 34–56). Malden, MA: Blackwell Publishing.

Allmark, P., & Tod, A. M. (2013). Can a nudge keep you warm? Using nudges to reduce excess winter deaths: Insight from the Keeping Warm in Later Life Project (KWILLT). *Journal of Public Health, 36*(1), 111–116.

Al-Najjar, B., & Kans, M. (2006). A model to identify relevant data for problem tracing and maintenance cost-effective decisions: A case study. *International Journal of Productivity and Information Management, 55*(8), 616–637.

Altheide, D. L. (1996). *Qualitative media analysis*. Thousand Oaks, CA: SAGE Publications.

American Sociological Association (1999). *Code of ethics and policies and procedures of the ASA Committee on Professional Ethics*. Washington, DC. Retrieved from http://www.asanet.org/images/asa/docs/pdf/CodeofEthics.pdf

Anderson, C. (2001). Heat and violence. *Current Directions in Psychological Science, 10*(1), 33–38.

Angrosino, M. (2007). *Doing ethnographic and observational research*. London: SAGE Publications.

Armstrong, D., Gosling, A., Weinman, J., & Marteau, T. (1997). The place of inter-rater reliability in qualitative research: An empirical study. *Sociology, 31*(3), 597–606.

Ary, D., Jacobs, L. C., Sorensen, C., & Walker, D. A. (2014). *Introduction to research in education* (9th ed.). Boston: Cengage Learning.

Australian Psychological Society (2007). *Code of ethics*. Melbourne. Retrieved from https://www.psychology.org.au/Assets/Files/APS-Code-of-Ethics.pdf

Axinn, W. G., & Pearce, L. D. (2006). *Mixed method data collection strategies*. Cambridge: Cambridge University Press.

Babbie, E. (2011). *The basics of social research* (5th ed.). Belmont, CA: Wadsworth, Cengage Learning.

Bachman, R., & Schutt, R. K. (2007). *The practice of research in criminology and criminal justice* (3rd ed.). Thousand Oaks, CA: SAGE Publications.

Bacon, C., Mendez, E., & Brown, M. (2005). Participatory action research and support for community development and conservation: Examples from shade coffee landscapes in Nicaragua and El Salvador. Research Brief #6 by the Center for Agroecology and Sustainable Food Systems. Retrieved from http://escholarship.org/uc/item/1qv2r5d8

Baker, A. J. L., & Charvat, B. J. (2008). *Research methods in child welfare*. New York: Columbia University Press.

Balnaves, M., & Caputi, P. (2001). *Introduction to quantitative research methods: An investigative approach*. London: SAGE Publications.

Banks, J. (2014). Online gambling, advantage play, reflexivity and virtual ethnography. In K. Lumsden & A. Winter (Eds.), *Reflexivity in criminological research: Experiences with the powerful and the powerless* (pp. 289–300). New York: Palgrave Macmillan.

Banks, M. (2007). *Using visual data in qualitative research*. London: SAGE Publications.

Basch, C. H., Hillyer, G. C., Basch, C. E., & Neugut, A. I. (2012). Improving understanding about tanning behaviors in college students: A pilot study. *Journal of American College Health, 60*(3), 250–256.

Bauernfeind, R. H. (1968). The need for replication in educational research. *The Phi Delta Kappan, 50*(2), 126–128.

Bazeley, P. (2007). *Qualitative data analysis with NVivo*. London: SAGE Publications.

Bazeley, P. (2013). *Qualitative data analysis: Practical strategies*. London: SAGE Publications.

BBC News (2008). 1952: London fog clears after days of chaos. *BBC News*. Retrieved from http://news.bbc.co.uk/onthisday/hi/dates/stories/december/9/newsid_4506000/4506390.stm

Becker, H. S. (1970). Practitioners of vice and crime. In R. W. Habenstein (Ed.), *Pathways to data: Field methods for studying ongoing social organizations* (pp. 30–49). Chicago: Aldine Publishing Company.

Beebe, J. (2014). *Rapid qualitative inquiry: A field guide to team-based assessment* (2nd ed.). Lanham, MD: Rowman & Littlefield.

Beer, A., & Faulkner, D. (2014). How to use primary and secondary data. In R. J. Stimson (Ed.), *Handbook of research methods and applications in spatially integrated social science* (pp. 192–209). Cheltenham: Edward Elgar.

Begun, A. L., & Gregoire, T. (2014). *Conducting substance use research*. New York: Oxford University Press.

Bell, M. L., & Davis, D. L. (2001). Reassessment of the lethal London fog of 1952: Novel indicators of acute and chronic consequences of acute exposure to air pollution. *Environmental Health Perspectives, 109*(s3), 389–394.

Bell, P. (2001). Content analysis of visual images. In T. Van Leeuwen & C. Jewitt (Eds.), *The handbook of visual analysis* (pp. 10–34). London: SAGE Publications.

Berg, B. L. (1995). *Qualitative research methods for the social sciences* (2nd ed.). Needham Heights, MA: Allyn & Bacon.

Bergin, T. (2013). *The evidence enigma: Correctional boot camps and other failures in evidence-based policymaking*. Farnham: Ashgate.

Bethlehem, J., Cobben, F., & Schouten, B. (2011). *Handbook of nonresponse in household surveys*. Hoboken, NJ: John Wiley & Sons.

Bhattacharya, K. (2015). Coding is not a dirty word: Theory-driven data analysis using NVivo. In S. Hai-Jew (Ed.), *Enhancing qualitative and mixed methods research with technology* (pp. 1–30). Hershey, PA: Information Science Reference (IGI Global).

Biemer, P. P., & Lyberg, L. E. (2003). *Introduction to survey quality*. Hoboken, NJ: John Wiley & Sons.

Biordi, D. L., & Nicholson, N. R. (2013). Social isolation. In I. M. Lubkin & P. D. Larsen (Eds.), *Chronic illness: Impact and intervention* (8th ed., pp. 97–132). Burlington, MA: Jones & Bartlett.

Blaikie, N. (2003). *Analyzing quantitative data: From description to explanation*. London: SAGE Publications.

Blankenship, D. C. (2010). *Applied research and evaluation methods in recreation*. Champaign, IL: Human Kinetics.

Boeije, H. (2010). *Analysis in qualitative research*. London: SAGE Publications.

Book, S. A. (1979). Why n – 1 in the formula for the sample standard deviation? *The Two-Year College Mathematics Journal, 10*(5), 330–333.

Boulmetis, J., & Dutwin, P. (2005). *The ABCs of evaluation: Timeless techniques for program and project managers* (2nd ed.). San Francisco: Jossey-Bass.

Bowen, G. A. (2009). Document analysis as a qualitative research method. *Qualitative Research Journal, 9*(2), 27–40.

Box, J. F. (1987). Guinness, Gosset, Fisher, and small samples. *Statistical Science, 2*(1), 45–52.

Brain, C. (2000). *Advanced subsidiary psychology: Approaches and methods*. Cheltenham: Nelson Thornes.

Brandt, M. J., Ijzerman, H., Dijksterhuis, A., Farach, F. J., Geller, J., Giner-Sorolla, R., Grange, J.A., Perugini, M., Spies, J. R., & van 't Veer, A. (2014). The replication recipe: What makes for a convincing replication? *Journal of Experimental Social Psychology, 60*, 217–224.

Bray, G.A. (1994). Commentary on classics in obesity research 1. Quetelet: Quantitative medicine. *Obesity Research, 2*(1), 68–71.

Brimblecombe, P. (1987). *The big smoke: A history of air pollution in London since medieval times*. London: Methuen.

British Society of Criminology (2015). *Statement of ethics 2015*. Retrieved from http://www.britsoccrim.org/new/?q=node/22

Brower, R. S., & Jeong, H.-S. (2008). Grounded analysis: Going beyond description to derive theory from qualitative data. In K. Yang & G. J. Miller (Eds.), *Handbook of research methods in public administration* (pp. 823–840). Boca Raton, FL: CRC Press.

Bryman, A. (1989). *Research methods and organization studies*. Abingdon: Routledge.

Bryman, A. (2006). Integrating quantitative and qualitative research: How is it done? *Qualitative Research, 6*(1), 97–113.

Bryman, A., & Cramer, D. (1994). *Quantitative data analysis for social scientists* (revised ed.). London: Routledge.

Burnard, P., Gill, P., Stewart, K., Treasure, E., & Chadwick, B. (2008). Analysing and presenting qualitative data. *British Dental Journal, 204*(8), 429–432.

Butke, P., & Sheridan, S. C. (2010). An analysis of the relationship between weather and aggressive crime in Cleveland, Ohio. *Weather, Climate, and Society*, 2, 127–139.

Campbell, E., & Lassiter, L. E. (2010). From collaborative ethnography to collaborative pedagogy: Reflections on the other side of Middletown project and community-university research partnerships. *Anthropology & Education Quarterly, 41*(4), 370–385.

Caplow, T., Bahr, H. M., Chadwick, B.A., Hill, R., & Williamson, M. H. (1982). *Middletown families: Fifty years of change and continuity*. Minneapolis, MN: University of Minnesota Press.

Caracelli, V. J., & Greene, J. C. (1993). Data analysis strategies for mixed-method evaluation designs. *Educational Evaluation and Policy Analysis, 15*(2), 195–207.

Cardinal, R. N., & Aitken, M. R. (2006). *ANOVA for the behavioural sciences researcher*. Mahwah, NJ: Lawrence Erlbaum Associates.

Carter, B. (2014). The mystery of the most fatal week of the year. *BBC News Magazine*, 1 January. Retrieved from http://www.bbc.com/news/magazine-25680933

Cartwright, N., & Runhardt, R. (2014). Measurement. In N. Cartwright & E. Montuschi (Eds.), *Philosophy of social science: A new introduction* (pp. 265–287). Oxford: Oxford University Press.

Center for Middletown Studies (2018). About the Center. Muncie, IN: Ball State University. Retrieved from http://cms.bsu.edu/academics/centersandinstitutes/middletown/about

Centers for Disease Control and Prevention (CDC) (2012). Obesity and overweight for professionals: Adult: Defining overweight and obesity. Retrieved from http://www.cdc.gov/obesity/adult/defining.html

Chalmer, B. J. (1987). *Understanding statistics*. New York: Marcel Dekker.

Chambliss, D. F., & Schutt, R. K. (2010). *Making sense of the social world: Methods of investigation* (3rd ed.). Los Angeles: Pine Forge Press.

Chan, L., & McGarey, P. (2012). Using large datasets for population-based health research. In J. I. Gallin & F. P. Ognibene (Eds.), *Principles and practice of clinical research* (3rd ed., pp. 371–380). London: Academic Press.

Charmaz, K. (2015). Grounded theory. In J. A. Smith (Ed.), *Qualitative psychology: A practical guide to research methods* (3rd ed., pp. 53–84). London: SAGE Publications.

Christopher, A. N. (2017). *Interpreting and using statistics in psychological research*. Thousand Oaks, CA: SAGE Publications.

Chui, W. H., & Cheng, K. K.-Y. (2017). Perceptions of fairness and satisfaction in lawyer–client interactions among young offenders in Hong Kong. *Journal of Mixed Methods Research, 11*(2), 266–285.

City and County of San Francisco. (n.d.). San Francisco Police Department CrimeMAPS. Retrieved from https://data.sfgov.org/Public-Safety/SF-Crime-Heat-Map/q6gg-sa2p/data

Clarke, A., & Dawson, R. (1999). *Evaluation research: An introduction to principles, methods and practice*. London: SAGE Publications.

Cleveland, W. S. (1994). *The elements of graphing data* (revised ed.). Summit, NJ: Hobart Press.

Cochran, W. G. (1952). The χ^2 test of goodness of fit. *Annals of Mathematical Statistics, 23*(3), 315–345.

Cochran, W. G. (1977). *Sampling techniques*. New York: John Wiley & Sons.

Coffey, A., & Atkinson, P. (1996). *Making sense of qualitative data: Complementary research strategies*. Thousand Oaks, CA: SAGE Publications.

Cohn, E. G. (1990). Weather and crime. *British Journal of Criminology, 30*(1), 51–64.

Cohn, E. G., & Rotton, J. (2000). Weather, seasonal trends and property crimes in Minneapolis, 1987–1988. A moderator-variable time-series analysis of routine activities. *Journal of Environmental Psychology, 20*, 257–272.

Cole, A. L., & Knowles, J. G. (2001). *Lives in context: The art of life history research*. Lanham, MD: AltaMira Press.

Column Five. (n.d.). Most valuable players. Retrieved from http://bit.ly/2lXnb9O

Court, M. (2004). Using narrative and discourse analysis in researching co-principalships. *International Journal of Qualitative Studies in Education, 17*(5), 579–603.

Cryer, P. (2006). *The research student's guide to success* (3rd ed.). Maidenhead: Open University Press.

Curty, R., Yoon, A., Jeng, W., & Qin, J. (2016). Untangling data sharing and reuse in social sciences. *Proceedings of the Association for Information Science and Technology, 53*(1), 1–5.

Dale, A., Wathan, J., & Higgins, V. (2008). Secondary analysis of quantitative data sources. In P. Alasuutari, L. Bickman, & J. Brannen (Eds.), *The SAGE handbook of social research methods* (pp. 520–536). Thousand Oaks, CA: SAGE Publications.

Data Management Services, Massachusetts Institute of Technology (MIT) Libraries (n.d.a). Documentation & metadata. Retrieved from http://libraries.mit.edu/data-management/

Data Management Services, Massachusetts Institute of Technology (MIT) Libraries (n.d.b). File naming and folder hierarchy. Retrieved from http://libraries.mit.edu/data-management/

Data Management Services, Massachusetts Institute of Technology (MIT) Libraries (n.d.c). Confidentiality & intellectual property. Retrieved from http://libraries.mit.edu/data-management/

Data Services, University of Tennessee Knoxville (2017). Data services: Data documentation and description. Retrieved from http://libguides.utk.edu/dataservices/metadata

Davies, C. A. (1999). *Reflexive ethnography: A guide to researching selves and others*. London: Routledge.

Davis, D., & Cosenza, R. M. (1988). *Business research for decision making* (2nd ed.). Boston: PWS-Kent Publishing Company.

Death Penalty Information Center (2017). States with and without the death penalty. Retrieved from http://www.deathpenaltyinfo.org/states-and-without-death-penalty

de Tocqueville, A. (1835). *Democracy in America*. London: Saunders and Otley.

Denscombe, M. (2008). Communities of practice: A research paradigm for the mixed methods approach. *Journal of Mixed Methods Research, 2*(3), 270–283.

Deschaux-Beaume, D. (2013). Studying the military in a comparative perspective: Methodological challenges and issues – The example of French and German officers in European security and defence policy. In H. Carreiras & C. Castro (Eds.), *Qualitative methods in military studies: Research experiences and challenges* (pp. 132–147). Abingdon: Routledge.

Dey, I. (1993). *Qualitative data analysis: A user-friendly guide for social scientists.* London: Routledge.

Doering, B. K., & Rief, W. (2013). Nocebos in daily clinical practice. In L. Colloca, M.A. Flaten, & K. Meissner (Eds.), *Placebo and pain: From bench to bedside* (pp. 257–266). London: Academic Press.

Doering, C. (2014). Big data means big profits, risks for farmers. *USA Today*, 11 May. Retrieved from http://usat.ly/1gbj0ac

Dooley, D. (2001). *Social research methods* (4th ed.). Upper Saddle River, NJ: Prentice Hall.

Driscoll, D. L., Appiah-Yeboah, A., Salib, P., & Rupert, D. J. (2007). Merging qualitative and quantitative data in mixed methods research: How to and why not. *Ecological and Environmental Anthropology*, *3*(1), 19–28.

Duckett, P. (2011). Future directions for qualitative research. In P. Banister, G. Bunn, E. Burman, J. Daniels, P. Duckett, D. Goodley, R. Lawthom, I. Parker, K. Runswick-Cole, J. Sixsmith, S. Smailes, C. Tindall, & P. Whelan (Eds.), *Qualitative methods in psychology: A research guide* (2nd ed., pp. 165–178). Maidenhead: Open University Press.

Dudeney, G., Hockly, N., & Pegrum, M. (2014). *Digital literacies.* Abingdon: Routledge.

Dunn, O. J., & Clark, V. A. (2009). *Basic statistics: A primer for the biomedical sciences* (4th ed.). Hoboken, NJ: John Wiley & Sons.

Edinburgh Napier University (2015). Edinburgh Napier University: Research data management policy. Retrieved from http://staff.napier.ac.uk/services/research-innovation-office/Documents/Research%20Data%20Management%20Policy.pdf

Edinburgh Napier University (2017a). Research data management: Storing data. LibGuides. Retrieved from http://libguides.napier.ac.uk/rdm/storingdata

Edinburgh Napier University (2017b). Research data management: Sharing data. LibGuides. Retrieved from http://libguides.napier.ac.uk/rdm/sharing

Eknoyan, G. (2008). Adolphe Quetelet (1796–1874) – the average man and indices of obesity. *Nephrology Dialysis Transplantation*, *23*(1), 47–51.

Ely, M., Vinz, R., Anzul, M., & Downing, M. (1997). *On writing qualitative research: Living by words.* London: Falmer Press.

Emerson, R. M., Fretz, R. I., & Shaw, L. L. (1995). *Writing ethnographic fieldnotes.* Chicago: University of Chicago Press.

Emmel, N. (2013). *Sampling and choosing cases in qualitative research: A realist approach.* Los Angeles: SAGE Publications.

Farrington, D. P. (2003). Methodological quality standards for evaluation research. *Annals of the American Academy of Political and Social Science*, *587*(May), 49–68.

Feinberg, C. (2013). The placebo phenomenon. *Harvard Magazine*, January/February. Retrieved from http://harvardmagazine.com/2013/01/the-placebo-phenomenon

Feinberg, J. (2014). Wordle. Retrieved from http://www.wordle.net/

Feldman, M. S. (1995). *Strategies for interpreting qualitative data.* Thousand Oaks, CA: SAGE Publications.

Felsenstein, F., & Connolly, J. J. (2015). *What Middletown read: Print culture and cosmopolitanism in an American city.* Amherst, MA: University of Massachusetts Press.

Fetterman, D. M. (2010). *Ethnography: step-by-step* (3rd ed.). Thousand Oaks, CA: SAGE Publications.

Fetters, M. D., Curry, L. A., & Creswell, J. W. (2013). Achieving integration in mixed methods designs – Principles and practices. *Health Services Research*, *48*(6.2), 2134–2156.

Fink, A. (2003). *The survey handbook* (2nd ed.). Thousand Oaks, CA: SAGE Publications.

Fink, A. (2009). *How to conduct surveys: A step-by-step guide* (4th ed.). Thousand Oaks, CA: SAGE Publications.

Fletcher, J. (2014). Spurious correlations: Margarine linked to divorce? *BBC News Magazine*, 26 May. Retrieved from http://www.bbc.co.uk/news/magazine-27537142

Flick, U. (2007a). About this book. In M. Angrosino, *Doing ethnographic and observational research* (pp. xiii–xiv). London: SAGE Publications.

Flick, U. (2007b). *Designing qualitative research*. London: SAGE Publications.

Fontes, L.A. (2008). *Interviewing clients across cultures: A practitioner's guide*. New York: Guilford Press.

Foster, H. (2014). The reason for the season: Why flu strikes in winter. *Harvard Science in the News*, 1 December. Retrieved from: http://sitn.hms.harvard.edu/flash/2014/the-reason-for-the-season-why-flu-strikes-in-winter/

Fox, C., Levitin, A., & Redman, T. (1994). The notion of data and its quality dimensions. *Information Processing & Management, 39*(1), 9–19.

Framingham Heart Study (2018). Research application overview, review process and procedures. Retrieved from https://www.framinghamheartstudy.org/fhs-for-researchers/research-application-overview/

Freeman, J., & Walters, S. (2010). Examining relationships in quantitative data. In K. Gerrish & A. Lacey (Eds.), *The research process in nursing* (6th ed., pp. 455–474). Chichester: Wiley-Blackwell.

Fritz, C. O., Morris, P. E., & Richler, J. J. (2012). Effect size estimates: Current use, calculations, and interpretation. *Journal of Experimental Psychology, 141*(1), 2–18.

Frost, N., Nolas, S. M., Brooks-Gordon, B., Esin, C., Holt, A., Mehdizadeh, L., & Shinebourne, P. (2010). Pluralism in qualitative research: The impact of different researchers and qualitative approaches on the analysis of qualitative data. *Qualitative Research, 10*(4), 441–460.

Fyrand, L., Moum, T., Finset, A., & Glennås, A. (2003). The effect of social network intervention for women with rheumatoid arthritis. *Family Process, 42*(1), 71–89.

Gastel, B. (1983). *Presenting science to the public*. Philadelphia: ISI Press.

Gee, J. P., Michaels, S., & O'Connor, M. C. (1992). Discourse analysis. In M. D. LeCompte, W. L. Millroy, & J. Preissle (Eds.), *The handbook of qualitative research in education* (pp. 227–291). San Diego, CA: Academic Press.

Geelhoed, E. B. (2000). *Muncie: The Middletown of America*. Chicago: Arcadia Publishing.

George, A. L., & Bennett, A. (2004). *Case studies and theory development in the social sciences*. Cambridge, MA: MIT Press.

Gibbs, G. R. (2007). *Analyzing qualitative data*. London: SAGE Publications.

Gibson, W. J., & Brown, A. (2009). *Working with qualitative data*. London: SAGE Publications.

Gill, C. E. (2011). Missing links: How descriptive validity impacts the policy relevance of randomized controlled trials in criminology. *Journal of Experimental Criminology*, 7, 201–224.

Gill, P., Stewart, K., Treasure, E., & Chadwick, B. (2008). Methods of data collection in qualitative research: Interviews and focus groups. *British Dental Journal, 204*(6), 291–295.

Glaser, B., & Strauss, A. (1965). *Awareness of dying*. Chicago: Aldine.

Glaser, B., & Strauss, A. (1967). *The discovery of grounded theory*. Chicago: Aldine.

Gläser, J. & Laudel, G. (2013). Life with and without coding: Two methods for early-stage data analysis in qualitative research aiming at causal explanations. *Forum Qualitative Sozialforschung/Forum: Qualitative Social Research, 14*(2), Article 5. Retrieved from http://www.qualitative-research.net/index.php/fqs/article/view/1886/3528

Glicken, M. D. (2003). *Social research: A simple guide*. Boston: Allyn & Bacon.

Gliner, J. A., Leech, N. L., & Morgan, G. A. (2002). Problems with null hypothesis significance testing (NHST): What do the textbooks say? *Journal of Experimental Education, 71*(1), 83–92.

Gohil, A. (2015). *R data visualization cookbook*. Birmingham: Packt Publishing.

Gonzalez, R. (2009). *Data analysis for experimental design*. New York: Guilford Press.

Gonzalez, R., Yu, T., & Volling, B. (2012). Analysis of experimental and quasi-experimental data: Pinpointing explanations. In B. Laursen, T. D. Little, & N. A. Card (Eds.), *Handbook of developmental research methods* (pp. 247–264). New York: Guilford Press.

Goodman, R., Meltzer, H., & Bailey, V. (1998). The strengths and difficulties questionnaire: A pilot study on the validity of the self-report version. *European Child & Adolescent Psychiatry, 7*(3), 125–130.

Graham, J. W., Cumsille, P. E., & Elek-Fisk, E. (2003). Methods for handling missing data. In J. A. Schinka, W. F. Velicer, & I. B. Weiner (Eds.), *Handbook of psychology: Research methods in psychology* (Vol. 2, pp. 87–114). Hoboken, NJ: John Wiley & Sons.

Gratton, C., & Jones, I. (2010). *Research methods for sports studies* (2nd ed.). Abingdon: Routledge.

Gravetter, F. J., & Wallnau, L. B. (2009). *Statistics for the behavioral sciences* (8th ed.). Belmont, CA: Wadsworth.

Greene, J., Caracelli, V., & Graham, W. (1989). Toward a conceptual framework for mixed method evaluation designs. *Educational Evaluation and Policy Analysis, 11*, 255–274.

Greenwood, D. J., & Levin, M. (2007). *Introduction to action research: Social research for social change* (2nd ed.). Thousand Oaks, CA: SAGE Publications.

Groves, R. M., & Couper, M. P. (1998). *Nonresponse in household interview surveys*. Hoboken, NJ: John Wiley & Sons.

Hair, J. F., Celsi, M. W., Money, A. H., Samouel, P., & Page, M. J. (2011). *Essentials of business research methods* (2nd ed.). Armonk, NY: M. E. Sharpe.

Handler, R. (2005). *Critics against culture: Anthropological observers of mass society*. Madison, WI: University of Wisconsin Press.

Hanneman, R. A., Kposowa, A. J., & Riddle, M. (2013). *Basic statistics for social research*. San Francisco: Jossey-Bass.

Harrison, L. (1997). The validity of self-reported drug use in survey research: An overview and critique of research methods. In L. Harrison & A. Hughes (Eds.), *The validity of self-reported drug use: Improving the accuracy of survey estimates* (pp. 17–36). Rockville, MD: National Institute on Drug Abuse.

Harrison, R. L., & Reilly, T. M. (2011). Mixed methods designs in marketing research. *Qualitative Market Research: An International Journal, 14*(1), 7–26.

Hatch, J. A. (2002). *Doing qualitative research in education settings*. Albany, NY: State University of New York Press.

Häuser, W., Hansen, E., & Enck, P. (2012). Nocebo phenomena in medicine: Their relevance in everyday clinical practice. *Deutsches Ärzteblatt International, 109*(26), 459–465.

Häussling, R. (2014). A network analytical four-level concept for an interpretation of social interaction in terms of structure and agency. In S. Domínguez & B. Hollstein (Eds.), *Mixed methods social networks research: Design and applications* (pp. 90–120). New York: Cambridge University Press.

Healey, J. F., & Prus, S. G. (2010). *Statistics: A tool for social research*. Toronto: Nelson Education.

Healy, J. D. (2003). Excess winter mortality in Europe: A cross country analysis identifying key risk factors. *Journal of Epidemiology & Community Health, 57*, 784–789.

Heath, D. (1995). *An introduction to experimental design and statistics for biology*. Boca Raton, FL: CRC Press.

Hesse-Biber, S. (2010). Qualitative approaches to mixed methods practice. *Qualitative Inquiry, 16*(6), 455–468.

Higgins, J. P. T., & Green, S. (Eds.) (2011). *Cochrane handbook for systematic reviews of interventions,* Version 5.1.0. Cochrane Collaboration. Retrieved from http://handbook-5-1.cochrane.org/

Hine, C. (2000). *Virtual ethnography.* Thousand Oaks, CA: SAGE Publications.

Hipp, J. R., Bauer, D. J., Curran, P. J., & Bollen, K. A. (2004). Crimes of opportunity or crimes of emotion? Testing two explanations of seasonal change in crime. *Social Forces, 82*(4), 1333–1372.

Hirschl, R. (2006). On the blurred methodological matrix of comparative constitutional law. In S. Choudhry (Ed.), *The migration of constitutional ideas* (pp. 39–66). Cambridge: Cambridge University Press.

Hirsh-Pasek, K., & Golinkoff, R. (2007). From the lab to the living room: Stories that talk the talk and walk and the walk. In M. K. Welch-Ross & L. G. Fasig (Eds.), *Handbook on communicating and disseminating behavioral science* (pp. 185–202). Thousand Oaks, CA: SAGE Publications.

Hodson, R., Chamberlain, L. J., Crowley, M., & Tope, D. (2011). Coding ethnographies for research and training: Merging qualitative and quantitative sociologies. *Sociological Perspectives, 54*(1), 125–131.

Hoffer, J. A., Prescott, M. B., & McFadden, F. R. (2002). *Modern database management* (6th ed.). Englewood Cliffs, NJ: Prentice Hall.

Hofmann, A. H. (2010). *Scientific writing and communication: Papers, proposals, and presentations.* New York: Oxford University Press.

Hoggart, K., Lees, L., & Davies, A. (2014). *Researching human geography.* Abingdon: Routledge.

Hollstein, B. (2014). Mixed methods social networks research: An introduction. In S. Domínguez & B. Hollstein (Eds.), *Mixed methods social networks research: Design and applications* (pp. 3–34). New York: Cambridge University Press.

Horowitz, I. L. (2004). *Tributes: Personal reflections on a century of social research.* Piscataway, NJ: Transaction Publishers.

House, E. (1993). *Professional evaluation.* Newbury Park, CA: SAGE Publications.

Howe, K. R. (1988). Against the quantitative-qualitative incompatibility thesis or dogmas die hard. *Educational Researcher, 17*(8), 10–16.

Howell, D. C. (2007). *Statistical methods for psychology* (6th ed.). Belmont, CA: Thomson Wadsworth.

Hsiao, C. (2014). *Analysis of panel data* (3rd ed.). New York: Cambridge University Press.

Huff, A. S. (2009). *Designing research for publication.* Thousand Oaks, CA: SAGE Publications.

Hukkinen, J., Roe, E., & Rochlin, G. I. (1990). A salt on the land: A narrative analysis of the controversy over irrigation-related salinity and toxicity in California's San Joaquin Valley. *Policy Sciences, 23,* 307–329.

Hussmanns, R., Mehran, F., & Verma, V. (1990). *Surveys of economically active population, employment, unemployment and underemployment: An ILO manual on concepts and methods.* Geneva: International Labour Office.

Iarossi, G. (2006). *The power of survey design: A user's guide for managing surveys, interpreting results, and influencing respondents.* Washington, DC: The World Bank.

Institute for Work & Health (2015). What researchers mean by ... cross-sectional vs. longitudinal studies. *At Work, 81* (Summer). Toronto. Retrieved from: https://www.iwh.on.ca/wrmb/cross-sectional-vs-longitudinal-studies

Ioannidis, J. P. A. (2005). Why most published research findings are false. *PLoS Med, 2*(8), e124. Retrieved from https://doi.org/10.1371/journal.pmed.0020124

Israel, M., & Hay, I. (2006). *Research ethics for social scientists.* London: SAGE Publications.

Jacoby, W. G. (1997). *Statistical graphics for univariate and bivariate data.* Thousand Oaks, CA: SAGE Publications.

James, A. (2012). Seeking the analytic imagination: Reflections on the process of interpreting qualitative data. *Qualitative Research, 13*(5), 562–577.

Jansen, H. (2010). The logic of qualitative survey research and its position in the field of social research methods. *Forum Qualitative Sozialforschung/Forum: Qualitative Social Research, 11*(2), Article 11. Retrieved from http://www.qualitative-research.net/index.php/fqs/article/view/1450/2946

Jekel, J. F., Katz, D. L., Elmore, J. G., & Wild, D. M. G. (2007). *Epidemiology, biostatistics, and preventive medicine* (3rd ed.). Philadelphia: Saunders Elsevier.

Jensen, K. B. (1989). Discourses of interviewing: Validating qualitative research findings through textual analysis. In S. Kvale (Ed.), *Issues of validity in qualitative research* (pp. 93–108). Lund: Studentlitteratur.

Jick, T. D. (1979). Mixing qualitative and quantitative methods: Triangulation in action. *Administrative Science Quarterly, 24*, 602–611.

'John Laub and Robert Sampson awarded Stockholm Prize' (2011). National Institute of Justice, About the NIJ Director. Retrieved from http://www.nij.gov/about/director/pages/stockholm-prize.aspx

Johnson, R. B., & Onwuegbuzie, A. J. (2004). Mixed methods research: A research paradigm whose time has come. *Educational Researcher, 33*(7), 14–26.

Kassebaum, G. (1970). Strategies for the sociological study of criminal correctional systems. In R. W. Habenstein (Ed.), *Pathways to data: Field methods for studying ongoing social organizations* (pp. 122–138). Chicago: Aldine.

Kault, D. (2003). *Statistics with common sense.* Westport, CT: ABC-CLIO.

Kelle, U. (2004). Computer assisted qualitative data analysis. In C. Searle, G. Gobo, J. F. Gubrium, & D. Silverman (Eds.), *Qualitative research practice* (pp. 443–460). London: SAGE Publications.

Kelle, U. (2006). Combining qualitative and quantitative methods in research practice: Purposes and advantage. *Qualitative Research in Psychology, 3*(4), 293–311.

Kent State University Libraries (2018a). Independent samples t test. Retrieved from https://libguides.library.kent.edu/SPSS/IndependentTTest

Kent State University Libraries (2018b). Statistical & qualitative data analysis software: About NVivo. Retrieved from http://libguides.library.kent.edu/statconsulting/NVivo

Kernler, D. (2014). A visual representation of selecting a random sample using the cluster sampling technique. Licensed under CC BY-SA 4.0 (https://creativecommons.org/licenses/by-sa/4.0/). Retrieved from https://en.wikipedia.org/wiki/Sampling_(statistics)#/media/File:Cluster_sampling.PNG

Kernler, D. (2014). A visual representation of selecting a random sample using the stratified sampling technique. Licensed under CC BY-SA 4.0 (https://creativecommons.org/licenses/by-sa/4.0/). Retrieved from https://commons.wikimedia.org/wiki/File:Stratified_sampling.PNG

Kernler, D. (2014). A visual representation of selecting a random sample using the systematic sampling technique. Licensed under CC BY-SA 4.0 (https://creativecommons.org/licenses/by-sa/4.0/). Retrieved from https://commons.wikimedia.org/wiki/File:Systematic_sampling.PNG

Kernler, D. (2014). A visual representation of selecting a simple random sample. Licensed under CC BY-SA 4.0 (https://creativecommons.org/licenses/by-sa/4.0/). Retrieved from https://commons.wikimedia.org/w/index.php?curid=36506020

Keys, A., Karvonen, N., Kimura, N., & Taylor, H. L. (1972). Indices of relative weight and obesity. *Journal of Chronic Diseases, 25*, 329–343.

King, G., Keohane, R. O., & Verba, S. (1994). *Designing social inquiry: Scientific inference in qualitative research.* Princeton, NJ: Princeton University Press.

King, N., & Horrocks, C. (2010). *Interviews in qualitative research*. London: SAGE Publications.

Kirk, A. (2016). *Data visualisation: A handbook for data driven design*. London: SAGE Publications.

Kitchin, R. (2014). *The data revolution: Big data, open data, data infrastructures & their consequences*. London: SAGE Publications.

Klein, S. (Ed.). (2012). *Action research methods: Plain and simple*. New York: Palgrave Macmillan.

Klenke, K. (2008). *Qualitative research in the study of leadership*. Bingley: Emerald Group Publishing.

Kline, T. J. B. (2005). *Psychological testing: A practical approach to design and evaluation*. Thousand Oaks, CA: SAGE Publications.

Konstantopoulos, W. M., Ahn, R., Alpert, E. J., Cafferty, E., McGahan, A., Williams, T. P., Castor, J. P., Wolferstan, N., Purcell, G., & Burke, T. F. (2013). An international comparative public health analysis of sex trafficking of women and girls in eight cities: Achieving a more effective health sector response. *Journal of Urban Health, 90*(6), 1194–1204.

Kostelnick, C., & Roberts, D. D. (2011). *Designing visual language: Strategies for professional communications* (2nd ed.). Boston: Longman.

Kreuter, F., Olson, K., Wagner, J., Yan, T., Ezzati-Rice, T. M., Casas-Cordero, C., Lemay, M., Peytchev, A., Groves, R. M., & Raghunathan, T. E. (2010). Using proxy measures and other correlates of survey outcomes to adjust for non-response: Examples from multiple surveys. *Journal of the Royal Statistical Society, Series A, 173*(2), 389–407.

Kromrey, J. D. (1993). Ethics and data analysis. *Educational Researcher*, 22(4), 24–27.

Kumar, R. (2005). *Research methodology: A step-by-step guide for beginners* (2nd ed.). London: SAGE Publications.

Kumar, S. (2010). *Quantitative techniques and methods*. New Delhi: Gennext Publication.

Kureishy, S., Khan, G. N., Arrif, S., Ashraf, K., Cespedes, A., Habib, M. A., Hussain, I., Ullah, A., Turab, A., Ahmed, I., Zaidi, S., & Soofi, S. B. (2017). A mixed methods study to assess the effectiveness of food-based interventions to prevent stunting among children under-five years in Districts Thatta and Sujawal, Sindh Province, Pakistan: Study protocol. *BMC Public Health, 17*, 24.

Kurweil, E. (1999). What Tocqueville might say about our NEA. In J. T. Marcus (Ed.), *Surviving the twentieth century* (pp. 153–162). New Brunswick, NJ: Transaction Publishers.

Lacey, A., & Luff, D. (2007). *Qualitative research analysis*. Nottingham and Sheffield: NIHR RDS for the East Midlands/Yorkshire & the Humber. Updated 2009. Retrieved from: https://www.rds-yh.nihr.ac.uk/wp-content/uploads/2013/05/9_Qualitative_Data_Analysis_Revision_2009.pdf

Lambert, C., Jomeen, J., & McSherry, W. (2010). Reflexivity: A review of the literature in the context of midwifery research. *British Journal of Midwifery, 18*(5), 321–326.

Landau, S., & Everitt, B. S. (2004). *A handbook of statistical analyses using SPSS*. Boca Raton, FL: Chapman & Hall/CRC.

Lanum, C. L. (2017). *Visualizing graph data*. Shelter Island, NY: Manning Publications.

Lassiter, L. E., Goodall, H., Campbell, E., & Johnson, M. N. (2004). *The other side of Middletown: Exploring Muncie's African American community*. Walnut Creek, CA: AltaMira Press.

Laub, J. H., & Sampson, R. J. (1993). Turning points in the life course: Why change matters to the study of crime. *Criminology, 31*, 301–325.

Laub, J. H., & Sampson, R. J. (2003). *Shared beginnings, divergent lives: Delinquent boys to age 70*. Cambridge, MA: Harvard University Press.

Lee, E. S., & Forthofer, R. N. (2006). *Analyzing complex survey data* (2nd ed.). Thousand Oaks, CA: SAGE Publications.

LeGates, R. (2005). *Think globally, act regionally: GIS and data visualization for social science and public policy research*. Redlands, CA: ESRI Press.

Lehren, A.W., & Hauser, C. (2009). In New York City, fewer murders on rainy days. *New York Times*, 3 July. Retrieved from http://www.nytimes.com/2009/07/03/nyregion/03murder.html?_r=0&pagewanted=print

Leon, A. C., Davis, L. L., & Kraemer, H. C. (2011). The role and interpretation of pilot studies in clinical research. *Journal of Psychiatric Research*, *45*(5), 626–629.

Li, J., Lovatt, M., Eadie, D., Dobbie, F., Meier, P., Holmes, J., Hastings, G., & MacKintosh, A. M. (2017). Public attitudes towards alcohol control policies in Scotland and England: Results from a mixed-methods study. *Social Science & Medicine*, *177*, 177–189.

Liebowitz, J. (Ed.) (2013). *Big data and business analytics*. Boca Raton, FL: CRC Press.

Lima, M. (2011). *Visual complexity: Mapping patterns of information*. New York: Princeton Architectural Press.

Lindlof, T. R., & Taylor, B. C. (2011). *Qualitative communication research methods* (3rd ed.). Thousand Oaks, CA: SAGE Publications.

Lingenfelter, P. E. (2016). *'Proof,' policy, and practice: Understanding the role of evidence in education*. Sterling, VA: Stylus Publishing.

Little, R. J. A. & Rubin, D. B. (1987). *Statistical analysis with missing data*. New York: John Wiley & Sons.

Lohr, S. (2013). Big data is opening doors, but maybe too many. *New York Times*, 23 March. Retrieved from http://www.nytimes.com/2013/03/24/technology/big-data-and-a-renewed-debate-over-privacy.html?pagewanted=all&_r=0&pagewanted=print

Lombard, M., Snyder-Duch, J., & Bracken, C. C. (2002). Content analysis in mass communication: Assessment and reporting of intercoder reliability. *Human Communication Research*, *28*(4), 587–604.

Love, P. (2003). Document analysis. In F. K. Stage & K. Manning (Eds.), *Research in the college context: Approaches and methods* (pp. 83–96). New York: Brunner-Routledge.

Lozada, C. (2015). The book every new American citizen – and every old one, too – should read. *Washington Post*, 17 December. Retrieved from https://www.washingtonpost.com/news/book-party/wp/2015/12/17/the-book-every-new-american-citizen-and-every-old-one-too-should-read/?utm_term=.de79f34e8060

Lui, K. J., & Kendal, A. P. (1987). Impact of influenza epidemics on mortality in the United States from October 1972 to May 1985. *American Journal of Public Health*, *77*, 712–716.

Luker, K. (2008). *Salsa dancing into the social sciences: Research in an age of info-glut*. Cambridge, MA: Harvard University Press.

Lupton, D. (1992). Discourse analysis: A new methodology for understanding the ideologies of health and illness. *Australian and New Zealand Journal of Public Health*, *16*(2), 145–150.

Lynd, R. S., & Lynd, H. M. (1929). *Middletown: A study in modern American culture*. Orlando, FL: Harcourt Brace & Company.

Lynd, R. S., & Lynd, H. M. (1937). *Middletown in transition: A study in cultural conflicts*. Orlando, FL: Harcourt Brace & Company.

Ma, W., Yang, C., Chu, C., Li, T., Tan, J., & Kan, H. (2013). The impact of the 2008 cold spell on mortality in Shanghai, China. *International Journal of Biometeorology*, *57*(1), 179–184.

MacNee, W. and Donaldson, K. (2008). Environmental factors in chronic obstructive pulmonary disease. In N. F. Voelkel and W. MacNee (Eds.), *Chronic obstructive lung diseases* (Vol. 2, pp. 121–140). Hamilton, Ontario: BC Decker.

Madden, R. (2010). *Being ethnographic: A guide to the theory and practice of ethnography*. London: SAGE Publications.

Majchrzak, A., & Markus, M. L. (2014). *Methods for policy research: Taking socially responsible action* (2nd ed.). Thousand Oaks, CA: SAGE Publications.

Makel, M. C., & Plucker, J. A. (2014). Facts are more important than novelty: Replication in the education sciences. *Educational Researcher, 43*(6), 304–316.

Manikandan, S. (2011). Frequency distribution. *Journal of Pharmacology & Pharmacotherapeutics, 2*(1), 54–56.

Manzi, J. (2012). *Uncontrolled: The surprising payoff of trial-and-error for business, politics, and society.* New York: Basic Books.

Marcus, G., & Davis, E. (2014). Eight (no, nine!) problems with big data. *New York Times*, 6 April. Retrieved from http://www.nytimes.com/2014/04/07/opinion/eight-no-nine-problems-with-big-data.html?src=me&ref=general&_r=0

Mark, M. M., & Henry, G. T. (2006). Methods for policy-making and knowledge development evaluations. In I. F. Shaw, J. C. Greene, & M. M. Mark (Eds.), *The SAGE handbook of evaluation* (pp. 317–339). London: SAGE Publications.

Marshall, C., & Rossman, G. B. (1995). *Designing qualitative research* (2nd ed.). Thousand Oaks, CA: SAGE Publications.

Marvasti, A. B. (2004). *Qualitative research in sociology: An introduction.* London: SAGE Publications.

Mass Observation. (n.d.). The original mass observation. Brighton: Mass Observation Archive, University of Sussex. Retrieved from http://www.massobs.org.uk/original_massobservation_project.htm.

Maxwell, J. A. (2013). *Qualitative research design: An interactive approach* (3rd ed.). Thousand Oaks, CA: SAGE Publications.

Mayer-Schönberger, V., & Cukier, K. (2013). *Big data: A revolution that will transform how we live, work, and think.* Boston: Houghton Mifflin Harcourt.

Mayo Clinic (n.d.). Institutional Review Board (IRB): Definition of terms. Retrieved from http://www.mayo.edu/research/institutional-review-board/definition-terms

Mayring, P. (2004). Qualitative content analysis. In U. Flick, E. von Kardoff, & I. Steinke (Eds.), *A companion to qualitative research* (pp. 266–269). London: SAGE Publications. (Translation of Qualitative Forschung – Ein Handbuch, published 2000, by Rowohlt Taschenbuch Verlag, Reinbek bei Hamburg.)

Mays, N., & Pope, C. (1995). Rigour and qualitative research. *British Medical Journal, 311*, 109–112.

McDowall, D., Loftin, C., & Pate, M. (2012). Seasonal cycles in crime, and their variability. *Journal of Quantitative Criminology, 28*, 389–410.

McKnight, P. E., McKnight, K. M., Sidani, S., & Figueredo, A. J. (2007). *Missing data: A gentle introduction.* New York: Guilford Press.

McNabb, D. E. (2002). *Research methods in public administration and nonprofit management: Quantitative and qualitative approaches.* Armonk, NY: M. E. Sharpe.

Meaden, G. J., & Chi, T. D. (1996). *Geographical information systems: Applications to marine fisheries.* FAO Fisheries Technical Paper No. 356. Rome: Food and Agriculture Organization of the United Nations.

Mendenhall, W., Beaver, R., & Beaver, B. (2013). *Introduction to probability & statistics* (14th ed.). Boston, MA: Brooks/Cole, Cengage Learning.

Merriman, S. B. (2009). *Qualitative research: A guide to design and implementation.* San Francisco: Jossey-Bass.

Miles, M. B., Huberman, A. M., & Saldaña, J. (2014). *Qualitative data analysis: A methods sourcebook* (3rd ed.). Thousand Oaks, CA: SAGE Publications.

Miller, F. G., Colloca, L., Crouch, R. A., & Kaptchuk, T. J. (Eds.) (2013). *The placebo: A reader.* Baltimore, MD: Johns Hopkins University Press.

Mitchell, C. (2012). Visual methodologies and social change. In J. Arthur, M. Waring, R. Coe, & L. Hedges (Eds.), *Research methods and methodologies in education* (pp. 290–296). Thousand Oaks, CA: SAGE Publications.

Mitchell, M. L., Jolley, J. M., & O'Shea, R. P. (2004). *Writing for psychology*. Belmont, CA: Wadsworth/ Thomson Learning.

Mohr, L. B. (1990). *Understanding significance testing*. Thousand Oaks, CA: SAGE Publications.

Monette, D. R., Sullivan, T. J., & DeJong, C. R. (2011). *Applied social research: A tool for the human services* (8th ed.). Belmont, CA: Brooks/Cole, Cengage Learning.

Monette, D. R., Sullivan, T. J., DeJong, C. R., & Hilton, T. P. (2014). *Applied social research: A tool for the human services* (9th ed.). Belmont, CA: Brooks/Cole.

Monge, P. R., & Contractor, N. S. (1988). Communication networks: Measurement techniques. In C. H. Tardy (Ed.), *A handbook for the study of human communication: Methods and instruments for observing, measuring, and assessing communication processes* (pp. 107–138). Westport, CT: Ablex Publishing.

Montello, D. R., & Sutton, P. C. (2013). *An introduction to scientific research methods in geography and environmental studies* (2nd ed.). Thousand Oaks, CA: SAGE Publications.

Morabia, A. (2007). Epidemiological methods and concepts in the nineteenth century and their influences on the twentieth century. In W. W. Holland, J. Olsen, & C. D. V. Florey (Eds.), *The development of modern epidemiology: Personal reports from those who were there* (pp. 17–30). Oxford: Oxford University Press.

Morçöl, G. (2002). *A new mind for policy analysis: Toward a post-Newtonian and postpositivist epistemology and methodology*. Westport, CT: Praeger.

Morgan, D. L., & Morgan, R. K. (2009). *Single-case research methods for the behavioral and health sciences*. Thousand Oaks, CA: SAGE Publications.

Morgan, G. A., Leech, N. L., Gloeckner, G. W., & Barrett, K. C. (2004). *SPSS for introductory statistics: Use and interpretation* (2nd ed.). Mahwah, NJ: Lawrence Erlbaum Associates.

Morse, J. M., & Niehaus, L. (2009). *Mixed method design: Principles and procedures*. Walnut Creek, CA: Left Coast Press.

Moser, W. (2012). Heat and crime: It's not just you feeling it. *Chicago*, 15 March. Retrieved from http://www.chicagomag.com/Chicago-Magazine/The-312/March-2012/Heat-and-Crime-Its-Not-Just-You-Feeling-It/

Mouton, J., & Marais, H. C. (1996). *Basic concepts in the methodology of the social sciences* (5th impression). Pretoria: HSRC Publishers.

Munro, B. H. (2005). *Statistical methods for health care research* (5th ed.). Philadelphia: Lippincott Williams & Wilkins.

Murchison, J. M. (2010). *Ethnography essentials: Designing, conducting, and presenting your research*. San Francisco: Jossey-Bass.

Myers, M. D. (1997). Qualitative research in information systems. *MIS Quarterly, 21*(2), 241–242.

Nathan, R. P. (2000). *Social science in government: The role of policy researchers* (new ed.). Albany, NY: Rockefeller Institute Press.

National Research Council (2012). *Using science as evidence in public policy*. Committee on the Use of Social Science Knowledge in Public Policy. K. Prewitt, T. A. Schwandt, & M. L. Straf (Eds.). Washington, DC: National Academies Press.

National Research Council (2013). *Nonresponse in social science surveys: A research agenda*. R. Tourangeau & T. J. Plewes (Eds.), Panel on a Research Agenda for the future of Social Science Data Collection, Committee on National Statistics. Division of Behavioral and Social Sciences and Education. Washington, DC: National Academies Press.

Newman, I., & Benz, C. R. (1998). *Qualitative-quantitative research methodology: Exploring the interactive continuum*. Carbondale, IL: Southern Illinois University Press.

Newton, R. R., & Rudestam, K. E. (2013). *Your statistical consultant: Answers to your data analysis questions* (2nd ed.). Thousand Oaks, CA: SAGE Publications.

Neyland, D. (2008). *Organizational ethnography*. Thousand Oaks, CA: SAGE Publications.

Ng, M., Fleming, T., Robinson, M., Thomson, B., Graetz, N., Margono, C., …, Gakidou, E. (2014). Global, regional, and national prevalence of overweight and obesity in children and adults during 1980–2013: A systematic analysis for the Global Burden of Disease Study 2013. *The Lancet, 384*(9945), 766–781.

Noaks, L., & Wincup, E. (2004). *Criminological research: Understanding qualitative methods*. London: SAGE Publications.

Noble, H., & Smith, J. (2014). Qualitative data analysis: A practical example. *Evidence-Based Nursing, 17*(1), 2–3.

Norman, G. R., & Streiner, D. L. (2008). *Biostatistics: The bare essentials* (3rd ed.). Shelton, CT: People's Medical Publishing House.

Norman, J. M. (2009). Got trust? The challenge of gaining access in conflict zones. In C. L. Sriram, J. C. King, J. A. Mertus, O. Martin-Ortega, & J. Herman (Eds.), *Surviving field research: Working in violent and difficult situations* (pp. 71–90). Abingdon: Routledge.

O'Dwyer, B. (2008). Qualitative data analysis: Illuminating a process for transforming a 'messy' but 'attractive' 'nuisance'. In C. Humphrey & B. Lee (Eds.), *The real life guide to accounting research: A behind-the-scenes view of using qualitative research methods* (pp. 391–408). Oxford: Elsevier.

Office for National Statistics (2015). What are the top causes of death by age and gender? (Data file). Retrieved from: http://visual.ons.gov.uk/what-are-the-top-causes-of-death-by-age-and-gender/

O'Neill, T., Jinks, C., & Squire, A. (2006). 'Heating is more important than food': Older women's perceptions of fuel poverty. *Journal of Housing for the Elderly, 20*(3), 95–108.

Osborn, C. E. (2006). *Statistical applications for health information management* (2nd ed.). Sudbury, MA: Jones and Bartlett Publishers.

Panik, M. J. (2012). *Statistical inference: A short course*. Hoboken, NJ: John Wiley & Sons.

Parkin, S. (2014). *An applied visual sociology: Picturing harm reduction*. Farnham: Ashgate.

Patterson, M., & Monroe, K. R. (1998). Narrative in political science. *Annual Review of Political Science, 1*, 315–331.

Perry, A. E. (2010). Descriptive validity and transparent reporting in randomised controlled trials. In A. R. Piquero & D. Weisburd (Eds.), *Handbook of quantitative criminology* (pp. 333–352). New York: Springer-Verlag.

Peters, J. D., & Simonson, P. (Eds.) (2004). *Mass communication and American social thought: Key texts 1919–1968*. Lanham, MD: Rowan & Littlefield.

Pett, M. A. (1997). *Nonparametric statistics for health care research: Statistics for small samples and unusual distributions*. Thousand Oaks, CA: SAGE Publications.

Pin, P. S., Golmard, J. L., Cotto, E., Rothan-Tondeur, M., Chami, K., & Piette, F. (2012). Excess winter mortality in France: Influence of temperature, influenza like illness, and residential care status. *Journal of the American Medical Directors Association, 13*(3), 309.e1–309.e7.

Pink, S. (2007). *Doing visual ethnography* (2nd ed.). London: SAGE Publications.

Podesta, J. (2014, 1 May). Findings of the big data and privacy working group review. *The White House blog*. Retrieved from http://www.whitehouse.gov/blog/2014/05/01/findings-big-data-and-privacy-working-group-review

Polit, D. F., & Hungler, B. P. (1999). *Nursing research: Principles and methods* (6th ed.). Philadelphia: J. B. Lippincott.

Polkinghorne, D. E. (2005). Language and meaning: Data collection in qualitative research. *Journal of Counseling Psychology, 52*(2), 137–145.

Pollo, A., & Benedetti, F. (2012). Pain and the placebo/nocebo effect. In R. J. Moore (Ed.), *Handbook of pain and palliative care: Behavioral approaches for the life course* (pp. 331–346). New York: Springer.

Popper, K. (2002). *The logic of scientific discovery*. London: Routledge. Originally published 1959.

Powell, H., Mihalas, S., Onwuegbuzie, A. J., Suldo, S., & Daley, C. E. (2008). Mixed methods research in school psychology: A mixed methods investigation of trends in the literature. *Psychology in the Schools, 45*(4), 291–309.

Pulsipher, L. M., & Pulsipher, A. A. (2006). *World regional geography: Global patterns, local lives* (3rd ed.). New York: W. H. Freeman.

Quetelet, L. A. J. (1842). *A treatise on man and the development of his faculties*. Edinburgh: William and Robert Chambers. (Reprinted in: Hawkins, F. B. (1973). *Comparative statistics in the 19th century*. Farnborough: Gregg International Publishers.)

R Core Team (2017). R: A language and environment for statistical computing. R Foundation for Statistical Computing, Vienna, Austria. Retrieved from http://www.R-project.org/

Ragin, C. C. (1987). *The comparative method: Moving beyond qualitative and quantitative strategies*. Berkeley, CA: University of California Press.

'Rainy days help cut crime stats' (2011). *Evening Times*, 15 August. Retrieved from http://www.eveningtimes.co.uk/news/news-editors-picks/rainy-days-help-cut-crime-stats.14743503

Rajacich, D., Kane, D., Williston, C., & Cameron, S. (2013). If they do call you a nurse, it is always a 'male nurse': Experiences of men in the nursing profession. *Nursing Forum, 48*(1), 71–80.

Rajan, A. (2017). Can democracy survive Facebook? *BBC News*, 1 November. Retrieved from http://www.bbc.com/news/entertainment-arts-41833486

Rao, P. S. R. S. (2000). *Sampling methodologies with applications*. Boca Raton, FL: Chapman & Hall/CRC.

Raudenbush, B. (2004). *Statistics for the behavioral sciences: A short course and student manual*. Lanham, MD: University Press of America.

Reason, P., & Bradbury, H. (2006). Introduction: Inquiry and participation in search of a world worthy of human aspiration. In P. Reason & H. Bradbury (Eds.), *Handbook of action research* (concise paperback ed., pp. 1–14). London: SAGE Publications.

Redwood, R. (1999). Information point: Narrative and narrative analysis. *Journal of Clinical Nursing, 8*, 663–674.

Rees, D. G. (2001). *Essential statistics* (4th ed.). Boca Raton, FL: Chapman & Hall/CRC Press.

Reid, K., Flowers, P., & Larkin, M. (2005). Exploring lived experience. *The Psychologist, 18*(1), 20–23.

Research & Enterprise Services, University of Reading (n.d.). What is research data management? Retrieved from https://www.reading.ac.uk/internal/res/ResearchDataManagement/AboutRDM/reas-WhatisRDM.aspx

Richards, L. (2005). *Handling qualitative data: A practical guide*. London: SAGE Publications.

Riegelman, R. K. (2005). *Studying a study and testing a test: How to read the medical evidence* (5th ed.). Philadelphia: Lippincott Williams & Wilkins.

Riessman, C. K. (1993). *Narrative analysis*. Newbury Park, CA: SAGE Publications.

Riessman, C. K. (2004). Narrative analysis. In M. S. Lewis-Beck, A. Bryman, & T. Futing Liao (Eds.), *Encyclopedia of social science research methods* (pp. 705–709). Newbury Park, CA: SAGE Publications.

Robson, D. (2015a). The contagious thought that could kill you. *BBC News*, 11 February. Retrieved from http://www.bbc.com/future/story/20150210-can-you-think-yourself-to-death

Robson, D. (2015b). The real reason germs spread. *BBC Future*, 19 October. Retrieved from http://www.bbc.com/future/story/20151016-the-real-reason-germs-spread-in-the-winter

Rose, G. (2007). *Visual methodologies: An introduction to the interpretation of visual materials* (2nd ed.). London: SAGE Publications.

Rossman, G. B., & Rallis, S.F. (2003). *Learning in the field: An introduction to qualitative research* (2nd ed.). Thousand Oaks, CA: SAGE Publications.

Rottenberg, D. (Ed.). (1997). *Middletown Jews: The tenuous survival of an American Jewish community.* Bloomington, IN: Indiana University Press.

Rotton, J., & Frey, J. (1985). Air pollution, weather, and violent crimes: Concomitant time-series analysis of archival data. *Journal of Personality and Social Psychology, 49*(5), 1207–1220.

Rubin, D. B. (1987). *Multiple imputation for nonresponse in surveys.* Hoboken, NJ: John Wiley & Sons.

Russell, N. (2010). *Communicating science: Professional, popular, literary.* Cambridge: Cambridge University Press.

Russell, R. (1889). *Smoke in relation to fogs in London.* London: National Smoke Abatement Institute.

Saldaña, J. (2016). *The coding manual for qualitative researchers* (3rd ed.). Thousand Oaks, CA: SAGE Publications.

Sale, J. E. M., Lohfeld, L. H., & Brazil, K. (2002). Revisiting the quantitative-qualitative debate: Implications for mixed-methods research. *Quality & Quantity, 36*, 43–53.

Salsburg, D. (2001). *The lady tasting tea: How statistics revolutionized science in the twentieth century.* New York: Henry Holt and Company.

Sampson, R. J., & Laub, J. H. (1993). *Crime in the making: Pathways and turning points through life.* Cambridge, MA: Harvard University Press.

Sandelowski, M. (2000). Combining qualitative and quantitative sampling, data collection, and analysis techniques in mixed-method studies. *Research in Nursing & Health, 23*, 246–255.

Santamouris, M., Alevizos, S. M., Aslanoglou, L., Mantzios, D., Milonas, P., Sarelli, I., Karatasou, S., Cartalis, K., & Paravantis, J. A. (2014). Freezing the poor – Indoor environmental quality in low and very low income households during the winter period in Athens. *Energy and Buildings, 70*, 61–70.

Schreier, M. (2012). *Qualitative content analysis in practice.* London: SAGE Publications.

Schreier, M. (2018). Sampling and generalization. In U. Flick (Ed.), *The SAGE handbook of qualitative data collection* (pp. 84–98). London: SAGE Publications.

Schwandt, T. A. (2006). Constructivist, interpretivist approaches to human inquiry. In J O'Brien (Ed.), *The production of reality: Essays and readings on social interaction* (4th ed., pp. 40–43). Thousand Oaks, CA: Pine Forge Press.

Scott, G., & Garner, R. (2013). *Doing qualitative research: Designs, methods, and techniques.* Boston: Pearson Education.

Seale, C. (2011). Secondary analysis of qualitative data. In D. Silverman (Ed.), *Qualitative research* (3rd ed., pp. 347–364). London: SAGE Publications.

Seidel, J., & Kelle, U. (1995). Different functions of coding in the analysis of textual data. In U. Kelle (Ed.), *Computer-aided qualitative data analysis: Theory, methods and practice* (pp. 52–61). London: SAGE Publications.

Shaw, I. F. (2003). Ethics in qualitative research and evaluation. *Journal of Social Work, 3*(1), 9–29.

Sheridan, D., Street, B., & Bloome, D. (2013). Writing ourselves: The mass-observation project. In H. Callan, B. Street, & S. Underdown (Eds.), *Introductory readings in anthropology* (pp. 345–353). New York: Berghahn Books.

Sheskin, D. (2004). *Handbook of parametric and nonparametric statistical procedures* (3rd ed.). Boca Raton, FL: Chapman & Hall/CRC Press.

Shoemaker, D. J. (2010). Conduct problems in youth: Sociological perspectives. In R. C. Murrihy, A. D. Kidman, & T. H. Ollendick (Eds.), *Clinical handbook of assessing and treating conduct problems in youth* (pp. 21–48). New York: Springer.

Shopes, L. (2011). Oral history. In N. K. Denzin & Y. S. Lincoln (Eds.), *The SAGE handbook of qualitative research* (4th ed., pp. 451–466). Thousand Oaks, CA: SAGE Publications.

Siddique, H. (2015). Huge rise in winter deaths last year blamed on ineffective flu vaccine. *The Guardian*, 25 November. Retrieved from https://www.theguardian.com/society/2015/nov/25/excess-winter-deaths-rose-more-than-150-43900-2014

Sieber, J. (1991). Openness in the social sciences: Sharing data. *Ethics & Behavior, 1*(2), 69–86.

Silverman, D. (2010). *Doing qualitative research* (3rd ed.). London: SAGE Publications.

Simons, H. (2014). Case study research: In-depth understanding in context. In P. Leavy (Ed.), *The Oxford handbook of qualitative research* (pp. 455–470). Oxford: Oxford University Press.

Sims, R. L. (2004). *Bivariate data analysis: A practical guide*. Hauppauge, NY: Nova Science Publishers.

Singapore Statement on Research Integrity (2010). Singapore Statement on Research Integrity. Retrieved from https://wcrif.org/statement

Sirkin, R. M. (2006). *Statistics for the social sciences* (3rd ed.). Thousand Oaks, CA: SAGE Publications.

Smith, K., Todd, M., & Waldman, J. (2009). *Doing your undergraduate social science dissertation*. Abingdon: Routledge.

Smith, L. F., Gratz, Z. S., & Bousquet, S. G. (2009). *The art and practice of statistics*. Belmont, CA: Wadsworth, Cengage Learning.

Smyth, T. R. (2004). *The principles of writing in psychology*. Basingstoke: Palgrave Macmillan.

Speight, J. G. (2012). *Clear and concise communications for scientists and engineers*. Boca Raton, FL: CRC Press.

Spicker, P. (2011). Ethical covert research. *Sociology, 45*(1), 118–133.

Stahl, B. C. (2008). *Information systems: Critical perspectives*. Abingdon: Routledge.

Stephenson, W. (2013). BMI: Does the Body Mass Index need fixing? *BBC News Magazine*, 28 January. Retrieved from http://www.bbc.com/news/magazine-21229387?print=true

Stevens, S. S. (1951). Mathematics, measurement and psychophysics. In S. S. Stevens (Ed.), *Handbook of experimental psychology* (pp. 1–49). New York: Wiley.

Stikeleather, J. (2013). The three elements of successful data visualizations. *Harvard Business Review*, 19 April. Retrieved from https://hbr.org/2013/04/the-three-elements-of-successf

Stommel, M., & Wills, C. E. (2004). *Clinical research: Concepts and principles for advanced practice nurses*. Philadelphia: Lippincott Williams and Wilkins.

Storey, J. (2014). *From popular culture to everyday life*. Abingdon: Routledge.

Strauss, A. (1987). *Qualitative analysis for social scientists*. Cambridge: Cambridge University Press.

Strauss, A., & Corbin, J. (1990). *Basics of qualitative research*. Newbury Park, CA: SAGE Publications.

Strauss, A., & Corbin, J. (1998). *Basics of qualitative research: Grounded theory procedures and techniques* (2nd ed.). Thousand Oaks, CA: SAGE Publications.

Sullivan, G. M., & Feinn, R. (2012). Using effect size – Or why the p value is not enough. *Journal of Graduate Medical Education, 4*(3), 279–282.

Taleb, N. N. (2013). Beware the errors of 'big data'. *Wired*, 8 February. Retrieved from http://www.wired.com/opinion/2013/02/big-data-means-big-errors-people/

Taris, T. (2000). *A primer in longitudinal data analysis*. London: SAGE Publications.

Taylor, S. J., Bogdan, R., & DeVault, M. L. (2016). *Introduction to qualitative research methods: A guidebook and resource* (4th ed.). Hoboken, NJ: John Wiley & Sons.

Teddlie, C., & Tashakkori, A. (2009). *Foundations of mixed methods research: Integrating quantitative and qualitative approaches in the social and behavioral sciences*. Thousand Oaks, CA: SAGE Publications.

Thomas, A. B. (2006). *Research concepts for management studies*. Abingdon: Routledge.

Thornberg, R. (2012). Grounded theory. In J. Arthur, M. Waring, R. Coe, & L. Hedges (Eds.), *Research methods and methodologies in education* (pp. 85–93). Thousand Oaks, CA: SAGE Publications.

Thorsheim, P. (2004). Interpreting the London fog disaster of 1952. In E. M. DuPuis (Ed.), *Smoke and mirrors: The politics and culture of air pollution* (pp. 154–169). New York: New York University Press.

Thorsheim, P. (2006). *Inventing pollution: Coal, smoke, and culture in Britain since 1800*. Athens, OH: Ohio University Press.

Tod, A. M., Lusambili, A., Homer, C., Abbott, J., Cooke, J. M., Stocks, A. J., & McDaid, K. A. (2012). Understanding factors influencing vulnerable older people keeping warm and well in winter: A qualitative study using social marketing techniques. *BMJ Open, 2*, e000922.

Tonkiss, F. (2004). Analysing text and speech: Content and discourse analysis. In C. Seale (Ed.), *Researching society and culture* (2nd ed., pp. 36–382). London: SAGE Publications.

Torres, R. T., Preskill, H., & Piontek, M E. (2005). *Evaluation strategies for communicating and reporting: Enhancing learning in organizations* (2nd ed.). Thousand Oaks, CA: SAGE Publications.

Tracy, S. J. (2013). *Qualitative research methods: Collecting evidence, crafting analysis, communicating impact*. Chichester: Wiley-Blackwell.

Tu, R. (2008). Bar chart. In S. Boslaugh (Ed.), *Encyclopedia of epidemiology* (Vol. 1, p. 69). Thousand Oaks, CA: SAGE Publications.

Tukey, J. W. (1977). *Exploratory data analysis*. Reading, MA: Addison-Wesley.

United States Department of Justice (2016). *Crime in the United States, 2015*. Uniform Crime Reports Series, Federal Bureau of Investigation. Retrieved from https://ucr.fbi.gov/crime-in-the-u.s/2015/crime-in-the-u.s.-2015

United States Department of Labor, Bureau of Labor Statistics (2017). Civilian noninstitutional population and associated rate and ratio measures for model-based areas. Retrieved from http://www.bls.gov/lau/rdscnp16.htm

University of Illinois at Urbana-Champaign (2015). Qualitative data analysis: Your options for programs: Free software. Retrieved from: http://guides.library.illinois.edu/c.php?g=348074&p=2346107

University of Surrey (n.d.). Choosing an appropriate CAQDAS package. Retrieved from: http://www.surrey.ac.uk/sociology/research/researchcentres/caqdas/support/choosing/

Vacha-Haase, T., & Thompson, B. (2004). How the estimate and interpret various effect sizes. *Journal of Counseling Psychology, 51*(4), 473–481.

Van Beveren, J. (2002). A model of knowledge acquisition that refocuses knowledge management, *Journal of Knowledge Management, 6*(1), 18–22.

Van den Eynden, V., Corti, L., Woollard, M., Bishop, L., & Horton, L. (2011). *Managing and sharing data* (3rd ed.). Colchester: University of Essex, UK Data Archive.

Vartanian, T. P. (2011). *Secondary data analysis*. New York: Oxford University Press.

Viegas, F., & Wattenberg, M. (2011). How to make data look sexy. *CNN*, 19 April. Retrieved from http://edition.cnn.com/2011/OPINION/04/19/sexy.data/index.html?_s=PM:OPINION

Vik, P. (2014). *Regression, ANOVA, and the general linear model: A statistics primer*. Thousand Oaks, CA: SAGE Publications.

Vogt, W. P. (2005). *Dictionary of statistics & methodology: A nontechnical guide for the social sciences* (3rd ed.). Thousand Oaks, CA: SAGE Publications.

Wagner, S. A. (2003). *Understanding green consumer behaviour: A qualitative cognitive approach*. London: Routledge.

Walker, W. (2005). The strengths and weaknesses of research designs involving quantitative measures. *Journal of Research in Nursing, 10*(5), 571–582.

Wallace, J. M., & Hobbs, P.V. (2006). *Atmospheric science* (2nd ed.). Burlington, MA: Academic Press.

Wallgren, A., Wallgren, B., Persson, R., Jorner, U., & Haaland, J.-A. (1996). *Graphing statistics & data: Creating better charts*. Newbury Park, CA: SAGE Publications.

Ware, C. (2008). *Visual thinking for design*. Burlington, MA: Morgan Kaufmann.

Wasserman, L. (2004). *All of statistics: A concise course in statistical inference*. New York: Springer.

Weathington, B. L., Cunningham, C. J. L., & Pittenger, D. J. (2010). *Research methods for the behavioral and social sciences*. Hoboken, NJ: John Wiley & Sons.

Weber, R. (2004). Editor's comments: The rhetoric of positivism versus interpretivism: A personal view. *MIS Quarterly, 28*(1), iii–xii.

Webster, S., Lewis, J., & Brown, A. (2014). Ethical considerations in qualitative research. In J. Ritchie, J. Lewis, C. M. Nicholls, & R. Ormston (Eds.), *Qualitative research practice: A guide for social science students and researchers* (2nd ed., pp. 77–110). London: SAGE Publications.

'Week of London fog killed 2,800' (1952). *Milwaukee Journal*, 21 December. Retrieved from http://news.google.com/newspapers?nid=1499&dat=19521221&id=R7UdAAAAIBAJ&sjid=uCMEAAAAIBAJ&pg=5889,1947998

Welch-Ross, M. K., & Fasig, L. G. (2007). Conclusion: Current themes and future directions. In M. K. Welch-Ross & L. G. Fasig (Eds.), *Handbook on communicating and disseminating behavioral science* (pp. 407–425). Thousand Oaks, CA: SAGE Publications.

Wells, J. C. K. (2014). Commentary: The paradox of body mass index in obesity assessment: Not a good index of adiposity, but not a bad index of cardio-metabolic risk. *International Journal of Epidemiology, 43*(3), 672–674.

Wells, R. E. (2012). To tell the truth, the whole truth, may do patients harm: The problem of the nocebo effect for informed consent. *American Journal of Bioethics, 12*(3), 22–29.

Westerman, M. A. (2006). Quantitative research as an interpretive enterprise: The mostly unacknowledged role of interpretation in research efforts and suggestions for explicitly interpretive quantitative investigations. *New Ideas in Psychology, 24*(3), 189–211.

Wetherell, M., & Potter, J. (1992). *Mapping the language of racism: Discourse and the legitimation of exploitation*. New York: Columbia University Press.

Whitley, R. (2008). Social capital and public health: Qualitative and ethnographic approaches. In I. Kawachi, S.V. Subramanian, & D. Kim (Eds.), *Social Capital and Health* (pp. 95–116). New York: Springer.

Wildbur, P., & Burke, M. (1998). *Information graphics: Innovative solutions in contemporary design*. New York: Thames and Hudson.

Wilkinson, A., Pettifor, A., Rosenberg, M., Halpern, C. T., Thirumurthy, H., Collinson, M. A., & Kahn, K. (2017). The employment environment for youth in rural South Africa: A mixed-methods study. *Development Southern Africa, 34*(1), 17–32.

Willis, J. W., Jost, M., & Nilakanta, R. (2007). *Foundations of qualitative research: Interpretive and critical approaches*. Thousand Oaks, CA: SAGE Publications.

Wimmer, R. D., & Dominick, J. R. (2014). *Mass media research: An introduction* (10th ed.). Boston: Wadsworth, Cengage Learning.

Winton, R., & Lee, N. (2005). As rain falls, so does crime. *Los Angeles Times*, 13 January. Retrieved from http://articles.latimes.com/2005/jan/13/local/me-crime13

Wisdom, J. P., Cavaleri, M. A., Onwuegbuzie, A. J., & Green, C. A. (2012). Methodological reporting in qualitative, quantitative, and mixed methods health services research articles. *Health Services Research, 47*(2), 721–745.

Wolcott, H. F. (1992). Posturing in qualitative inquiry. In M. D. LeCompte, W. L. Millroy, & J. Preissle (Eds.), *The handbook of qualitative research in education* (pp. 3–52). San Diego, CA: Academic Press.

Wolcott, H. F. (2008). *Ethnography: A way of seeing* (2nd ed.). Lanham, MD: AltaMira Press.

Wolcott, H. F. (2009). *Writing up qualitative research* (3rd ed.). Thousand Oaks, CA: SAGE Publications.

World Bank (2017). GDP per capita, PPP (current international $). World Bank, International Comparison Program database. Retrieved from: https://data.worldbank.org/indicator/NY.GDP.PCAP.PP.CD

World Medical Association (2015). WMA Declaration of Helsinki – Ethical principles for medical research involving human subjects. Retrieved from https://www.wma.net/policies-post/wma-declaration-of-helsinki-ethical-principles-for-medical-research-involving-human-subjects/

Wright, R. T., & Decker, S. (1994). *Burglars on the job: Streetlife and residential break-ins*. Boston: Northeastern University Press.

Xiao, L. D., Paterson, J., Henderson, J., & Kelton, M. (2008). Gerontological education in undergraduate nursing programs: An Australian perspective. *Educational Gerontology, 34*(9), 763–781.

Yan, Y. Y. (2004). Seasonality of property crime in Hong Kong. *British Journal of Criminology, 44*, 276–283.

Yazici, H., Lesaffre, E., & Yazici, Y. (2014). Ethical issues in study design and reporting. In H. Yazici, Y. Yazici, & E. Lesaffre (Eds.), *Understanding evidence-based rheumatology* (pp. 247–264). Cham: Springer.

Zammar, G. R., Shah, J., Ferreira, A. P. B., Cofiel, L., Lyles, K. W., & Pietrobon, R. (2010). Qualitative analysis of the interdisciplinary interaction between data analysis specialists and novice clinical researchers. *PLoS ONE, 5*(2), e9400.

Ziliak, S. T., & McCloskey, D. N. (2008). *The cult of statistical significance: How the standard error costs us jobs, justice, and lives*. Ann Arbor, MI: University of Michigan Press.

Index